D0684071

THE POLICY CYCLE

SAGE YEARBOOKS IN POLITICS AND PUBLIC POLICY

Sponsored by the

Policy Studies Organization

Series Editor:

Stuart S. Nagel, *University of Illinois, Urbana*

International Advisory Board

Albert Cherns, *University of Technology, England*
John P. Crecine, *University of Michigan*
Kenneth M. Dolbeare, *University of Massachusetts*
Yehezkel Dror, *Hebrew University, Israel*
Joel Fleishman, *Duke University*
Matthew Holden, Jr., *University of Wisconsin*
Charles O. Jones, *University of Pittsburgh*
Harold Lasswell, *Yale University*
Leif Lewin, *University of Uppsala, Sweden*
Klaus Lompe, *Technical University of Braunschweig, Germany*
Julius Margolis, *University of Pennsylvania*
Henry Mayer, *University of Sydney, Australia*
Joyce Mitchell, *University of Oregon*
Jack Peltason, *American Council on Education*
Eugen Pusic, *University of Zagreb, Yugoslavia*
Austin Ranney, *University of California, Berkeley*
Peter Szanton, *Rand Corporation*
Enrique Tejera-Paris, *Venezuela Senate*

Books in this series:

1. What Government Does (1975)
   MATTHEW HOLDEN, Jr. and DENNIS L. DRESANG, *Editors*

2. Public Policy Evaluation (1975)
   KENNETH M. DOLBEARE, *Editor*

3. Public Policy Making in a Federal System (1976)
   CHARLES O. JONES and ROBERT D. THOMAS, *Editors*

4. Comparing Public Policies: New Concepts and Methods (1978)
   DOUGLAS E. ASHFORD, *Editor*

5. The Policy Cycle (1978)
   JUDITH V. MAY and AARON B. WILDAVSKY, *Editors*

VOLUME 5. SAGE YEARBOOKS IN POLITICS AND PUBLIC POLICY

THE POLICY CYCLE

JUDITH V. MAY
and
AARON B. WILDAVSKY
Editors

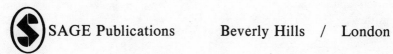SAGE Publications   Beverly Hills / London

Copyright © 1978 by Sage Publications, Inc.

All rights reserved. No part of this book may be reproduced or utilized in any form or by any means, electronic or mechanical, including photo-copying, recording or by any information storage and retrieval system, without permission in writing from the publisher.

For information address:

SAGE PUBLICATIONS, INC.
275 South Beverly Drive
Beverly Hills, California 90212

SAGE PUBLICATIONS LTD
28 Banner Street
London ECIY 8QE

Printed in the United States of America

Library of Congress Cataloging in Publication Data

Main entry under title:

The Policy Cycle.

    (Sage yearbooks in politics and public policy; v. 5)
    Includes bibliographical references.
    1. Policy sciences—Addresses, essays, lectures.
2. Evaluation research (Social action programs)—
United States—Addresses, essays, lectures. I. May,
Judith V. II. Wildavsky, Aaron B.
H61.P58573   300   78-15351
ISBN 0-8039-0825-3
ISBN 0-8039-0826-1 pbk.

FIRST PRINTING

H
61
P58573

CONTENTS

143129

SERIES EDITOR'S INTRODUCTION

This is the fifth volume in the series of Yearbooks in Politics and Public Policy published by Sage Publications in cooperation with the Policy Studies Organization. Each volume has dealt with a different general approach to analyzing the causes and effects of alternative public policies. The first volume on *What Government Does,* edited by Matthew Holden, Jr., and Dennis L. Dresang, provides an overview of various substantive policy problems from a political science perspective. The second volume on *Public Policy Evaluation,* edited by Kenneth M. Dolbeare, provides an analysis of the methodological problems involved in seeking to evaluate alternative public policies. The third volume on *Public Policy Making in a Federal System,* edited by Charles O. Jones and Robert D. Thomas, deals with the influence of the federal form of government on policy formation and implementation in a variety of policy fields. The fourth volume on *Comparing Public Policies,* edited by Douglas E. Ashford, emphasizes the influence of alternative forms of national governments, economies, and cultures on policy formation and implementation.

This fifth volume on *The Policy Cycle* edited by Judith V. May and Aaron B. Wildavsky, like the first four, deals with a general approach to public policy analysis rather than with one or a few specific substantive policy problems. Also like the previous volumes, this symposium is mainly based on the best papers presented at the last annual meeting of the American Political Science Association, the regional political science associations, other disciplinary meetings, and specially commissioned or submitted papers. Many of the papers were presented on the public policy panels at the 1977 APSA meeting. Bringing those papers together in this symposium format brings out their coherence in discussing the cycle of public policies from agenda-setting, issue analysis, service delivery, implementation, utilization of policy evaluation, through policy termination.

In discussing the policy process, political science has traditionally emphasized just policy formation, which tends to mean how a bill becomes a law. In this volume, however, the policy process is treated from a much broader perspective. First, the editors and chapter authors are concerned with how a bill becomes a bill, when they discuss agenda-setting. Second, they are concerned with how a law becomes either a nullity, a goal-achieving act, or something in between, when they discuss service delivery and implementation. Third, they are concerned not only with both policy formation and policy administration (which are traditional political science subjects), but also with policy evaluation (which in the past has often been left to philosophers, journalists, social activists, and economists). Fourth, the editors and chapter authors go beyond the traditional political science emphasis on the legislative process (particularly at the federal level) in discussing the policy process. Rather, they display in their analyses an interest in the policy process in all branches and levels of government.

The chapters or process-stages can be grouped into three sets, namely those dealing with policy formation, administration, and evaluation. An especially interesting process in policy formation is agenda-setting, whereby society decides that some occurrence is now (1) a problem, i.e., a socially undesirable occurrence about which something should be done, and is also now (2) a political matter, i.e., a subject in which the society collectively by way of its government should make and implement some decisions concerning what is the right thing to do. Child abuse and urban growth are provided as illustrations of occurrences that were not formally considered political problems, but have now become important matters on the agendas of policy makers. Another important part of policy formation is issue analysis, whereby policy makers implicitly or explicitly analyze the options available for dealing with a political problem. Issue analysis has traditionally been a loose incremental procedure, but it is increasingly becoming more carefully thought out as the methods of policy analysis and program evaluation become more a part of governmental policy-making. The chapters in this section of the book particularly emphasize how one option rather than another gets chosen, using neighborhood preservation and automobile passenger protection as examples.

Policy administration can essentially take two forms. One form involves service delivery, which tends to emphasize providing people with goods such as a tangible park or road, the labor of a fireman or school teacher, or money or food stamps as part of a welfare program. The illustrative examples in chapters 5 and 6 deal with the labor services of policemen and garbage collectors. A second form of policy administration is implementation or regulation where the emphasis is more on trying to influence the behavior of people rather than trying to provide people with goods or services. The examples in chapters 7, 8 and 9 deal with regulating unemployment, auditing government subsidies, and the economic regulation of the federal independent regulatory agencies. The distinctions between service delivery and implementation may sometimes be unclear since the same government institutions often do both. A key element both process-stages have in common, however, is that they can often dash or at least change the expectations of the policy makers in forming policies before the effects can reach the ultimate policy consumers.

Policy evaluation can be defined as the attempt to determine the effects of alternative public policies in light of their goals and side effects. It is often also concerned with determining the relative benefits and costs of the alternative policies, either after or before the policies are adopted. Closely related to policy evaluation is the subject of research utilization, since evaluations are not of much value unless they are used. Chapters 10 and 11 combine evaluation and utilization in the context of federal funding of local programs and the work of the Agency for International Development. Also closely related to policy evaluation is the decision to continue or terminate the policy in question. The termination process, or how a law ceases to be a law, is especially illustrated in chapter 13, by the phasing out of California's state mental institutions. As with all the chapters, the illustrative examples are accompanied by an attempt to draw broader generalizations concerning the process-stages that go beyond the examples.

The next volume in the Sage-PSO Yearbooks in Politics and Public Policy will be *Policy Studies and Public Choice* edited by Douglas Rae and Stephanie Cameron. It will emphasize the use of deductive modeling and a benefit-cost perspective to obtain a better understanding of why the policy process operates the way it does and how it can be made to operate more effectively. That volume will be followed by *Why Policies Succeed or Fail* edited by Helen Ingram and Dean Mann, plus *Urban Policies: Causes and Consequences* edited by Dale Rogers Marshall. Both volumes will be partly based on the public policy papers presented at the 1978 APSA convention. Robert Lineberry will be doing a volume for the Yearbook series based on the policy panels which he is coordinating for the 1979 convention. That tenth volume will bring the series into the 1980s.

Stuart S. Nagel
Urbana, Illinois

VOLUME EDITORS' INTRODUCTION

The articles in this volume were selected from among those delivered at panels organized under the Public Policy Section of the 1977 American Political Science Association meeting in Washington, D. C. Like the panels, the articles are organized according to stages in the policy cycle. Focusing upon the policy cycle is a convenient way of organizing research being done on public policy. Depending upon the stage of the policy cycle under examination, researchers ask different questions. Compared to organizing research by roles (policy analysts, city councilmen), functional areas (health, housing), institutions (Congress, Office of Management and Budget), or processes (coordination, bargaining), organizing research by stages of the policy cycle focuses attention upon generic activities integrally linked with the policy process. It directs attention to the ways in which political actors identify problems for collective action, conceptualize issues and identify strategic points of intervention, mobilize support and enact policies, design institutions to carry them out, implement programs to achieve policy objectives, evaluate whether those objectives have been achieved, and modify or, more rarely, terminate unsuccessful or outmoded institutions, policies, and programs. Arranged by stage in the policy cycle, the articles in this volume lend themselves to modest but interesting comparisions.

In her article, "Setting the Public Agenda: The Case of Child Abuse," Barbara Nelson develops a framework for examining the emergence on state and national political agendas of the issue of child abuse. Characterizing child abuse as a domestic social policy issue about which there is little controversy, she identifies four stages in the policy agenda-setting process through which the issue passed as it was moved from the private to the public agenda. In "Growth and Its Discontents: Origins of Local Population Controls," Nelson Rosenbaum presents and compares four case studies of cities in which the issue of growth management was placed on the municipal agenda. Analyzing the relationship between the emergence of the issue and the attributes of the communities, he is able to suggest some of the reasons why the issue was highly controversial in three of the cities and not very controversial in the fourth.

In "Neighborhood Preservation: An Analysis of Policy Maps and Policy Options," Eric Moskowitz relates how political actors understand society to function to how they conceptualize issues and policy positions. From interviews with high-level federal policy makers, he shows that their attitudes toward the nature of neighborhoods, the causes of their decline, and the relative efficacy of the market and governmental action are associated with the policies that they advocate. With remarkable success, he illuminates the range of policy positions in the murky area of neighborhood preservation. In his article on automobile passenger restraint systems, "The Politics of Automobile Passenger Protection: Behavioral versus Environmental Control," Stephen Merrill shows how a nonobvious distinction between types of automobile restraint systems can be used with elegant simplicity to interpret patterns of political behavior. Together these articles suggest that much more work should be done relating the attributes of issues to the patterns of political behavior associated with them.

The two articles in the section on service delivery systems address different aspects of efficiency in the production of services. In "Policing: Is There a System?" Elinor Ostrom, Roger Parks, and Gordon Whitaker focus on the production of a number of different police services and show that a multiplicity of police agencies need not prevent the realization of economies of scale in the production of specialized police services. In their article, "Solid Waste Collection: Organization and Efficiency of Service Delivery," E. S. Savas, Barbara Stevens, and Eileen Berenyi assess the relative efficiency of different public and private institutional arrangements for solid waste collection and show that, in cities over 50,000 population, private firms working under contract within exclusive territories were more efficient than municipal agencies, apparently because they were motivated to use more efficient management practices and achieved higher labor productivity.

In the section on implementation, the articles by Donald Baumer, "Implementing Public Service Employment," and Floyd Stoner, "Federal Auditors as Regulators: The Case of Title I of ESEA," make an interesting pair. Both describe the implementation of decentralized Federal programs aimed at disadvantaged groups. While Baumer argues that federal officials should play a more active role in assuring that the public service employment titles of the Comprehensive Employment and Training Act program provide new employment opportunities for the structurally unemployed, Stoner shows that federal officials, specifically regulation writers and auditors, have played an aggressive role in targeting Elementary and Secondary Education Act Title I assistance upon educationally disadvantaged children. Apparently, federal program decentralization is potentially compatible with strong federal leadership and technical assistance in guiding program implementation and with strong federal oversight in the form of performance audits. It appears that all tales of implementation need not be accounts of how administrators gave way before pressures to undercut progressive social policy objectives. In fact, HEW regulation writers and auditors appear to have exceeded Congressional intent. While Stoner's case study undercuts facile assumptions about the direction of change during the implementation of social programs, liking the outcome should not obscure the underlying issues of how to define responsibility, responsiveness, and accountability in a pluralistic political system.

John Plumlee and Kenneth Meier address these issues in the context of regulatory administration. In their article, "Capture and Rigidity in Regulatory

Administration: An Empirical Assessment," they develop an empirical test of the assumption (derived from the concept of an organizational life cycle) that regulatory agencies must inevitably become captives of the interests that they were established to regulate and consequently become organizationally rigid—slow, inefficient, and unresponsive to external demands. They examine the relationships among age, diffuse political support (from the President and Congress), specific political support (from the regulated industry), capture, and rigidity in selected regulatory agencies, and find that capture of an agency by the regulated industry need not lead to organizational rigidity. Their study, too, warns against overly facile assumptions about the direction of change during program implementation.

Both of the articles on utilization of evaluation examine how evaluations are used by different federal agencies in making decisions to fund community development activities. In their article, "The Federal Decision To Fund Local Programs: Utilizing Evaluation Research," Rita Mae Kelly and Bruce Frankel examine how the Office of Economic Opportunity's (OEO's) decisions to fund community development corporations (CDCs) were influenced only indirectly by third-party evaluations of the CDCs' past performance. In his article, "Use of Evaluations in A.I.D.: The Influence of Roles and Perceptions," Douglas Shumavon shows that actors located at different levels in the AID hierarchy (the project level, country mission level, and bureau level) desired different information from project evaluations. Interestingly, these articles suggest that both OEO and AID bureau level personnel desired similar information in making community development project funding decisions. Both were less interested in what CDCs had actually done in the past than what they could do to achieve the bureau's objectives in the future. Whereas the evaluators were interested in what the CDC's projects had accomplished, which was all they could study, bureau-level personnel were interested in who could perform for them in the future, which was their principal worry.

Finally, in the section on termination, Peter de Leon presents "A Theory of Policy Termination," and argues for more attention to this phenomenon. It must be possible to create a welfare state because so many nations have done it. But is it possible to march down the hill as well as march up it? If it were as easy to end programs as to say "zero-base budgeting" or "sunset legislation," there would be no doubt. Yet as big government matures, the question of termination is bound to assume ever greater importance. In "Ideology and Policy Termination: Restructuring California's Mental Health System," James Cameron presents a case study of the process by which California's state mental hospitals were phased out with deleterious results for severely disabled patients who received few services upon discharge. By showing how a change in the definition of the problem lead to the phasing out of state hospitals in favor of community mental health centers, this article illustrates as well as could be hoped the continuity in the policy cycle between policy termination and policy initiation.

"The policy cycle," in its usage here, does not refer to some predetermined, definitive number of steps through which all policies must inevitably go, but refers instead to how, in thinking about the policy process, one's attention is drawn to

Judith V. May and Aaron B. Wildavsky   13

beginnings, middles, and endings that may lead to new beginnings. As the "policy space" becomes more crowded—i.e., as governments assume responsibility for a wider range of activities in a growing number of areas, then it becomes apparent that the activities examined here (policy initiation, implementation, termination, etc.) become more problematic as policies, so to speak, grow larger and bump into each other. Past policies become an important (and sometimes, the most important) part of the environment to which future policies must adapt. Policies intended as solutions to certain problems are themselves the causes of new problems for which policy solutions must be designed.

Whether one focuses upon initiation or termination, beginning or ending, it sometimes appears that the force required to move a policy through the system may be at odds with the finesse required to make the policy work. As Cameron shows, the deinstitutionalization of mental patients was pursued with single-minded ferocity by those who held the view that institutionalization equaled incarceration and the loss of civil liberties. To achieve deinstitutionalization, they blinded themselves to the difficulties of continuing to meet the needs of emotionally troubled patients once they left the hospital. Cameron properly labels policy disputes of this sort "ideological." Had the terminators admitted the drawbacks of their position to themselves or others, they might have incapacitated themselves through ambivalence, or have given ammunition to their opponents and never achieved their objective. But a great deal of social evil is done in the name of doing social good.

Even when pursuit of a policy does not generate a contest between conflicting ideologies, it does not mean that ideological blinders are not being worn. Nelson describes the issue of child abuse as noncontroversial, but a moment's reflection reveals, and Nelson in part affirms, that alternative definitions of the issue were simply less politically palatable at the time. Policy-makers were unresponsive to the view that caretakers who assault or otherwise abuse children are criminals and should be punished. Neither were they inclined to the view that allegedly abused children should be assisted in seeking compensatory damages from their caretakers or the state. They were inclined to believe that perpetrators of child abuse were themselves victims of past child abuse, ignorance of acceptable childrearing practices, and social and economic stress, and could be treated in rehabilitation programs. Of course, if one's aim is to promote the welfare of the family, then one might be reluctant to encourage the state to intrude upon internal family relations. It appears that the process of designing public policy has ultimately to do with the allocation of pain and suffering. How does one weigh the preservation of the family against the suffering of a child? Is it any wonder that policy-makers prefer ideological blinders?

It may be that the study of activities associated with the stages of the policy cycle can procede without too much attention to the content of the policies used as vehicles for hypothesis testing and development. In this respect, it may differ little from past and continuing efforts to understand decision-making, bureaucracy, or leadership, and other topics without reference to the content of the decisions being made, programs being administered, or directions being offered. It is interesting to note, however, that several of the authors contributing to this volume have found it useful to apply their analytic talents to the attributes of the policies and programs as well as the activities that they are studying. This suggests the possibility that it may someday be possible to compare policies across functional lines on the basis of their substantive attributes. Moskowitz shows how closely policy preferences follow from a policy-maker's notions about how society functions. Is the distinction between behavioral and environmental measures used so fruitfully by Merrill equally useful in interpreting behavior in other issue arenas?

It may be that we will discover that certain kinds of concerns are regularly associated with certain kinds of policies. For example, implicit in Rosenbaum's treatment of growth management is the question of whether land use standards should be determined by a higher level of government. Controversy over what level of government should set the standards may be typical of regulatory policy. Implicit in Plumlee and Meier's treatment of regulatory agency capture and rigidity is the question of whether preservation of the public interest through standard-setting and enforcement is possible at all. These questions are quite different from those raised by the two articles on the provision of public services which raise the issues of the relative merits of centralization and decentralization and the relative efficiency of public and private service providers.

Public service employment appears to be the solution to the problem of what the public sector can be when its inducements are inadequate to motivate the private sector to hire the cyclically and structurally unemployed: the answer— hire them itself. Community development corporations are also intended to overcome market failures and to increase the opportunities of targeted groups. Will it someday be possible to say what community development corporations and public service employment have in common so that the successes and failures of one may be used as object lessons for the other? For example, if the private sector fails to purchase the goods and services of a CDC, will the public sector purchase them itself (as it in fact does in many instances through preferential contracting)? Once one has confidence that two things are the same, only different, one has a base from which to begin to construct theory.

The articles in this volume, then, not only contribute to our understanding of the generic activities associated with the policy cycle; they suggest that more patterns of activity have to be discovered if we are to find effective ways of treating policy content as an explanatory variable. Progress may be made if we begin with how problems are conceptualized—what does the policy-maker see as wrong, and, by implication, as the proper state of affairs from which it deviates; and how solutions are crafted—who promises to do what to whom in order to move from what is to what ought to be. Conceptually, at least, the range of policy options may turn out to be considerably more limited than one might suppose.

Judith V. May
Department of Housing and Urban Development
Aaron B. Wildavsky
University of California, Berkeley

PART I

AGENDA SETTING

1

SETTING THE PUBLIC AGENDA:
The Case of Child Abuse

BARBARA   J.   NELSON

Princeton University

with the assistance of
THOMAS   LINDENFELD

INTRODUCTION

In the winter of 1655 the frozen body of John Walker, a 12-year old boy apprenticed to Robert Latham, was examined by a dozen men of the Plymouth Colony, who testified that bruises, mutilations, malnutrition, and exposure caused Walker's death. For this "cruelty and hard usage" of his apprentice, Latham was "burned in the hand" and "all his goods confiscated" (Bremmer, 1970:123-124). Although the Walker case was not the first record of child abuse in the American colonies, it was the first time the name of the child was

AUTHOR'S NOTE: *I would like to express my thanks to the Guggenheim-supported Research Program in Criminal Justice, Jameson W. Doig, Director, for support for this research. My thanks also go to the many people who generously contributed to this work: Zaida Dillon for tireless research assistance; Jack Walker, Jerry Webman, and Julian Wolpert for their helpful comments; and Lu Crooks, Marjorie Quick and Jean Nase for able administrative support. My very deep gratitude is extended to the 32 public-spirited people who gave their time and continuing interest to the search for knowledge. An earlier version of this paper was presented at the 1977 American Political Science Association meetings.*

mentioned. John Walker, then, can be considered a symbol of a condition which has always been part of American life and, indeed, has always been part of social interaction as far back as human records go (DeMause, 1975; Light, 1973; Thomas, 1972).

In 1957, a report issued by the U.S. Children's Bureau (CB) entitled "Proposals . . . for Legislation on Public Child Welfare and Youth Services" suggested that each state's Child Welfare Department[1] investigate neglect, abuse, and abandonment; offer social services; or bring the situation to the attention of a law enforcement agency. This recommendation is the first major public sector recognition of child abuse as an issue of *public policy* as opposed to an occasional field work problem of social workers. In the three centuries separating the John Walker case and the 1957 "Proposals . . . for Legislation," any response evoked by the problem of child abuse and neglect came from the private sector, primarily from the "protective societies" which began forming in the late 19th century. However, in the 20 years *since* the "Proposals . . . for Legislation," the problem of child abuse and neglect has achieved a secure niche on the agendas of the federal bureaucracy, all 50 state legislatures, and Congress.

The research reported here focuses on the transformation of the problem of child abuse and neglect from a private sector charity concern to, additionally, a public sector social welfare issue. It is a report on issue creation and agenda setting, specifically investigating how the political, economic, and moral burdens for response to child abuse were shifted away from private charity and on to government. It is a case study, then, of the first step of the policy process—the step whereby the large number of problems government *could* address is reduced to the much smaller number of problems government *will* address.

The research is presented in three sections. The first section presents our conceptualization of the agenda-setting process. This section covers four topics: the analytic stages in the agenda-setting process, the exigencies of empirical research on agenda setting, a framework for case finding in the study of agenda setting, and problems of hypothesis selection in agenda-setting research. The second section uses the conceptual discussion as a basis for recounting and analyzing the history of how the federal bureaucracy, the 50 state legislatures, and Congress each in turn added the problem of child abuse and neglect to their agendas. This section also presents a summary of the media's role in setting the governmental agendas. The third and final section offers several summary thoughts on directions for agenda-setting research.

It is important to delay briefly the beginning of the next section to speak to the issue of what kind of case study this is. Very frequently case studies are lauded for their "hypothesis generating" power. (Lijphart, 1971). This important role for case studies is seen as the mining effort which provides the raw materials for that segment of empirical research which follows the mold of:

HYPOTHESIS → TEST → AFFIRMATION/CONTRADICTION →
EVALUATION → INTEGRATION

A less frequent but perhaps more important function for case studies is what may be called "hypothesis organization."[2] Hypothesis organization is valuable for pointing out the logical consistency of groups of hypotheses, designating the centrality of certain hypotheses, and directing our attention to the contexts in which the behaviors we want to explain occur. Hypothesis-organizing case studies are especially important when examing complex behaviors, undertaken by a number of people, extending over a long period of time.

CONCEPTUALIZING AND STUDYING AGENDA SETTING

A large portion of political inquiry has been directed at *how* problems are resolved; much less attention has been given to the question of *which* problems reach arbitration. The process by which conflicts and concerns come to receive governmental attention and thus the potential for action by the public sector has been called "agenda-building" or "agenda-setting" (Cobbs and Elder, 1972: Cobb et al., 1976; Walker, 1974; McCoombs and Shaw, 1972). Cobb and Elder (1972:85) define the governmental agenda as "all issues that are commonly perceived by members of the political community as meriting public attention and . . . involving matters within the legitimate jurisdiction of existing governmental authority." They further state that there are many semi-independent governmental agendas in the United States as a result of the numerous access points (Gergen, 1968) to governmental decision makers and the relatively high level of autonomy between governmental units (Aldrich, 1973).

Agenda setting per se is a relatively new topic in political science. However, the apparent novelty is partially the result of a new label for older concerns such as issue definition, interest group activity, and the policy effects of expanding enfranchisement. Three approaches have emerged to explain the causes of expansion or shifts in the content of governmental agendas: (1) economic growth, (2) issue careers and issue cycles, and (3) organizational behavior. The approaches are not mutually exclusive. Rather, each approach designates a set of scholarly traditions providing sources of research hypotheses.

Depending on their perspectives, economic growth analysts look with alarm or satisfaction at the fact that public expenditures in America (measureed in constant dollars) have risen from 6.8% of the GNP in 1902 to 34.1% in 1970 (Borcherding, 1977: 26). Today the most vocal economic growth theorists are "public choice" advocates who look with dismay at the rise in public expenditures. Among them Borcherding estimates (1977: 64) that "only" about 50% of this century's growth in public expenditures is a function of changes in relative prices, incomes, and population, and their associated interdependencies. He suggests that a combination of pressure from interest groups, a low level of efficiency in public bureaucracies, and an increasing sophistication in methods of taxation account for the growth in more discretionary public expenditures. Although considerations of economic growth are very important in agenda setting, there are two problems with the public choice approach. First, notwithstanding valid arguments for minimalist government, there is no reason to believe that the early 1900s reflect the optimum level of public expenditures and therefore should be used as a baseline. More importantly, the public choice approach only hints at the broad categories where increased expenditures are expected (i.e., the service sector) without specifying in more detail what issues or types of issues will experience increased expenditures.

A second approach to agenda setting emphasizes issue careers or issue cycles. Cobb, Keith-Ross, and Ross (1976:127) define issue careers in terms of issue initiation, specification, expansion, and entrance. They propose three patterns of issue careers based on whether critical actors are inside or outside government, and the extent to which these actors attempt to engage the support of the citizenry as well as public servants. Others emphasize the public's and especially the media's span of attention to particular issues. (Downs, 1972; Nadel, 1976). Professional journalists constantly judge the extent to which additional coverage of an issue will cause overexposure and the loss of audience interest (Lazarsfeld and Merton, 1971).

The issues approach has roots in interest group research, roots which tend to stress the conflictual nature of agenda setting. In the issues approach, the search for a place on a governmental agenda is often portrayed as one where contenders for government favors spar with each other in the hallways of power. Unfortunately, this characterization is misleading in many cases of agenda setting in domestic social policy. A large segment of agenda-setting for domestic social issues is typified by Kotz's (1969) discussion of the initiation of the food stamp program, a program which excited much concern and controversy, but which lacked a sharply adversarial tone. The adversarial tone of the issue approach is a result of an emphasis on cases where the opponents were highly organized (e.g., the mine workers versus the mine owners (Cobbs and Elder, 1972:64-67, 77; Groennings, 1970)) and the empirical difficulties in separating agenda setting from the consideration of solutions.

Increasingly, research on agenda setting reflects organizational themes. Walker (1974:4-8) notes the importance of professional career patterns and the influence of professional associations on agenda setting. Zaltman and associates (1973) propose that organizations that are small, young, competitive, and pressed by rapid technological changes accept new ideas more readily. The organizational approach quite appropriately highlights the fact that governmental agenda setting occurs when high-level public servants act in their policy-making roles, roles which are, with rare exceptions, organizational. Thus, although issues clearly have careers and cycles which are in turn influenced by economic variables, the most important task of agenda-setting research is to conceptualize how organizations set their agendas.

From an organizational perspective we propose four analytically distinct stages in the agenda-setting process: (1) issue recognition, (2) issue adoption, (3) issue prioritizing, and (4) issue maintenance. Stage (1), issue recognition, is the juncture where an issue is noticed and felt to be a potential topic for action. Stage (2), issue adoption, focuses on the decision to respond or not to respond to an issue. It is important to emphasize that the decision to consider an issue is analytically distinct from the decision made between competing policy alternatives. Two conditions must prevail for an issue to be adopted. First, decision makers must share a perception of the legitimacy of government responsibility for action on this issue. Second, they must believe that an appropriate response *could* be found if the issue is adopted. In stage (3), prioritizing, the existing agenda is reordered to include the new issue. This prioritizing frequently constitutes more than slipping the new issue between two older ones. A new issue may completely dislodge one or more older issues or may cause substantial shifts in the intensity of consideration given to older issues. If interest in the newer issue is not maintained (Stage 4), the issue will never reach the point of substantive decision making. Similarly, in order for an issue to remain on the agenda after it has had consideration and perhaps response, its merit as part of the ideas in "good currency" (Walker, 1974:2) must be maintained. Without this long-term maintenance an issue fails to become an addition to the enduring concerns of government.[3] That failure is not necessarily regretable; the government agenda would be incredibly crowded if there were no mechanisms to remove from public consideration the myriad of horse-and-buggy issues which no longer evoke general interest.

The implementation of research based on the stages of agenda setting requires answers to four methodological questions: (1) how to provide working definitions of the agenda setting stages, (2) how to separate agenda-setting from other phases of the policy process, (3) how to choose cases for study, and (4) how to find or formulate hypotheses.

It is difficult to provide working definitions of the agenda-setting stages for (at least!) six reasons: (1) the necessity of having detailed institutional information because working definitions must be sensitive to organizational context, (2) the fact that a specific behavior in a designated institution may cover more than one of the analytic categories of agenda setting, (3) the problem of the asymmetry of proof, i.e., it is easier by far to tell when an issue has achieved the agenda than when it has not (Bachrach and Baratz, 1963), (4) the problems of unit and level of analysis, i.e., does one properly investigate the actions of people or institutions? (5) the linguistic, if not analytic, pull toward personifying the activities of institutions, and (6) the temptation of inevitability, or how even the most complex decisions become simple when you know how they turned out (Proscio, 1977).

It is also difficult to know where agenda setting stops and deliberation on an issue begins. The line between the two phases of the policy process will always be somewhat arbitrary. Once again, attention to the procedures of public institutions alerts us to situations when the policy process moves from an emphasis on issue recognition and predecision procedures to an emphasis on the choice among substantive alternatives.

The third methodological concern in studying agenda setting is the need to devise a research strategy to locate and select cases to pursue. This choice is no small task. For instance, how do we determine if an issue has ever been addressed by government? If a government policy maker has dealt with the issue earlier, deciding at first not to act, does a second consideration of the problem constitute a new case or an old case? The constant redefinition of issues, their enlarging and shrinking, also makes case definition difficult.

Creative case choice is a strategy for building a general understanding of agenda setting. We can argue that existing case studies on agenda setting represent an implicit acknowledgment of important characteristics of issues or institutions. Agenda-setting research needs to develop an explicit case-finding rationale.

What criteria should we use to choose cases? To supplement the organizational focus of the analytic stages of agenda setting, we propose a case-finding typology based on important issue characteristics. Three dimensions provide a framework for case finding: (1) the consensual or controversial nature of the issue, (2) its characterization as scientific/technical or social, and (3) its designation as domestic or international.

On the consensual-controversial dimension, we identify two types of issues: valence issues and position issues (Campbell, 1966:170-174).[24] We define valence issues as those which elicit strong, fairly uniform affective responses and thus do not have an adversarial quality, in contrast to position issues for which there are at least two alternative sets of preferences. On the second dimension, issues are designated scientific/technical or social in part by whether they deal with things or people. However, it is not merely the definition of the problem which is important. Additionally, scientific/technical issues elicit mechanistic solutions more frequently than do social issues. On the third dimension, issues are designated as domestic or international not only on the basis of geographical focus, but also by the tradition of secrecy or openness surrounding the decision-making process.

Of course, not every actor labels an issue in the same manner. Indeed, one common denominator in agenda-setting research is the recognition that labeling is an important decision which eventually dictates the kind of attention an issue attracts. One of the most frequent labeling tactics used by issue partisans is characterizing a problem as a valence (highly consensual and affective) issue. As we shall see in the next section, those who set the child abuse agendas agreed that the problem was a social valence issue. In fact, the phrase most commonly used to describe child abuse is a "motherhood issue," a phrase ironic in its old-fashionedness, for nothing is more controversial these days than motherhood.

Figure 1 displays the case-finding typology for agenda setting. As is frequently the case with graphic rendition of ideas, the boundaries between the dimensions

| | Domestic | | International | |
	Social	Scientific/ Technical	Social	Scientific/ Technical
Valence	Child Abuse and Neglect			
Position				

Figure 1: CASE FINDING MATRIX FOR THE STUDY OF AGENDA SETTING

appear more solid than they are in reality. Nonetheless, it is useful to have a visual image of the agenda-setting case-finding typology and the place of the child abuse case within it.

The fourth implementation question is how to choose appropriate hypotheses to study agenda setting. Within the three previously mentioned approaches to agenda setting are smaller traditions which can provide specific hypotheses. Differences in the consumer, producer, and financial perspectives on economic growth provide a wide range of hypotheses for agenda-setting research (Tarschys, 1975). Studies of group affinity and legitimacy (e.g., Truman, 1951; Olson, 1971), media attention (e.g., McCoombs and Shaw, 1972; Downs, 1972), labeling (e.g., Erikson,1967; Mercer, 1973), and political leadership (e.g., Miller and Levitan, 1976) provide hypotheses in the issues approach. Analyses of corporate leadership,[4] professional career building (e.g., Becker, 1970; Walker, 1974:4-29), innovation, and diffusion of innovation (e.g., Wilson, 1966; Walker, 1969; Gray, 1973; Eyestone, 1977) provide hypotheses in the organizational behavior approach. Each research tradition contributes to understanding segments of the agenda-setting process. The association of particular hypotheses with specific analytic stages or specific agendas is left for the next section. It is important, however, to mention here that we did not expect that one research tradition would have enough power and breadth to explain all the facets of this complex set of behaviors. The final section presents our judgment as to which traditions were most productive and why.

GOVERNMENTAL RECOGNITION OF CHILD ABUSE AND NEGLECT

Governmental recognition of the problem of child abuse was based in part on cultural and institutional readiness, or what Smelser (1962) calls the structural conduciveness for change. Generally, the growth of the public sector, and most notably the growth of the public social service and benefit sector (Tarschys, 1975), has increased the range and extent to which government intervenes in the lives of its citizens. However, the willingness of government to accept new responsibilities or expand old ones is cyclical. Government expands not only in times of war,[5] but also in periods when equity is an important political concern. Conversely, government constricts when efficiency is of paramount political interest.[6]

A long period of concern with a variety of equity issues began with the civil rights movement in the mid and late 1950s. The 1962 amendments to the Social Security Act requiring child welfare services in every county or parish of every state demonstrated that the interests of children were part of the equity cycle. The amendments were followed by the "War on Poverty" which emphasized the importance of services to children as a method of eliminating poverty. The equity cycle was given tremendous impetus by the Supreme Court's 1967 *In re Gault* opinion which gave children Bill of Rights protections. Later, the months spent crafting the Comprehensive Child Development Act (CCDA) (ultimately vetoed by President Nixon) educated members of Congress to the importance of providing adequately for the needs of all children.

The concern for children was not limited to government. Pediatricians, the most prestigious group dealing with youngsters, enjoyed two decades of notable success conquering child-killing microbes. Having cured or prevented many children's diseases, pediatricians had the status, skills, and the slack resources to invest in research on pathologies which were at least partly behavioral in origin.

With this cultural readiness in mind, we shall show how child abuse achieved the agendas of the Children's Bureau in the Department of Health, Education and Welfare (HEW), the 50 state legislatures, and Congress. The discussions of achieving these agendas follow the agenda-setting stages presented above: issue recognition, issue adoption, issue prioritizing, and issue maintenance. We will emphasize the agenda-setting process, including information on the final policy decision only when it illuminates that process.

The data for this analysis derive from two sources: (1) the written record as found in books, journals, memos, correspondence, and unpublished reports; and (2) confidential interviews with 32 public- and private-sector leaders who participated in the agenda-setting process. The interviews, which lasted from 30 minutes to three hours, were conducted with past and present high-ranking officials in the executive branch, members of Congress, and with several of their past and present personal and committee staff, noted researchers, professors, legal and medical practitioners in the child abuse field, and national leaders in relevant private charity groups.

SETTING THE AGENDA IN THE CHILDREN'S BUREAU

Child abuse first received mass media attention in 1874 with the famous Mary Ellen case. Stated briefly, Mary Ellen, a foster child/indentured servant, was severely treated by her caretakers. Henry Bergh, the founder of the American Society for Prevention of Cruelty to Animals, brought suit to have Mary Ellen removed from her dangerous surroundings. The grounds for removal were not the oft-told myth that as a member of the animal kingdom Mary Ellen deserved protection, but rather a petition for a writ *de homine replegiando,* an old English writ to remove the custody of one person from another (Thomas, 1972:307-308). The uproar caused by the case precipitated the forming of the New York Society for the Prevention of Cruelty to Children (NYSPCC), and other prevention societies quickly formed in a number of eastern cities. In the late 1800s and early 1900s such societies were frequently licensed by states to receive and place "destitute, neglected, and wayward children" (1972:311). So powerful were some of these groups that it was, for example, a misdemeanor for anyone to interfere with the work of the NYSPCC. Thus, several eastern state legislatures were the first public institutions to recognize child abuse and neglect. In the spirit of the day, these states enfranchised, as it were, private groups to take action.

Eighty years after the Mary Ellen case, the private prevention movement was practically nonexistent. Highly moralistic charity did not enjoy the same social sanction, and charity dollars had dwindled during the Depression, primarily replaced by public monies available under a variety of titles of the Social Security Act (Trattner, 1974:228-229). Professional social work had turned away from coercing clients into accepting services to emphasizing responsiveness to the expressed needs of clients. The result of changed funding sources and service methods was an increasingly articulate, middleclass clientele. By the end of World War II an activist interest in child protection services had largely disappeared.

What then sparked the Children's Bureau into recognizing an issue which had consistently been losing supporters? Interest did not initiate in the Bureau. Rather it was the result of the Bureau's responding to research on child protection carried out by the American Humane Association (AHA), a private charity dedicated to child and animal protection. Unlike the prevention societies, the AHA did not provide direct service, preferring to undertake research, thus providing scholarly and training materials to pediatric and family-focused social workers.

In the fall of 1954, the AHA's Children's Division under the leadership of its new director, Dr. Vincent DeFrancis, began the first nationwide survey on neglected, abused, and exploited children. The results, published in 1955 (DeFrances, 1956:1), were distributed to state Child Welfare Departments and other interested professionals, then later sold to the public for a minimal fee. The findings were also presented at one of the then semi-annual meetings of child welfare experts coordinated by the AHA. Approximately 15 to 20 professionals were present at these meetings, the CB being represented by Annie Lee Sandusky. Other participants included representatives of the Child Welfare League, Family Service Association of America, National Council of Crime and Delinquency, United Community Chests and Councils of America, the National Social Work Association, and American Public Welfare Association. These meetings helped to convey the full impact of child abuse as a national problem to the CB.

The AHA's 1955 report emphasizing child protective services was congruent with the social work perspective of the CB (Steiner, 1976:36-89). Because the proposed method of dealing with child abuse (case work) was the CB's preferred response to most child welfare problems, the CB immediately began considering policy options, virtually bypassing the issue adoption, prioritizing, and maintenance stages. With the 1957 publication of "Proposals for Drafting Principals and Suggested Language for Legislation on Public Welfare and Youth Services," it was evident to the attentive public that the CB had a policy interest in child abuse.

The importance of child abuse to the CB was demonstrated by the research it supported. As we shall see, the CB's early support for research on child abuse developed a small, but vocal, group of professionals whose recommendations woud be important in precipitating state response to child abuse. In the late 1950s the CB supported Dr. C. Henry Kempe, a noted pediatrician at Denver General Hospital and the University of Colorado School of Medicine, to explore with his colleagues the physical abuse of children. Early in his career Dr. Kempe had specialized in immunology, a field requiring an interest in the behavorial as well as the microbiological aspects of illness. But his interest in child abuse and neglect

did not develop solely from his professional awareness of the social aspects of the
etiology of illness. He had a more central and practical concern. His personal
agenda with regard to child abuse was set by his dissatisfaction with the diagnoses
of the interns and residents under his tutelage. Rather than diagnose deliberate
injuries to children as such, these young physicians frequently reported the
possibility of rare blood and bone diseases. Kempe realized that a problem cannot
be treated if it is not identified correctly.

Kempe reported his research findings on several occasions. The first was at the
November 1961 meetings of the American Academy of Pediatrics. As a long-
time member of the program committee, Kempe had the opportunity to organize a
seminar on the topic of his choice, choosing not surprisingly, the physical abuse of
children. Fellow members of the program committee suggested that a title such as
physical abuse which emphasized legally liable and socially deviant behavior
might make some members wary of attending the seminar. Kempe agreed,
renaming the seminar the "Battered Child Syndrome." In one stroke he labeled
the problem in a manner which downplayed the deviant aspects while highlighting
the medical aspects. From an agenda-setting perspective the effect of the label
cannot be overestimated.

In 1962 Kempe and his associates published "The Battered Child Syndrome"
in the *Journal of the American Medical Association* (JAMA). The article, and
the accompanying editorial, electrified the medical profession. The small number
of medical and social work articles on child abuse published prior to 1962 either
failed to mention the problem in the title or employed the then-scary term "child
abuse."[7] As a follow-up to the successful American Academy of Pediatrics'
seminar, Kempe's well-titled article in a prestigious journal gave the problem of
child abuse professional legitimacy. National media attention to the problem
dates from the publication of this article, as we shall discuss in the section on the
media.

Also in 1962, the CB held a conference to present Kempe's research to a group
of interested lawyers, doctors, and social workers. The conference recommended
that the CB draft a model child abuse reporting statute and disseminate it to the
states with a strong recommendation for adoption. Such a model statute was
written and widely distributed in 1963. This action mounted the assault on the
second agenda, that of the 50 state legislatures.

After circulating the model reporting law, the CB maintained its interest in and
support for research on child abuse by initiating a series of nationwide studies in
1965. Five years later the results were published by the principal investigator,
David G. Gil, in *Violence Against Children: Physical Child Abuse in the United
States.* Like Kempe's work, *Violence Against Children* was widely read by both
professionals and interested lay people. Thus, the research supported by the CB
provided public servants and the general public with scholarly, concerned, but not
titillating information about the existence and extensiveness[8] of child abuse. This
critical information legitimized the call for legislation.

While the research of child abuse sponsored by the CB kept the issue visible to
the public, the child abuse issue would ultimately keep the Bureau alive. The CB,
created by an Act of Congress in 1912 to research and document the status of

children in the United States, was handicapped by opponents who objected to any possible "control" of child rearing by the government. Although the CB never posed a threat to parental authority, it did not respond well to institutional authority. Beginning in 1967, the CB was administratively subordinate to Social and Rehabilitation Services (SRS) within HEW. In 1968 and 1969, Mary Switzer, administrator of SRS, encouraged the CB to shift its focus from middle-class children to poor and minority children. The CB refused to retreat from its traditional position.[9]

In early 1969, Secretary of HEW Robert H. Finch was pressed to find a home for Head Start, which was being ousted from the Office of Economic Opportunity. Finch created the Office of Child Development (now the Administration for Children, Youth and Families) to house the intransigent CB and homeless Head Start Program. Despite high-flown rhetoric, OCD only had two important tasks: managing Head Start and supporting research on child abuse. SRS administered such important concerns as maternal and child health and other child welfare programs. Without the ground swell of public interest in child abuse, a benefit derived from research sponsored by the CB, OCD would have had no important programs under its auspices.

THE MEDIA AND GOVERNMENT RECOGNITION OF CHILD ABUSE

Before analyzing how child abuse achieved the state and Congressional agendas, it is important to ascertain the role of the media in informing political elites of the existence and extensiveness of the problem, and building mass consensus for government activities. Cobb and associates (1976:127) have correctly stated that some issues are generated within institutions and then attract the attention of the mass media while in other cases the order is reversed. The child abuse case affords the opportunity to examine the role of the media in setting a sequence of governmental agendas.

Although there were scattered articles on child abuse in the 1950s, the first article of importance was, as noted before, Kempe's "Battered Child Syndrome." However, its publication should not be regarded as the Children's Bureau's attempt to engage media support for an issue not yet on the agenda. By the time Kempe's article was published, child abuse was firmly established on the CB's agenda. Rather, the "Battered Child Syndrome" is more appropriately considered a regular product of professional research.

The Kempe article did, however, set the stage for issue recognition by the mass printed media. Many mass circulation magazines[10] regularly cover new medical developments. Some, especially traditional "women's" magazines, have health columns. The first mass media article was the "Battered Child Syndrome" published in the July 20, 1962, *Time* magazine, two weeks after Kempe's article appeared. This article reported Kempe's research as part of the regular medicine section of *Time*. The four other mass media articles in 1962 and 1963 also relied heavily on Kempe's work.

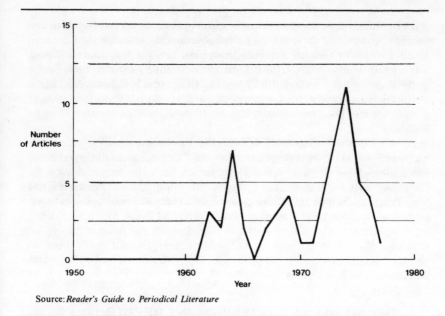

Source: *Reader's Guide to Periodical Literature*

Figure 2: MASS MEDIA COVERAGE OF CHILD ABUSE AND NEGLECT

We suggest that the increasing coverage of child abuse in the mass media not only informed the general public, but also caught the attention of some state legislators. As Figure 2 shows, between 1962, when the first mass media article appeared, and 1967, when every state had passed a reporting law, 16 articles appeared in mass circulation magazines. During the same period 51 articles on the subject appeared in *The New York Times,* although some of them were the more titillating child murder stories. In addition, there were two television programs featuring child abuse (episodes in "Ben Casey, M.D.," and "Dragnet") which reached millions of viewers.

The professional media[11] demonstrated the growing awareness and interest in child abuse within many different professions. Figure 3 shows that between 1961 and 1967, there were 137 articles on child abuse listed in professional indexes.[12] The authors of these professional articles formed the core of an attentive public who supported federal legislation and who stood to benefit most from the availability of increased research funding.

Media attention to child abuse in the period of setting the state agendas (1963-1967) cannot be characterized as specifically directed at provoking governmental response. As we shall see, however, Congress, or more specifically the Subcommittee on Children and Youth,[13] did actively encourage media coverage. In 1973, the year when federal legislation was introduced, *The New York Times* published 43 articles on child abuse, more than any other year before or since. In 1974, the year when federal legislation became effective, *The New York Times* carried 34 child abuse articles and the *Readers' Guide* indexed 11 stories, its all-time high.

In addition to generating coverage of child abuse, members of Congress who were initially uninvolved in the child abuse issue may have learned about it from the *Washington Post's* coverage of a local case. The Washington newspapers, especially the *Post,* are an integral part of national political communication. On March 27, 1973, the *Post* reported that Keith and Bonnie Volk were guilty of the beating death of their two-year-old daughter, Dawn Marie. Several members of Congress reported that the article brought home to them the problem of child abuse.

The coverage of child abuse suggests two conclusions about the role of the media and agenda setting. First, issues which are brought to the attention of elected officials may have had their genesis in the activities, especially the research support, of appointed officials. Undoubtedly, the ground swell of general interest in child abuse to which Congress responded in 1973 had its origins in the

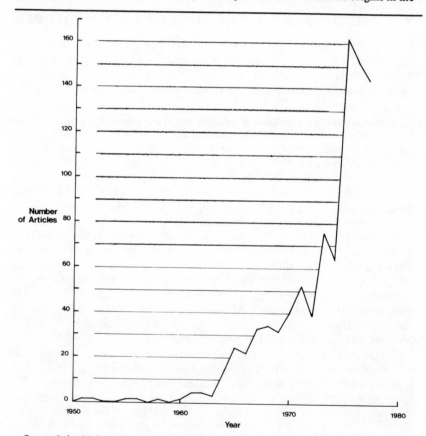

Source: *Index Medicus, The Index of Legal Periodicals, The Social Science Index, The Humanities Index,* and *The Current Index to Journals in Education*

Figure 3: PROFESSIONAL MEDIA COVERAGE OF CHILD ABUSE AND NEGLECT

work of the Children's Bureau 15 years earlier. Second, the issue attention cycles of the professional and mass media may differ, or even be at odds with each other. Whereas the mass media may be in a constant search for novel topics to amuse its consumers (Downs, 1972:42), the professional media may sustain interest in a topic for a much longer period of time, especially if funds for research remain available. Continued professional interest frequently provides pressure for the reconsideration of issues which have been eclipsed in the interest of the general population. This pressure is the source of a classic democratic dilemma. Professional pressure provides continuities, elevating political life above the sole consideration of immediate concerns. However, professional pressure is also the source of the abuse of special interests which may thrive because they are not subject to continual scrutiny.

SETTING THE AGENDAS OF THE STATE LEGISLATURES

As was mentioned, in 1963 the CB published and disseminated its booklet, "The Abused Child: Principles and Suggested Language for Legislation on Reporting of the Physically Abused Child." This booklet did not go to state legislators; instead it travelled the CB's regular dissemination route to state Child Welfare Departments and interested private groups, although some booklets were no doubt forwarded to sympathetic legislators. Other legislators independently learned about the new developments in this field. Armed with the CB guidelines, members of some private charities and professional groups approached legislators in various states. As a result, in 1963, the same year the CB promulgated their guidelines, 18 states recognized child abuse as a public issue by introducing legislation. Thirteen states passed child abuse laws that year (Children's Division, no date:1). By 1967 every state had passed some form of legislation acknowledging child abuse as a public problem.

Only four years elapsed before all states passed child abuse reporting laws, an adoption rate five times faster than the average for other innovations between 1933 and 1966 (Walker, 1969:895). Even the four-year time span understates the rate of adoption. In 1963 and 1965 three states did not convene regular sessions of their legislatures, and in 1964 and 1966 27 and 26 states respectively did not convene regular sessions. Altogether more than half the state legislatures were not meeting regularly at least half of the time period during which this policy diffused (Council of State Governments, 1962-1969).

Similar to the situation in the CB, the period between agenda setting and action was so short in many states that the empirical distinction between recognition and response is difficult to maintain. Analysis of the first 13 child abuse statutes helps us to understand why issue recognition moved so quickly to institutional action. Similarly, analysis of the many model statutes and guidelines which followed those promulgated by the CB demonstrate why diffusion proceeded so quickly.

By 1967 every state had responded to the problem of child abuse (and sometimes child neglect) by instituting voluntary or mandatory reporting laws. Of the *initial* 13 state child abuse laws, however, only 10 were reporting laws. The other three defined the crime of child abuse and discussed the limits of the sentence for this crime. Eight of the laws were incorporated in the criminal codes, while five were placed in statutory sections on welfare or general administration (Children's Division, no date:1-3). Illinois was the only state which appropriated funds for implementing its original child abuse law.

Despite this statutory diversity, these 13 original laws had one trait in common: each can be considered an invocation of social norms to protect children. Each was a public statement of the values of the community. That some of the laws stressed reporting as a protection for children and others stressed punishment for offenders only reemphasizes that the norms being tapped were complex and multidimensional.

Whichever norms were invoked, politicians were indeed pleased to associate themselves with a valence issue as impervious to attack as child abuse. When rectitude made no demands on the public purse, they were all the more eager to be associated with the issue. The legislators' practice of not appropriating extra service money while setting up a mechanism which created more service users was eventually to have serious consequences. For example, when Florida adopted a toll-free 24-hour WATS line and mounted a public education campaign, the number of reported child abuse and neglect cases rose from 17 to 19,120 (Sussman and Cohen, 1975:125). It is doubtful that the agencies receiving those reports could process let alone respond to them.

From a pragmatic point of view, support for child abuse legislation was a sure-win situation for virtually all of the state legislators involved in the passage of the first laws. It allowed them to be on record supporting a central ideal of American culture—the importance of children—without spending public money. This fact helps to explain the rapid pace between issue recognition and action; however it is not sufficient to explain the extremely rapid adoption of child abuse laws by all 50 states.

The rapid diffusion of reporting laws was facilitated by the litany of model statutes and legislative guidelines formulated and distributed between 1963 and 1967. In its 1963 publication, the CB recommended that reports of child abuse be made to peace officers on the principle that officers are always available.[14] In the same year, the American Humane Association published legislative guidelines urging reporting to child welfare agencies on the principle that the law should emphasize the service outcomes of reporting, not the punitive ones, if reporting were to be encouraged. Then in 1965 the Council of State Governments published a model statute, a compromise between those of the CB and AHA, but which did support reporting to the police. Also in 1965, the American Medical Association (AMA), unhappy with mandatory reporting under penalty of criminal prosecution applicable only to physicians, contributed its own model statute. The prestigious AMA proposed voluntary reporting by professional groups such as doctors, nurses, teachers, and social workers to either the police or a child welfare agency. The American Academy of Pediatrics devised still another model statute, published in 1966, favoring mandatory reporting only by physicians to social service agencies.[15]

In widely distributing their guidelines, each of these groups increased the pressure for state action. State legislatures responded promptly and deliberately.

As the "experts" began to offer advice, states began to revise the child abuse reporting laws they had so recently passed. A state-by-state comparison of child abuse reporting laws between 1963 and 1976 shows a movement toward similarity of statutes. These laws can no longer merely be considered invocations of public values. Additionally, they reflect the collective judgments of experts about how to maintain and review this public responsibility.

What caused the continual changes in child abuse reporting laws? Revisions to reflect current professional expertise only account for part of the activity. Other changes were the result of the legislative mandate of the federal Child Abuse Prevention and Treatment Act (CAPTA) passed in 1974. In order to receive discretionary service funds, CAPTA required states to enact reporting laws completely conforming to a list of stringent professional standards. Because of the detail of the requirements, only 42 states presently have reporting laws in compliance with federal standards.[16] To aid the states not in compliance, in 1977 the National Center for Child Abuse and Neglect (created by CAPTA and reporting to the Chief of the Children's Bureau) prepared a draft of a model child protection act. It has been criticized by some legal scholars and policy analysts as being too long and cumbersome for state adoption. Therefore, the model act may not precipitate a "supply driven" adoption of changes in state reporting laws, a goal of the National Center.

SETTING THE AGENDA OF THE CONGRESS

Unlike the state legislatures, considerable time separated the first Congressional recognition of child abuse and the first Congressional action, making it possible to trace easily the stages of agenda setting. The movement to promote federal legislation on child abuse began in 1969 with action by Congressman Mario Biaggi (D-N.Y.). During that and subsequent years Biaggi introduced legislation and spoke periodically on the floor of the House about the increasing epidemic of child abuse. All of these bills languished and eventually died in the House Ways and Means Committee. This failure can be attributed in part to a series of tactical miscalculations. Biaggi's early bills suggested a child abuse amendment to the Social Security Act which "automatically" referred the bills to Ways and Means. Ways and Means is noted for its indifference to social service legislation. But probably more important than poor committee assignment, lack of interest in child abuse by Congressional leaders accounts for the four-year span between issue recognition and adoption.

Indeed, the Senate, not the House, provided the initial leadership on the issue of child abuse. Senate interest was first marked by the Subcommittee on Children and Youth's fall 1972 publication of a book of readings on the topic. In 1971, as a new subcommittee of the Committee on Labor and Public Welfare, the senior staff had worked with Subcommittee Chairman Walter F. Mondale on the ill-fated Comprehensive Child Development Act. The new subcommittee, without a fixed agenda, was looking for interesting issues—issues which might succeed where the CCDA had failed. The first interest of the Subcommittee was the legal rights of children. This movement, with its strong emphasis on child advocacy, is intimately linked to the child abuse issue because child abuse cases are persuasive examples of the situation when the legal needs of children differ from the legal needs of their caretakers. It was a short and easy move to a separate interest in child abuse. In both these areas the subcommittee acted like the classic young organization, rich with the organizational gold of no prior issue commitments and ready to create an agenda to establish its organizational credentials.

On February 27, 1973, the senior staff of the subcommittee wrote a memo to then-Senator Mondale suggesting several issues, child abuse prominent among them, that the subcommittee could pursue, and outlining the strategies for action. Mondale chose to concentrate on child abuse, later joking that not even Richard Nixon could be for child abuse—a fact which might make it possible to enact child abuse legislation in a climate otherwise hostile to service legislation. Mondale introduced legislation and the committee staff immediately began to prepare for hearings. Mondale's decision to proceed indicated that the issue had been adopted, and the speed with which legislation was introduced and hearings scheduled indicated its high priority.

Committee hearings are a strong but not certain indication that a chamber will eventually vote on an issue. The Senate hearings were quite deliberately designed to generate and maintain Congressional interest in child abuse and to activate the vocal interest, if not outrage, of the citizenry. The Senate hearings were packaged to emphasize the most extreme cases of child abuse, or as described by one of those involved with the hearings, "an effort was made to present the human side of child abuse." Staff felt that child neglect was more extensive than child abuse but realized that less consensus existed on the definition of neglect. Some administration representatives regarded the tenor and coverage of the hearings as yellow journalism. However, sensationalism succeeded. National coverage of the Senate hearings brought the expected spate of mail. The House hearings, held several months later, were more sedate because House staff recognized that the media would not respond with as much interest to a second round of sensationalism, and because the Senate regularly receives better media coverage than the House.

Although Congressman Biaggi joined by Congressman Peter Peyser (then R., N.Y.) had introduced House legislation early in 1973, the companion legislation to the Mondale bill was introduced by novice Congresswoman Patricia Schroeder (D., Colo.). In addition to being a *new* member of Congress, Schroeder also was *not* a member of the Subcommittee on Select Education (of the Labor and Education Committee) which received the bill. She therefore needed to rely on the leadership of Congressman John Brademas (D. Ind.), who chaired the subcommittee. Friction arose between them over control of the bill. Brademas was a prominent, respected, and experienced Congressional leader noted for his interest in child development. Schroeder was a concerned Congressional newcomer with Kempe as a constituent. Schroeder overcame her low status as a freshman member by using her role as a woman to promote interest in child abuse. In some ways, Schroeder violated the norms of freshman behavior, upsetting the clear expectations which allow the House to run predictably. The friction was overcome, however, by a sincere concern on both parts for the issue.

The hearings in both Houses maintained, even increased, Congressional interest in child abuse, facilitated the movement from subcommittee to committee, and ensured, along with strong leadership, that the issue would be brought to a vote. The valence quality of the issue was reflected in the vote: 57 for CAPTA versus seven against in the Senate, and 354 for versus 36 against in the House. Because the Nixon administration opposed CAPTA, virtually all the nay votes came from Republicans, all seven in the Senate and 24 of 36 in the House.

On April 24, 1978, after a one year pro forma renewal, CAPTA was reenacted under the guise of the Child Abuse Prevention and Treatment and Adoption Reform Act (CAPTARA). The reconsideration of CAPTA was affected by two related issues, subsidized adoption[17] and child pornography. Title II of S. 961, the Opportunities for Adoption Act of 1977, proposed the reenactment of CAPTA for two years at the same level of funding but with slightly different emphasis on the types of expenditures to be made. By including the reauthorization of CAPTA in this legislation it was hoped that a large and committed constituency already interested in children's issues would lend support to subsidized adoptions. In final form CAPTARA fell short of legislating subsidized adoption. However, supporters of subsidized adoption employed a classic technique in their legislative attempt: they tied a strong issue with almost no detractors to one which was more problematic.

In the House, the reauthorization of CAPTA was not related to subsidized adoption. Rather, the House bill (H.6693) included a new section which imposed a $50,000 fine and maximum imprisonment of 20 years (or both) for willfully causing or allowing child pornography. The problem of child pornography has been the particular interest of Dr. Judiann Densen-Gerber. Through her efforts, the media were replete with news articles and editorials on the issue. We asked those we interviewed about the relationship of child pornography to child abuse. From an agenda maintenance perspective there were two possible relationships: (1) that child abuse and neglect needed the infusion of concern generated by an even more heinous behavior in order to retain public or Congressional support, or (2) that child pornography was capitalizing on the legitimacy of child abuse because it was doubtful that it would or should stand as a separate issue. Most legislators and administrators, regardless of partisanship, felt that the issue of child pornography was exaggerated, that it was best left to the state legislators (who, not surprisingly, have proposed a rash of child pornography bills), and that it was riding on the established legitimacy of child abuse. If the federal government became active in the child pornography issue, most preferred that it be directed away from Subcommittee on Select Education toward the Judiciary Committee.

Recently in both the Senate and the House, the consensual quality of child abuse was used to promote more controversial issues. We asked the people who set the Congressional agenda in 1973 whether they thought that child abuse was a politically divisive issue. Most, again regardless of partisanship, reported that they did not think it was. They were defining "politically divisive" in terms of hostile partisanship or extreme ideology. It is interesting to note that routine partisanship, such as that present in the Administration's position, was not considered divisive.

Administrators occasionally reported that in 1973 child abuse was divisive in the sense that it set the Administration and Congress against each other. This response is perhaps best interpreted in the light of the cross-pressures felt by the professional staff in OCD and CB. Professional staff members were sympathetic to the necessity for strong action to prevent and treat child abuse. They were also aware very early in the legislative process that a law would be enacted. Yet they were required to present the Administration's position against any separate legislation on child abuse. Feeling among them ran so high that one staff member, Dr. Frederick Green, then Associate Director of the CB, refused to testify against the bill. Believing that he should not retain his position if he could not support the Administration, he chose to resign, waiting only until the Senate hearings had closed so as not to politicize the issue. Other professional staff expressed discomfort with the conflict between professional beliefs and required institutional roles. This highlights a particularly important aspect of valence issues: they provide a respite from the acrimony of politics. When no respite occurs, officials are less likely to view an issue as noncontroversial. If politics is one's job, an issue must be consensual within one's own sphere as well as socially consensual to be considered a true valence issue.

CONCLUSION

As mentioned in the introduction, this research was planned to be hypothesis organizing: that is, to evaluate which hypotheses or groups of hypotheses were especially useful in understanding agenda setting. For the federal bureaucracy, the state legislatures, and Congress we recounted how the issue of child abuse and neglect was recognized, adopted, prioritized, and maintained. This account, coupled with the literature on agenda setting, suggests that two groups of hypotheses—those dealing with slack resources and those dealing with labeling— are consistently useful in explaining agenda setting. The first part of the conclusions elaborates on the role of slack resources and labeling in agenda setting. The second part speculates on the role of valence issues in personal career building and institutional maintenance.

Each agenda set in this case study demonstrates that slack resources encourage the adoption of new issues (Cyert and March, 1963:278-279; Walker, 1977:444). However, in each instance, organizational resources, not surplus funds, provided the slack. The Subcommittee on Children and Youth is the clearest example of slack organizational resources. Newly organized in 1971, the subcommittee's staff was young, energetic, ambitious, and searching for an issue after completing work on child advocacy. The Subcommittee Chairman, Walter F. Mondale, was contemplating running for President. Personal interest, political ambition, the availability of trained subcommittee staff without other policy commitments, and the vehicle of Senate hearings catapulted Mondale into providing the leadership necessary for child abuse to achieve the Congressional agenda.

For states, slack resources did not take the form of staff or legislators looking for a new issue. Rather, the recognition of child abuse by the states was the result of the absence of political or economic costs associated with the issue. A "no cost" activity performs the same function as expansion to take up slack resources: it allows for greater productivity, perhaps greater power, without initially requiring extra resources.

The Children's Bureau is a less forceful case of slack resources. Steiner (1976:36-46) argues that the Children's Bureau was never a particularly well-respected organization and it never appeared to be overworked. Following this train of thought, the CB perpetually had slack organizational resources. However, the CB retained a well-defined although somewhat narrow definition of mission. Thus, when an issue congruent to the CB's mission was brought to its attention, there existed both the consensus and the resources with which to respond.

As noted, surplus funds were the least important slack resource in each instance of agenda setting. Even the general state of the economy was not overly important. For example, the agendas of the CB and Congress were set during recessions. Of course, the extremely limited cost of the CB's response to child abuse made the state of the economy a trivial factor. But congressional response did have a price tag: $57 million for the first three and one-half years. In FY76 an additional $46.5 million was spent on child abuse and neglect under Title IVb (Child Welfare Services) of the Social Security Act (SSA). Title XX of the SSA, born about the same time as CAPTA, expressly allowed the expenditures of social service money for child abuse and neglect cases. In FY76, approximately $200 million of Title XX money was spent on child abuse and neglect. These monetary resources *followed* organizational willingness. For Congress, fiscal expenditures were the *product* of willingness to recognize and adopt the issue.

In addition to slack organizational resources, careful labeling and promotion of the child abuse issue helped it to achieve professional and governmental agendas. The dominant label for the issue changed in the process of agenda setting. Kempe established the legitimacy of the problem for physicians by naming it the "battered child syndrome." That label highlighted the medical aspects of the issue. In government forums, however, the problem was almost uniformly labeled "child abuse." The transformation was deliberate, the result of the issue partisans recognizing that "child abuse" was the term which encouraged the most consensus among political elites because it denoted the most extreme behavior. The 1973 Senate hearings exemplify the political necessity of maintaining the child abuse label. In an exchange between Dr. David Gil, a researcher, and Senator Jennings Randolph (D., W. Va.) the Senator took umbrage with Gil's insistence that any corporal punishment was child abuse. Physical discipline was not child abuse, asserted Randolph, who added, "I think if we were to draw sides, I would rather have more paddling and less pampering of children." The example demonstrates that when child abuse was explicitly expanded to include anything more than deliberately brutal behavior it lost its valence quality.

The powerful role of the child abuse label also demonstrates a more general characteristic of issue naming: that issue labels have an implicit message for those not directly interested in a topic as well as for those directly affected. For example, most professionals agreed that child neglect was more pervasive and harder to remedy than child abuse, yet neglect was downplayed in the agenda setting process. By design, those who promoted governmental recognition and action for child abuse emphasized that aspect of the issue on which there was the *most* consensus and the *strongest* emotions, namely abuse rather than neglect. Such a strategy reassures the inattentive public. An inattentive public remains inattentive by receiving messages reaffirming its ideal images of the polity. Thus, in political arenas, labeling frequently emphasizes the valence aspects of issues. However, the strategy of employing valence labels has two weaknesses. First, if the label is a sham, the attentive public may denounce it. Second, ideal images of the polity vary among people and over time, and finding an adequate, enduring valence label may be difficult. Issue labels, then, must be conferred with considerable political wisdom.

The child abuse case also allows us to comment on how valence issues may be used in personal career development and institutional survival. In discussing election campaigns, Campbell and associates (1966:170-171) suggest that valence issues are good issues on which to mount a campaign. We can further suggest that one of the advantages accruing to incumbents is the opportunity to promote institutional recognition of valence issues.[18] Mondale, for example, benefitted politically from championing federal response to child abuse, gaining national press coverage and probably increased name recognition. State legislators derived similar benefits from their attachment to the issue. The opportunity to foster one's political career by promoting a valence issue definitely provided leadership on the issue of child abuse. Without that energetic leadership, interest in the issue would have died.

The findings on the political advantages of association with valence issues raise many questions for further research. We need to know, for instance, what determines the mix of valence and position issues in a governmental unit at any given time; what kind of politicians (e.g., work horses or show horses) initiate recognition of valence issues; and whether valence issues perform the "latent function" (Gans, 1972) of diffusing hostilities and reestablishing consensus within political forums.

Similarly, we need to know more about how valence issues are employed to ensure institutional survival. For a long time, the issue of child abuse and neglect ensured the survival of the Office of Child Development. No one in OCD originally planned to save a job or even to save a declining institution. Rather, the OCD (and the CB within it) was given the task of coordinating research on child abuse and neglect at a time when the issue had relatively low federal visibility. The times changed, however; Congress became interested, and the existing expertise on child abuse and neglect proved to be OCD's saving grace. By emphasizing the issue of child abuse and neglect, OCD focused on a particularly imperiled group of children, a strategy which was preferred in HEW. There are, of course, many imperiled groups of children: e.g., minority children or juvenile delinquents. OCD was fortunate that the group of children in which they unwittingly specialized was a group whose needs no one assailed. This suggests that other governmental units may recognize and then adopt valence issues to ensure organizational longevity.

The child abuse issue may lend one final insight into the study of agenda setting. When a new issue achieves a governmental agenda it sets a precedent, indeed paves the way, for governmental consideration of similar issues. Government agendas are approached, if not set, by clusters of issues. Governmental recognition of child abuse has encouraged demands for governmental recognition and remedies for battered women, sexual abuse of children, rape, and child pornography. In the same vein, Walker (1977:435-43) showed that once traffic safety made the Congressional agenda, coal mine safety and general occupational safety followed right behind. There are two related reasons for the clustering of issues in agenda setting. First, as is the case for sexual abuse of children or child pornography, broadly defined issues are increasingly specified. Second, groups with similar problems see the success of parallel issues, want a slice of the pie and recognize, if they are knowledgeable, that informal elite coalitions exist if they act quickly. Thus, the acceptance of one issue on the discretionary agenda may substantially limit the size and flexibility of that agenda, not only because of the direct consequences of the first issue (Crenson, 1971:172), but also because the first issue's siblings may demand attention.

In sum, we have briefly described the important steps which transformed child abuse from a private charity concern to a prominent social welfare issue. Child abuse sequentially achieved the agendas of the Children's Bureau, the state legislatures, and Congress. Focusing on the steps of the agenda setting process (issue recognition, adoption, prioritizing and maintenance), we presented a history of how each of these agendas was achieved. We found that without organizational slack resources, a powerful and mobilizing label for the problem, and the incentives for leadership arising from valence issues, child abuse would have remained in the private sector. But these situations did occur and child abuse has a secure place on the domestic social agenda in America.

NOTES

1. We employ the term "Child Welfare Department" to cover any state administrative unit dealing with child welfare services and benefits, regardless of name.

2. Lijphart has two categories of case studies similar to our "hypothesis organizing" category called "theory confirming" and "theory infirming" cases. See Lijphart, 1971.

3. For a discussion of long-term issue maintenance in the Senate, see Walker, 1977.

4. For examples particularly relevant to governmental agenda setting, see Anthony and Herzlinger, 1975; McGregor, 1976.

5. Conventional wisdom states that since the mid-1930s there has been a tradition of government expansion during times of depression and recession as a counter to the business cycle. Using public employment as a proxy for exhaustive spending, Borcherding (1977:37) found that state and local government activity is counter-cyclical but federal activity has been mainly procyclical or of negligible consequence.

6. The relationship of equity and efficiency cycles to the business cycle is largely unexplored. It appears, however, that equity cycles are somewhat related to periods of relatively high economic growth and efficiency cycles are somewhat related to periods of lower economic growth. See Mishan, 1977.

7. For a review of the early literature on child abuse, see Gil, 1970:18-25.

8. The extensiveness of child abuse is unknown. Hortatory articles frequently suggest it is on the increase, but the true incidence and prevalence is extremely difficult to ascertain. For an excellent discussion of incidence and prevalence rates, see Nagi, 1977:31-58.

9. Steiner, 1976:36-46, and Children Today, 1972.

10. Mass circulation magazines are defined as those indexed in the *Readers' Guide to Periodical Literature.*

11. The professional media are defined as those articles listed on *Index Medicus, The Index of Legal Periodicals, The Social Science Index, The Humanities Index,* and *The Current Index to Journals in Education.*

12. The figure of 137 professional articles on child abuse was derived by summing all the professional index entries, without eliminating double entries, if any.

13. The Subcommittee on Children and Youth is now called the Subcommittee on Child and Human Development.

14. The CB eventually moved away from its original preference for reporting child abuse to police officers.

15. The discussion on model statutes is based on Thomas, 1972:331-333.

16. P.L. 93-247, Sect. 4(b)(2)(A-J).

17. The argument in favor of subsidized adoption is that foster care is supported out of the public treasury, but relatives of an orphaned or abandoned child, or foster paresnts who want to provide a permanent home for a child receive no monetary support.

18. Politicians must be careful in their choice of valence issues, making sure that the problem is defined in such a way as not to seem frivolous.

REFERENCES

ALDRICH, H. (1973). "Organizational boundaries and interorganizational conflict." Pp. 379-393 in F. Baker (ed.), Organization systems. Homewood, Ill.: Richard D. Irwin.

ANTHONY, R. N., and HERZLINGER, R. E. (1975). Management control in nonprofit organizations. Homewood, Ill.: Richard D. Irwin.

BACHRACH, P., and BARATZ, M. (1963). "Decisions and non-decisions: An analytic framework." American Political Science Review, 57(September):632-642.

BECKER, M. H. (1970). "Sociometric location and innovativeness: Reformulation and extension of the diffusion model." American Sociological Review, 35(April):267-282.

BORCHERDING, T. E. (1977). "One hundred years of public spending, 1870-1970." In T. E. Borcherding (ed.), Budgets and bureaucrats: The sources of government growth. Durham, N.C.: Duke University Press.

────── (1977). "The sources of growth of public expenditures in the United States, 1902-1970." In T. E. Borcherding (ed.), Budgets and bureaucrats: The sources of government growth. Durham, N.C.: Duke University Press.

BREMMER, R. H. (ed.) (1970). Children and youth in America: A documentary history, Vol. I: 1600-1865. Cambridge, Mass.: Harvard University Press.

CAMPBELL, A., et al. (1966). Elections and the political order. New York: Wiley.

Children Today (1972). "Six decades of action for children." March-April, 1:4.

Children's Division, American Humane Association (no date). Review of legislation to protect the battered child: A study of laws enacted in 1963. Denver: author.

COBB, R. W., and ELDER, C. D. (1972). Participation in American politics: The dynamics of agenda-building. Boston: Allyn and Bacon.

COBB, R. W., et al. (1976). "Agenda-building as a comparative process." American Political Science Review, 70(March):126-138.

Council of State Governments (1962-1965). The book of the states. Lexington, Ky.: author.

────── (1966-1967). The book of the states. Lexington, Ky.: author.

────── (1968-1969). The book of the states. Lexington, Ky.: author.

CRENSON, M. A. (1971). The un-politics of air pollution. Baltimore: John Hopkins Press.

CYERT, R. M., and MARCH, J. G. (1963). A behavioral theory of the firm. Englewood Cliffs, N.J.: Prentice-Hall.

DeFRANCIS, V. (1956). Child protective services in the United States: Reporting a nation-wide survey. Denver: Children's Division, American Humane Association.

DeMAUSE, L. (1975). "Our forebears made childhood a nightmare." Psychology Today, 8 (April):85-88.

DOWNS, A. (1972). "Up and down with ecology—'The issue attention cycle.' Public Interest, 32(Summer):38-50.

ERIKSON, K. T. (1967). "Notes on the sociology of deviance." Pp. 294-304 in T. J. Scheff (ed.), Mental illness and social processes. New York: Harper and Row.

EYESTONE, R. (1977). "Confusion, diffusion, and innovation." American Political Science Review, 71(June):441-447.

GANS, H. J. (1972). "The positive functions of poverty." American Journal of Sociology, 78(September):275-276.

GERGEN, K. J. (1968). "Assessing the leverage points in the process of policy formation. Pp. 181-203 in R. A. Bauer and K. G. Gergen (eds.), The study of policy formation. New York: Free Press.

GIL, D. G. (1970). Violence against children: Physical child abuse against children. Cambridge, Mass.: Harvard University Press.

GRAY, V. (1973). "Innovation in the states: A diffusion study." American Political Science Review, 67(December):1174:1185.

GROENNINGS, S. (1970). "Patterns, strategies and payoffs in Norwegian coalition forma-tion." Pp. 60-79 in S. Groennings et al. (eds.), The study of coalition behavior: Theoretical perspectives and cases from four continents. New York: Holt, Rinehart, and Winston.

In re Gault (1967) 387 U.S. 1, 61.

KEMPE, C. H., et al. (1962). "The battered child syndrome." Journal of the American Medical Association, 181(July 7):17-42.

KOTZ, N. (1969). Let them eat promises: The politics of hunger in America. Englewood Cliffs, N.J.: Prentice Hall.

LAZARSFELD, P. F., and MERTON, R. K. (1971). "Mass communication, popular taste, and organized social action." Pp. 554-578 in W. Schramm and D. F. Roberts (eds.), The process and effects of mass communication. Urbana, Ill.: University of Illinois Press.

LIGHT R. J. (1973). "Abused and neglected children in America: A study of alternative policies." Harvard Educational Review, 43(November):556-598.

LIJPHART, A. (1971). "Comparative politics and the comparative method." American Political Science Review, 65(September):682-693.

McCOOMBS, M. E., and SHAW, D. L. (1972). "The agenda-setting function of mass media." Public Opinion Quarterly, 36(Summer):176-187.

McGREGOR, D. (1976). "The human side of enterprise." Pp. 214-221 in R. J. Stillman, II (ed.), Public administration: Concepts and cases. Boston: Houghton Mifflin.

MERCER, J. R. (1973). Labeling the mentally retarded. Berkeley: University of California Press.

MILLER, W. E., and LEVITAN, T. E. (1976). Leadership and change: The new politics and the American electorate. Cambridge, Mass.: Winthrop.

MISHAN, E. J. (1977). The economic growth debate. London: George Allen and Unwin.

NADEL, M. V. (1976). "Consumer protection becomes a public issue (again)." Pp. 22-34 in J. E. Anderson (ed.), Cases in public policy making. New York: Praeger.

NAGI, S. Z. (1977). Child maltreatment in the United States: A challenge to social institu-tions. New York: Columbia University Press.

National Center on Child Abuse and Neglect (1977). Model child protection act with commentary. Washington, D.C.: H.E.W., Office of Human Development Services, Administration for Children, Youth and Families, Children's Bureau.

OLSON, M., Jr. (1971). The logic of collective action. New York: Schocken.

PROSCIO, A. J. (1977). A pernicious charity: Being an inquiry into how even the most complicated decisions become simple when you know how they turned out. Princeton: Woodrow Wilson School, Princeton University, May 26, xerox.

SMELSER, N. (1962). Theory of collective behavior. New York: Free Press.

STEINER, G. Y. (1976). The children's cause. Washington, D.C.: Brookings.

SUSSMAN, A. and COHEN, S. J. (1975). Reporting child abuse and neglect: Guidelines for legislation. Cambridge, Mass.: Ballinger.

TARSCHYS, D. (1975). "The growth in public expenditure, nine modes of explanation." Pp. 9-31 in Scandinavian political studies, vol. 10. Norway: Universitetsforlaget; and Beverly Hills, Cal.: Sage.

THOMAS, M. P., Jr. (1972). "Child abuse and neglect, part I: Historical overview, legal matrix and social perspectives." North Carolina Law Review, 50(February):293-349.

TRATTNER, W. I. (1974). From poor law to welfare state. New York: Free Press.

TRUMAN, D. B. (1951). The governmental process. New York: Knopf.

United States Children's Bureau (1957). Proposals for drafting principles and suggested language for legislation on public child welfare and youth services. Washington, D.C.: H.E.W., Social Security Administration.

_____ (1963). The abused child: Principles and suggested language for legislation on reporting of the physically abused child. Washington, D.C.: H.E.W., Welfare Administration.

WALKER, J. L. (1969). "The diffusion of innovations among the American states." American Political Science Review, 63(September):880-899.

_____ (1974). "The diffusion of knowledge and policy change: Toward a theory of agenda-setting." Paper presented at the 1974 Annual Meeting of the American Political Science Association, Chicago, August 29-September 2.

_____ (1977). "Setting the agenda in the U.S. Senate: A theory of problem selection." British Journal of Political Science, 7(October):423-445.

Washington post (1973). "Two guilty in death of baby." March 27.

WILSON, J. Q. (1966). "Innovation in organization: Notes toward a theory." Pp. 194-218 in J. D. Thompson (ed.), Approaches to organizational design. Pittsburgh: University of Pittsburgh Press.

ZALTMAN, G., et al. (1973). Innovations and organizations. New York: Wiley Interscience.

2

GROWTH AND ITS DISCONTENTS:
Origins Of Local Population Controls

NELSON ROSENBAUM

The Urban Institute

INTRODUCTION

It is 50 years since the Standard State Zoning Enabling Act and the Standard City Planning Enabling Act were developed as model statutes through which states could delegate police power authority over land use to local governments. Under the impetus of a wave of enthusiasm for zoning and planning, most states rapidly passed enabling acts during the 1930s and 1940s. Counties and municipalities exercising regulation under these statutes were allowed to control the spatial pattern of land development through the standard techniques of "Euclidian" zoning, comprehensive land use planning, and subdivision plat approval.

Among local government officials exercising police power regulation over land use, satisfaction with the standard techniques of spatial control remained substantial through the early 1960s. At that point, however, a number of jurisdictions—particularly suburban municipalities that were feeling the full weight of population migration from the great metropolitan cities—began to experiment with additional regulatory methods that would provide some control

AUTHOR'S NOTE: *An earlier version of this paper was presented at the 1977 annual meeting of the American Political Science Association. The author would like to thank Miriam Kohler of the Urban Institute for her invaluable research assistance and Paul Sabatier, Robert Johnston, Jack Walker, Worth Bateman, and Daniel Mandelker for their constructive comments and critiques.*

over the *timing* or *sequence* of land development. The objective of these techniques was to prevent new development from overwhelming the fiscal capacities and public services of the established community. Dramatic property tax increases, double sessions at the public schools, and water supply crises were among the most common stimuli of experimentation with timing control mechanisms such as Planned Unit Development Zoning, Capital Facilities Programming, Sewer and Water Hookup Moratoria, Performance Permit Systems, and Urban Service Area Designations. While these new methods are still undergoing an elaborate and expensive series of legal attacks across the nation, there is general recognition among land use professionals that they fall within the broad scope of the legitimate exercise of the police power. Almost all of the controls are officially based upon some type of documented health and safety rationale—inadequate sewage capacity, over-crowding in the schools, and so forth. In addition, all of the new techniques incorporate some provision for flexibility—whether through the allocation of official variances and special exceptions, or through the willingness of the developer to defray the cost of public services himself. Under these circumstances, the courts have generally viewed such methods as a logical extension of and supplement to the standard land use controls exercised under state enabling authority.[1] These types of controls are rapidly diffusing across the nation in the 1970s as legal uncertainty diminishes.

Innovation in land use control has not stopped with regulation of the timing or sequencing of land development. In the last few years, an entirely new dimension of police power control has arisen which seeks to impose through regulatory permit requirements *an absolute numerical limit upon the number of dwelling units or residents allowed in a community.* While proponents of population control have attempted to link the imposition of absolute limits on growth to the established tradition of land use controls based upon protection of "health, safety, and general welfare," the explicit limitation of population clearly represents a dramatic and distinct departure from past practice. Utilization of land use control authority for population limitation was certainly never envisioned in the enabling statutes of most states.

The new crop of land use controls is currently under furious legal attack in state and federal courts. A large part of the scholarly commentary on these controls has focused on the statutory and constitutional issues involved in these cases such as the right to travel. As yet, however, there has been no attempt to focus upon the political origins and implications of such limits to growth. Why have these communities challenged the American gospel of growth? How did the idea of population limitation get on the public agenda? Are these jurisdictions idiosyncratic aberrrations or is the innovation likely to spread until the United States becomes a confederation of autarchic city-states?

The objective of this chapter is to address these issues through a detailed comparative analysis of the origins of population controls in the three "pioneer" cities that initiated the innovation: Boca Raton, Florida; Boulder, Colorado; and Petaluma, California. As the original innovators, these three small cities have been in the forefront of litigation over population controls and are the most familiar of the jurisdictions that have implemented population control through land use regulation.

Within the context of a brief narrative of the specific events leading up to the imposition of population controls in each city, the comparative analysis is organized around three themes. First, the major antecedent conditions of innovation will be examinaed. Identification of common dispositional factors among the three cities is a critical task in estimating the likely future diffusion of the policy innovation. Second, the pattern of policy initiation in the three cities will be explored. Who originated the idea of imposing a numerical limit on housing units and residents? How did the idea get on the agenda of official action? How much cross-fertilization was there between the three innovative municipalities? Third, the politics of adoption will be assessed. Which groups supported and opposed the proposal for population controls? What accounts for differing degrees of public support for population controls in the three communities. Based upon these three points of comparison, we will attempt to project the likely future spread of population control ordinances.

BOULDER

The city of Boulder, Colorado, is located approximately 30 miles from Denver in a valley surrounded by plateaus and the Rocky Mountain foothills. Owing to its status as a university center and to its attractive natural setting, Boulder has attracted considerable research activity and other white-collar professional employment. As a result of growth in these sectors of the economy, the city and its surrounding area have experienced a dramatic increase in population. From 1960 to 1970, Boulder's total population nearly doubled, from 37,718 to 68,634. Over the same time period, the proportion of its professional and technical workers also increased by 7.4%.

As early as the mid-1950s, Boulder initiated major steps to control the pattern and timing of its growth. In 1958, an urban service line was drawn around the city, beyond which water service would not be extended. This action, the purpose of which was to preserve Boulder's scenic foothills, was formalized and expanded in 1965 through adoption of a "Service Area Plan," which charted future directions for extension of urban services. In 1970, the Boulder Valley Comprehensive Plan was adopted. The plan emphasized that further residential development should be limited to the core area of the city to protect the scenic resources of the Boulder Valley. The plan also proposed that no further employment centers should be established in the Boulder area. Employers should henceforth be limited to areas already zoned for their needs. Despite these policies, the plan predicted that Boulder's population would rise to 140,000 by 1990 if present migration trends continued. This prediction called into question the ultimate ability of traditional land use controls to preserve the uncrowded small-town atmosphere and the magnificent scenery that attracted people to Boulder in the first place.

Public debate on the comprehensive plan was the crucial catalyst to the idea of explicitly limiting population growth. Profoundly shocked by the projection of 140,000 residents, a group of students and young citizen activists called "People United to Reclaim the Environment" conducted a survey of local residents in which alternative population limits lower than 140,000 were offered for consideration. An overwhelming majority of responses indicated that existing residents favored no more than a maximum population of 100,000 in the Boulder area. This figure of 100,000 was then adopted as an optimum population target by the local affiliate of Zero Population Growth. Looking for a dramatic issue, the ZPG group sucessfully circulated initiative petitions to place a referendum issue on the November 1971 ballot which would establish 100,000 as the official population goal for the city.

The Boulder City Council, while sympathetic to the concept of limiting growth, nevertheless looked upon the Boulder Valley Comprehensive Plan and attempts by the Planning Department to develop new timing controls as the prime means of restraining the rate of development. In opposition to the ZPG initiative, the council therefore proposed a rival referendum issue on the November ballot calling for further study of the optimum population and growth rate for the Boulder Valley.

In the election of November 1971, the ZPG referendum was defeated by a ratio of 60% to 40%. The City Council's measure was approved by 70% to 30%. The council was thus given further time to experiment with adaptations of traditional land use controls. The council took a number of actions to implement this opportunity. In March 1972, it officially adopted the Interim Growth Policy which dedicated the city to slowing significantly the rate of population growth, and discouraged any further primary employers from locating in the area. In addition, the council revised the city zoning ordinance to place severe restrictions on development in areas of steep slopes and flood plains. In conjunction with this action, Boulder County placed a moratorium on new subdivisions in unincorporated areas while it prepared a stringent new subdivision control ordinance. The centerpiece of this growth control system was, however, the city's policy on sewer and water hookups. Through a substantial hookup fee for sewer and water service and restrictions on extension of public services beyond the Urban Service Line, the city hoped to keep the growth of new housing units to a significantly lower rate than in the 1960s.

With this extensive array of timing controls in place and an intensive study of future growth underway by the Planning Department and the Boulder Growth Study Commission, the advocates of explicit population control temporarily remained quiescent. However, this equilibrium was soon upset by a dramatic court ruling.

On August 1, 1972, Lawrence Robinson filed an applicaton with the city to extend water services to his property, which lay outside the Urban Service Line. The city denied Robinson's request, and he subsequently took the city to court. On May 20, 1974, the District Court of Boulder ruled that the city in its role as a public utility had a legal obligation to provide the plaintiff with water and sewer services.[2] Two years later, the city lost an appeal to the Colorado Supreme Court.

As a result of the setback to timing controls in the *Robinson* decision, citizen groups in Boulder began to question the wisdom of relying upon the development of the growth timing system. Advocates of explicit population limitation again became active in 1975 and 1976, this time focusing upon the approach to population control utilized by Petaluma, California—i.e., restriction of the absolute number of dwelling units constructed in the community each year. The concept was developed by a number of groups into the "Slow Growth Ordinance," which established an overall limit of 450 housing units per year—half to be constructed in the core area and half in outlying areas of the city. This plan projected a population growth rate of only 1.5% per year, less than half the rate of the early 1970s and one-sixth the rate of the 1960s.

The "Slow Growth Ordinance" was proposed to the City Council by one of its own members in early 1976. By a narrow 5 to 4 margin, the council refused to submit the issue to the citizenry for a referendum vote. Initiative petitions were then successfully circulated, which placed the issue on the November 1976 ballot.

The campaign over the referendum issue was bitter and divisive. As the city planning director noted (Rosall, 1977):

> Citizens and organizations who opposed the ordinance argued that it was exclusionary, would generate higher priced housing, would actually accelerate pressures for urban sprawl by directing greater land speculation and development efforts outside of the city limits where appropriate services were not available, and threatened the free market system by the direct infringement of property rights.

On the other side, the advocates of population control argued that the *Robinson* case conclusively demonstrated that traditional land use controls and capital facilities programming could not restrict the rate of growth. They also overcame reservations about the Slow Growth Ordinance by arguing that a no vote would be interpreted as endorsement of a more permissive attitude toward growth.

The Slow Growth Ordinance was adopted by referendum in November 1976 by the narrowest of margins, 18,783 to 18,231. Support for the innovation was greatest in the core areas of the city. Support dropped off dramatically in outlying areas where housing prices would be most affected by absolute restrictions on new development.

The City of Boulder is now in the process of attempting to integrate the new population control ordinance into its revised comprehensive plan and existing building permit system. Along the lines of the Petaluma experience, the city will allocate housing unit permits by a "merit system" in which developers compete for approval of their plans. To date, Boulder's population limitation ordinance has not been subjected to legal attack, but a suit is expected by the city.

BOCA RATON

Forty miles north of Miami, on the "Goldcoast" of Florida, lies the city of Boca Raton. Until the 1960s, this city was a small, quiet community of large single-family homes built around an exclusive country club. In the last decade, however, Boca Raton became one of the state's fastest growing jurisdictions, attracting middle-class retirees and the overspill of Miami's urban population to a rapidly expanding array of apartments and multi-family dwellings.

The 1960 census recorded Boca Raton's population at 6,961. By 1970, this figure had jumped to 28,506. Between 1970 and 1973, the city's population increased by another 10,000. Most of this growth in population was composed of older persons with high incomes. Between 1960 and 1970 Boca Raton's population aged 65 and over increased by approximately 480%, and over the same time period the percentage of families with income above the national median family income rose from 43% to 61.3%.

Due to the wealth of migrants and their relatively low service demands, Boca Raton did not suffer any fiscal burden from its rapid growth. In terms of real property tax revenues, the city more than doubled its receipts in the five-year period from 1970 to 1975. The city's annual revenues were significantly in excess of its expenditures during this period. Neither did Boca Raton suffer from the public service deficiencies characteristic of rapid-growth communities. Due to farsighted planning as well as the fiscal surplus, Boca Raton enjoyed ample services to meet the needs of its growing population.

Instead of the fiscal and service concerns that traditionally stimulate efforts to restrict the rate of development, it appears that the strongest motivating factor behind Boca Raton's experiment with population controls was the concern of existing residents about preserving Boca's quiet, single-family, small-town "way of life." From 1970 to 1972, seven multi-family units were constructed for every new single-family unit. Most of these were in large moderate-income garden apartment developments in newly annexed sections of Boca. By 1972, Boca Raton no longer had a majority of single-family units. This change in the traditional image of Boca Raton profoundly disturbed many long-time residents, as well as many recent well-to-do migrants.

Public concern came to a head over the City Council's refusal to use traditional land use controls to control the new developments. Despite public protests, the council voted four to one, in February 1972, to approve an application from the Arvida Corporation to rezone 1,818 acres of land west of Boca Raton from single-family to multi-family density. This action was the catalyst that spurred citizen's groups into action. Immediately, several residents organized a petition campaign demanding that the council rescind its action on the rezoning. Bowing to citizen pressure, the City Council rescinded the rezoning on March 8, and on April 11, the legislative body imposed a 60-day moratorium on all rezoning throughout the city.

Following their initial victory, advocates of restricted growth began a campaign to ensure that future rezonings would not endanger what they viewed as the unique character of their city. Leading this campaign was the Royal Palm Audubon Society—an activist group whose concerns extended to urban development issues. The Audubon Society prepared and submitted to the City Council a special report on "The Problems of Growth in Boca Raton." The idea of a population cap to restrict future growth was first introduced in this report.

The Society's report was based largely upon the experience of Boulder, Colorado in attempting to establish limits to growth. The report cited many similarities between the setting and problems of Boulder and Boca Raton and praised the efforts of Zero Population Growth to establish a 100,000 population limit in Boulder.

Based upon the Audubon Society's report and the projections of future growth by the City Planning Department, the figure of 100,000 population became a symbol of potent significance to citizen activists in Boca. Future growth control activity centered around how this "optimum" population figure could be achieved. In July 1972, Councilman Norman Wymbs—who was elected on a controlled growth platform—introduced a motion in City Council to restrict the future growth of Boca Raton to no more than 40,000 dwelling units, which would accommodate approximately 100,000 residents. Despite strong support from citizen groups, the majority of the City Council rejected Wymbs' plea to submit the 40,000 dwelling unit proposal to a referendum vote. This set the stage for an initiative petition drive by the Royal Palm Audubon Society and a coalition of smaller groups, organized in a "Citizens for Responsible Growth" committee. By late August, these groups collected more than 5,000 signatures on their petitions, thus easily qualifying the 40,000 dwelling unit cap issue for a November referendum.

Like the Boulder debate of 1976, Boca's referendum campaign aroused a great deal of emotion and conflict. Opponents attacked the growth cap proposal as an improper and inflexible use of the police power. Lawyers questioned its constitutionality and the city's leading newspaper advised citizens to vote no. On the other hand, proponents maintained that the nondiscretionary "growth cap" was the only way to prevent the City Council from administering traditional land use controls in an arbitrary and pro-development manner. They warned that Boca Raton's population could easily grow to 140,000 by 1990 if present trends were not drastically changed.

On November 7, 1972, the citizens of Boca Raton adopted the 40,000 dwelling unit growth cap as an amendment to the City Charter. The vote was 7,722 to 5,626. The following day, the city council enacted a moratorium on all future building permits for multi-family dwellings until the comprehensive plan and zoning ordinances were changed to reflect the 40,000 figure. These changes were accomplished by April 1974, at which time the moratorium was limited and a merit system for the issuance of building permits was introduced.

Support for the 40,000 dwelling unit population limit was strongest in the wealthiest and oldest precincts of the city where citizens were most insulated from concern about dwelling costs and most attached to the image of Boca Raton as a small and exclusive community. Support was weakest among less affluent and newer residents on the outskirts of Boca Raton, who were principally concerned about low housing prices.

In early 1973, the Boca Raton growth cap came under legal attack by the Boca Villas Corporation and the Arvida Corporation—two of the largest landowners in Boca. The suit wound its way through court proceedings until October 1976, at which time Boca Raton's population cap was ruled unconstitutional by the Florida Circuit Court as an abridgement of due process and the right to travel from one city to another.[3] The "cap" was ordered rescinded and ordinances changed back to their status prior to November 1972. The case is currently on appeal by the city to the Florida Supreme Court.

PETALUMA

The city of Petaluma lies 35 miles north of San Francisco in Sonoma County, California. It is bisected by the Petaluma River and U.S. Highway 101. From its founding in 1858 through the late 1960s, Petaluma was a rural market town that served as the center of a large cattle and poultry farming region in Sonoma and Marin counties.

In response to growing concern about the economic risk implicit in heavy dependence on agriculture, Petaluma annexed a large tract of land along Highway 101 during the early 1960s and provided it with sewer and water service as a means of attracting industry. However, the city had little success in promoting industrial development. Instead, by 1970 Petaluma found itself well on the way to becoming yet another commuter suburb of San Francisco. As the cost of housing soared in neighboring Marin County, much of the land in the new industrially zoned section was gobbled up by developers of moderately priced single-family housing. The city government, faced with paying off the heavy capital costs of the sewer and water connections, erected few obstacles to rezoning for residential use.

From 1960 to 1970, the total population of Petaluma almost doubled from 14,035 to 24,780. In 1970 and 1971 alone, the population increased by another 5,000 people. Along with this increase came significant changes in population composition. Most of the new residents were younger, more educated, and more culturally tied to Marin County and San Francisco than the existing residents of the city. Nearly 75% of the households east of Highway 101 commuted to work outside the city, while almost all of the population in "old Petaluma" west of Highway 101 worked locally. This created fears among many residents in old Petaluma of a "loss of community," a division of their town into two opposing and potentially hostile camps.

Even more serious than the psychological threat to the comfortable small town atmosphere of Petaluma was the strain on public facilities produced by the influx of new residents. The initial and most visible "pressure point" was public education. In the fall of 1970, public schools on the east side of Highway 101 in the new residential area were forced to introduce double sessions because of the inability of the local school districts to construct classrooms fast enough to keep up with the dramatic pace of population growth. This situation outraged the parents of school-age children among the new residents, because one of the primary attractions of a small town such as Petaluma was to escape from urban congestion and overcrowding. Indeed, the discontent of parents was the single most important catalyst for the population control movement.

The other major strain on public facilities was inadequate sewage treatment capacity. During 1971 the Public Works Department in Petaluma warned the City Council that sewage treatment capacity would be exhausted within one year if present rates of development continued. Considering the enormous cost of constructing new sewage treatment plants, this threat was enough to push the newly elected council strongly in the direction of growth limitation.

In response to the growing citizen discontent, the City Council and the City Manager initiated a set of actions designed to address the problems posed by growth. First, in January 1971, the City Council imposed a moratorium on all further rezoning in the city until a revision of the Petaluma General Plan could be completed. The original General Plan of 1962 projected a total population of 77,000 residents in 1990, a level that was consistent with the rapid growth of the late 1960s. The City Council's action clearly indicated that this level of population was unacceptable, thus raising the issue of what specific number was appropriate. Second, in February 1971, the council established a moratorium on further annexations of land surrounding the city, thus limiting one of the major sources of growth in the past. Third, the council authorized a major study of Petaluma's future growth. The study was directed by an appointed citizen's commission called the Petaluma Planning Conference, with the assistance of the city planning staff and a consultant. It was this study group that was charged with defining the acceptable limits of future growth.

As the cornerstone of the study, the Petaluma Planning Conference sent out questionnaires to 10,000 residents in April 1971 asking for responses to various projected levels of population. Fifty-six percent of the 2,400 citizens who responded favored control of growth at a target population of 40,000 citizens or less while over 30% favored an optimum level of between 40,000 and 70,000. The survey demonstrated that what residents liked most about Petaluma was its "small town atmosphere," an atmosphere that would be impossible to maintain as population expanded over 70,000. Significantly, the questionnaire responses indicated strong support for growth control measures on both sides of Highway 101, thus avoiding the cleavage between old and new residents found in Boulder and Boca Raton.

The survey thus provided a strong mandate for the Planning Conference and the study team to recommend the imposition of stringent controls on further population growth. On the basis of an intensive analysis of Petaluma's growth during the 1960s and its future fiscal capacities, the study group came up with an optimal target population of 55,000 residents. This limit was to be achieved through downzoning of existing development sites as well as the establishment of an annual quota of no more than 500 residential building permits. The 55,000 figure was, in essence, a compromise between the 40,000 target favored by a majority of citizens and the 77,000 projection found in the 1962 general plan. The quota of 500 building permits per year was based on the average number of permits issued by Petaluma during the 1960s. While far below the frenetic pace of development in 1969, 1970, and early 1971, the annual quota of 500 permits still provided ample opportunity for development in the view of the study group.

The Petaluma City Council was highly receptive to the recommendations of its citizen's commission and study group. Public opinion was so strongly supportive of population control that any other posture was politically infeasible. In June 1971, the City Council adopted the recommendations of the Planning Conference as the Official Development Policy for the city. Over the next nine months, the City Planning Commission and various citizen advisory groups worked out a series of implementing measures to ensure the effective execution of policy. These included the following:

1. *The Environmental Design Plan,* adopted March 1972. This plan officially established an urban service line for Petaluma within which an annual total of 500 residential units could be constructed.

2. *The Residential Development Control System,* adopted in August 1972 to implement the Environmental Design Plan. This ordinance established a Residential Development Evaluation Board to allocate the annual quota of 500 residential building permits under a "merit" allocation principle. Permits were to be divided equally between East and West Petaluma.

Once these implementing techniques were in place, the City Council went back to the voters for approval of the overall population control plan. In an advisory referendum in June 1973, Petaluma's citizens endorsed the annual quota of 500 building permits by a margin of 4,444 to 953, an 82% affirmative response. Support for the population control plan was overwhelming on both sides of Highway 101.

The city of Petaluma has successfully limited its growth to 500 housing units per year since 1973. Utilizing the detailed criteria in the Housing Element of the General Plan, the Residential Development Evaluation Board has established a mix of multi-family and single-family housing at a variety of income levels. Petaluma is extremely sensitive to the charge of exclusionary zoning and has gone out of its way to ensure a balanced housing stock.

The most serious challenge to Petaluma's population control measures arose from a suit brought by the Construction Industry Association of Sonoma County in federal court. This initial District Court judgment, issued in April 1974 found that the city's growth control system violated the fundamental right to travel guaranteed by the Constitution and was thus invalid.[4] However, on appeal to the Circuit Court of Appeals, Petaluma's control program was upheld due to the plaintiff's lack of standing. The Supreme Court subsequently refused to hear the case, allowing Petaluma's plan to remain in force.

POLITICS OF POPULATION CONTROL: A COMPARATIVE ANALYSIS

ANTECEDENTS OF INNOVATION

Why did these three communities prove receptive to such a radical innovation as population control? What common antecedent conditions, if any, explain the disposition of citizens and officials to initiate and implement such a departure from past practice? The three cities share at least six common factors which played a major role in stimulating the movement for population control.

Population Increase

The most obvious common dispositional antecedent of innovation was an extraordinarily rapid rate of increase in population and total housing units during the decade preceding the imposition of population controls.

Table 1. COMPARATIVE RATES OF POPULATION AND HOUSEHOLD GROWTH

City	1950 Total	1960 Total	1960 Av. Annual % Increase	1970 Total	1970 Av. Annual % Increase	1973 Total	1973 Av. Annual % Increase	1975 Total	1975 Av. Annual % Increase
BOCA RATON									
*Households	—	2,494	—	10,605	32.5	17,875	22.8	18,767	1.6
Population	922	6,961	66.5	28,506	31.0	38,079	11.2	42,363	3.7
BOULDER									
*Households	5,572	10,902	9.6	21,564	9.8	25,278	5.7	25,992	0.9
Population	19,999	37,718	8.9	68,634	8.2	75,904	3.5	78,560	1.2
PETALUMA									
*Households	3,614	4,725	3.1	7,795	6.5	9,133	5.7	9,650	2.8
Population	10,315	14,035	3.6	24,870	7.7	30,452	7.5	30,810	0.4

Sources: U.S. Bureau of the Census: Census of Population, Census of Housing, and Current Population Reports.

*Total number of occupied housing units.

As Table 1 shows, Boulder and Petaluma grew by approximately 8% *per year* during the 1960s, while Boca Raton expanded by over 31% annually. This extraordinary population influx, sparked by the proximity of the three cities to major metropolitan cities as well as their own natural attractiveness, was the primary catalyst of innovation.

Rapid growth alone, however, is clearly not a sufficient condition of innovation. During the 1960s, 154 American cities with more than 5,000 population grew by more than an 8% annual rate, yet only a handful have followed the lead of the three innovators in imposing population controls during the 1970s.

Compositional Change

An additional contributing factor in the three innovating cities was a significant change in the composition of the population due to in-migration. The existing residents of Boca Raton reacted strongly to an influx of less affluent apartment dwellers. In Petaluma, concern was aroused about the social gulf between the San Francisco commuters and those who worked locally. Compositional change does not appear to have been as important a factor in the Boulder experience, although the survey conducted by the Boulder Area Growth Study Commission uncovered considerable concern about the influx of transients and young people without ties to the community.

Economic Independence

Each of the three cities is a "freestanding" employment center, with significant numbers of stable jobs for its residents. None of the three was dependent upon further population growth for economic advancement. In contrast to the fealty of bedroom suburbs that depend entirely on their commuting populations, economic independence played a key role in convincing residents of Petaluma, Boulder, and Boca Raton that the cities could "go it alone" outside the growth orbit of the metropolitan area. Economic independence also reinforced a psychological sense of uniqueness.

Small Town Amenities and Lifestyle

With 1970 populations of between 24,000 and 68,000, all three cities were still relatively small towns where citizens could enjoy a more relaxed and uncongested lifestyle. Many of the newcomers were attracted to the cities for exactly this reason. Preservation of the small-town lifestyle was a common rallying cry and dispositional antecedent in all three towns. Preservation of unique environmental resources was also a significant facet of lifestyle concerns. Particularly in Boulder and Boca Raton, the magnificent natural setting was a focus of citizen activism.

Land Use Planning Experience

Despite their small town character, each of the cities was large enough to enjoy extensive prior experience with traditional land use controls and to recognize their limitations in controlling growth. Perhaps most importantly, each city

Table 2. COMPARATIVE GROWTH OF PROPERTY TAXATION

City	Property Tax Revenues (000s)	Total Market Value of Assessed Property (000s)	Effective Tax Ratio (% of Market Value)
BOCA RATON			
1960	$ 1,926	$ 171,666	1.12
1965	3,883	390,387	0.99
1970	8,583	625,289	1.37
1975	19,203	1,518,977	1.26
BOULDER			
1960	$ 3,911	$ 190,582	2.05
1965	7,126	283,302	2.51
1970	12,130	449,021	2.70
1975	17,871	604,049	2.96
PETALUMA			
1960	$ 1,676	$ 85,302	1.96
1965	2,528	102,145	2.47
1970	4,893	155,337	3.15
1975	9,770	292,339	3.34

enjoyed a large cadre of experienced land use activists capable of coming up with an innovative idea independently. Proximity to universities aided considerably in this regard. Towns with a population of less than 10,000 to 15,000 would be unlikely to have this experience.

Fiscal Strain and Public Service Deficiencies

In both Petaluma and Boulder, strains upon public services and rising property taxes were major stimuli of favorable attitudes toward population controls. The dramatic increase in effective property tax ratios in these two cities during the 1960s is illustrated in Table 2. In Boca Raton, on the other hand, property tax increases were less of a problem, but concern about sewage capacity entered into the debate over the 40,000 dwelling unit cap.

Summary

While this list of factors is clearly tentative, it does lead to some explicit testable propositions about receptivity to population controls. Stated as a predictive theory, the chances for adoption of population controls are greatest in small cities with population growth of at least 8% to 10% per year, a total population between 15,000 and 75,000, an independent employment base, prior land use planning experience, a rising effective property tax ratio, and a sewer, school, or water supply crisis.

PATTERNS OF POLICY INITIATION

The three cities display some remarkable similarities in patterns of policy initiation. First, the concept of population control came from outside city government in all three cities. The policy initiative arose within citizen's groups that were discontented with traditional land use controls. Their motives were mixed, but focused around the idea of preserving the small-town way of life.

Second, in each case, the starting point for the policy initiative was an alarming projection of future population growth contained in the city's general plan. In response to this projection, each citizen's group sent out a community question-naire asking for public comment on alternative levels of population growth. Responses to these surveys served as the crucial underpinning of the population control proposals.

Third, each of the cities relied on the experience of another to strengthen and legitimize its own population control proposal. Boca Raton carefully studied Boulder's population control proposal of 1971. Boulder relied upon Petaluma's 1972 quota system in enacting its 1976 Slow Growth Ordinance. Petaluma cited Boca Raton's successful 1972 referendum as support for its own 1973 referen-dum vote. This mutual interaction was a crucial source of support for citizen's groups that might otherwise have felt hesitant about the legitimacy of their proposals.

In short, the population control proposals were initiated by similar citizens groups with similar perspectives reacting to similar phenomena. This similarity of circumstance and perspective was noted by the three groups involved and was utilized as a resource in their efforts to get the population control issue on the agenda.

Beyond these commonalities in policy initiation, the agenda-setting process also differed somewhat between the three cities. Most obviously, the policy initiative was opposed by the City Councils in Boulder and Boca Raton, forcing citizens to conduct a mass petition campaign to place the issue on the referendum ballot. In Petaluma, on the other hand, the initiative of the Planning Conference was welcomed by the City Council and the agenda of population control was established with official assistance. This difference can be attributed to variation in the severity of fiscal strain and public service crises. In 1971, Petaluma faced immediate and direct crises in its public schools and sewage treatment plants. This required the newly elected council to focus on the need for some drastic measures to limit growth. In Boulder, deficiencies in water and sewer supply were also evident, but these were problems of a more long-standing nature that the city had grappled with previously. There was no immediate crisis that forced the City Council to support a departure from the land use controls that Boulder traditionally relied upon. Similarly, in Boca Raton, the relatively good fiscal condition of the city provided no immediate stimulus for the council to go along with the citizen initiative on population control.

The other major difference in agenda setting was that the Petaluma citizen's group, with assistance from the city government, became much more deeply involved in oversight of implementation than the groups in Boulder and Boca Raton. In Boulder and Boca Raton, the population control initiative was a great symbolic issue, which, once enacted, was left to city authorities to implement. In Petaluma, on the other hand, the citizen's group followed up its initial victory in securing adoption of the Official Development Policy with intensive agenda-setting work on the entire set of ordinances which were designed to implement the policy.

In sum, the principal vehicle of policy initiation in the area of municipal population controls appears to be a large, active citizen's coalition with sufficient knowledge and commitment to generate an innovative proposal for limitation of growth. Policy initiatives on population control are unlikely to come from municipal governments themselves unless they are faced with an overwhelming fiscal or public service crisis.

ADOPTION POLITICS

Each of the cities held a referendum vote on population controls. In each referendum a majority of the voting public supported the innovation. Beyond these essential similarities, however, the style and substance of adoption politics varied substantially from city to city. In Petaluma, 82% supported the quota system, whereas in Boulder only 50.5% supported the Slow Growth Ordinance. Boca Raton fell in between with 57% in favor of the 40,000 dwelling unit cap. Adoption politics in Petaluma was highly consensual. In Boulder, there was extensive conflict and opposition between citizens groups. Boca Raton's campaign was conducted in an atmosphere of distrust and contention between proponents and the City Council.

Analysis of the referendum data by precinct for the three cities provides some insight into this variation. The referendum data reveals that socio-demographic cleavages reliably predict differences in support for population controls across the three cities. Of great import are three types of socio-demographic variables:

1. Residents of older core areas in each city provided greater support for population controls than residents of new built-up areas.

2. Residents of areas with a high level of home ownership provided greater support for population controls than residents of areas high in multi-family dwellings.

3. Areas with low rates of housing turnover provided more support for population controls than those with high rates of mobility.

These findings make sense intuitively. Older core areas benefit from population controls by slowing the rate of public investment in newly developing areas. Homeowners benefit from population controls by a decrease in the rate of property tax increases and an increase in the price of the existing housing stock. Apartment dwellers, on the other hand, suffer from higher home prices as an obstacle to their ultimate mobility into single-family housing. Residents in low-turnover areas favor population controls because they have a greater "stake" in maintaining the community's character than those who are likely to move on in the near future.

In light of these findings, the differences between cities begin to make sense. The less extensive these cleavages, the greater the consensual support for population controls should be in a given city. For example, in Petaluma, the residents were quite homogeneous on the homeownership dimension. Almost all of the housing in the city is single-family detached stock, thus providing a uniform incentive to minimize property tax increases. The entire city of Petaluma is also an area of relatively slow housing turnover, giving all the residents a stake in preserving the small-town "way of life." These uniformities cut across the cleavage between the residents of the older and newer parts of town and enabled the proponents of population control to build a strong coalition of support for the proposals.

In Boulder, by contrast, the cleavage among the population was substantial on all dimensions. Boulder is a town of transients who circulate in and out of universities and research institutions with rapidity. Boulder also has a wide diversity of housing stock. There is much multi-family housing, particularly in the fringe areas. The impact of these cleavages is illustrated by the strong negative vote on the population control proposal in the outlying precincts, while the areas of low-turnover single-family housing gave substantial majorities to the proposition. The principal factor that overcame these cleavages and allowed the Slow Growth Ordinance to be adopted was the common dedication to the environment among residents of all these areas. The magnificent Rocky Mountain scenery that drew many residents to Boulder in the first place was a major focus of the referendum campaign. The environmental preservation issue apparently drew enough support for the innovation among residents of the outlying areas to swing the total vote in favor of population control.

The circumstances in Boca Raton were quite similar to those in Boulder. Overlapping cleavages produced little support for the dwelling unit cap in the newer areas of Boca Raton. Support was concentrated among the established, upper middle class, single-family neighborhoods and the expensive retirement condominiums. The difference in the percentage of support for population controls between Boulder and Boca Raton may be attributed to two factors. First, Boca Raton has a greater proportion of single-family housing stock than Boulder. Second, the population control proposal in Boca Raton became entwined with the more general issue of citizen participation in government. Proponents of the population control initiative portrayed it as a necessary antidote to the arbitrary actions of city government. Public debate during the campaign centered far more around the propriety of "government by petition" than upon the merits of the 40,000 housing unit figure. Thus, a vote against population control was construed by many as a vote against participatory democracy. This swayed a significant number of citizens who might have otherwise voted against the proposition on its merits.

In sum, the prospects for adoption of population control measures through popular referendum appear best when:

1. The relevant socio-demographic cleavages are small or cross-cutting.

2. Some overarching issue such as protection of the environment or enhancing citizen participation in government provides a common groundwork of public support.

CONCLUSION: POLICY IMPLICATIONS

As long as population controls are limited to three cities, no significant national policy issue is raised. But what if the innovation begins to spread rapidly? What if many communities decide that they wish to establish population limits? The broad policy implications under these circumstances are deeply troubling, not only from the perspective of restrictions on freedom to travel and relocate, but also with regard to the nation's ability to meet the housing needs of its younger and less affluent citizens.

The analysis presented in previous sections of this chapter enables us to make some estimate of the likely future spread of the innovation. From 1960 to 1970, 154 communities across the country experienced a population growth rate of over 8% annually. This group of localities constitutes the potential target group for population control measures. These rapid-growth communities are concentrated primarily in four states—California (53), Illinois (31), Florida (27), and Texas (14).

How many of these communities appear likely candidates for the adoption of population control measures? An intensive analysis of this question is currently being conducted as part of a larger project, but preliminary findings indicate that very few of these communities possess the array of qualities and characteristics which disposed Boulder, Boca Raton, and Petaluma toward limiting future population growth. For example, most of the communities in Illinois are suburban bedroom communities without any independent employment base, without a sense of special small-town identity, and without any major public service or fiscal crisis.

In Texas, the general orientation toward land use controls is so negative that an innovative use of police power regulation is extremely unlikely. Indeed, most of the rapid growth communities, including Houston, the state's largest city, have no prior experience with traditional land use controls.

Experience with traditional land use controls is also spotty among the Florida cities in the rapid-growth category. However, many of these cities have experienced public service crises and enjoy an independent employment base. Considering the successful legal challenge to Boca Raton's "growth cap," the most likely response to population strains among Florida communities is experimentation with the timing or sequencing of development rather than adoption of explicit population controls. To date, none of the rapid growth communities in Illinois, Texas, or Florida have adopted explicit population controls.

The prospects for diffusion of population controls are best in California where many of the rapid-growth communities are freestanding small towns with an independent employment base. Under the state's mandatory planning and zoning laws, all of these communities enjoy previous experience with land use controls. California cities have also experienced some of the most severe service problems in water supply and sewage treatment capacity.

An examination of the rapid growth communities in California reveals that six communities besides Petaluma have adopted explicit population controls from 1973 through 1977. These are Vacaville, Roseville, Davis, Rohnert Park, Santa Rosea, and Livermore. These communities display a striking resemblance to Petaluma. Each is a small town of between 12,000 and 70,000 population on the periphery of a large metropolitan area. Each suffered from a severe fiscal crisis or public service deficiency in the early or mid-1970s. Each enjoyed an extremely active citizen's group which pressed strongly for adoption of land use controls to limit population. As in Petaluma, city councils in each of the cities supported population controls under strong citizen pressure.

A crucial factor at work in the California experience is the close proximity of the innovating communities. Davis, Vacaville, and Roseville are located within 30 miles of each other in the Sacramento Valley and they reacted to the same phenomenon of rapid growth in the Sacramento area. Indeed, to some extent the communities exacerbated the problem for each other. By artificially restricting new development within its own boundaries, each jurisdiction displaced growth to surrounding communities, which in turn imposed their own controls.

Livermore, Petaluma, and Rohnert Park are part of the San Francisco metropolitan region. Petaluma and Rohnert Park are adjacent jurisdictions. Rohnert Park's action was largely a response to new development displaced from Petaluma.

Other rapid-growth communities in both the Sacramento and San Francisco areas are currently considering the imposition of population controls, posing the threat of even greater distortions in the regional housing markets.

Outside of California, however, the imposition of local population controls does not appear to be a phenomenon that will rapidly sweep the country. While any generalization based upon a sample of three cases is obviously suspect, the antecedent conditions, agenda-setting mechanisms, and adoption politics in the three jurisdictions seem sufficiently unusual that extensive diffusion is unlikely over the immediate future. Over the longer term, however, any prediction must be hedged with caution. As in California, the dynamic of emulation and competition among neighboring jurisdictions is strong across the United States. One or two adoptions in a metropolitan area may be all that is required to start a rapid wave of competing adoptions designed to restore the equilibrium. Thus, the diffusion of local population controls bears continuous study and monitoring as a potential policy problem of substantial national importance.

NOTES

1. For example, the widely publicized "Residential Development Control System" in Ramapo, N.Y. does not aim to halt population growth explicitly. Rather, this policy ties residential construction to capital facilities availability and gives developers the option of advancing development by providing necessary public facilities themselves. *Golden v Planning Board of Ramapo* (1972) 285 N.E.2d 291, the validated timing amendments as "proper zoning techniques, exercised for legitimate zoning purposes."

2. *Robinson v City of Boulder* (1974) District Court of Boulder, Action No. 72-2033-1. For commentary on this case and similar actions in other states, see Note (1976).

3. *Boca Villas Corp. v Pence* (1976) Circuit Court of Palm Beach County, Florida, September 30. This case is currently on appeal to the Florida Supreme Court. Significantly, the trial judge did not hold that the concept of a growth cap was unconstitutional, but rather maintained that the 40,000 unit figure was an arbitrary infringement of constitutional rights because no scientific and planning studies had been conducted to justify the figure. Thus, a unit/population figure that was validated by such studies might be upheld.

4. *Construction Industry of Sonoma County v City of Petaluma* (1975) 522 F2d 897. The Appeals Court rejected the District Court judgment solely on the ground of plaintiff's lack of standing to sue, leaving the substantive issues resolved. Petaluma's plan was in no way validated by this action. However, the Supreme Court's denial of certiorari indicates a reluctance to wade into this particular "political thicket," indicating that further legal challenge to growth caps in federal court are unlikely.

REFERENCES

ALONSO, W. (Fall 1973). "Urban zero population growth." Daedalus, 102(4):191-206.
Ashley Economic Services (1973). The economic and environmental impacts of the 40,000 unit cap on the city of Boca Raton. Newport Beach, Cal.: author.

BOSSELMAN, F. (1973). "Can the town of Ramapo pass a law to bind the rights of the whole world?" Florida State University Law Review, 1(2):234-265.

Boulder Area Growth Study Commission (1973). Exploring options for the future: A study of growth in Boulder County. Boulder: Municipal Government Reference Center.

COKE, J., and LIEBMAN, C. (1961). "Political values and population density control." Land Economics, 38(3):347-361.

ELLICKSON, R. (1977). "Suburban growth controls: An economic and legal analysis." Yale Law Journal, 86(2):385-511.

FIELDING, R. (1972). "Putting a speed limit on growth." Planning, 38(10):263-265.

FINKLER, E. et al. (1976). Urban nongrowth: City planning for people. New York: Praeger.

FRANKLIN, H. (1973). Controlling urban growth: But for whom. Washington, D.C.: Potomac Institute.

LAMM, R., and DAVISON, S. (1973). "The legal control of population growth and distribution in a quality environment: The land use alternatives." Denver Law Journal, 49(1):1-51.

McGIVERN, W. (1972). "Putting a speed limit on growth." Planning, 38(10):263-265.

Note (1976). "The thirst for population control: Water hookup moratoria and the duty to augment supply." Hastings Law Journal, 27(3):753-774.

PART II
ISSUE ANALYSIS

3

NEIGHBORHOOD PRESERVATION:
An Analysis of Policy Maps and Policy Options

ERIC S. MOSKOWITZ

University of Illinois, Chicago Circle

INTRODUCTION

Much of the policy-making literature in American political science has explicitly or implicitly been concerned with the question of whether the policy process can best be described as pluralist or elitist. This is a dispute between those who see policy as the result of bargaining among a multiplicity of groups and those who see policy as the will of an interlocked dominant elite.[1] Both pluralist and elitist analyses focus upon the actions of individuals seeking power and/or a specific set of policy outputs. Neither school emphasizes the subtle effects which the social and economic environment might have on the political process and its policy outputs.[2]

POLITICAL ECONOMY AND POLICY-MAKING

One contemporary variant of Marxist analysis, structural Marxism, offers some trenchant suggestions for the construction of a political model which is more sensitive to the impact of social and economic structures on the political process.[3] Structuralists reject the elitist notion that governmental policy makers either are

AUTHOR'S NOTE: *I wish to thank the Brookings Institution for its provision of Guest Scholar privileges to facilitate this research. Of course, the Brookings Institution takes no responsibility for the views expressed in this article. I also want to thank Jeff Fishel and Elaine Grunwald for their generous assistance.*

members of the economic elite or are directly controlled by that economic elite. They point out that such individualistic instrumental theories of power cannot explain government actions which are opposed by economic elites. Nonetheless, structuralists maintain that the government's functions are to encourage economic growth and preserve social equilibrium, both of which benefit the economic elites. The government strives toward these ends, not because it is controlled by economic interests, but because these ends will enhance the government's autonomy and self-interest. Essentially, the structuralists maintain that the socioeconomic system in which the government is situated helps to determine the government's perception of its own self-interest. The self-interest of the government and the needs of the dominant segment of the society overlap.

There are two important weaknesses in this structural approach for an analysis of policy making. Despite the structuralists' portrayal of government policy as the result of cross pressures from the corporate economic sector and the general public, there is a strong tendency in their analyses to depict all government actions as only a response to the functional needs of the private corporate sector. Government policy makers are rarely described as servants of the public interest. The end result is a model which comes much closer to the elitist school than is at first apparent.

More importantly, the structural model, like many macro-political models, offers few details about the policy process. There is a lengthy discussion of the functional requisites which the government must provide to the socio-economic system but there is little description of how that output is produced. Given the structuralist rejection of the proposition that economic elites directly control the policy process, some alternative hypothesis should be offered to explain why actors in the political process should behave in a manner which fulfills the functional requisites of the system.

There is, however, an inchoate strand within the structural model which may yield a useful tool to probe this problem. Claus Offe's (1972) conceptualization of positive selective mechanisms is most relevant here. He asserts that these positive mechanisms operate within the political process to produce the requisite policy outputs. Unlike negative selective mechanisms which merely filter out policy alternatives before they reach the governmental decision process, positive selective mechanisms ensure that particular requisite policy choices are made by the policy makers. The crux of the positive mechanism is a general governmental goal of "cautious crisis management and long-term avoidance strategy" (1972:99). Offe indicates that only certain types of problems are readily recognized by the political structure. The actors' understanding of what is essential for the stability of the social system will help explain what issues are treated and how they are treated. This insight implies that the cognitive structures of the policy makers must be taken into account. Cognitive studies of decision making indicate that given a very complex, uncertain environment, decision makers "depend on preset cognitive images to process information, to order, understand, remember, and interpret it, and to reach judgements quickly" (Stassen, 1972:99).

The cognitive concept of a policy map, therefore, is a useful tool to investigate the policy-making process.[4] As employed here, the policy map consists of problems which are perceived, goals which are valued, explanatory calculi which are accepted, and policy positions which are decided upon. The policy map has the potential to mesh a micro-oriented analysis such as pluralism and a macro-oriented analysis such as structural Marxism. By focusing on the policy map, it may be possible to combine pluralism's insights about the intricacies of the political process with structural Marxism's recognition that the social and economic environment of a political system consistently influences the outputs of that political structure. This environment may transmit particular cognitive patterns to the policy makers. The policy maps, in turn, may then influence the actors' policy choices.

In order for the policy map to link the socio-economic environment and the policy-making process, there are two minimum requirements. Certain core components of the policy maps must be held almost universally by the policy makers. In addition, this core policy map must be relevant to the pattern of policy choices produced by the political process. If the first requirement cannot be met, the policy map approach would not extend beyond the aggregation of individual attitudes rather than being a systemic trait. The map would have no meaningful implications for the general relationship between the socio-economic environment and the policy process. If the second requirement cannot be met, the core policy map found would have little utility as a tool of policy analysis. If the requirements are met, then it is possible that the content of the core policy map may add to the understanding of how a relatively autonomous pluralistic policy process might systematically produce outputs which tend to support, or at least not threaten, the interests of the predominant economic structures in society. This linkage model of the political economy portrays a genuine multi-group political bargaining process constrained by the parameters of a core policy map held by most of the policy makers.

NEIGHBORHOOD PRESERVATION AS A POLICY ISSUE

Neighborhood preservation is a particularly attractive policy issue upon which to apply the above political economy perspective. It is an issue which has important social and economic components. Community groups tend to see neighborhood preservation as a program which would enable the residents to maintain long-standing social structures. The desire to assure that adequate financial resources are made available for the stable maintenance and transfer of homes in a community has become one of a cluster of demands designed to guard the socio-cultural attributes of neighborhoods. Attacks on school busing, pornography shops, zoning decisions, and now neighborhood disinvestment have all spread outward from the residents' desire to protect their social community and its cultural style. The policy demands of those seeking to preserve neighborhoods have important implications for private financial institutions. Much of the controversy surrounding neighborhood decline involves the question of how extensively the government should intrude into the private housing and mortgage markets to redirect financial investments toward mature urban neighborhoods. Government intervention in the private mortgage market has the potential for a significant economic impact.

RESEARCH STRATEGY

The remainder of this study provides a classification and analysis of the policy maps of federal decision makers who participated in the making of neighborhood preservation policy during the mid-1970s. Policy decisions concerned with providing adequate levels of private investment in mature urban neighborhoods were of particular interest.

The policy maps of 34 actors are treated. Of the 34 policy actors analyzed, there were 12 HUD officials, 11 Congressional policy actors, seven officials from financial regulatory agencies (FRA), and four policy makers in the Institutional Presidency.[5] There were 19 Republicans, 13 Democrats, and two Independents. All were identified as significant participants through archival research, secondary source research, or interviews. Interviews provided the major source for the content of the policy maps. Public statements were used to supplement the interview material.[6] A schedule of open-ended questions was used to draw out the logic of the respondents' understanding of the neighborhood preservation issue. This material was then qualitatively analyzed to determine if there was a pattern in the respondents' understanding of the issue.

CAUSES OF DECLINE

The policy makers' understanding of the causes of neighborhood decline is the most logical point to initiate the analysis of the policy maps. The responses tended to revolve around five concepts. The policy makers explained neighborhood decline in terms of the general relationship of the neighborhood to the private economic sector, the level of municipal services provided, the unintended consequences of federal programs, the social attitudes of the neighborhood population, and the perceptions and activities of key private economic institutions. All but one of the actors individually emphasized a single cause of decline. The one exception emphasized two causes and was included under both explanatory categories.

AN ECONOMIC DEMAND EXPLANATION:
EMPLOYMENT BASE OR CONSUMER CHOICE

Nine of the policy makers attributed decline to the general relationship of the neighborhood to the private economic sector. In this regard, two points were most frequently raised. Decline was seen either as the consequence of an inadequate employment base or the result of an unsuccessful competition against other neighborhoods for desirable new residents. Four policy makers supported the first position and five the second position. Of the nine actors in this overall category, seven were Republicans, one was a Democrat, and one was an Independent.

Actors in the employment base subcategory believed that without the income which a healthy neighborhood employment base provides, there will not be adequate resources for the maintenance of neighborhood housing. The resulting under-maintenance will produce deterioration of the housing. In effect, there was not sufficient effective demand to support these neighborhoods.

The other subset of actors in this general category emphasized a different definition of economic demand. They argued that neighborhoods declined when consumer-residents wei e no longer willing to pay an adequate price to live in the housing located there. These consumer choice analysts maintained that some older housing was no longer attractive in the more competitive, modern housing market. There was simply no demand to live in this housing and consequently the neighborhood declined. The consumer choice theorists were more concerned with the economic characteristics of the buildings while the employment base theorists focused on the economic characteristics of the people.

A MUNICIPAL SERVICES EXPLANATION

The municipal services interpretation bears some similarity to the consumer choice model. According to this second diagnosis, the inadequate delivery of municipal services—road repairs, street lighting, curbs, sewers, garbage removal, crime protection, and the educational system—made particular neighborhoods less attractive as places to live. This rationale was often used as a rebuttal to the insinuation that financial institutions were the prime cause of neighborhood decline. This interpretation was held by four Republican policy actors.

These policy makers claimed that the deficiencies in public service delivery put a neighborhood at a competitive disadvantage in the metropolitan housing market. Because it stressed the importance of the quality of the neighborhood in determining its value and fate in a competitive market, this explanation resembled the consumer choice model. They differed in the type and source of the neighborhood quality upon which they focused. The consumer choice actors looked at the relative quality of the neighborhood's housing units (which are primarily in the private sector) while the municipal services proponents pointed to the relative neighborhood-wide qualities dependent on local government provision. As one HUD official observed, "Decline should not only be seen as a problem of bricks and mortars but also in the delivery of municipal services."

A FEDERAL PROGRAMS EXPLANATION

A third cluster of policy makers emphasized the role which federal programs played in the destruction of urban neighborhoods. All four actors in this category were Republicans. The actor with the dual explanation of decline was in this group and the municipal services group.

In a joint presentation made to an academic conference in 1974, two HUD actors stated:

> [T]he record of federal subsidized housing programs shows with stunning clarity the *harmful* impact these programs have had on neighborhoods. In some cases, the programs destroy the neighborhoods. . . . [T]he programs show an astonishing lack of understanding of the basic economic factors determining supply and demand in housing markets.

Most of the actors in this category viewed the neighborhood as a fragile social institution much too susceptible to the disruptions caused by outside influences like federal programs. Only locally run programs based on local accommodations among all the affected groups could avoid these sharply destructive disruptions.

A NEIGHBORHOOD AFFINITY EXPLANATION

The fourth set of policy actors explained neighborhood decline in terms of the social attitudes of the residents. This group was made up of four Republicans, three Democrats, and one Independent. According to these policy makers, the fate of a neighborhood was largely determined by the will of its residents.

These actors believed that neighborhood stability was enhanced by the existence of a social affinity for the particular geographic site as a communal environment. A member of a financial regulatory agency stated: "Two or three things can explain neighborhood decline but the most important factor is the residents' perception of the neighborhood as a place to live. . . . Without neighborhood pride, nothing can be done." These neighborhood affinity actors asserted that residents who were proud of their neighborhood would somehow see to it that their housing units were maintained and adequate municipal services were delivered.

Unlike the actors who fell either into the consumer choice or municipal services categories, these neighborhood affinity analysts saw housing conditions and municipal services primarily as intervening variables rather than as independent variables explaining neighborhood conditions. The neighborhood affinity analysts claimed that, if the residents truly value their neighborhood, they will see to it that the mediating factors of housing conditions and municipal services are produced. Without neighborhood pride, even the provision of sound housing and municipal services will not be sufficient to preserve a neighborhood.

AN INSTITUTIONAL MISPERCEPTION EXPLANATION

The last cluster of policy makers focused on the role which private economic institutions played in the decline of neighborhoods. This group was made up of one Republican and nine Democrats. This is the only group with a majority of Democrats. Almost three quarters of all the Democratic policy makers included in the study are in this group.

Actors in this category believed that the failure of financial institutions to invest in older neighborhoods could cause these areas to decline. A Congressional policy maker noted: "When the neighborhood cannot get mortgage credit, property values drop; new homeowners cannot move in because they cannot get mortgages. Eventually, the neighborhood starts to deteriorate." The policy makers in this cluster blamed this pattern of disinvestment on the inability of financial institutions to process accurately economic information on the investment potential of mature urban neighborhoods. According to this argument, there was a profit to be made in many declining neighborhoods, but private institutions failed to recognize the opportunity. An official in an FRA stated: "The market cannot work if its perceptions are erroneous. Reinvestment is both essential to and economically feasible in these older neighborhoods, but there must be a change in the perceptions."

The actors in this category maintained that this institutional misperception of the profit potential of older neighborhoods is due to the fact that these areas are more difficult to assess accurately. Not only can investment conditions change more rapidly in older areas, but investment potential is not as susceptible to superficial appraisal. These actors believed that both factors demand a greater effort in information processing than financial institutions are presently willing to put forth. The result is a style of decision making which the institutional misperception analysts called "lazy lending." "Lazy lending" is arbitrarily biased toward suburban lending, thereby contributing to the disinvestment of mature urban neighborhoods.

Several of the categories used cognitive structures in their explanation. But the use of this approach varied. Institutional misperception theorists looked at private economic institutions and the way in which they misperceived profitability. Neighborhood affinity theorists emphasized the social groups in the neighborhood and their affection for that neighborhood. Consumer choice proponents also stressed the role of economic evaluation by private actors but they focused principally on the consumer-resident's economic evaluation and found no evidence of misperception.

INEVITABILITY OF DECLINE

Attitudes about the inevitability of neighborhood decline also need to be considered in this investigation of policy maps. An actor's image of the mutability of a social condition should influence the actor's policy response to that condition. Of the 34 policy makers, only seven were committed to the unqualified position that neighborhood decline was a natural and inevitable process. They agreed that as buildings age and become obsolescent, their value diminishes and people are less willing to live in them. The other 27 policy actors asserted that the decline of viable neighborhoods was not inevitable. Moreover, they believed that the neighborhood decline process was causing otherwise structurally sound housing to be prematurely destroyed.

A positive feeling about the value of neighborhood preservation was associated with the belief that decline was not a natural and inevitable event. A single motif ran through the comments of those policy makers who rejected the inevitability of decline. All paid homage to the need for the conservation of economic and social resources. A HUD official observed:

Neighborhood preservation has several advantages. It is cost effective. It utilizes existing resources, not just housing but also the physical infrastructure and social systems. Neighborhood preservation also copes with a human want and desire to stay where you feel comfortable.

Conversely, policy makers who saw decline as inevitable made little or no mention of neighborhood preservation's conservation virtues. Quite the opposite, most looked on neighborhood preservation as a waste of resources. "Many areas are declining for good reason. They are no longer feasible areas of growth. To put money into these areas would be throwing good money after bad."

For all of the policy makers, there was a fortuitous harmony between nature and analysis. Those who saw decline as inevitable believed neighborhood preservation had few benefits in any case. On the other hand, those who saw the benefits of neighborhood preservation believed that neighborhood decline was preventable.

POSITIVE VIEWS OF THE MARKET

Given the fact that most of the policy actors saw neighborhood decline as a valid issue of public concern, the next logical topic is their analysis of suitable methods to respond to the decline problem. A broad consensus held that neighborhood preservation was an extremely complex phenomenon which required huge amounts of resources. Only the private sector held those resources on a requisite scale. Furthermore, the policy actors believed that the role of government was to garner those private resources for neighborhood preservation.

Two features of the private sector attracted the attention of these policy makers. One aspect was the sheer magnitude of the private economy. A HUD official remarked: "The largest assets of the urban system are in private resources, not public ones. To be effective, government programs on neighborhood preservation must leverage these private funds." The concept of leveraging private resources for the public cause of neighborhood preservation ran throughout the comments of the policy actors. "Leverage" has two connotations. At its simplest, leveraging is merely an attempt to add the weight of private resources to those of the smaller public sector. But more importantly, leveraging requires an understanding of the workings of the private sector in order to thrust the small governmental program (or lever) into the appropriate part of the private market mechanism. If done adroitly, the lever will produce the optimal private output necessary for the desired social goal.

The decentralized market mechanism was the second feature of the private sector emphasized by these policy actors. Their attitude toward the market helps explain their adoption of the leverage approach to neighborhood preservation. A hypothetical policy actor might agree that the private sector was the only sector large enough to handle the resources needed for neighborhood preservation, but he need not conclude that the government's primary response should be to leverage these resources. Instead, one might opt to take public command of a sufficient amount of these private resources to perform the tasks perceived to be necessary for neighborhood preservation. This option, however, was only offered by one policy maker. The other 33 policy makers' perceptions of the value and power of the private market led them to advocate a minimal manipulation of the existing private economy for public purposes. The most prevalent basis for supporting the private market was its efficiency as an allocator of resources. All but one of the policy actors agreed that overall the market was the most efficient economic mechanism. The market produced the most desirable output from a given resource base.

EXTENSIVE MARKET ADVOCATES

The most fervent supporters of the market included four of the policy actors who had explained the decline of neighborhoods as the result of consumer choice. This could be expected since the consumer choice interpretation is a pure market model. It explains decline in terms of consumer demand and housing supply mediated by a private market mechanism. Three other policy actors also evidenced extensive confidence in the market solution. They all had diagnosed neighborhood decline as a disease which resulted from ill-advised federal programs. In general, these three policy makers saw governmental intervention as a distortion and disruption of the market equilibrium.

While there was almost complete unanimity about the great utility of the private market as a resource allocator, these seven policy makers were distinctive because of the extensive scope which they would allow the market. They will be labeled extensive market advocates. These actors saw far fewer imperfections in the market distribution of goods in society than did the others. One such Congressional actor asserted:

> The private market, if allowed to work, can do a better job than the public sector, either Federal or local. The private sector functions better because it will seek out the more effective and efficient uses of resources. It does so much more readily than government mandate. It is more efficient because it has the discipline of the profit system to control its processes. You do not do something unless you know you will make a profit or, at least, a good chance to get a return for your money.

This distinction was a matter of degree, of course. All of these extensive market advocates would agree that the private market was not well constructed to provide certain basic public goods such as streets and sewers. One should not caricature them as absolutely opposed to any government intrusion into the market. But compared to the other policy actors, they were much more inclined toward this view. In discussing the possibility that private financial institutions might contribute to neighborhood decline, one Congressional actor in this category responded:

> Many areas are declining for a good reason. They are no longer feasible areas for economic growth. To put money into these areas would be throwing good money after bad. You cannot have a goal of neighborhood preservation at any cost. People often forget that we are dealing with scarce resources. The needs and demands of the system are endless. The political system cannot distribute these resources efficiently. The best way of determining the ultimate distribution of goods, even though it may sometimes be harsh, is the market. Allocation by Congress will needlessly chew up resources. In the end, you must only help those who help themselves.

The fact that these actors found the market mechanism the most efficient does not mean that they failed to realize that the market could have detrimental effects on persons caught in its wake. As one of the extensive market advocates said about neighborhood change: "Cities are always in a state of flux. Unfortunately, some people get caught in this flux."

MODIFIED MARKET ADVOCATES

Twenty-six policy actors took the position that the basic market mechanism was the best resource allocator, but certain modifications were necessary. Nevertheless, these actors did not reject the market. An official in an FRA who was one of the strongest proponents of neighborhood preservation made an observation typical of the modified market position. He said one should be "leery of most direct government action. You should always seek the most private solution possible." In general, these policy makers felt it was best to leave maximum decision-making power with the private market. Only if irremedial flaws were shown in the market should government activity be taken. Where they found a flaw, these actors sought to correct it while still maintaining the basic market mechanism.

Like those in the extensive market group, the modified market advocates praised the allocational efficiency of the market. But modified market advocates portrayed this efficiency in relative rather than absolute terms. They saw the market as the best practical alternative. Often their rationale for the market was shaped in terms of their rejection of an alternative policy option—government allocation of credit. Typical comments in this category were:

> I would be very wary of any attempt to replace completely the decision of the market with the judgement of legislators.

> The free market is still capable of responding to the investment needs of older areas. There is no need to alter the system, but only to facilitate the market and change some erroneous perceptions. The alternative of government planned investment is not feasible. There is not enough wisdom to dictate politically where resources should go.

> Government allocation of investment would write neighborhood policy in stone. It would be too inflexible.

The modified market explanation for the better performance of the market is very similar to that of the extensive market explanation. Both emphasized that the market is made up of a multiplicity of competing actors. Therefore, it is better able to amass a greater amount of information necessary for the proper allocation of resources. The profit motive forces the market actors to seek the best and latest information about productivity and consumer demand. Both explanations assert that there is greater responsiveness because the market's profit motive provides a clear statement by which one can immediately judge results. In addition, a new idea need only be adopted by one private firm, not an entire political bureaucracy, in order to have an initial effect.

MARKET DEFICIENCIES

The two schools of market advocacy are distinguishable by their treatment of market deficiencies. Two types of market imperfections were readily perceived by policy makers in the modified market cluster, but they were not as willingly accepted by those in the extensive market category. The two market imperfections involved the processing of information and the handling of externalities resulting from private goods.

MISINFORMATION

Internal flaws of the market were predominantly described in terms of a lack of information on the part of the market actors. As might be expected, those policy makers, who had stressed institutional misperception as the cause of neighborhood decline, reiterated their observations about the lack of accurate information when evaluating the market.

In addition, some policy makers who had emphasized other causes of neighborhood decline also mentioned the problem of a lack of information within the market. The comments usually were made when more direct questions were asked about the relationship of the market to neighborhood preservation requirements. These actors felt that the rapidly changing conditions in marginal neighborhoods made it difficult for the market to process information accurately. One policy maker who had explained decline as a result of the lack of neighborhood pride acknowledged:

> Of course, lenders in the market place do not always act with perfect rationality. . . .
> Changing neighborhood conditions justify modifications in the investment instrument, but often lenders may act erroneously and completely write off a still viable neighborhood, once it is in doubt.

These actors integrated the misperception theme into their preferred explanation of decline. For instance, an actor who favored a neighborhood affinity explanation maintained that the evidence of organized civic pride could force lenders to re-evaluate their information about the viability of a neighborhood.

Generally, extensive market advocates rejected the claims of market misinformation. One such actor countered, "I am not comfortable with some government employee making $20,000 telling a businessman making $50,000 that he is mistaken about where the profits lie. If there is one thing businessmen know, it is how to make a profit."

All told, 20 of the policy makers attributed some significance to the problem of misinformation within the market decision process. They were made up of 12 Democrats and eight Republicans. Ten had previously stressed institutional misperception, five neighborhood affinity, two economic base, and one each consumer choice, federal programs, and municipal services as causes of decline. Only one actor in this group was an extensive market advocate.

NEIGHBORHOOD EXTERNALITIES

The second market imperfection involved the problem of negative neighborhood externalities resulting from privately held goods. An official in one of the FRAs described the problem in the following way:

There is a piece left out of the free market system and it is a valid public policy to supply that piece. A car which is broken down and left at the curb will soon be carried off, but a similar house will just sit there and pull the whole neighborhood down with it. The private market cannot cope with such a problem.

Neighborhood externalities were given significant mention by a great variety of policy makers. They were distributed in the following pattern: one consumer choice, one federal programs, two municipal services, and three each in the economic base, institutional misperception, and neighborhood affinity categories. All 13 of the policy makers who treated the issue of externalities were modified market advocates. Nine were Republicans, three Democrats, and one Independent.

Not surprisingly, this market deficiency is theoretically compatible with most explanations of neighborhood decline. In fact, the interrelationship of property values among all residential structures in a given area forms the basis for seeking neighborhood preservation as opposed to merely individual structural rehabilitation. It is perhaps most closely associated to the neighborhood affinity explanation of decline. Social cohesion can be a force which will push recalcitrant owners to keep their property up to standards, thereby protecting the value of the entire neighborhood. The inadequate income perspective also is compatible with the neighborhood externality flaw. The lack of income may force an owner to neglect the maintenance of his home. This individual's neglect may have a negative impact on the whole neighborhood. From the perspective of those who stress institutional misperception, neighborhood externalities simply quicken the process by which neighborhoods are written off by these institutions. They believed that the first signs of under-maintenance in individual structures trigger an exaggerated negative response by private institutions. Concern about neighborhood externalities also is compatible with the municipal services approach because both treat the issue of decline in terms of an area-wide scope rather than the individual unit.

Extensive market advocates (who dominated both the consumer choice and federal programs categories) were much less sympathetic to the neighborhood externalities argument. They tended to emphasize the uniformity of neighborhood conditions rather than the uneven quality of neighborhoods. In discussing neighborhood externalities, one extensive market advocate stated, "The National Housing Policy Review never was able to find any evidence of the existence of such externalities."

In conclusion, the two schools of market advocacy reacted to alleged market imperfections differently. The modified market analysts accepted the problems of misinformation and neighborhood externalities while, for the most part, the extensive market advocates did not.

PUBLIC POLICY OPTIONS

Having already explored cognitions concerning the causes of neighborhood decline and the strengths and weaknesses of the market as a resource allocator, neighborhood preservation public policy options will now be analyzed. The policy options offered fell into three main divisions. One group would not attempt to stem neighborhood decline arising from private sector activity. The second set would offer compensatory material incentives to reattract private investment to declining neighborhoods. The third cluster would seek to change the attitudes of the private sector in order to stimulate private investment in mature neighborhoods.

OPTION ONE: DO NOTHING TO STOP DECLINE

Of the 34 policy makers, seven found the decline of neighborhoods to be a reasonable and efficient response to changing social and economic conditions. Six of these seven perceived such decline as inevitable. All seven of these actors were extensive market advocates. Six were Republicans and one was an Independent. Quite logically, they did not see a strong need for a governmental program in neighborhood preservation. Nonetheless, there was some policy variation among these actors.

Laissez Faire

The three federal programs analysts in this group stressed the need to cut back federal housing programs as their policy option.[7] They claimed such programs were useless in already declined areas and destructive in healthier areas.

Triage

The four consumer choice actors in this category took a more active stance. To one degree or another, they adopted neighborhood triage as a policy option. Government policy should seek to cut off the unsupportable areas of cities. They observed that if a section is going to decline in any case, the rational response would be to write it off quickly.

OPTION TWO: PROVIDE MATERIAL INCENTIVES

A second group of policy makers (made up of eight Republicans, four Democrats, and one Independent) opted for a policy which would provide additional material incentives to encourage greater private sector investment in marginal neighborhoods. These policy options employ the material resources of the government to leverage greater private sector activity. The suggested inducement took two forms: infrastructure improvements and subsidies.

Infrastructure Improvements

Nine policy makers sought to improve the infrastructure of the city which, in turn, would make private investment there look more promising. These infrastructure improvements included physical development projects, basic municipal services, and social services. These improvements were designed to make particular neighborhoods more attractive to private investors. A HUD official remarked:

The market may have to be supplemented. It is crucial that public money be targeted to those areas which need it and can use it. This money must be directed to forces which will attract back the private capital.

This policy option is distinguishable from a coercive regulatory policy which would directly intrude on the business decision-making process. The HUD official cited above also stated that the actual investment process must be left to the private sector. "The government is ill-equipped to determine where private investment must go." The infrastructure improvement option avoided mandating the use of private resources by legal coercion. It functioned by making certain activities and/or geographic areas relatively more attractive to the private business sector. But the private sector would make the final choice.

Subsidies

The other material inducement was supported by four policy makers. This policy entailed direct subsidies to private corporations for handling socially desirable business transactions. The two most frequently discussed incentives for neighborhood preservation were co-insurance for mortgage lending and tax credits for rehabilitation activity. These incentives differ from the infrastructure improvements in that they work more directly within the private sector's decision-making process. The infrastructure improvements are meant to enhance the relative profitability of alternative investment areas by changing the characteristics of a certain number of those areas. These improvements, if successful, would then be taken into account by the private institutions when calculating the profitability of potential investments there. Co-insurance and/or tax benefits would not change the evaluation of an investment target area prior to the profit calculation. Rather, they would add a direct subsidy to the transaction after the normal profit calculations were made. The neighborhood, per se, would not be any more or less profitable as an investment, but the added government subsidy would change the final profit estimation of the transaction.

A Comparison of the Two Material Incentive Policies

According to the policy makers, the important feature of the direct subsidies approach and the infrastructure improvements mode was the ability not to run counter to basic market principles. The incentives only skew incrementally the direction of the market. These policy makers rejected government mandated private investments. This rejection was based on the belief that the government, which functions outside the market's parameters, could not be trusted to judge the utility of particular investments. The discipline of the market—especially the risk of material losses—forces the private sector to analyze investments more carefully. At the same time, the rewards of the market—profits—encourage enthusiastic private implementation activity. Government action does not benefit from these guidelines. Incremental government incentives, however, allow these mechanisms to function.

A HUD official described how HUD's nonincremental use of excessive subsidies and complete risk insurance resulted in large numbers of mortgage defaults in marginal neighborhoods during the late 1960s. He contrasted that approach with one of incremental incentives.

This forced attempt to avoid market constraints resulted in massive wastes of public resources. This is not to say that there must not be any government interference with the market. But it is preferable to use incentives for investments (like tax legislation) rather than the mandating of investments. At least by using incentives which work through the market, the most outrageous misuses of resources will be avoided. Incentives which are processed through the market will continue to be constrained by market rules.

For this actor's policy preference to be effective, the subsidy must only be incremental. The subsidy must not be so large as to be profitable by itself. Such a circumstance would remove all risk and discipline from the market process.

Policy makers interested in either the infrastructure improvement or the incremental subsidy modes also stressed the utility of the profit motive as an incentive system. The possibility for profit was believed to be a more effective incentive than government regulation. One policy maker noted, "When you mandate something, you only achieve the bare minimum and that's not enough. You need more." These actors viewed profit not only as an efficient incentive system, but also as the core of a socially productive economic system. Profits were seen as a self-sustaining pool of resources which are used to support a growing base of socially productive business transactions. Profits were not viewed as contradictory to social goals, but rather supportive of them. An official of a financial regulatory agency stated, "Without profits, the savings and loan industry would not be able to accomplish its social purpose of fostering thrift and homeownership."

The infrastructure proponents were more sensitive to the neighborhood externality issue than were the subsidy advocates. Seven of the nine in the former category mentioned neighborhood externalities while only one of the four in the latter category did. This relationship is not surprising. Appreciation of neighborhood-wide impact is very compatible with a policy preference emphasizing neighborhood infrastructure improvements.

Misinformation, however, was not an important factor in the analysis of either the infrastructure or the direct subsidy proponents. Only five of these 13 policy makers gave any credence to a problem of misinformation in the market place. But even these five viewed misinformation only as a marginal problem of the market. This pattern may be explained by the fact that all 13 of these policy actors were very concerned with the profit margins of the private institutions. These actors considered it highly unlikely that private institutions entering transitional neighborhoods on government orders would find it sufficiently profitable. This concern for the profitability of the financial institutions evidently made it more difficult for these policy actors to accept the possibility that misinformation seriously flawed the market.

OPTION THREE: CHANGE MARKET ATTITUDES

A third major policy category was made up of those actors who hoped to change the behavior patterns of private institutions without offering any compensatory material incentives. Fourteen policy makers (nine Democrats and five Republicans) fell in this category. All perceived misinformation as a flaw in the market process. Ten of these actors had supported institutional misperception as a primary cause of neighborhood decline. Three others had analyzed decline as a function of a lack of neighborhood affinity and one as due to an insufficient employment base. All of the policy actors in this category hoped to get the private institutions to change their evaluation of transitional neighborhoods as targets of investment. These actors suggested that persuasion, informal coercion, and additional market competition were the best policy options.

Persuasion

Seven of the policy actors opted for persuasion or cooperation as the best means to increase private investment in transitional neighborhoods. They were made up of four Republicans and three Democrats. These policy makers thought that by employing calm rational discussion, they could prove to the private sector that it could make sufficient profits in transitional neighborhoods. Material incentives were considered unnecessary to change institutional lending habits. One HUD official stated:

> Resources from the private sector might be garnered for marginal neighborhoods if the Federal government could show them with facts, figures, and experiences from Federal demonstration programs what the private sector could realistically expect in the way of profits. With these facts, you can change the attitudes of businessmen. Don't just make a regulatory policy statement with no proof of its validity.

This same official found that a regulatory policy of mandatory investments was ineffective.

> Credit allocation is self-defeating. The required percentage of neighborhood investment will either be set too low, or the classification system will be biased to exempt the truly needy areas, or the program will be so dismal that it will threaten the confidence of financial institutions, resulting in less business activity. Credit allocation has a nice ring to it, but it just may not be possible.

In general, these actors rejected comprehensive regulatory policies on the grounds that the regulations were too inflexible to deal with the full range of neighborhood conditions. Moreover, they believed these regulations might give the intended beneficiary neighborhood a bad reputation. Voluntary private investment would then become even more scarce since government action would reinforce private attitudes about the riskiness of a neighborhood. The private sector was seen as a skittish structure whose confidence must always be preserved if optimal results are to be achieved.

Informal Coercion

Another coterie of policy makers also believed that compensatory material incentives were inappropriate. This set of actors thought that coercion should be used to stimulate private lending in mature neighborhoods. Four actors, all Congressional Democrats, took this position.

In several ways, this group's attitude toward comprehensive regulation was similar to that of the persuasive policy adherents. Both groups felt that government regulators had neither sufficient information nor adequate means of evaluating that information to prescribe individual business transactions successfully. In addition, both agreed that bureaucratic decision making was prone to the inefficiencies of red tape. But the proponents of a coercive policy also showed a greater skepticism about the purity and fragility of business relations with government. They emphasized the difficulty of protecting regulatory bodies from the influence of the regulated industries. Furthermore, this group was not as fearful of destroying the fragile confidence of the business sector. These promoters of a coercive solution evidenced little faith in the honor of the business sector and for this reason did not find persuasion or voluntary cooperation a viable alternative. The difference between the coercive and persuasive schools of thought is related to their views on human nature. A policy maker, who had suggested the importance of cooperation along with subsidies as a policy, commented:

> Some reformers suggest compulsion as the first response to a problem. They do this because they believe that the private sector is out to cheat the average person. I believe that public policy should be premised on the belief that all people in the public and private sectors are willing to cooperate for the public good.

Caught up in their lack of faith in either voluntary cooperation or comprehensive regulation, these proponents of a coercive policy opted for a more sporadic style of political pressure on the private sector. This coercion was not meant to take the form of a comprehensive plan for the regulation of urban investments, but rather periodic pungent reminders to the private sector that there was an obligation to serve the cities and this service could be profitable.

Proponents of coercion did not reject the market process. A Congressional actor explained the value of mortgage disclosure as a tool for community pressure groups in market terms: "The attraction of the disclosure approach is that it leaves regulation to the market place and to the newly informed public." This same actor praised the decision-making ability of the market process.

> I have a great admiration for our banking system. . . . I think that bankers sit right at the heart of our economic system, and I think they do have much better judgement than we have here. But the record shows we have to do something to nudge them, influence them, persuade them to invest in their community.

Policy actors in the coercive category spoke of the market process in positive terms. They said market actors had "know-how" and "better judgment."

82

Competition in the market was called powerful and efficient. Nevertheless, a tendency was noted for financial institutions to fail to meet some of the investment needs of their communities.

In order to ameliorate these investment oversights, the coercive actors sought to stimulate both citizen-consumer pressure and regulatory pressure on financial institutions. But it is important to note how that regulatory pressure was defined. "Mandatory loans," "comprehensive credit allocation," "mandatory quotas," or "a bureaucratic credit allocation scheme" were all excluded. There would be no attempt to "substitute the judgement of the regulator for the judgement of a banker on individual loans." A comprehensive regulatory policy which had clear mandatory investment quotas and would infringe upon the individual portfolio decisions of financial institutions was rejected. Instead, terms like "nudge," "influence," "persuade," "carrot and stick," "jawboned," "a little talk," and "a signal" were used to describe the style of enforcement procedures envisioned.

Coercive actions would be noninstitutionalized and informal. A large bureaucracy and reams of codified regulations would not be necessary. The basic efficiency of the market would not be disrupted by mandating specific investments or requiring the comprehensive approval of every investment. Informal coercion simply would create a climate which predisposed the private sector to be more aware of the desirability of investments in mature neighborhoods.

Policy makers in both the informal coercion and the persuasion groups believed that the market overall was the most efficient economic mechanism. However, their attribution of market efficiency was limited to the implementation of specific transactions within investment categories. Both policy groups assumed that the market could overlook a profitable class of investments, such as investments in mature neighborhoods. But if that oversight was brought to the market's attention, these policy makers believed that the market once again would be the most efficient mechanism to implement these investments. Disagreement arose over the best method to bring this oversight to the attention of the private institutions. One subset suggested persuasion while the other advocated informal coercion.

Additional Market Competition

A third subset of policy makers also hoped to change the investment pattern of private institutions without offering material incentives to either the urban environment or the existing private institutions. One Republican and two Democratic policy makers proposed the encouragement of alternative private institutions to provide the necessary investments for urban neighborhoods. One Congressional policy maker said of the existing financial institutions:

> It is hopeless to think you can regulate these institutions and change their behavior. It is better and easier to set up alternative institutions. This would not be a subsidy. Market rates would still be used by the new institutions. It is just an attempt to get access to capital—not a subsidy of its use. . . . The market concept is fine. I would look like an idiot if I rejected the market economy. What is necessary is the amelioration of problems arising from the market.

These actors believed that there was little hope that the existing institutions would change their behavior either by persuasion or coercion. Two of them were quite skeptical of the government's ability to get an honest effort by the private sector in an endeavor which might have a smaller rate of return. All three of the policy makers in this group thought that a private institution with a more specialized mission could better provide the social goal of neighborhood preservation while still remaining within the context of a private market economy. Their critique was of the market participants rather than the market process. They wanted to increase the number of competitors in the market process. They sought to get some recognition for community needs, not by regulation, but by encouraging community participation in these alternative institutions. These three policy makers were less concerned with correcting the mistaken attitudes of the existing private institutions than with encouraging new competitors who already had the correct attitudes.

While only a few of the policy makers who favored a noncompensatory policy mode thought the rate of return in mature neighborhoods would be as high as other residential investments, all 14 believed that such investments would be both secure and sufficiently profitable. On the other hand, the actors who sought to offer compensatory material incentives to encourage private investments in mature neighborhoods did not believe unassisted private investments in these areas would be sufficiently safe or profitable. But both sets of policy makers thought that the older neighborhoods had virtues which, though not perfectly communicable within the market, were nonetheless real. The preservation of neighborhoods would contribute toward the nation's more efficient use of its social and economic resources. One advocate of subsidies philosophized:

> It is important to save our cities and the neighborhood is what holds our cities together. . . . They provide necessary order in society. . . . It will be cheaper socially and economically to provide the necessary urban concentration by building on what presently exists.

CONCLUSION

Two dimensions are important for understanding the policy positions of the actors analyzed in this study. The policy maker's evaluation of whether urban disinvestment is detrimental to society and the policy maker's evaluation of whether private urban investment is detrimental to private investors are the significant dimensions. The intersection of these two evaluations produces four possible policy contexts. The first context is made up of findings that urban disinvestment is nondetrimental for society and private investment is nondetrimental for individual investors. The second context consists of conclusions that urban disinvestment is nondetrimental for society and private investment is detrimental for the individual investors. A third cognitive context is composed of conclusions that urban disinvestment is detrimental for society, but private investment is also detrimental for individual investors. The fourth context is comprised of beliefs that urban disinvestment is detrimental for society and private urban investment is nondetrimental for individual investors.

TABLE 1. A POLICY MATRIX: THE EFFECT OF PUBLIC AND PRIVATE CONSEQUENCES ON NEIGHBORHOOD POLICY CHOICES

		Nondetrimental	Detrimental
Policy Actor's Perception of the Consequences of Urban Disinvestment for Society:	Nondetrimental	I. Halt growth A. Zoning	II. Do nothing to stop decline A. Laissez faire B. Triage
	Detrimental	IV. Change market attitudes A. Persuasion B. Informal coercion C. Additional market competition	III. Provide material incentives A. Infrastructure improvements B. Subsidies

Policy actors whose cognitions fall within a particular context had similar policy responses. The first context would logically be associated with a no growth or zoning policy. Because the interviews predominantly focused upon the problem of encouraging further investment from a reluctant private sector, the problem of an overactive private sector was not relevant to these discussions. It is not surprising then that none of the policy makers fell into this context. It will not be treated any further in this analysis. Those actors in the second context responded with a policy of either governmental inaction or governmental action meant to hasten decline in selected neighborhoods. Policy makers in the third context espoused programs to compensate for the possible detrimental consequences private investors might suffer. The compensation took the forms of improvements to the investment environment or subsidies to the investors. Those in the fourth cognitive context responded with a policy which either attempted to change the attitudes of the leadership of existing private business institutions or to encourage the formation of new competing private institutions which would have a better attitude on urban investment.

Thus, each of the three relevant contexts are associated with one of the three major policy clusters described in the last section. The policy choices typical of contexts three and four are of particular interest for an evaluation of a political economy analysis of the policy-making process. These are the two contexts which suggest that some public action might be necessary to supplement private activity with regard to neighborhood preservation.

Context three presumes that increased private investments in mature neighborhoods would be detrimental for those private investors. The respondents who held these views indicated a desire to improve the public infrastructure in order to reattract private investments or a direct subsidy to the private sector for preservation investments. Given the premises of these policy actors, both of these policy options were logical. Another option, however, might also be logical. Direct public investment for neighborhood preservation could have been proposed. A healthy housing environment might have been classified as a legitimate public service. Such public services need not be as constrained by the lack of sufficient profitability as private activities. Context four presumes that additional private urban investment will not be detrimental to the private investors. The policy was to change the attitudes of the private sector or to encourage the establishment of new private competitors who would hold the sought after attitudes. Again, another option is plausible. One might have selected a program which included a more comprehensive, direct government mandating of private investment for neighborhood preservation.

That both these possible options did not arise can be attributed to the way that these policy makers understood the functioning and relative benefits of the market mechanism. Despite the fact that these actors believed that the present neighborhood decline situation was unacceptable, direct action by the government as a housing developer, housing lender, or mandator of private housing investment was not suggested. Such policy choices were unlikely because the actors felt that the private market was the most efficient economic instrument for achieving specific goals. The policy makers in these two contexts believed that under some circumstances the market may not provide an optimal distribution of essential goods. But the market was still perceived as the most economically efficient administrative tool for reaching a particular social goal. Thus, their policy response was to attempt to refocus indirectly the market process toward the desired social goal without unduly disrupting the internal market process.

One can distinguish the various policy choices presented in this study by where they attempt to change the market. Those policy actors contiguous with the second context sought no appreciable change in the present market system. Two types of changes were found in the third context. One group sought to change the investment environment (through the improved delivery of public goods) which was then expected to influence indirectly the resulting investment decisions of the private sector. The other group sought to change the investment decision by adding a direct subsidy after the normal calculations were made. Policy makers in the fourth context sought an increase in private investments by a change in the attitudes of the private sector which would then affect how they evaluated the investment calculations. In brief, policy makers differed on the point in the decision process they wished to affect. One sought to change the investment environment, one the investment calculations, and one the investors' minds.

The policy makers' recognition of neighborhood decline as a problem was triggered by a concern for the apparent social pain and disruption decline caused as well as the physical resources it wasted. These concerns channeled policy attention toward the neighborhood decline issue. The widespread positive evaluation of the market process, however, shaped the policy responses to the perceived problem of decline. The actors believed the market was the most efficient allocator of resources and should be given the maximum feasible autonomy consistent with basic public goals. This belief filtered out policies calling for major government intrusions into the private economy. Once the more direct forms of government intervention were excluded by this negative selective mechanism, the policy maker's evaluation of the potential profitability of neighborhood preservation activity by the private sector became important. Perceptions of profitability helped determine the choice of specific policy options. If sufficient profitability was adjudged unlikely, compensatory material incentives were thought the best policy. If sufficient profitability was deemed likely, attitudinal change was selected as the policy option. Further variations within the general attitudinal change policy option were chosen on the basis of the actor's perception of the willingness of the private sector to work for public goals. The policy maker skeptical of that willingness would opt for informal coercion or competition from alternative private institutions. Those more trusting would advocate persuasion as the policy best suited to achieve the necessary private sector activity. Thus, notions about the profitability of the task and the motivations of the private institutions acted as positive channeling mechanisms in the selection of a final policy option from among the remaining choices.

Despite differences about whether and how to leverage the market process, there was general concurrence about the value of the market process. All but one of the policy makers thought the market was the preferable method for resource allocation. Any revisions of market results were to be achieved only through minimal interference in the market process. The cognitive material concerning the role of the market in neighborhood preservation presented in this chapter indicates that the basic requirements of a core policy map were met. There was a widely held set of beliefs and these beliefs were relevant to the policy options chosen. Policy preferences were shaped and constrained by the content of the core policy map.

NOTES

1. For a description of these two schools of thought, see Connolly, 1969; Dahl, 1956; Domhoff and Ballard, 1968; Latham, 1965; Mills, 1956; Polsby, 1963; and Prewitt and Stone, 1973.

2. For this critique, see Balbus, 1971; Lukes, 1974; and Parry and Morriss, 1974.

3. See David Gold, et al., 1975; O'Connor, 1973; Offe, 1972; and Poulantzas, 1973.

4. For the cognitive approach, see Eulau and Prewitt, 1973; Shapiro and Bonham, 1973; Stassen, 1972; and Steinbruner, 1974.

5. Congressional actors refer to actors in both the Senate and the House. Financial regulatory agencies refer to the Federal Reserve System and the Federal Home Loan Bank System.

6. All of the respondents were promised complete confidentiality. The sources of quotations will not be identified in order to honor that commitment. In the case of three actors, public statements comprised the bulk of the cognitive material. But even public statements will not be identified in order to minimize the chances of linking an actor to her or his confidential statements.

7. One of the federal programs analysts in this category was also classified as a municipal services analyst.

REFERENCES

BALBUS, I. (1971). "The concept of interest in pluralist and Marxian analysis." Politics and Society, 1, 2(February):151-177.

CONNOLLY, W. (ed.) (1969). The bias of pluralism. New York: Atherton.

DAHL, R. (1956). A preface to democratic theory. Chicago: University of Chicago Press.

DOMHOFF, G. W. and BALLARD, H. (eds.) (1968). C. Wright Mills and the power elite. Boston: Beacon.

EULAU, H. and PREWITT, K. (1973). Labyrinths of democracy. Indianapolis: Bobbs-Merrill.

GOLD, D. et al. (1975). "Recent developments in Marxist theories of the capitalist state—Parts I and II." Monthly Review, 27(October/November):29-43, 36-51.

LATHAM, E. (1965). The group basis of politics. New York: Octagon.

LUKES, S. (1974). Power. London: Macmillan.

MILLS, C. W. (1956). The power elite. New York: Oxford.

O'CONNOR, J. (1973). The fiscal crisis of the state. New York: St. Martin's.

OFFE, C. (1972). "Political authority and class structures." International Journal of Sociology, 2(Spring):73-108.

PARRY, G. and MORRISS, P. (1974). "When is a decision not a decision?" Pp. 317-336 in I. Crewe (ed.), British political sociological yearbook, Vol. 1. London: Croom Helm.

POLSBY, N. (1963). Community power and political theory. New Haven: Yale University Press.

POULANTZAS, N. (1973). "On social classes." New Left Review, March/April:27-54.

PREWITT, K. and STONE, A. (1973). The ruling elites. New York: Harper and Row.

SHAPIRO, M. and BONHAM, G. M. (1973). "Cognitive processes and foreign policy decision making." International Studies Quarterly, 17(2):147-174.

STASSEN, G. (1972). "Individual preference vs. role-constraint in policy making." World Politics, 25(October):96-119.

STEINBRUNER, J. (1974). The cybernetic theory of decision. Princeton: Princeton University Press.

4

THE POLITICS OF AUTOMOBILE PASSENGER PROTECTION:

Behavioral Versus Environmental Control

STEPHEN A. MERRILL

Committee on Commerce, Science and Transportation,
United States Senate

CLASSIFYING PUBLIC POLICY ISSUES

More than a decade ago, political scientists welcomed Theodore Lowi's proposition that the substance of public policy not only matters to the people who are affected, but it also determines political relationships among them (1964:688-690). The ability to categorize government policies and identify corresponding differences in political process combined relevance and rigor. It promised to liberate policy analysis from the limitations of case histories and studies of conventional issue areas.[1] It also compensated for the rather disturbing finding that structural political variables, constitutions and institutions, seemingly have little effect on some policy outcomes, at least on levels of public expenditures.[2]

The promise of substantive policy analysis using complex categories unfortunately fell considerably short of fulfillment. Froman (1968) pointed out several difficulties in an assessment of Lowi's distributive-regulatory-redistributive typology and others of comparable abstractness.[3] Although the categories

AUTHOR'S NOTE: *This chapter was written in large part before the author joined the staff of the Senate committee on Commerce, Science and Transportation and does not necessarily represent the views of the committee.*
The author is grateful to William Haddon, Jr., and Judith May for their criticisms of earlier drafts of this chapter.

appeared to correlate with other political phenomena and thus to have considerable theoretical power, they presented formidable methodological obstacles to application. The categories were not necessarily mutually exclusive, had low reliability, and were exceedingly difficult to operationalize (Froman, 1968:51).[4] One source of these problems was the effort to develop an all-inclusive classification. Even Froman (1968:46), despite his skepticism, proposed that a key test of a policy typology be whether "all policies" can be classified in one or another category.[5] Much of the best recent policy analysis has been less ambitious.[6] Theoretically interesting policy distinctions can be found even within supposedly single political issues. An example is the long controversy over seat belts and air bags to protect people in car crashes.

THE CASE OF AUTOMOBILE OCCUPANT CRASH PROTECTION

For nearly a generation, deaths and injuries to occupants in car crashes have been a well-documented social problem capable of substantial amelioration. Using data and hypotheses derived from aviation studies and studies of falls from extreme heights, researchers in the late 1940s and early 1950s showed that automobile occupants can survive even relatively severe collisions without serious injury if they are not thrown out of the vehicle and do not strike unyielding or lacerating surfaces. Short of preventing crashes altogether, there are several complementary ways of providing the necessary protection: reducing the speed of vehicles at impact; designing vehicle structures capable of dissipating much of the energy of impact and preventing collapse or penetration of the passenger compartment; securing the doors and windshield so that occupants are not ejected; substituting energy-absorbing steering assemblies, windshields and instrument panels for conventional rigid structures; and restraining drivers and passengers with belts or other devices. Occupant restraint was not only among the more practical of these measures; it also promised benefits exceeding those of any other known means of reducing traffic accident fatalities and injuries.[7]

The slow pace at which seat belts and other measures were adopted, nonetheless, led the federal government in 1966 to adopt a policy of attempting to "reduce the risks to motorists of having a collision and of being killed or injured in the event a crash occurs."[8] To the latter end, the government has taken a series of discrete actions in the form of regulations issued in accordance with this statutory policy, although on occasion it has later revoked or significantly modified various of these actions by amending the law.

TWO TYPES OF OCCUPANT RESTRAINT MEASURES

Largely as a result of government regulation, belts were installed in all seating positions of cars manufactured or sold in the United States and have been gradually improved in comfort and convenience, but a large majority of American motorists have failed to use them consistently. The government's actions, therefore, represent two different approaches to occupant restraint. On the one hand, it has tried to persuade, induce, or compel motorists to protect themselves by using seat belts; on the other, it has required manufacturers to install equipment or make design changes that directly provide greater protection. These two approaches entail different costs for individuals and producers. Consequently, they have been associated with different groups of partisans favoring and opposing various measures. Most partisans have viewed and decision makers acted as if they were alternatives, although they are not mutually exclusive. Proposals to improve vehicle safety have repeatedly generated proposals to increase belt use. Federal government regulators have more readily adopted measures directly or indirectly regulating motorists even though evidence of their effectiveness is lacking or they have been shown to be inferior to available vehicle modifications. Congress, on the other hand, has intervened to suspend only actions regulating motorists, *particularly* when they appear to be somewhat successful in promoting seat belt use.

This distinction, which has parallels in other issues of public policy, is between measures intended to change the behavior of individuals who are at risk and measures intended to change the physical environment in order to reduce the risk. For convenience, I shall call these behavioral and environmental measures.[9] As illustrated in Table 1, the categories encompass and clearly distinguish all of the major changes in manufacturer policy, federal safety standards,[10] and law relating to occupant restraint. They do not, as many policy classifications do, raise the possibility that political actors' perceptions of measures differ markedly from observers' (Froman, 1968:50).

Table 1. TWO TYPES OF OCCUPANT RESTRAINT MEASURES

Behavioral Measures	Environmental Measures
• educational programs and advertising messages	• lap belts
• buzzer-light reminder system	• shoulder belts
• ignition-interlock system	• automatic restraints (air bags and passive belts)
• compulsory belt use laws	• structural modification of the vehicle to provide crash protection at higher speed (e.g., 45-50 mph.)

Exhortations, educational programs, and criminal laws are typical ways of trying to change personal behavior. Examples in this case are public service advertising campaigns, educational materials for schools, and laws, proposed in many states and in force in Puerto Rico and several foreign countries, making failure to wear a seat belt a misdemeanor subject to a fine. Less typical are the buzzer-light reminder system, which activates when occupants in certain seating positions neglect to fasten seat belts, and the starter-interlock system, which prevents the car from starting under the same conditions. The sole purpose of these additions to belt systems was to promote belt use; they provided no additional protection to motorists. The distinction, therefore, is not between social action and technological innovation.

Government-imposed environmental measures change the behavior of a small number of manufacturers without directly attempting to influence the conduct of millions of motorists. These measures include installing lap belts and shoulder belts, inertia-reel retracting mechanisms which lock belts on sudden deceleration, air bag restraints which inflate on impact in a frontal crash of sufficient severity to cause injury, and so-called "passive" seat belts, which are permanently fastened to the floor and door frame of the car and wrap around the passenger as the door closes.[11] Standard belts require individual action to be effective; retractors, air bags, and passive belts provide protection automatically. Further structural vehicle modifications that prevent collapse of the passenger compartment and improved air cushions that operate in lateral and rollover crashes are other environmental measures that may be the subjet of future federal standards.

PARTISAN ALIGNMENTS

Some broad policy classifications purport to identify different sets of political activists behaving in characteristic ways.[12] The behavioral and environmental categories reveal reasonably stable coalitions of producers and professionals supporting each approach, respectively, to occupant crash protection. Although both manufacturers and professionals have occasionally split over particular measures, the most important change in 20-odd years of debate has been not a realignment of partisans but an expansion of both coalitions.[13] Consumer interest representatives established a group of professional advocates specializing in auto safety issues. The once dormant casualty insurance industry perceived an economic stake in reducing accident costs and, among other actions, transformed a public relations body into a professional automobile and highway safety research institute. Foreign automobile manufacturers and importers organized trade associations and hired lobbyists as their share of the American market increased. Domestic seat belt producers also organized to protect their market.

Crash-injury researchers who originally advocated the use of lap belts worked in small university-based projects supported mainly by the military services, the federal Public Health Service, and the major automobile manufacturers. When their laboratory tests and field data confirmed the limitations of lap belts alone in preventing serious injuries, they proposed to add an upper torso restraint, preferably in combination with a retracting mechanism that would permit flexibility under normal driving conditions but lock in the event of a crash. These measures were strongly supported by a number of doctors, primarily surgeons, and a handful of public health specialists, lawyers, and engineers not affiliated with the auto industry. In recent years, consumer organizations, insurers, and insurance trade associations have joined researchers, physicians, and other professionals in advocating conversion to automatic restraint systems.

In part because safety is an important social value and also because other strategies have been available, the automobile industry has rarely opposed environmental measures outright, but it has consistently attempted to delay their adoption or to weaken federal requirements relating to them. The manufacturers voluntarily implemented one measure, front seat lap belts on 1965 model cars, but only after several states had passed laws requiring the equipment on cars sold in their jurisdictions (U.S. Dept. of Transportation, 1972). In 1970, General Motors, Chrysler, and Ford each advised the federal agency of plans to produce air bag systems "in volume" or to make them available as options on all models by 1975. Their combined production over five years did not exceed 12,000 air bag-equipped cars, however, since the manufacturers succeeded in their appeals to postpone a proposed federal mandate.[14] In both cases, the industry's position has been identical; the restraint systems, they argued, were insufficiently tested, possibly hazardous to motorists, too costly, and lacked public demand. Nevertheless, the industry generally supported public efforts to encourage the purchase and use of seat belts, even when that entailed additional manufacturing costs. Ford Motor Company proposed the ignition interlock to the National Highway Traffic Safety Administration in 1971 and promoted it in advertising. The four major domestic companies and the Motor Vehicle Manufacturers Association have lobbied for belt use laws in various states and in petitions to the federal agency.

Behavioral measures have lacked organized opposition. Public service advertising campaigns are rarely controversial; the buzzer and interlock systems were adopted speedily without significant public debate. Professional groups, researchers and doctors, have often supported educational efforts and belt use laws, if less actively than they have environmental measures. The principal allies of the automobile companies in promoting the use of belts since their adoption, however, have been the manufacturers of seat belts and their trade association, the American Safety Belt Council. Air bag producers have been more cautious advocates of their introduction as standard equipment. It appears that suppliers of safety components to the automobile industry are more aggressive in retaining an established market than in creating a new one.

ACCEPTABILITY TO DECISION MAKERS

Other important political differences between behavioral and environmental measures are the speed and facility of their adoption by individuals who are in positions to make binding decisions and, once adopted, the willingness of authorities to maintain them.[15] In automobile and highway safety, as in other issues, decision making authority is shared, not unitary, and the reasons are constitutional, statutory, and political.

In regulating vehicle traffic, for example by enforcing seat belt use, the states' police power is primary, the role of Congress and the federal executive distinctly secondary. Under the 1966 Highway Safety Act, the Secretary of Transportation or his designee, the Administrator of NHTSA,[16] may issue standards requiring states to enact and enforce traffic regulations, but their only sanction is to withhold financial assistance for highway safety programs and highway construction. In addition to granting or repealing this authority, Congress may order that a particular standard be issued or withdrawn. Under these circumstances, the

Secretary and the Administrator have strong incentives to consult states before standards are drafted, to seek voluntary compliance once they become effective, and to impose sanctions for noncompliance very sparingly.[17]

In regulating the safety of vehicles, for example by deciding to have restraint systems installed, Congress has largely preempted the power of the states and delegated broad authority to the Executive agency, but left manufacturers considerable discretion. The 1966 National Traffic and Motor Vehicle Safety Act authorizes the Secretary to issue minimum vehicle safety standards which manufacturers may exceed if they choose. In order to encourage innovation, moreover, the law requires that standards be couched in terms of performance criteria rather than design specifications; thus the agency may not require air bags but simply some means of automatically reducing crash forces in certain laboratory tests. Furthermore, a vehicle standard may explicitly give the manufacturer quite different options such as installing either belt or automatic restraint systems. Within these limits, automobile company executives are decision makers as well as partisans.

Federal regulations, in any event, are not imposed by fiat, but are subject to formal and informal negotiation between the agency and the manufacturers. One purpose of administrative rule-making procedures is to obtain the industry's acquiescence, even though authority to decide the outcome lies with the agency.[18] Failure to do so may result in appeal and delay or reversal of the agency's decision and in weakening of the agency's influence in future proceedings. Again, Congress may intervene to change the agency's authority or to demand that a particular safety standard be issued or revoked.

Actions having the broadest effect include decisions by Congress, the Secretary and the Administrator, and automobile company executives, but not by individual states. With regard to vehicle modifications, they are decisions resulting in changes on all new automobiles. In these cases, a rough measure of the speed and facility with which occupant restraint measures are adopted is the elapsed time between their earliest consideration and their being instituted voluntarily or mandated by federal standards. To identify the inception of an idea is inevitably a matter of judgment subject to differing opinions. For present purposes, however, the history of a proposed measure dates from the approximate start of advocacy by private interests, primarily researchers or manufacturers, or of rulemaking proceedings by NHTSA and its predecessor agency.

As shown in Table 2, behavioral measures have been much more readily adopted by public and corporate decision makers than have environmental measures. Most behavioral measures have been adopted within two or three years, while environmental measures have been considered and debated for ten years or longer. A significant difference remains even if two or three years' lead-time is considered necessary for manufacturers and suppliers to produce and install restraint systems as standard equipment, but a comparable time is not allowed for buzzer reminder and ignition interlock devices.

The implementation of environmental measures has also been characterized by extreme gradualism and frequent setbacks. When the automobile companies were under pressure to install lap belts, they agreed first to offer them as optional extra-

Table 2. ACCEPTABILITY TO DECISION MAKERS OF OCCUPANT RESTRAINT MEASURES

Type of Measure	Approximate Interval Between Proposal and Adoption	Comments
Environmental Measures		
Lap belts	10 years	Installed in front seat positions of all domestic models, 1964, though required by law in a few states beginning in 1961; mandatory in all positions, 1968.
Shoulder belts	10 years	Mandatory in front-seat outboard positions, 1968; combined 3-point lap and shoulder belt system required in lieu of automatic restraints, 1973.
Inertia reel retractors	15 years	Required in lieu of automatic restraints, 1973.
Automatic restraints	12-14 years	Optional since 1973; subject to congressional veto, required in full-size cars in 1981, intermediate and compact cars in 1982, and subcompacts in 1983.
Occupant protection at crash speed of 45-50 mph	———	Rulemaking proposed in 1974 to be effective no earlier than 1980.
Behavioral Measures		
Educational programs and advertising	2 years	Conducted by public agencies and private organizations intermittently since the mid-1950s.
Buzzer-light reminder system	2 years	Continuous warning required in lieu of automatic restraints, 1972; limited by Congress to 8-second warning, 1974.
Ignition interlock system	3 years	Required in lieu of automatic restraints, 1973; requirement revoked by Congress, 1974.
Compulsory belt use laws	———	Proposed as a Federal Highway Safety Program Standard, 1972; states eligible for federal incentive grants, 1974; enacted by Puerto Rico, 1974; incentive grant funds withheld by Congress, 1974.

Sources: See footnote 13.

cost equipment, then to make depressions in the floor pan to indicate the proper location of attachment points, then to install attachment points, all before making belts standard equipment in front seat positions.[19] Until 1973, the federal occupant restraint standard issued in 1967 allowed and most American manufacturers preferred to install detachable shoulder belts.[20] This interval between the introduction of shoulder belts and combined three-point belt systems was not characteristic of many foreign car makes nor even of some American makes manufactured abroad. NHSB originally proposed to require automatic restraints beginning in 1972 and subsequently issued a rule applying to front seat positions in cars manufactured after July 1, 1973.[21] The deadline was repeatedly postponed and the specifications revised, in one instance under federal court order resulting from a suit brought by Chrysler and other manufacturers.[22] One revision of the standard allowed manufacturers to install either automatic restraints or belt systems; overwhelmingly, they close the latter option. Behavioral measures, on the whole, have encountered similar resistance only after they have been adopted.

Congress has rarely resorted to legislation to compel executive agencies to issue new regulations, but in recent years it has frequently intervened to restrict the uses of appropriated funds, reserve to its committees or to one or both Houses the right to veto future actions, and repeal regulations already in effect. What is noteworthy in the case of occupant restraint is that Congress has acted almost exclusively against behavioral measures. A year after the introduction of the ignition interlock system in 1974 model cars, the House approved an amendment repealing the requirement by a vote of 339 to 49. The Senate passed a similar amendment, though advisory in nature, 64 to 21.[23] The provision agreed to by both houses also barred the agency from reverting to a continuous buzzer reminder system by limiting the warning signal to 8 seconds.[24] This was the first instance of repeal or delay of a vehicle safety standard by legislation.

Although Congress has not acted to forbid NHTSA from issuing a Highway Safety Program Standard that would make federal assistance conditional upon states' adoption of belt use laws, the 1974 Department of Transportation Appropriations Act prohibited the Department from carrying out a previously authorized program of incentive grants to states enacting such laws.[25] In the following session, moreover, Congress temporarily suspended the penalty provisions of the 1966 Highway Safety Act in ordering NHTSA to repeal its requirement that states enforce the use of motorcycle helmets, another behavioral measure.[26] Secretaries Coleman and Adams both cited congressional sentiment in rejecting promotion of belt use laws as an alternative to mandating automatic restraints (U.S. Dept. of Transportation, 1976:58-59; 1977:14). The only obstacle that Congress has raised to the adoption of an environmental measure is a provision of the 1974 Motor Vehicle and Schoolbus Safety Amendments subjecting any future automatic restraint standard to a 60-day review by both houses and a possible veto by concurrent resolution.[27]

FEASIBLITY AND EFFECTIVENESS

Even if Congress had not stipulated that federal safety standards "shall be practicable" and "shall meet the need for vehicle safety,"[28] practical and political factors would dictate that decision makers consider the technical feasibility and effectiveness of proposed occupant restraint measures. Problems encountered in research and development do not account for the longer delays of environmental measures enumerated in Table 2; but decision makers appear to demand considerably more evidence that environmental measures will reduce deaths and injuries than that behavioral measures will increase belt use. At least, decisions to provide means of protection other than as extra cost options to purchasers have generally awaited the accumulation of a significant body of proof of their protective value. Behavioral measures are instituted in the presence of conflicting or absence of supporting evidence of their utility. Ironically, Congress has repealed or blocked them after they have shown some promise of success.

The technology of belt restraints, including lap belts, shoulder belts, and inertia reel retractors, was employed in aviation before its application to private automobiles. The technology was not transferable without adaptation to the vehicle passenger compartment, uses of the automobile, and forces experienced in car crashes; but questions concerning appropriate belt configurations, materials, and attachment points did not take long to resolve. The buzzer-light reminder and ignition interlock systems were, by comparison, novel devices when instituted. Only the air bag, therefore, represents an environmental measure originally proposed to be mandated in advance of technological refinement and large-scale production. Yet in 1972, the Sixth Circuit Court of Appeals judged the pending automatic restraint standard to be practicable within the meaning and intent of the 1966 Act, with the minor exception of its specifications for dummies to be used in compliance testing.[29]

Similarly, environmental measures have usually been shown to be effective in reducing deaths and injuries long before their adoption. At least by 1960, field studies of real-world crashes and experimental crash tests both supported the efficacy of lap belts in preventing ejection and ameliorating injury.[30] Crash tests, in addition, demonstrated the superiority of upper torso restraints of various configurations to lap belts alone.[31] Air bag restraints have been tested experimentally on numerous occasions and have performed to specifications in the great majority of crashes involving cars so equipped in the course of more than 300 million miles of driving exposure.[32] Although the number of crashes that have occurred does not yield statistically significant conclusions,[33] a recent study comparing injuries to air bag-restrained and three-point-belt-restrained occupants of cars involved in similar crashes showed the automatic system to be superior.[34]

Only two studies of the buzzer-light reminder system were conducted before its installation on most 1972 models. A 1970 NHSB survey of belt use by government employees driving cars equipped with different combinations of belts, lights, and buzzers reported an increase in belt use with the reminder system, but ignored the documented discrepancy between claimed and actual belt use, the effect of the study on changes in behavior, and the existence of an agency directive that employees fasten their belts (U.S. Dept. of Transportation, 1971). In a Ford Motor Company interview survey of 100 drivers of cars equipped with the reminder system, belt use was found to increase from less than 50% to between 60 and 80%. Pre-study interviews and personal observations by researchers, however, made it possible that subjects were influenced by researchers' expectations (Shaw, 1971a).

Two reports on belt use associated with the ignition interlock were available to NHTSA prior to the agency's decision to adopt the device as an interim substitute for automatic restraint systems. Neither study found any significant difference in belt use in vehicles equipped with the interlock mechanism compared with that in vehicles with buzzer-warning systems (Shaw, 1971b; U.S. Dept. of Transportation, 1973). Rigorously controlled studies of the effects of the reminder and interlock systems after their adoption yielded contrary conclusions. Buzzers and warning lights induced no more frequent belt use, while the interlock raised the proportion of drivers wearing lap or shoulder belts or both in 1974 model cars observed in urban areas from 28% to nearly 60%.[35] Both sets of results were published prior to congressional action banning the interlock and retaining a modified buzzer device.

Positive effects of compulsory belt use laws on both usage and injury rates were documented by studies conducted in Australia, where such laws were enacted in 1971 (Foldvary and Lane, 1974). Elsewhere seat belt laws have produced less dramatic but not wholly discouraging results, with the possible exceptions of Puerto Rico, Japan, and Ontario (Robertson, 1977; and other IIHS surveys). In any event, Congress withdrew its support for the incentive grant program when only the Australian data were available.

BEHAVIORAL VERSUS ENVIRONMENTAL MEASURES

Behavioral and environmental measures have been introduced gradually. The pattern in both cases, preceding and following passage of the National Traffic and Motor Vehicle Safety Act and the National Highway Safety Act, is a classic example of incremental decision making, whereby changes of policy differ only marginally from existing policies as a consequence of decision makers' efforts to cope with limited information, capability, and financial resources, as well as with conflicting values.[36]

This process, nonetheless, might have resulted in any one of three outcomes that did not occur or appear unlikely to occur in the future: (1) an earlier decision to opt for automatic restraint systems as the most effective and, for the driving public, least obtrusive solution to the problem of low seat belt usage; (2) a decision to opt for seat belt use laws and forego development of new technology whose cost and reliability were uncertain; or (3) a decision to enforce seat belt usage in vehicles already on the road and mandate automatic restraints in future automobiles. Behavioral and environmental approaches are, after all, compatible and complementary,[37] in the short run as the vehicle population is replaced with cars equipped with automatic restraints and, indeed, as long as lap belts are required in conjunction with air bag systems, rear seat passengers are not provided automatic restraints, and car owners are able to detach and thus defeat passive seat belts.

The crucial additional factor is that behavioral and environmental measures are not advanced independently of each other. It is not simply that partisans have represented them as alternatives. On a series of occasions, proposals originating from research and development to change vehicle design in order to increase protection of occupants have actually generated counter-proposals to induce motorists to protect themselves. Proponents of environmental measures frequently endorse behavioral measures when the obstacles to the former seem insuperable in the short run or when they prefer to avoid conflict in the hope of persuading their opponents. Federal regulators have usually adopted one or more behavior modification alternatives, often as interim substitutes. Neither approach, as a result, has been pursued exclusively nor have both been implemented simultaneously.

When, in the early 1950s, professional groups began to urge the installation and use of lap belts, the automobile manufacturers agreed to offer them as optional equipment but resisted their standard installation. They proposed instead a national education effort to persuade consumers to purchase and wear belts. Many crash-injury researchers and physicians endorsed this alternative, and a campaign was undertaken by the U.S. Public Health Service in cooperation with the American Medical Association and the National Safety Council. In 1969, after examining the progress of air bag technology, NHSB notified the industry of its intention to require conversion to automatic restraint systems in two years' time. In a series of comments and petitions to the agency between 1969 and 1973, some automobile and safety belt manufacturers urged postponement of the deadline and substitution of the buzzer reminder and ignition interlock systems which they were developing. The agency accepted each of the proposed alternatives in turn as an interim option and deferred the automatic restraint deadline, in the latter case apparently under pressure from the White House.[38] The manufacturers, in the meantime, advocated passage of state belt use laws. The federal agency indicated in 1972 that it would issue a Highway Safety Program standard requiring such laws, but later settled for the incentive grant or "carrot' approach to encourage state action to enforce belt use.

Not only does the advancement of one type of measure encourage opponents to pursue the other, but also controversy about one can favorably or adversely affect the acceptability of the other. The industry's extreme reaction to the proposed automatic restraint standard, for example, facilitated adoption of the buzzer and interlock devices even though government regulators had ample reason to suspect that they would be unpopular with the public. The agency's original schedule represented an effort to force the pace of technological development rather than, as has been customary, to follow its lead;[39] the manufacturers charged that this was a flagrant case of standard-setting out of hand.[40] Individually and severally, the major domestic companies appealed to the federal courts, the White House, and the public to delay or defeat the requirement. In June 1971, for example, Ford ran a newspaper advertisement citing numerous purported air bag hazards such as inadvertent firings and extreme noise. NHTSA released an unusual rebuttal questioning the company's motives as well as its veracity (U.S. Dept. of Transportation, 1971). The efforts to discredit the air bag were damaging nonetheless.

The ignition interlock system, on the other hand, generated intense public hostility imperiling both behavioral and environmental measures. In the course of repealing the interlock requirement, Congress narrowly defeated an amendment prohibiting an automatic restraint only by adopting a provision allowing a legislative veto after publication of such a rule. Shortly before leaving office,

Secretary Coleman rejected both a compulsory belt use standard and an immediate automatic restraint mandate. Although convinced that "passive restraints are technologically feasible, would provide substantial protection to the public, and can be produced economically," he argued that "the public record and our experience with the ignition interlock system and motorcycle helmet use requirements indicate that the public would react adversely to a Federal mandate of unfamiliar devices directed towards self-protection which also add substantially to the price of an automobile" (U.S. Dept. of Transportation, 1976:1,6).

Industry opposition to air bags and public opposition to the starter-interlock adopted as a substitute have generated considerable controversy about both environmental and behavioral methods of increasing occupant crash protection.[41] The conflict appears to have exhausted the behavioral remedies, leaving federal regulators the choice only of whether or not to proceed to require automatic restraints. Having decided to do so, Secretary Adams for a time faced the possibility of an unprecedented congressional veto of an environmental measure.

BENEFITS AND COSTS

Occupant crash protection has become more controversial as its benefits and costs have increased. The most vigorously criticized measures, air bags, belt laws, and the ignition interlock, appear to be more effective than previous measures in reducing deaths and injuries. According to Department of Transportation estimates, front seat automatic restraints will save an additional 9,000 lives and prevent a much greater number of serious injuries annually when all automobiles are so equipped. Belt systems could produce substantial if not equal savings with usage rates of 70% or more, a result achievable only by enforcement of belt use laws. The interlock system temporarily raised the use rate in 1974 model cars to 60% in some urban areas, nearly three times the present average.[42]

Air bags, belt laws, and interlock systems also impose greater costs of various types than previous measures. Estimates of the retail price of full-front air bags range from slightly less than $100 to $235, a substantial increase in either case over the retail cost of current belt systems and a significant addition to the $249 attributed to all federal safety requirements combined (U.S. Dept. of Transportation, 1977:54, 1976:5). Compared with previous efforts to encourage belt use, the interlock system and enforced use impose relatively severe sanctions on affected individuals who neglect or decline to comply.[43]

Increments in costs imposed by changes in occupant restraint policy account for differences in the amount of controversy provoked by various measures, but not its sources and political impact. As the air bag, belt law, and interlock cases suggest, behavioral and environmental measures entail different kinds of costs differently distributed between producers and the general population and differently perceived by them. Only "cash costs" have been analyzed and documented, subjects' perceptions hardly at all,[44] but the following are plausible hypotheses.

The economic burden of changes in vehicle design and equipment falls ultimately on the consumer, but most immediately and perceptibly on the manufacturer. Installing air bags, for example, will require manufacturers to make a substantial prior investment in production equipment, redesign interior features of most models, and negotiate contracts with suppliers of components. It may foreclose other investments and design changes that the manufacturer would prefer to make. The eventual price increase, even though it includes a margin of profit, may affect future demand for new cars. If small cars are equipped with passive belts, air bag-equipped large models will be comparatively even more expensive. Manufacturers' market shares could increase or decline as a result. Because of these commitments and uncertainties, the automobile companies resist such changes to a greater or lesser degree depending upon their ability to bear those costs and risks. They have been willing to incur the additional costs of buzzers and interlocks in order to avoid the greater cost of air bags and in order to shift the burden of protection to individual motorists. They have brought their influence to bear through the communications media, in the courts, and in negotiations with the Executive branch.

Behavioral measures command personal attention. They occupy time, irritate, prevent driving, or carry the possibility of a fine or other legal sanction. They are far more repetitive than price increases and allow individuals little choice as to whether they will be affected. They impinge on all motorists, not just purchasers of automobiles. Consumers, in any event, are unable to distinguish price increases resulting from federal safety regulations from other price increases unless, as in the case of the air bag, they are widely publicized. The more obtrusive but apparently not the more expensive the measure, therefore, the more strongly the public has resisted it. Elected representatives have responded promptly to such opposition.

ANALYSIS OF OTHER SOCIAL PROBLEMS

At the root of the distinction between behavioral and environmental remedies are opposing definitions of a social problem. The first attributes the problem to the deviant characteristics of the persons involved, their willful or neglectful failure to protect themselves. The other attributes the problem to situational, structural, or environmental factors such as the inadequate protection afforded by the automobile and the failure of manufacturers to provide means of protection that are available. These attributions do not necessarily determine proposed remedies; they may be rationalizations of them. They are indicative, however, of efforts by political actors to control the process of policy making and obtain a favorable outcome.[45]

As William Ryan (1971) has illustrated, personal and structural attributions are characteristic of a wide range of social issues, including health, poverty, and crime. Similarly, accidents of various sorts are attributed to victims' carelessness, drunkenness, and ineptitude or to environmental hazards. Lack of business competition is variously blamed on conduct such as price-fixing or on corporate size and market structure. A note of caution, however, should be introduced here. Definitions of social problems are far more useful guides to policy analysis than issue labels. The objective of occupant crash protection policy, as it happens, is clear and undisputed; in other cases, the identity of the problem is very much at issue.

The categories "behavioral" and "environmental" are also not necessarily the most enlightening and least troublesome in other contexts, although they correspond closely to personal and structural attributions. Another way to describe different occupant restraint measures is to say that one set restricts the alternatives of individuals by raising the costs of noncompliance. The other increases their opportunities for protection. Perhaps this is what Lowi meant by his statement (1964:690) that "the impact of regulatory decisions is clearly one of directly raising costs and/or reducing or expanding the alternatives of private individuals."

NOTES

1. Dahl had previously confirmed that community political activists "specialize" in issues such as urban redevelopment, public education, and political nominations. His examination of political interaction in these areas, however, showed no other general variations among them; one issue, education, exhibited no internal pattern at all. Dahl, 1961; Polsby, 1963:70-84.

These community studies were more interested in using policy to demonstrate the structure of local power than in explaining policy per se. Some analysts of predefined policy areas, however, have conceded that there are few political characteristics that are common to issues in a certain area and distinguish them from all other issues. In a study of consumer protection policy, for example, Mark Nadel reported that his scaling of congressional roll call votes showed that (1971:145):

in consumer protection, as in other issues areas, the degree of partisanship is modified by the cross-cutting effect of the "conservative coalition" of Republicans and Southern Democrats. . . . Consumer protection issues break the same way as other issues.

Furthermore, his comparison of the legislative histories of several consumer bills revealed "no single sine qua non for the passage of consumer protection legislation. . . . There are a variety of substitutive factors which may lead to the passage of legislation" (1971:149-150).

2. This concern is reflected in Salisbury, 1968. Salisbury describes his elaboration of Lowi's typology as an effort at "rehabilitating political variables," particularly policy content as a "crucial component variable in the analysis of any political system" (1968:151, 174).

3. The other typologies mentioned by Froman are Berelson, Lazarsfeld, and McPhee's distinction between "style" and "position" issues; Edelman's dichotomy in terms of "material" and "symbolic" satisfaction; Huntington's distinction between "strategic" and "structural" defense issues; Riker's "zero-sum" versus "non-zero-sum" distinction; and Froman's own "areal" and "segmental" types of city policies.

4. Others have made a similar judgment of the Lowi typology. See Heclo, 1972:105.

5. Lowi and others expended considerable effort trying to devise an appropriate fourth category and apply the classification to foreign policy issues.

6. As Salisbury (1968:156) observed:

The object of analysis may not always be the building of more general theory. We are not so rich in lower level descriptive statements that we can afford to stop seeking them, even if we were agreed, as we are not, that we are never to be interested in explaining, let us say, variations in educational policy because we are interested in educational policy. . . . The prudent strategy will surely be one of critical pluralism,with many scholars exploiting a variety of approaches at different levels of generality while critically and continuously reviewing and refining the work of other participants in the enterprise.

7. The decrease in driving and imposition of the 55-mile-per-hour national speed limit, both in response to the fuel shortage of 1973-1974, contributed to a dramatic reduction of 9,000 traffic deaths in one year. However, lap belts, standard lap and shoulder belts, air cushion restraints, and "passive" belt systems all have greater life-saving potential, according to Department of Transportation estimates. For example: 10,900 fewer deaths annually with lap belts at 100% usage; 11,500 fewer deaths with lap and shoulder belts at 70% usage; 12,100 fewer with full front air bags and lap belts at 20% usage; and 9,800 fewer with passive belts at 60% usage. Approximately 60% of all traffic fatalities occur to vehicle occupants. U.S. Department of Transportation, 1977:53.

8. National Traffic and Motor Vehicle Safety Act, 15 U.S.C. sec. 1392(a) (1966). The pertinent provisions authorized the Secretary of Commerce (subsequently Transportation) to issue and enforce safety standards for vehicles manufactured or sold in the United States. The companion Highway Safety Act of 1966, 23 U.S.C. 402, authorized grants to states whose highway safety programs, such as traffic law enforcement, conform to standards issued by the Secretary. Both laws are administered by the National Highway Traffic Safety Administration, NHTSA (formerly the National Highway Safety Bureau, NHSB).

The federal role had previously been limited to establishing safety requirements for certain commercial vehicles, maintaining a register listing persons whose drivers' licenses had been revoked, setting safety standards for hydraulic brake fluid and for seat belts sold or shipped in interstate commerce, and establishing safety standards for passenger vehicles purchased by the federal government.

9. Despite their apparent similarity, the behavioral-environmental distinction should not be confused with that between "active" and "passive" crash protection and other public health measures. The former refers to the change intended by a policy proposal, the latter to the amount of cooperation required of individuals for protective measures to be effective once they are adopted. "Active" seat belts require millions of individual actions daily for complete success; "passive" air bags operate automatically. While poles apart in this respect, seat belts and air bags have very similar political histories, in contrast with measures aimed directly at changing motorists' behavior. For obvious reasons, however, the active-passive distinction is extremely useful in predicting the efficacy of a variety of public health strategies, including those used in combating infectious diseases, preventing injury, and controlling population. See, for example, Haddon, 1974:353-354; Robertson, 1975:165-170.

10. Principally, Federal Motor Vehicle Safety Standard 208 (49 C.F.R. 571.208).

11. Passive belts are presently deemed appropriate only for smaller cars with bucket seats, whereas air bags can be designed for almost any size car. The passive belt consists of a single strap configuration similar to the standard shoulder belt; a padded knee panel is required to prevent the occupant from sliding under and out of the belt in a crash. Contemporary air bag systems function only in full frontal and front angle impacts; a standard lap belt is required to provide full protection in lateral and roll-over crashes.

12. Lowi (1964:689-690) intended to show that each national policy "arena" develops its own elites, group relations, and political structure.

13. These and subsequent generalizations in this section are based on a number of sources, principally, the series of hearings before the Special Subcommittee on Traffic Safety (later, Subcommittee on Health and Safety) of the House Committee on Interstate and Foreign Commerce (1956-1964), the National Highway Traffic Safety Administration dockets pertaining to rulemaking on FMVSS 208, and the public hearings on passive restraints conducted by Secretaries of Transportation William Coleman (August 3, 1976) and Brock Adams (April 27-28, 1977).

14. The commitments were made in individual comments to NHTSA on Docket 69-7, Notice 4, submitted in July and August, 1970. Chrysler has produced no air bag-equipped cars, Ford approximately 800 for use in business or government fleets, and General Motors approximately 11,000 both for lease and for sale to the public. Citing lack of public demand, GM ceased production in 1976. Insurance Institute for Highway Safety (1976); Status Report, 11:7 (May 3):3.

15. The present case supports Salisbury's observation (1968:154) that the simple adoption-nonadoption variable employed in some policy case studies is misleading. The longer the time span of one's observations, the more likely it is that some policies previously stalled or rejected will be successful and, one should add, existing policies revoked or changed.

16. The Secretary has formally delegated his authority under the Motor Vehicle and Highway Safety Acts to the Administrator of NHTSA, but may, of course, reassert it. In 1976, Secretary Coleman reserved the right to make a "final" decision on the question of mandating automatic restraints, and Secretary Adams followed suit in reconsidering and reversing Coleman's decision.

17. The Department of Transportation has only once initiated penalty proceedings, in 1975, against three states for failure to enact adequate motorcycle helmet use laws. The action almost immediately led Congress to suspend the Secretary's authority to withhold highway safety and construction funds.

18. The procedures, for the most part specified in the Administrative Procedure Act, can be characterized as follows. The federal agency, A, declares its general intent to achieve some statutory objective by publishing an advance notice of proposed rulemaking (ANPRM). The manufacturer, B, now on notice, responds with a general statement of the acceptability and practicability of the means necessary to achieve the objective. A specifies ends and means, often more modest ones, in a notice of proposed rulemaking (NPRM). B tells A what he is willing to accept and may advance an alternative rule by which he proposes to be bound. A issues a "final" rule which is subject to petitions for reconsideration, and so forth.

19. The sequence is chronicled in the hearings before the Subcommittee on Traffic Safety (later, Subcommittee on Health and Safety) of the House Committee on Interstate and Foreign Commerce: Traffic Safety, 84th Congress, 2nd session (1956); Automobile Seat Belts, 85th Congress, 1st session (1957); Motor Vehicle Safety, 85th Congress, 1st session (1959); and Motor Vehicle Safety Standards, 87th Congress, 1st session (1961).

20. Federal Register, XXXII, No. 23 (February 3, 1967), p. 2415. The requirement of combined 3-point belt systems was in conjunction with the ignition interlock as an option to installing automatic restraint systems. See Federal Register XXXVII, No. 37 (February 24, 1972), p. 3911.

21. Federal Register, XXIV, No. 126 (July 28, 1969), p. 11148 (Advance Notice of Proposed Rulemaking). The final rule appeared in Federal Register, XXV, No. 214 (November 3, 1970), p. 16927.

22. Chrysler Corp. v. Department of Transportation (6th Cir. 1972), 472 F.2d 636.

23. House vote on the Wyman Amendment to the Motor Vehicle and Schoolbus Safety Amendments of 1974, Congressional Record, 93rd Congress,2nd session(August 12, 1974), p. H8137; Senate vote on the Buckley-Eagleton Amendment to the Federal-Aid Highway Amendments of 1974, Congressional Record, 93rd Congress, 2nd session (September 11, 1974), p. S16439.

24. Motor Vehicle and Schoolbus Safety Amendments of 1974, 88 Stat. 1470, sec. 109.

25. Department of Transportation Appropriations Act, P.L. 93-391, 93rd Congress, 2nd session, 1974.

26. Federal-Aid Highway Act of 1976, 90 Stat. 425. Prior to congressional action, compulsory motorcycle helmet use laws had been challenged on constitutional grounds in 25

states, although they had been upheld in all but one of those cases. Information from the Office of Chief Counsel, National Highway Traffic Safety Administration, May 1975. At least nine states have since repealed their laws.

27. Motor Vehicle and Schoolbus Safety Amendments of 1974, 88 Stat. 1470, sec. 109. Following the presentation of this paper at the Annual Meeting of the American Political Science Association, congressional opponents of an automatic restraint requirement failed to obtain passage of resolutions overturning Secretary Adams' ruling within the 60 legislative days allowed by statute. By narrow majorities, the House Interstate and Foreign Commerce Committee tabled a resolution of disapproval; and the Senate Commerce, Science and Transportation Committee reported a similar resolution with a recommendation that it be rejected. The Senate then tabled the veto resolution by a substantial margin, 65 to 31; the House did not vote on the matter. Insurance Institute for Highway Safety (1977); Status Report, 12:16 (November 8):3-5.

28. National Traffic and Motor Vehicle Safety Act (1966). 15 U.S.C. sec. 1392(a).

29. See note 22.

30. For example, Tourin and Garrett, 1960; and testimony of Derwyn M. Severy, UCLA Institute of Transportation and Traffic Engineering, in Hearings Before the House Special Subcommittee on Traffic Safety, Automobile Seat Belts (1957), pp. 174-176.

31. For example, see the Severy testimony referred to in note 30.

32. Information from the Office of Multidisplinary Accident Investigation, National Highway Traffic Safety Administration, March 1977.

33. It should be noted that field studies of safety devices are always dependent on the cooperation of manufacturers in making the relevant number of cars or on obtaining data from countries where such changes have been accomplished. Thus, Secretary Adams rejected the argument made to him that the Department should not issue an automatic restraint rule in the absence of statistically significant real-world data. "Statistical 'proof' is certainly desirable in decision making, but it is often not available to resolve public policy decisions." DOT, "Occupant Restraint Systems: Final Rule" (June 30, 1977), p. 20.

34. Insurance Institute for Highway Safety, Submission to NHTSA Docket No. 74-14, Notice 10, May 1977.

35. See Roberton and Haddon, 1974:814-815; Robertson, 1974. A subsequent survey, however, showed a substantial drop in belt use in 1975 and 1975 interlock-equipped cars (Robertson, 1975).

36. The formulation is that of Braybrooke and Lindblom, 1963. Other examples abound both of incremental decision making and of decision makers' *assumption* that incrementalism is the norm. Transportation Secretary Adams has proposed to phase in automatic restraint systems over a three-year period beginning with 1982 model full-size cars and ending with 1984 model subcompacts. DOT, "Occupant Restraint Systems: Final Rule," June 30, 1977. NHTSA's short-lived incentive grant program provided a scale of bonuses for states enacting compulsory belt use laws. A state requiring drivers and front seat passengers to wear lap belts was to receive 10% more than its usual highway safety apportionment, 15% if the law applied to front seat lap and shoulder belts or lap belts in all positions, and so on. Federal Register, XXXVIII, No. 228 (November 28, 1973), p. 32818.

37. In April 1976, then NHTSA Administrator Gregory recommended to Secretary Coleman that he issue simultaneously a highway safety standard requiring states to enforce belt use beginning in 1980 and a vehicle standard requiring automatic restraints beginning with the 1980 model year. U.S. Department of Transportation, 1976.

38. According to former NHTSA Administrator Douglas Toms, Secretary Volpe opted for the interlock after a meeting with John Erlichman and other White House officials, subsequent to a discussion of the air bag between Ford and Chrysler executives and President Nixon. Toms has said, "If that meeting with White House officials had not taken place, DOT

would never have raised the interlock as an alternative to the air bag." Quoted in a memorandum from Michael Lemov, Counsel, to John Moss, Chairman of the House Subcommittee on Commerce and Finance (June 4, 1974).

39. For an analysis of the very different political circumstances surrounding another technology-forcing policy decision, see Jones, 1972. Some observers might consider the 1970 automatic restraint ruling as a case of "non-incremental" decision making.

40. For example: "problems of such technical complexity as are involved in the air cushion system cannot be legislated out of existence any more than the laws of nature can be overruled." General Motors Corporation Petition for Reconsideration of FMVSS 208, submission to NHTSA Docket 69-7, Notice 7 (December 3, 1970).

41. Industry efforts to involve the courts and the public, congressional intervention originating on the floors of both houses rather than in committee, and the personal involvement of the Secretary are all indicative of a greatly expanded arena of conflict, making policy outcomes more uncertain. See Schattschneider, 1960: Chaps. 1-2.

42. See notes 7 and 35.

43. The interlock system, in addition, cost purchasers approximately $32. U.S. Dept. of Transportation, 1974:47.

44. None of the government's various cost benefit, environmental impact, and inflation impact studies of proposed occupant restraint measures address their consequences as perceived by consumers and motorists. See, however, Robertson, 1976.

45. See Ross and Staines, 1972, for a discussion of the political determinants of personal and situational attributions of social problems. A variety of cognitive and motivational factors are analyzed in Staines, 1972.

REFERENCES

BRAYBROOKE, D., and LINDBLOM, C. E. (1963). A strategy of decision: Policy evaluation as a social process. New York: Free Press.

DAHL, R. A. (1961). Who governs? Democracy and power in an American city. New Haven: Yale University Press.

FOLDVARY, L. A., and LANE, J. C. (1974). "The effectiveness of compulsory wearing of seat belts in casualty reduction." Accident Analysis and Prevention, 6 (September):59-81.

FROMAN, L. A., Jr. (1968). "The categorization of policy contents." Pp. 48-52 in A. Ranney (ed.), Political science and public policy. Chicago: Markham.

HADDON, W., Jr. (1974). "Strategy in preventive medicine: Passive vs. active approaches to reducing human wastage." Journal of Trauma, 14:4(April):353-354.

HECLO, H. (1972). "Review article: Policy analysis. British Journal of Political Science, 2:1(January):105.

JONES, C. O. (1972). "Characteristics of environmental politics: The case of air pollution." Paper prepared for the Annual Meeting of the American Political Science Association, Washington, D.C., September.

LOWI, T. J. (1964). "American business, public policy, case-studies, and political theory." World Politics, 16(July):677-715.

NADEL, M. (1971). The politics of consumer protection. Indianapolis: Bobbs-Merrill.

POLSBY, N. W. (1963). Community power and political theory. New Haven: Yale University Press.

ROBERTSON, L. S. (1974). Safety belt use in automobiles with starter-interlock and buzzer-light reminder systems. Washington, D.C.: Insurance Institute for Highway Safety, June.

——— (1975). "Behavioral research and strategies in public health: A demur," Social Science and Medicine, 9:165-170.

_____ (1975). Belt use in 1975 cars: Initial data from one metropolitan area. Washington, D.C.: Insurance Institute for Highway Safety, May.

_____ (1976). Increased motor vehicle crash protection: Public preference and willingness to pay. Washington, D.C.: Insurance Institute for Highway Safety, August.

_____ (1977). Automobile seat belt use in selected countries, states and provinces with and without laws requiring belt use. Washington, D.C.: Insurance Institute for Highway Safety, April.

_____ and HADDON, W., Jr. (1974). "The buzzer-light reminder systems and safety belt use." American Journal of Public Health, LXIV(August):814-815.

ROSS, R., and STAINES, G. L. (1972). "The politics of analyzing social problems." Social Problems, 20:1(Summer):18-40.

RYAN, W. (1971). Blaming the victim. New York: Random.

SALISBURY, R. H. (1968). "The analysis of public policy: A search for theories and roles. Pp. 151-175 in A. Ranney (ed.), Political science and public policy. Chicago: Markham.

SCHATTSCHNEIDER, E. E. (1960). The semisovereign people: A realist's view of democracy in America. New York: Holt, Rinehart and Winston.

SHAW, D. J. (1971a). "Interim results from test drive II advanced features interest study." Ford Motor Company submission to NHTSA Docket No. 69-7, July 21.

_____ (1971b). "Interim results from test drive II advanced features interest study." Ford Motor Company submission to NHTSA Docket No. 69-7, October 20.

STAINES, G. L. (1972). The attributional dilemma in social problems: Person versus situation. Ann Arbor: Institute for Social Research, University of Michigan.

TOURIN, B., and GARRETT, J.W. (1960). Safety belt effectiveness in rural California automobile accidents. New York: Automotive Crash Injury Research of Cornell University.

U.S. Dept. of Transportation (1971). An evaluation of a safety belt interlock system. Washington, D.C.: National Highway Traffic Safety Administration.

_____ (1971). "Comments on Ford Motor Company's ad on air bags." Submitted to NHTSA Docket 69-7, June 24. Washington, D.C.: NHTSA Office of Crashworthiness.

_____ (1972). "Laws requiring seat belts." Report No. DOT HS-820-226. Washington, D.C.: U.S. Government Printing Office.

_____ (1973). "Effectiveness of safety belt warning and interlock systems." J.B. Cohen and A. S. Brown, Report No. DOT HS-800-859, April.

_____ (1974). "Analysis of effects of proposed changes to passenger car requirements of FMVSS 208." Washington, D.C.: NHTSA, August.

_____ (1976). "FMVSS 208, occupant restraint: Options, alternatives, and issues." Memorandum from James Gregory, NHTSA Administrator to the Secretary and Deputy Secretary, April 12.

_____ (1976). "The secretary's decision concerning motor vehicle occupant crash protection." Washington, D.C.: NHTSA, December 6.

_____ (1977). "Occupant restraint systems: Final rule." NHTSA Docket No. 74-14, Notice 10, June 30.

PART III
SERVICE DELIVERY SYSTEMS

5

POLICING: Is There a System?

E L I N O R   O S T R O M

Indiana University

R O G E R   B . P A R K S

Indiana University

G O R D O N   P . W H I T A K E R

University of North Carolina, Chapel Hill

Many writers, in discussing the ways police are organized in metropolitan areas, have assumed that systematic ways of working together are impossible among police agencies. Bruce Smith (1949:22) expressed this view in a frequently quoted statement:

> There is therefore no such thing in the United States as a police system, nor even a set of police systems within any reasonably accurate sense of the term. Our so-called systems are mere collections of police units having some similarity of authority, organization, or jurisdiction; but they lack any systematic relationship to each other.

Similarly, the President's Commission on Law Enforcement and Administration of Justice summarized this image in its report, *The Challenge of Crime in a Free Society* (1967:119):

The machinery of law enforcement in this country is fragmented, complicated and frequently overlapping. America is essentially a nation of small police forces, each operating independently within the limits of its jurisdictions. The boundaries that define and limit police operations do not hinder the movement of criminals, of course. They can and do take advantage of ancient political and geographic boundaries, which often give them sanctuary from effective police activities.

... coordination of activity among police agencies, even when the areas they work in are contiguous or overlapping tends to be sporadic and informal, to the extent that it exists at all.

However, this conventional wisdom is not supported by systematic study of how police do or do not work together in metropolitan areas. Anecdotes of feuds between departments have been used in place of systematic surveys of how police services are delivered in most metropolitan areas.

An empirical description of how police work together is now possible in light of recently completed research on police services delivery in 80 U.S. metropolitan areas. In this research we took an industry approach to the study of police organization. This analytical approach is neutral in regard to whether systematic relationships exist in metropolitan areas. However, using this approach forces one to *ask questions* about the nature of production of consumption relationships in a metropolitan area rather than *assume* the nature of these relationships from a simple list of agencies in the area. In this chapter we will first briefly describe the approach we utilized and the metropolitan areas included in our study. We will then present some findings on the structure of police service delivery in metropolitan areas.

THE INDUSTRY APPROACH

Instead of focusing solely on the agencies in a metropolitan area that met some basic definition of "police department," we looked for agencies producing specific public services for the area.[1] Each agency is considered in terms of what it produces or consumes, and who receives its products.

DEFINITION OF SERVICES

In order to determine unambiguously which agencies are part of a public service industry, we must first define a group of goods or services which are considered to be the industry products. No intrinsic feature of an agency places it exclusively in one public service industry rather than another. A police department, for example, may be considered in the health industry if it provides ambulance service, in the fire prevention industry if it inspects buildings, and in the recreation industry if it sponsors a softball league. One can tell if an agency is "in" or "out" or an industry only by knowing whether it produces one of the goods or services that are considered to be an industry product.

We selected a variety of law enforcement activities that are directed to citizens. We examined the delivery of three *direct services:*

- Patrol
- Traffic Control
- Criminal Investigation[2]

These three services include some of the more time-consuming and high priority police services to citizens. For our purposes, delivery of these services involves activity by officers who have *extraordinary powers of arrest* in the conduct of the service, thus excluding private watchmen, guards, and private investigators.

We also included a number of auxiliary services that are used by police agencies in their production of direct services. These are services used by the producers of policing rather than services directed to citizens. We analyzed the delivery of four *auxiliary services:*

- Radio Communications
- Adult Pretrial Detention
- Entry-Level Training
- Crime Laboratory Analysis[3]

The configuration of the police industry differs from service to service. In one metropolitan area many producers of patrol may exist while there is only one producer of detention. In another metropolitan area, the pattern may be quite different. Our first effort was to identify the producers of direct services and the citizens they served. Secondly, we determined from direct service producers whether they used each auxiliary service and, if so, how they obtained this service.

INDUSTRY AND ORGANIZATIONAL APPROACHES CONTRASTED

We can illustrate the difference between the industry approach taken here and the more conventional organizational approach. Observers, using an organizational approach to study police, find that most departments having fewer than 150 full-time sworn officers do not have their own crime laboratories. These observers typically conclude that citizens served by these departments are lacking the advantages crime labs can offer to investigators.

Using an industry approach, however, we are interested in determining whether the residents served by smaller police departments are, in fact, covered by crime lab services. We ask the small, direct service producers whether they use crime lab services and, if so, where they obtain them? Most frequently we find that agencies with overlapping jurisdictions, such as county or state police agencies, provide crime lab facilities to direct service producers. Some direct service producers contract for crime laboratory services from another local police department or a nonpolice agency, such as local hospital or a private laboratory.

Observers using an organizational approach may argue that, if economies of scale exist in the production of some police services, all police agencies should be made large enough (through consolidation or merger, for instance) to gain these economies. However, observers using an industry approach will ask whether these economies can be captured by organizing large, specialized agencies to produce a particular service rather than including all police service production within one agency.

In private goods and services market we are familiar with the difference between retailers and wholesalers. We are also familiar with the differences between neighborhood, quick-service, limited selection establishments, and broad-spectrum supermarkets or department stores. There is a role for a variety of different types of firms in private goods industries. The differences among types of firms in private goods industries can be instructive when examining organizational arrangements for supplying public services. Instead of assuming that there should be only one type of agency—a large, full-service agency—serving each area, one begins with no prior assumption about any ideal form of organization, and simply asks how goods and services are being produced and exchanged? Then, one develops a systematic way for measuring the structure of these relationships. Then, and only then, is it possible to begin evaluating the comparative performance of different kinds of industry structure.

SERVICE DELIVERY MATRICES

Once services have been defined and we have identified the producers and consumers for each service, we can depict the service by service structure of a police industry by constructing service delivery matrices. Measures of industry structure can be derived from the matrices.

All agencies that produce a given police service in a metropolitan area can be arranged as *rows* in the delivery matrix for that service. The *columns* in the matrix are the service recipients. For each direct service, service areas are the service recipients. We included as service areas any territory that had a resident population of at least 100, some way of making collective decisions about police services in the area, and a distinct legal arrangement with a producer of a direct police service. Thus, for each direct service, the population of the metropolitan area is divided into mutually exclusive service areas, each served by one or more producers. The service areas for one direct service may differ from the service areas for another direct service. A community of people may have one arrangement for general area patrol and another for traffic control or criminal investigation. Many service areas are cities, towns, or villages. A residential campus or military base may also be a service area.

The service recipients for auxiliary services are agencies that produce direct services. These agencies use auxiliary services in producing direct services. Thus, the columns of a radio communications service delivery matrix are those direct service producers who use radio communications. Although we found that most direct service producers use all auxiliary services, we did find some who did not require their recruits to have entry-level training, or that do not use any radio communications.

PRODUCTION RELATIONSHIPS: ENTRIES IN THE MATRIX

We use the cells of the matrix to characterize production relationships. When a producer does not deliver the service to a recipient, the cell in that recipient's column is left blank. We were not able to develop interval measures of service flow from each producer. Instead, we developed a typology of production types that differentiates only ordinally. One distinction we make is between regular and irregular production of the service. By regular production of a direct service, we mean that the producer makes the service available on a routine basis to individuals in the area it serves. Regular production of auxiliary services occurs when the service is routinely produced for the police agency being served. By "irregular" production we mean that the service is produced only in unusual circumstances. If, for example, a municipal police department investigates all reported homicides in a city, but the state police occasionally assist in homicide investigation, the municipal police would be considered a regular producer and the state police an irregular producer for that city. Although we have found some irregular production relationships for all services, our structural measures are computed excluding irregular relationships.

More important, we think, are several distinctions among types of regular service delivery. In observing police services we found that several forms of production involve *simultaneous regular production by more than a single producer for any given service recipient.* Three forms of simultaneous regular production are so important that we developed special ways to code and measure them. These are coordination, alternation, and duplication.

Coordination occurs when two or more producers interact in planning regular service production for the same service recipient. In many service areas homicide investigations are simultaneously conducted by several agencies who coordinate their activities. Even though two or more agencies work on the case, they maintain a single case record and share information. This is a strict definition of coordination requiring interaction in the planning and the production of the service.

Alternation occurs when two agencies produce a service for the same service area, but systematically divide their production activities over space, over time, or among clientele. The production of traffic control on a freeway within a city by the State Highway Patrol, and in the rest of the city by municipal police departments, is an example of alternation in space.

Duplication in service delivery occurs when two or more regular producers supply a service to the same consuming unit without coordination or alternation.

Thus, for each direct and auxiliary service, a producer and a service recipient may have either: (1) no production relationship, (2) an irregular production relationship, or (3) a regular production relation. If the production relationship is regular, it might be coordinated, alternated, duplicated, or independent (i.e., no simultaneous production). For each service we classify the relationship (or lack thereof) between each producer of that service and all service recipients, and enter the specific relationships in the cells of a service delivery matrix. (For examples of these matrices, see Ostrom et al., 1977; McIver, 1977; and Ostrom et al., 1974.)

SERVICE DELIVERY MEASURES

From these individual service delivery matrices for each direct and auxiliary service for each metropolitan area, we can construct service delivery measures that enable us to compare service delivery across the 80 Standard Metropolitan Statistical Areas (SMSAs). Some of the measures we developed are discussed below.

Multiplicity

We define multiplicity as the number of producers of a particular service in a metropolitan area. Comparison among metropolitan areas is facilitated by controlling for population size. Relative multiplicity for direct services is defined as the number of producing units for a given police service per 100,000 SMSA residents. For auxiliary services, relative multiplicity is defined as the number of producers of the auxiliary service divided by the number of direct service producers receiving the auxiliary service. This measure is an inverse indicator of the degree to which SMSA has consolidated production of each police service. The lower the value for relative multiplicity, the greater the consolidation.

Alternation

Alternation is the proportion of service recipients in the SMSA receiving the service from two or more regular producers, where at least one of the producers alternates in time, space, or clientele. For direct services, relative alternation is the sum of the residents living in service areas receiving alternative services divided by the total population of the metropolitan area.

Coordination

Coordination is the proportion of service recipients in the SMSA receiving the service from two or more producers that coordinate their service delivery. For direct services, relative coordination is the sum of the residents living in service areas receiving coordinated services divided by the total population of the metropolitan area.

Duplication

Duplication is the proportion of service recipients in the metropolitan area that regularly receive a service from more than one producer *without* coordination or alternation. This measures the amount of simultaneous production where some form of arrangement for either coordinating or alternating the production has not been worked out among multiple producers of the service. For direct services, relative duplication is measured by the sum of the population of the service areas receiving duplicate service divided by the total population of the metropolitan area.

Other Measures

In addition to those defined above, we have developed measures of fragmentation, dominance, independence, and autonomy. These are discussed in several recent publications. (For example, see Ostrom et al., 1977; McIver, 1977; and Ostrom et al., 1974.)

THE METROPOLITAN AREAS STUDIED

Our findings are based on data gathered in 1974 and 1975 in a study of police service delivery in small- to medium-sized metropolitan areas. In 1970 the U.S. Census Bureau identified 200 single-State Standard Metropolitan Statistical Areas (SMSAs) with populations of less than 1.5 million. More than 67 million Americans, one third of the U.S. population, lived in these 200 metropolitan areas. We selected 80 of these SMSAs in a stratified, random sample which included metropolitan areas in 31 states.

The 80 SMSAs include a wide variety of metropolitan area sizes, population densities, and types of communities. Three of them have more than one million residents. Ten have fewer than 100,000 residents. Population densities range from 32 persons per square mile to more than 3,000 persons per square mile. Major cities are included in this sample. Two cities have more than 500,000 residents and another nine have between 250,000 and 500,000 within city limits. Twenty-three cities have between 100,000 and 250,000 residents. This study also includes the full range of other types of areas that police agencies serve, including smaller central and suburban cities and towns, unincorporated county areas near more built-up cities, and rural areas.

THE PRODUCERS OF POLICE SERVICES

DIRECT SERVICE PRODUCERS IN EACH SMSA

Most metropolitan areas have local and state producers of direct services, and many have federal producers as well. State and federal agencies usually supply direct services to several SMSAs. Thus, the total number of *producers* for the 80 metropolitan areas is greater than the number of *agencies* supplying those services. Municipal police departments are the most numerous *producers* of direct services. Table 1 shows a regional breakdown of the type of agency producing the direct services studied.

More than 60% of the producers of patrol, traffic control, and criminal investigation in the 80 metropolitan areas are municipal police. This category includes not only the police departments of cities, towns, and villages, but also township and New England town police. Agencies of this type usually supply all three of the direct services to the jurisdictions they serve.

County sheriffs' departments, county police departments, and county prosecutors' police account for about 8% of the producers of patrol, traffic control, and criminal investigation in metropolitan areas outside New England (Region 1). New England town police conduct these services in rural parts of metropolitan areas in those states. In many other parts of the country, county sheriffs' departments or county police have responsibility for serving much of the territory within metropolitan areas, some of which is urban, but much of which is rural.

Table 1.　NUMBERS AND TYPES OF PRODUCERS SUPPLYING DIRECT POLICE SERVICE IN 80 METROPOLITAN AREAS

Location	Number of Direct Police Producers	Percent of Direct Police Producers That Are:						
		Municipal Police Departments	County Police and Sheriffs	State Police Agencies	Campus Police	Military Police	Federal Police Producers	Other Police Producers
All Direct Service Producers	1454	64	7	7	7	6	3	6
Northeast								
Region 1	87	69	0	18	10	0	0	2
Region 2	162	82	6	3	3	0	0	7
Region 3	143	78	1	4	6	4	2	5
Midwest								
Region 5	275	74	9	6	6	1	1	3
Region 7	54	65	7	7	4	2	4	11
South								
Region 4	305	62	9	7	10	6	2	4
Region 6	182	49	10	9	10	11	5	6
West								
Region 8	48	44	8	10	6	19	6	6
Region 9	170	43	7	4	9	15	8	13
Region 10	28	68	21	7	0	0	0	4

Rows may not total 100 percent due to rounding errors.

County agencies also often coordinate investigations with municipal and special district police departments and supply them with auxiliary services. Like municipal departments, most of them supply all three direct services.

State police, highway patrols, and state bureaus of investigation are another group of agencies producing direct services. State agencies control traffic on at least some highways in each of the 80 SMSAs. In half of the metropolitan areas, the highway patrol or state police also conduct criminal investigations. Thirteen other metropolitan areas in the sample of 80 receive the investigative service of state bureaus of investigation.

College and university police departments commonly supply patrol and traffic control, but fewer of them investigate crimes. We consider all campus police in a single category, regardless of the kind of governing authority responsible for the campus. State, county, and municipal colleges and universities are not the only kinds of campuses with their own law enforcement agencies. Many private colleges and universities also have campus police conducting patrol, traffic control, and criminal investigation. Campus police account for almost 7% of the producers of direct police services in the 80 SMSAs.

Military law enforcement agencies also supply direct police services in metropolitan areas. Forty-eight base police units serve Army, Navy, Air Force, and Marine Corps installations in the 80 SMSAs. Almost all of these patrol, and more than half also investigate burglary. Investigations of homicides and of more serious burglaries on federal military reservations are undertaken by military investigation agencies: the Army Criminal Investigations Division, the Naval Special Investigations Office, and the Air Force Office of Special Investigations. Several of the metropolitan areas have more than one installation of the same branch of the military and, therefore, have several base police producers, but only a single military investigation unit. Eighty of the 1,454 direct service producers are military units.

Nonmilitary federal agencies constitute another group of producers. The Federal Bureau of Investigation is regularly involved in burglary and homicide investigation on federal reservations in 26 of the 80 metropolitan areas. There are SMSAs with military or other federal reservations. The FBI and other federal investigative agencies such as the Bureau of Alcohol, Tobacco, and Firearms and the Drug Enforcement Administration, conduct investigations in all metropolitan areas, but the enforcement of federal laws is not within the scope of this study, except on federal reservations where federal law supplants state law as the general criminal code. Other federal agencies producing patrol, traffic control, or burglary and homicide investigation in federal jurisdictions include the Veterans' Administration, the National Park Service, and the Bureau of Indian Affairs. These agencies produce direct police services in a variety of combinations, usually including patrol and traffic control. Forty of the 1,454 direct service producers are nonmilitary federal agencies.

Table 2. NUMBER OF DIRECT SERVICE PRODUCERS IN AN SMSA WHO PRODUCE EACH OF THE DIRECT SERVICES BY REGION

Metropolitan Areas Grouped By 1973 Population	Number of SMSAs	Multiplicity: Median Number of Direct Service Producers in an SMSA				Relative Multiplicity: Median Number of Direct Service Producers in an SMSA per 100,000 Population			
		Patrol	Traffic Accident Investigation	Burglary Investigation	Homicide Investigation	Patrol	Traffic Accident Investigation	Burglary Investigation	Homicide Investigation
Nationwide	80	13	11	10	8	5.9	5.3	4.7	3.9
Northeast									
Region 1	8	6	7	6	6	3.9	4.2	3.9	3.9
Region 2	4	19	18	16	13	6.0	4.6	4.6	3.9
Region 3	6	14	11	12	7	6.6	5.5	5.5	4.7
Midwest									
Region 5	16	13	12	11	8	7.2	6.4	5.6	4.5
Region 7	4	7	7	8	6	4.6	5.8	4.8	3.7
South									
Region 4	15	18	16	15	10	5.3	4.1	4.2	3.2
Region 6	14	8	7	6	6	3.6	3.2	3.3	3.0
West									
Region 8	4	5	5	7	7	4.2	4.0	4.7	4.7
Region 9	7	20	16	17	16	4.8	2.9	3.6	3.3
Region 10	2	5-21	6-20	5-20	5-20	3.9-10.5	4.7-10.0	3.9-10.0	3.9-10.0

A final type of direct service police producers are the law enforcement departments or other agencies like housing authorities, airport authorities, park departments, state capitols, hospitals, and so on. A few of these investigate crimes, but most are patrol and/or traffic control producers. When we combine these "special district" producers, they make up about 6% of the producers of patrol, traffic control, and criminal investigation in the 80 SMSAs.

MULTIPLICITY AND RELATIVE MULTIPLICITY OF DIRECT SERVICES

The median number of patrol producers in the 80 SMSAs is 13. This means that half of the SMSAs have 13 or fewer patrol producers, while half have more than 13. But, a simple count of producers does not characterize police service delivery adequately. For example, one metropolitan area might have 10 agencies that produce patrol service for a population of one million. Another might have 10 agencies, but a population of one million. Another might have 10 agencies, but a population of only 100,000. The difference between the two areas is lost if one uses only a simple count of producers. Computing the number of producers for 100,000 inhabitants of a metropolitan area (relative multiplicity) provides a means of showing the difference between the two metropolitan areas of the example. They both would have 10 producers, but the number of producers per 100,000 population in the first is 1.0, while it is 10.0 in the second SMSA. In relative terms, there are many more producers in relation to consumers in the second metropolitan area than in the first. As Table 2 shows, the median number of patrol producers per 100,000 inhabitants in the 80 metropolitan areas is 5.9.

A smaller number of producers investigate homicides in metropolitan areas than conduct general area patrol: the median number of homicide investigation producers is eight. No more than four homicide investigation producers per 100,000 population operate in half of the 80 metropolitan areas. Most metropolitan areas have fewer producers of traffic accident investigation and residential burglary investigation than of patrol, but more producers of these services than of homicide investigation.

Considerable regional variation exists in the number of direct service producers in an SMSA. Metropolitan areas in California and Arizona (Region 9) and in New York and New Jersey (Region 2) generally have the largest number of producers of direct police services. Regional variation is less for number of producers per 100,000 inhabitants. A common pattern across all regions is for there to be more producers of patrol than of other direct services.

In general, metropolitan areas with more residents have more producers of direct police services. By computing the number of producers per 100,000 residents, we can see whether larger SMSAs also tend to have relatively more police service producers. We find that this is not the case. Relative to the number of people living in a metropolitan area, there are *fewer* producers in the very largest SMSAs than there are in the smallest ones. Metropolitan areas with

Table 3. NUMBER OF DIRECT SERVICE PRODUCERS IN AN SMSA WHO PRODUCE EACH OF THE DIRECT SERVICES BY SIZE OF SMSA

Metropolitan Areas Grouped By 1973 Population	Number of SMSAs	Multiplicity — Median Number of Direct Service Producers in an SMSA				Relative Multiplicity — Median Number of Direct Service Producers in an SMSA per 100,000 Population			
		Patrol	Traffic Accident Investigation	Burglary Investigation	Homicide Investigation	Patrol	Traffic Accident Investigation	Burglary Investigation	Homicide Investigation
Nationwide	80	13	11	10	8	5.9	5.3	4.7	3.9
50,000 to 124,999	20	5	5	4	4	5.9	5.8	4.7	4.6
125,000 to 249,999	26	10	10	10	8	6.4	6.4	5.7	4.4
250,000 to 499,999	21	19	16	15	12	6.0	5.1	4.8	3.7
500,000 and over	13	29	27	28	22	4.0	3.5	3.5	3.0

populations from 125,000 to 249,999 tend to have the most producers of direct services per 100,000 residents (Table 3).

The reason that more agencies produce patrol than the other direct services is that smaller cities, townships, and college campuses often organize part-time or small, full-time police agencies to *supplement* the patrol capability of other police agencies responsible for providing direct services to these areas. The municipal police departments, county sheriffs' departments, or state police that have authority to produce direct services for the areas, continue to undertake investigations—either independently or, in some cases, in coordination with the smaller agencies. Where the agencies with overlapping jurisdictions conduct investigations independently, the small patrol producers specialize in patrol and immediate response services and do not usually conduct investigations. We discuss some of these arrangements more fully in a later section.

AUXILIARY SERVICE PRODUCERS IN EACH SMSA

Auxiliary services are used by police agencies in the production of direct services for residents living in service areas. With the exception of radio communications, few direct service producers supply their own auxiliary services (Table 4). While 68% of the 1,454 direct service producers supply radio

Table 4. AUXILIARY SERVICES SUPPLIED BY DIRECT SERVICE PRODUCERS

Type of Direct Service Producer	Number of Direct Police Producers	Percent of Direct Producers That Supply:			
		Radio Communications	Adult Pre-Trial Detention	Entry-Level Training	Chemical Laboratory Analysis
All Direct Producers	1454	68	11	15	8
Municipal Police Departments	936	66	6	6	1
County Police and Sheriffs	108	87	81	7	7
State Police	97	88	0	86	60
Campus Police	108	84	0	8	0
Military Police	81	58	17	42	12
Federal Police	40	32	8	75	65
Other Police Producers	84	56	0	10	0

communications, only 11% supply adult pretrial detention, entry-level training, and chemical laboratory analysis. The type of agencies producing these auxiliary services varies considerably from the pattern found in direct service production. County police and sheriffs are the only type of direct service producer likely to produce detention services. State and federal police are the only types of direct service agencies that commonly produce entry-level training and chemical laboratory analysis. Very few municipal police departments produce any of the auxiliary services except radio communications.

MULTIPLICITY AND RELATIVE MULTIPLICITY FOR AUXILIARY SERVICES

Multiplicity for auxiliary services is much lower than that for direct services (Table 5). The median number of radio communications producers in an SMSA is nine, for entry-level training it is four, and median multiplicity is two for both detention and laboratory analysis. There is no more than one jail and one crime lab for approximately every seven patrol or investigation producers in half of the SMSAs. There is no more than one training academy for every three direct service producers. The median is less than one radio communications producer for each police agency using radio communications.

Multiplicity of auxiliary service producers is greater in larger SMSAs, but relative multiplicity is less. In the median SMSA of those over 500,000 in population, there is approximately one jail and one lab per ten direct service producers, while in the median SMSA of those under 125,000 there is one jail per five direct service producers and about one crime laboratory per four direct service producers.

It is true that there are a large number of police agencies serving metropolitan areas. Most of these agencies supply direct service and radio communications. The number of detention, entry-level training, and laboratory analysis producers is substantially smaller. The roles of different types of agencies vary considerably across the 80 SMSAs.

AGENCY COOPERATION AND SERVICE DELIVERY

Conventional wisdom holds that if many police agencies exist in a metropolitan area, it necessarily follows that there must be duplication of services. Police officers are pictured as tripping over one another as they weave in and out of fragmented jurisdictions. Officers are seen as isolated from their counterparts in nearby departments and as failing to cooperate across jurisdictional boundaries.

In this section we present findings that indicate otherwise. We find little duplication of services. We discuss the ways in which police agencies in fact organize their service delivery systems to avoid duplicating each other's work.

Table 5. NUMBER OF AUXILIARY SERVICE PRODUCERS IN AN SMSA WHO PRODUCE EACH OF THE AUXILIARY SERVICES BY SIZE OF SMSA

Metropolitan Areas Grouped By 1973 Population	Number of SMSAs	Multiplicity — Median Number of Auxiliary Service Producers in an SMSA				Relative Multiplicity — Median Number of Auxiliary Service Producers in an SMSA per Direct Service Producers Who Utilize Service			
		Radio Communications	Entry-Level Training	Adult Pre-Trial Detention	Crime Laboratory Analysis	Radio Communications	Entry-Level Training	Adult Pre-Trial Detention	Crime Laboratory Analysis
Nationwide	80	9	4	2	2	.86	.33	.15	.14
50,000 to 124,999	20	5	2	1	2	1.00	.50	.22	.25
125,000 to 249,999	26	8	3	1	1	.81	.33	.11	.11
250,000 to 499,999	21	16	7	2	3	.88	.35	.15	.15
500,000 and over	13	23	8	4	3	.82	.29	.11	.09

Then we examine fresh pursuit legislation which opens the boundaries between jurisdictions. Finally, we discuss the extent of emergency assistance, mutual aid agreements, and deputization among police agencies.

Although we present findings about many workable arrangements for policing among agencies, we are in no way recommending maintenance of the status quo. Police organization in each particular area can be examined to determine whether current service delivery patterns can be improved. Arrangements that work well in one metropolitan area may not work well in a different area. The recognition that policing has been organized in a variety of ways leads to the realization that many options are available for reorganizing police services delivery.

DUPLICATION OF SERVICES

Duplication of services has been a major concern of critiques of American policing. That concern has arisen from the observation that most metropolitan areas have numerous, separate direct service police agencies. The assumption is that these agencies are duplicating each other's work. In general, our findings refute this assumption.

The work of policing is, with few exceptions, divided among the various agencies of SMSA. Each agency is responsible for conducting a limited set of activities and for serving a limited territory.

Overlapping jurisdictions have also been viewed as indicative of duplicate service delivery. But again, the assumption is generally inconsistent with our findings. For example, county sheriffs' departments typically do *not* patrol in those parts of their legal jurisdiction patrolled by municipal police. Similarly, city police agencies usually do not patrol residential campuses or military bases within city limits when these special areas have their own police. It is, therefore, important to distinguish service areas from jurisdictions. A police service area is any territory with a resident population and a unique set of service delivery arrangements. Only where two or more producers conduct the same service in a single *service area* may they duplicate each other's work. Even this is not usual, however. Most producers conducting the same service in the same service area have adopted divisions of labor that eliminate duplication.

ALTERNATION OF DIRECT SERVICES

In most service areas where two or more producers supply the same service, the producers have divided the work between them. The most common type of division is alternation. Service delivery can alternate in time, in space, or with respect to specific clientele group. For example, some small municipal police departments patrol only from eight A.M. to midnight. From midnight to eight A.M., county sheriffs' departments patrol those municipalities. This is alternation in time. No duplication is involved. In such situations, county sheriffs' patrols substitute for the municipal police officers.

Alternation in space for patrol usually occurs where there is a special purpose patrol agency operating in the jurisdiction of another agency. Examples include municipal park police who patrol exclusively in the parks; school district or community college police who patrol only on campus; and special district police who patrol airports, bridges, or hospitals. The defining characteristics of alternation in space is the supply of patrol services to an enclave of another agency's jurisdiction, where the enclave does not have a resident population. Officers from the larger jurisdiction may or may not patrol the enclave; generally they do not.

For traffic patrol, a geographic division of responsibility by type of thoroughfare is often established. State agencies often patrol traffic on interstate freeways and major state highways, but not elsewhere in the jurisdiction. Municipal and county police rarely patrol freeways.

Alternation based on clientele served is exemplified by the relationship between municipal police departments and military police where municipalities adjoin large military bases. Both military police and municipal police officers may patrol the downtown area of the municipality. The military police limit their attention to military personnel, while the municipal police retain their responsibility for dealing with civilians.

For traffic accident investigation, the division of responsibility between agencies is often determined by the seriousness of the accident; i.e., fatalities may be investigated by an agency other than the one that investigates nonfatal personal injury accidents. Also, property loss limits may determine which agency will investigate a particular accident.

Figure 1 illustrates the extent of traffic patrol alternation in the 80 SMSAs. The SMSAs are ordered from left to right according to the percentage of their service areas with alternate traffic patrol producers. Above the line are bars indicating the percentage of service areas with alternate traffic patrol producers. Half of the metropolitan areas have alternation in more than 47% of their service areas. Half have 47% or less. (That is, the median SMSA has alternate producers in 47% of its service areas.) One-fourth of the SMSAs have alternation in 33% or fewer of their service areas. Another fourth have alternation of traffic patrol in more than 67% of their service areas. (That is, the inter-quartile range is between 33 and 67%.) Service areas with alternate producers of traffic patrol tend to be larger than those without alternate producers. In half of the SMSAs, over three quarters of the population is served by alternate traffic patrol producers.

As shown in Table 6, there is more alternation of patrol, traffic patrol, and accident investigation than of burglary or homicide investigation. Legal powers and duties assigned to different types of agencies by state law influence alternation of service delivery. In our sample of New England SMSAs, for example, all service areas receive accident investigation services from alternating producers because of state policy. In Massachusetts, the Registry of Motor

Table 6. ALTERNATION, COORDINATION, AND
         DUPLICATION OF DIRECT POLICE SERVICE
         DELIVERY IN 80 SMSAs

| Police Service | Percent of Service Areas in Each SMSA Receiving Service From: | | | | | |
| | Alternate Producers | | Coordinated Producers | | Duplicate Producers | |
	Median	Inter-Quartile Range	Median	Inter-Quartile Range	Median	Inter-Quartile Range
Patrol	21	4-38	0	0-0	0	0-14
Traffic Patrol	47	33-67	0	0-0	0	0-13
Traffic Accident Investigation	35	13-64	0	0-7	0	0-7
Residential Burglary Investigation	7	0-25	6	0-27	0	0-0
Homicide Investigation	0	0-15	33	13-70	0	0-0

Vehicles investigates all fatal accidents, and in Connecticut, the Connecticut State Police investigate all accidents on the freeways which are located in each of the four Connecticut SMSAs. Local police agencies investigate other traffic accidents in the SMSAs of these states.

There is usually more alternation of patrol and accident investigation in SMSAs with larger populations. These SMSAs are more likely to have airports, municipal parks,and other enclaves with specialized police forces. Larger SMSAs are also more likely to have major freeways crossing several municipalities, each with its own local police. This creates more service areas to receive alternate service from state police or highway patrols.

COORDINATION OF DIRECT SERVICES

Coordination occurs when two or more producers plan and execute service activities together in a single service area. Two agencies investigating homicides or residential burglaries in the same service area usually coordinate their work. Regular coordination of criminal investigation typically involves performance of two related sets of activities: one based on local contacts, the other on special investigative skills. Screening crime reports, conducting initial inquiries, and providing contacts and background information regarding the service area are

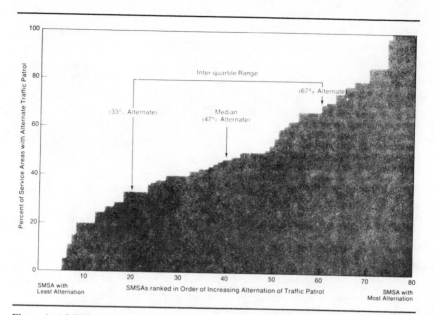

Figure 1: ALTERNATION OF TRAFFIC PATROL IN 80 SMSAs

typically carried out by a service area's own police department. Departments performing only these aspects of criminal investigation usually participate in investigations only in their own jurisdiction. They work with investigative specialists, who gather and assemble physical evidence and testimony. These specialists typically work with departments in numerous service areas.

Coordination in burglary investigation occurs primarily in small towns and in special police districts, e.g., college and university campuses. Most of the assistance to local police agencies in these service areas comes from the detectives employed by county and state investigative agencies.

Metropolitan areas vary widely in the percentage of their service areas for which agencies coordinate homicide investigation. This variation is displayed in Figure 2. In 16 of the 80 SMSAs, no service area has coordinated homicide investigation. These SMSAs are grouped at the left side of the figure. All service areas have coordinated homicide investigation in nine metropolitan areas. These are at the right side of the figure. The median SMSA has coordinated homicide investigation in 33% of its service areas. The interquartile range is from 13% to 70% of the service areas.

As Table 6 shows, coordination is a more common arrangement for criminal investigation than for patrol, traffic patrol, or accident investigation. Coordination is most extensive for homicide investigation. In over half of the SMSAs, at least one third of the service areas have coordinated homicide investigation. The

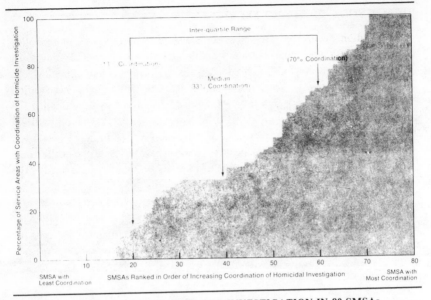

Figure 2: COORDINATION OF HOMICIDE INVESTIGATION IN 80 SMSAs

median for coordination of burglary investigation is 6%, with an interquartile range from zero to 27%. In half of the SMSAs, 7% or less of the population is served by coordinated homicide investigation, reflecting the smaller populations of most service areas with coordinated investigation services.

State laws and policies are important in determining the extent of coordination of homicide investigation. County prosecutors' detectives investigate all homicides and other major crimes in California and New Jersey SMSAs. State detective bureaus have been established to investigate homicides in Massachusetts and New Mexico. In many other states, state police regularly coordinate with police in some service areas where local investigative resources need to be supplemented.

In addition to producers who regularly coordinate all investigations of burglary or homicide, there is also considerable temporary or special purpose cooperation between departments. *Occasional cooperation* on investigations is practically universal. Few, if any, police agencies, whatever their resources, find it possible to gather all the information and evidence they need in all cases without the assistance of other agencies. In many metropolitan areas, *special inter-agency task forces* have been established to provide continuity to the cooperative efforts of the various criminal investigation agencies working in the area. Several SMSAs, including Des Moines, Iowa and Madison, Wisconsin, have developed multi-jurisdictional major case squads. The squads train together at regular intervals and are available to any jurisdiction in the area if a major case—usually a homicide—occurs and the local force needs the help of a specialized team.[4]

DUPLICATION OF DIRECT SERVICES

Duplication occurs only in those service areas where two or more police agencies supply the same service without alternating or coordinating their activities. As shown in Table 6, no duplication exists in over half of the SMSAs for all direct services. There is no duplication in residential burglary investigation and homicide investigation in three quarters of the SMSAs. More duplication exists in the supply of general area patrol than in the supply of the other direct services. Figure 3 displays the extent of patrol duplication for the 80 SMSAs. Forty-two of the 80 SMSAs have no duplication of patrol. The interquartile range is zero to 14%. Only about 10% of the SMSAs have more than one third of the service areas receiving duplicate patrol services. In the SMSA with the most duplication of patrol, 79% of the service areas (but only 48% of the population) are served by duplicate patrol producers. Duplication of patrol production occurs primarily in service areas with smaller populations, and this accounts for the smaller proportion of population being served by duplicate producers.

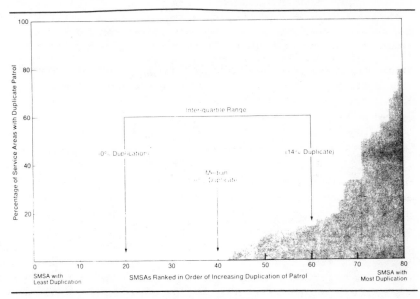

Figure 3: DUPLICATION OF PATROL IN 80 SMSAs

DUPLICATION, COORDINATION, AND ALTERNATION OF AUXILIARY SERVICES

Duplication and coordination of auxiliary services are rare. Only a few SMSAs have police agencies receiving an auxiliary service from two coordinating producers. In more than half of the SMSAs, no duplication exists for any of the auxiliary services (Table 7). Where duplication exists, for training and chemical analysis, it may be an advantage. Police agencies using two or more academies or labs have the the choice of where to send recruits or evidence. These are services for which a choice of suppliers may be particularly useful to the agency needing the service.

There is some alternation in radio communications. Some smaller municipal agencies are dispatched by a civilian employed by the agency during the day-time hours. (This person may also keep police records and do other secretarial work.) In the evening hours, these agencies are dispatched by a county sheriff or a neighboring city police department. Some alternation occurs in the delivery of pretrial detention where two agencies specialize: one holds male prisoners, while the other holds female prisoners. However, this type of alternation is not extensive. Alternation in entry-level training and crime laboratory analysis is very infrequent.

DUPLICATION AND DIVERSITY

Although there is almost no duplication in service delivery, there is certainly much diversity in service arrangements. Diversity, by itself, is likely to be neither everywhere useful nor everywhere harmful. It may or may not lead to confusion of responsibility. Most police chiefs with whom we spoke expressed little concern about the existence of a number of patrol, traffic control, and criminal

Table 7. **ALTERNATION, COORDINATION, AND DUPLICATION OF AUXILIARY POLICE SERVICE DELIVERY IN 80 SMSAs**

Police Service	Percent of Service Areas in Each SMSA Receiving Service From:					
	Alternate Producers		Coordinated Producers		Duplicate Producers	
	Median	Inter-Quartile Range	Median	Inter-Quartile Range	Median	Inter-Quartile Range
Ratio Communications	5	0-17	0	0-0	0	0-0
Detention	0	0-12	0	0-0	0	0-0
Entry-Level Training	0	0-0	0	0-0	0	0-11
Chemical Laboratory Analysis	0	0-0	0	0-0	0	0-7

investigation producers in their metropolitan areas, nor were they concerned about those other agencies serving in their own service areas. At the same time, some chiefs were concerned about ambiguities in the division of responsibilities between their own departments and others operating in the same areas. Clearly, some localities have not developed working relationships that are understood and accepted by all the agencies affected. Such localities are rare, however.

FRESH PURSUIT

The division of metropolitan areas into several separate police jurisdictions is seen by some observers as a deterrent to effective law enforcement. They assumed that police officers have no authority to pursue a fleeing suspect beyond jurisdictional boundaries. Because police officers' authority is largely determine by state legislation, we examined state laws regarding fresh pursuit both within and between states. We found that the police officers in most states have explicit authority to pursue suspects beyond the limits of their own jurisdictions.[5] However, that authority is subject to a variety of restrictions.

INTRA-STATE FRESH PURSUIT

Thirty-nine states have intra-state fresh pursuit legislation—statutes authorizing county or municipal peace officers to pursue suspected criminals across municipal and county lines. These states are shown in Map 1.

Intra-state fresh pursuit is generally not a problem for officers employed by state-level law enforcement agencies. Most state law enforcement agencies have, by definition, state-wide jurisdiction. State police may pursue suspected offenders anywhere within their state. County and local peace officers have more restricted jurisdictions. Fresh pursuit legislation is not always uniformly applicable to these peace officers. Pursuit authority may also be limited by the type of offense.

Of the 39 states having specific legislation on intra-state fresh pursuit, 22 authorize *all* county and municipal peace officers to engage in fresh pursuit throughout their state for *any* offense. An additional eight states authorize state-wide pursuit under at least some circumstances. That 30 states authorize some form of *state-wide* fresh pursuit contradicts any blanket assertion that police officers are unable to pursue beyond their own jurisdicitons. Of the nine additional states having other forms of legislation regarding intra-state fresh pursuit, eight authorize *county-wide* pursuit for any offense.

Eleven states have no legislation pertaining specifically to intra-state fresh pursuit. Lack of specific legislation does not, however, preclude intra-state fresh pursuit activity in these states. In states having no applicable statutes or case law, officers have the same right to arrest another person as do private persons under the common law. (Under common law, a citizen may make an arrest only for an offense committed in his/her presence.) So, even in states with no legislation or case law specifically applicable to intra-state fresh pursuit, law enforcement officers are not helpless if a suspected criminal crosses jurisdictional lines: the citizen's arrest right extends state-wide.

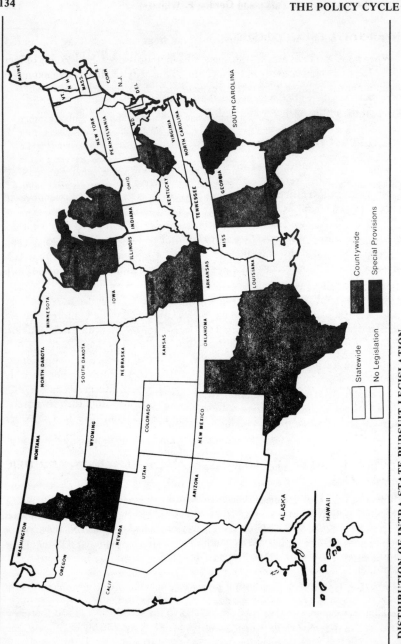

Map 1: DISTRIBUTION OF INTRA-STATE PURSUIT LEGISLATION

INTER-STATE FRESH PURSUIT

When a suspect flees across state lines, what authority does the pursuing officer have? Here the legislation is more specific. A majority of states have extended broad authority to the police officer as exemplified by this statute:

> Any member of a duly organized state, county or municipal peace unit of another state of the United States who enters this state in fresh pursuit, and continues within this state in such fresh pursuit, of a person in order to arrest him on the ground that he is believed to have committed a felony in such other state, shall have the same authority to arrest and hold such person in custody, as has any member of any duly organized state, county, or municipal peace unit of this state, to arrest and hold in custody a person on the ground that he is believed to have committed a felony in this state. [Kansas S.A. §62-632 (1937)]

A statute like this is designated a Uniform Act on Fresh Pursuit and has been enacted by 31 states. Ten more states have enacted variations of the Uniform Act. Of these 10, two have broadened the authority of the Uniform Act to include *any* offense. The other eight require reciprocity for their own act to authorize inter-state fresh pursuit. A police officer in any of these eight states can pursue across state lines into any other state that has passed a variant of the Uniform Act. By 1974, only nine states had not enacted any legislation on inter-state fresh pursuit. Most of these states are located in the South, as shown on Map 2.

Police officers in most states have relatively broad powers to pursue fleeing suspects, particularly when a felony is suspected. Some states without specific *intra*-state authority have used their authority under the Uniform Act authorizing *inter*-state fresh pursuit as authorization for fresh pursuit within their own state. So the actual practice concerning intra-state fresh prusuit may be somewhat understated.

EMERGENCY ASSISTANCE, MUTUAL AID AGREEMENTS, AND DEPUTIZATION

Presumed lack of cooperation among police agencies is a favorite topic of critics of metropolitan policing. In contrast, we find a great deal of mutual assistance. We deal only with local producers of general area patrol since they are the agencies usually viewed as most likely to need emergency assistance. (For further details, see McIver, 1977.)

PATTERNS OF INTER-AGENCY ASSISTANCE

Eighty-six percent of local patrol agencies in the 80 SMSAs report that they assist other police departments outside their jurisdictions (Table 8). Ninety-one percent report that they receive assistance from other agencies. Is this assistance "reciprocal"? In almost all cases, the answer is yes. Only 3% of local patrol producers report assisting other agencies, while not receiving assistance themselves. Eight percent report receiving assistance without themselves providing assistance. Together, both types of nonreciprocal assistance apply to only 11% of

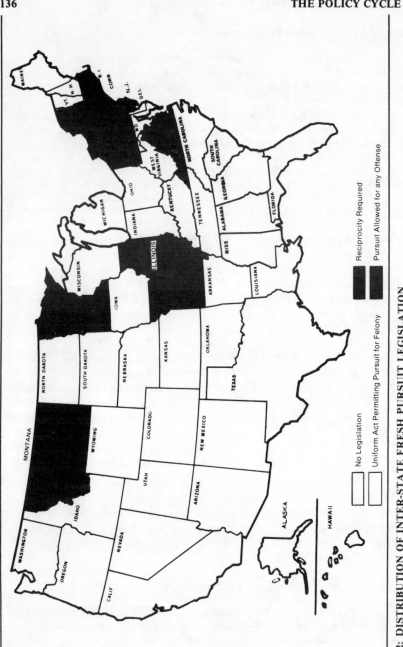

Map 2: DISTRIBUTION OF INTER-STATE FRESH PURSUIT LEGISLATION

the patrol agencies. Ninety-three percent of all local patrol agencies in the 80 SMSAs report providing *or* receiving assistance.

Municipal police departments provide assistance outside their jurisdictions more often than other types of local patrol agencies. More than 90% of municipal patrol agencies indicated that their officers go beyond jurisdictional boundaries to assist other agencies. County sheriffs are slightly less likely to assist *outside* their jurisdictions: 77% provide aid outside their jurisdictions. It should be noted, however, that out-of-jurisdiction for most county producers means beyond *county* lines. Almost all county sheriffs do assist the municipalities *within* their county. Special patrol producers and campus police agencies are much less likely to assist outside their jurisdictions. In some instances, the legal powers of these officers are limited to the jurisdictions of their employing agency by state law; for example, to a college or university campus. These agencies are also less likely to share radio frequencies with other agencies, and so their officers are not as likely to be aware of another agency's need for emergency help.

More than 90% of municipal police agencies, and about 80% of the county agencies, report receiving assistance. Similar proportions of campus and other special district patrol producers report receiving assistance.

Table 8.   PERCENT OF LOCAL PATROL PRODUCERS WHO GIVE OR RECEIVE ASSISTANCE AND WHO ARE MEMBERS OF FORMAL MUTUAL AID AGREEMENTS

Percent of Local Patrol Producers Who:	Nation-wide	Type of Producer			
		Municipal Police Departments	County Police	Campus Police	Other Police
Assist Others Outside Jurisdiction	86	92	77	56	53
Receive Assistance	91	92	79	87	97
Members of Formal Mutual Aid Agreements	47	51	30	32	32

MUTUAL AID AGREEMENTS

Although almost all local police agencies provide assistance to and receive assistance from other agencies, fewer local agencies enter into *formal* mutual aid agreements with other departments.

Nearly half of the patrol agencies have some type of mutual aid agreement with at least one other agency. Municipal police departments are the most likely to organize such aid agreements. Fifty-one percent of the municipal police departments, but only about 30% of county agencies, campus police, and other specialized producers belong to mutual aid pacts.

Significant regional differences exist in mutual aid pact membership. The West has the largest proportion of agencies who are parties to formal aid arrangements; the South has the smallest proportion.The large proportion of agencies in the West that have formal aid agreements is due principally to California law which requires all police agencies to be members of formal mutual aid pacts.

PATTERNS OF DEPUTIZATION

Deputization means that police officers from one jurisdiction are given police powers in a jurisdiction or jurisdictions other than their own. Almost two out of five local patrol agencies use some type of deputization arrangement. The most prevalent arrangement is a nonmutual one where one agency's officers are deputized by a second agency, but the first agency does not deputize the second agency's officers.

The officers of over one third of the local patrol agencies we studied are deputized by other police agencies. Seventeen percent of the patrol producers deputize officers from other jurisdictions. Examination of deputization patterns for county and municipal police departments provides a clue as to why a larger number of agencies have officers deputized by other agencies than deputize officers from other agencies.

Nearly 50% of the county agencies indicate that they deputize officers from other agencies, while only 16% of the municipal agencies and almost no campus agencies deputize officers from other agencies. In any instances, county sheriffs deputize officers from the smaller municipal agencies operating within their juriɔdictions. Deputization enables county sheriffs, who may have many municipal departments within their overall jurisdictions, to draw upon these departments for back-up assistance within the county as a whole.

Fewer than 20% of the county patrol agencies have officers who have been deputized by other departments. Sheriff's department officers do not need to be deputized by municipalities to have powers to arrest within the municipalities in their own county. This contrasts with municipal, campus, and other local police departments, which have more of their officers deputized by other agencies. Many of these are small departments. Across the country, more than 50% of the departments with only part-time officers and more than 30% of the departments with 1 to 10 officers have their officers deputized by another agency.

Campus police departments are most likely to have their officers deputized by city, county, or state police. This deputization may give campus police their formal police powers, since in some states college and university security departments are not empowered to authorize their own officers. Campus police are not likely to deputize others—other agencies with legal jurisdiction of a campus do not need their officers deputized.

PARTICIPATION IN EMERGENCY ASSISTANCE

Only 50% of the patrol producers who both give and receive emergency assistance outside their jurisdiction are members of mutual aid agreements. Clearly, assistance is available in many places without formal agreements. Twenty-six percent of the agencies that report neither giving nor receiving any external assistance belong to mutual aid agreements; so belonging to a mutual aid pact is no guarantee that assistance has been provided. (Of course, there may have been no need for assistance in some of these cases.) Almost 70% of the producers who report both giving and receiving emergency assistance are either members of mutual aid pacts or have some form of deputization agreement. Thus, most of the agencies reporting mutual assistance do have some formal arrangements between them, although the absence of formal arrangements does not preclude assistance.

Larger municipal police departments are less likely to give and receive emergency assistance than small departments (Table 9). More than 90% of municipal police departments smaller than 50 full-time sworn officers both give and receive emergency assistance. For municipal departments larger than 150 officers, this proportion falls to 80% giving assistance and 61% receiving assistance. About 50% of the municipal departments with 150 or fewer full-time sworn officers are parties to mutual aid agreements, while only 24% of the largest departments participate in such agreements. The relationship for county departments is the opposite. Larger county departments are more likely to both give and receive assistance than are their large municipal counterparts. Smaller county departments are not as likely to participate in a mutual aid agreement as are smaller municipal departments. Almost 50% of the county agencies with over 150 full-time sworn officers participate in such agreements. Department size has no relationship to assistance for campus and other local agencies.

COOPERATION, NOT ISOLATION

We find much more cooperation among police agencies producing patrol services than one would expect after reading many of the descriptions of metropolitan policing which have appeared in national reports. Nationwide, about 90% of all agencies give or receive emergency assistance outside their own jurisdictions. While the proportion of agencies who belong to formal mutual aid agreements is lower (nearly 50% of all patrol agencies), membership in such formal agreements is not necessary for emergency assistance to be given. Agencies operating in metropolitan areas with large numbers of patrol producers are more likely to engage in both formal and informal assistance.

Not only do the various agencies patrolling parts of metropolitan areas provide each other with needed emergency assistance in most cases, but they also have generally organized their work to avoid duplicating each other's activities. Patrol, traffic patrol, and traffic accident investigation are conducted in alternate times or places in most service areas that have more than one producer of the service. Coordination of criminal investigations is common.

Table 9. ASSISTANCE BY SIZE OF PRODUCER

		Percent of Patrol Producers That:		
Type of Patrol Producer	Number Reporting	Provide Assistance To Other Police Agencies	Receive Assistance From Other Police Agencies	Belong To A Mutual Aid Agreement
Municipal Police Departments By Number of Full-Time Officers	841	92	92	51
Part-Time Only	62	95	98	53
1 to 4	213	92	95	46
5 to 10	206	95	95	50
11 to 20	119	93	96	58
21 to 50	119	93	94	64
51 to 150	76	87	79	57
Over 150	46	80	61	24
County Police And Sheriffs By Number of Full-Time Officers	91	77	79	27
1 to 4	2	50	500	0
5 to 10	4	75	100	0
11 to 20	16	69	75	31
21 to 50	27	85	85	22
51 to 150	26	69	65	31
Over 150	16	88	94	50
Campus Police By Number of Full-Time Officers	93	56	87	32
Part-Time Only	3	0	100	67
1 to 4	13	31	77	46
5 to 10	36	64	92	28
11 to 20	18	61	78	17
21 to 50	20	65	95	40
51 to 150	3	33	67	33
Other Local Producers By Number of Full-Time Officers	38	53	97	32
Part-Time Only	2	0	100	50
1 to 4	11	73	100	55
5 to 10	10	60	90	0
11 to 20	8	50	100	25
21 to 50	6	33	100	33
51 to 150	1	0	100	100

Overlapping jurisdictions usually do not result in duplication of service delivery. Nor do many separate jurisdictions limit fresh pursuit. Most states have legislation explicitly authorizing pursuit beyond local boundaries. Cooperation between police agencies throughout the nation's metropolitan areas is extensive.

IS THERE A POLICE SYSTEM?

If a system is defined as a single, overarching hierarchical decision-making unit, then certainly the police industry in most U.S. metropolitan areas is not a system. However, the concept of a system is not limited to that of a simple hierarchy. Any collection of entities defined by a boundary and regular, predictable relationhsips among them is a system. The set of agencies producing specified services for a metropolitan area are a bounded collection and the police agencies included in such a collection do indeed have regular, predictable relationships among themselves in most SMSAs. Such a police industry should be considered a system.

Is this playing with words? Does it matter if a police industry is a system? We think it matters. For too long, proposed changes in the way police are organized in metropolitan areas have been made with a view toward an idealized hierarchical system, and without any careful research on current operational practices. There is certainly room for improvement in the way police services are delivered in many metropolitan areas. However, before changing from a system of separately organized service agencies to a system organized as a single unit, there should be a careful examination of the existing network of working relationships in their area. A large number of small police forces does not automatically mean chaos and lack of system. Nor does a single agency mean that chaos is avoided. The critical question for the organization theorist and for the reformer should be how well does the system produce the intended services, and not how well does it match a standard model. We need to be exploring alternative models for service delivery systems. The police services industry provides us with an abundance of models for closer examination.

NOTES

1. The importance of separating production from consumption relationships was stressed by Ostrom, Tiebout, and Warrent, 1961. A further elucidation of the theoretical approach was Ostrom and Ostrom, 1965. The approach taken here is described in more detail in Ostrom, Parks, and Whitaker, 1974; Ostrom, Parks, and Whitaker, 1977; and McIver, 1977.

2. Patrol is defined as organized surveillance of public places within a specified territory and response to reports of suspected criminal activities for the purpose of preventing crime, apprehending offenders, or maintaining public order. Officers assigned to patrol also typically respond to emergencies and other types of noncriminal calls.

Criminal investigation is activity undertaken to identify the persons suspected of alleged criminal acts, to gather evidence for criminal proceedings, or to recover stolen goods. Because the agencies and the methods of investigation differ with different crimes, depending on their degree of seriousness, we specifically focused our attention on investigation of *residential burglary* and investigation of *homicide.* Residential burglary is an often encountered felony. In contrast, homicide occurs less frequently, but is generally regarded as a more serious offense.

Traffic control includes the monitoring of vehicular traffic and the investigation of traffic accidents. Because *traffic patrol* assignments may differ from *traffic accident investigation* assignments, we examined the delivery of each.

3. Radio communications is the relaying of requests for police assistance to officers in the field and the receipt of radioed requests for information or assistance from officers in the field.

Adult pretrial detention is the holding of an adult after arraignment but prior to final court disposition of a case. Only agencies empowered to hold individuals in their facilities for more than 24 hours are included. We did not consider agencies that had temporary "lock-ups" as procedures of adult pretrial detention services.

Entry-level training is the department-required training of recruits for a direct service police agency. We do not disregard state requirements for entry-level training. For many departments, the state minimum is the departmental requirement. For some, the departmental requirement greatly exceeds the state minimum.

Crime laboratory analysis is the processing of evidence by persons whose testimony is accepted for presentation in court. Many kinds of laboratory analyses are required in criminal and accident investigation. We have limited our attention to the identification of *narcotics* and the *chemical analysis* of such substances as blood and hair.

4. Several of these Major Case Squads have been described in Fact Sheets available from the Workshop in Political Theory and Policy Analysis. These include: Elinor Ostrom, "The Topeka Major Case Squad;" Nancy M. Neubert, "The Major Investigative Team of Polk County;" Steve Mastrofski, "The Tuscaloosa County Homicide Unit;" Nancy M. Neubert, "A Comparison of Major Case Squads in Four Metropolitan Areas;" Staff Research Unit, Kansas City/Missouri Police Department, "Kansas City Area Metro Squad;" Eric Scott, "The Intra-Country Major Case Investigation Unit of Dane County;" and John P. McIver, "The Worcester County Fraudulent Check Association: Community Cooperation in Law Enforcement."

5. Specific citations to legislation and further detail about intra-state and inter-state fresh pursuit is available in Larry Wagner, "Patterns of State Laws Relating to 'Fresh Pursuit'." Bloomington, Indiana: Workshop in Political Theory and Policy Analysis, Technical Report T-1.

REFERENCES

McIVER, J. (1977). "The effects of state laws on municipal police departments: Mutual assistance in metropolitan areas." Bloomington, Ind.: Workshop in Political Theory and Policy Analysis, Technical Report T-20.
_____ (1977). "Cooperation between police agencies: Patterns of mutual aid and cross-deputization." Bloomington, Ind.: Workshop in Political Theory and Policy Analysis, Technical Report T-35.
OSTROM, E., PARKS, R. B., and WHITAKER, G. P. (1974). "Defining and measuring structural variations in interorganizational arrangements." Publius, 4, No. 4(Fall):87-108.
_____ (1977). Patterns of metropolitan policing. Cambridge, Mass.: Ballinger.
OSTROM, V., and OSTROM, E. (1965). "A behavioral approach to the study of intergovernmental relations." Annals of the American Academy of Political and Social Science, 359(May):137-146.

OSTROM, V., TIEBOUT, C. M., and WARREN, R. (1961). "The organization of government in metropolitan areas: A theoretical inquiry." American Political Science Review, 55(December):831-842.

President's Commission on Law Enforcement and Administration of Justice (1967). The challenge of crime in a free society. Washington, D.C.: U.S. Government Printing Office.

SMITH, B. (1949). Police systems in the United States. New York: Harper.

6

SOLID WASTE COLLECTION:

Organization and Efficiency of Service Delivery

E . S . S A V A S

Columbia University

B A R B A R A J. S T E V E N S

Columbia University

E I L E E N B. B E R E N Y I

Columbia University

Within the last decade, state and local government spending has grown to account for 80% of all non-defense government purchase of goods and services and nearly 15% of the GNP (Committee on Economic Development, 1976). Local governments are an integral part of the overall economic well-being of the nation. However, given the uncertain state of the economy over the last several years, the ability of local governments to finance themselves and deliver services has been severely threatened. The spectres of financial default and of serious

AUTHOR'S NOTE: *This material was prepared with the support of the Advanced Productivity Research and Technology Program, Research Applied to National Needs Division, National Science Foundation, under Contract No. SSH 74-02061 A01. The opinions, findings conclusions and recommendations herein are those of the authors and do not necessarily reflect the news of the National Science Foundation.*

The research reported in this paper is from the study by Savas and Stevens, "Evaluating the Organization of Service Delivery: Solid Waste Collection and Disposal". The findings are reported in detail in Savas, 1977.

curtailment in government services have stimulated nationwide concern about the costs and performance of local governments.

Within the context of rising financial burdens of local governments, the issue of productivity looms large. Public officials are being asked to evaluate what services local governments should provide and what organizational format can deliver these services most efficiently and effectively. Municipal agencies and workers can and do provide services, but many other alternatives are also to be found. Therefore, a fundamental policy issue can be raised: Under what structural arrangement can municipal services best be provided? Are public services best provided by public agencies using public employees and acting as public monopolies? Can competition—public or private—be introduced, and is it advantageous to do so? Under what circumstances, if any, can the private sector provide public services more efficiently and effectively than the public sector? How can the public interest be protected if vital public services are provided by the private sector?

Under the auspices of the National Science Foundation/RANN Division, the Center for Government Studies, Columbia University Graduate School of Business has been conducting an in-depth, nationwide study of these issues as applied to the delivery of solid waste collection services. Solid waste collection is eminently suited for such a study. It can be provided by both the private and public sector under a variety of organizational forms. It is a vital service with high political visibility and it is relatively easy to measure inputs and outputs. The research has been carried out by an interdisciplinary team at Columbia University with the assistance of the International City Management Association, Public Technology, Inc., and the Center for Policy Research.

This chapter will address the following questions: (1) How does one classify the basic organizational structures used by local governments for the provision of refuse collection services? (2) What is the national distribution of the major types of refuse collection arrangements? and (3) What are the efficiency and productivity differences among the various organizational forms of refuse collection?

Two important definitions must be kept in mind by the reader: (1) "Refuse" or "solid waste" refers to garbage (i.e., putrescible waste), dry trash, yard trash, newspapers, bulk items, etc. It does not include sewage sludge, agricultural wastes, or liquid wastes; and (2) solid waste collection includes the picking up and transporting of waste to a disposal site or transfer station.

CLASSIFYING BASIC ORGANIZATIONAL FORMS FOR PROVIDING REFUSE COLLECTION SERVICES

The first task of the research was to develop a classification scheme for alternative service delivery structures. Four descriptors were found necessary to distinguish organizational arrangements for refuse collection. (These issues are discussed in more detail in Savas, 1978). These were (1) the service recipient, (2) the service provider, (3) the service arranger, and (4) the service type. The *service recipient* is the consumer unit. However, a recipient can be a commercial establishment, institution, industrial establishment, or an individual household. The *service provider* is the entity which actually performs the service, i.e., collects the refuse. The provider can be a municipality, county, a special district, a private firm under contract to the municipality, or a private firm which has negotiated arrangements with individual customers (either commercial or industrial establishments or householders), or the service recipient himself. In the last instance, homeowners and industrial plants may haul their own refuse to a disposal site. The *service arranger* is the entity that assigns the provider to the recipient. This descriptor corresponds roughly to Ostrom's (1975) collective decision-making unit without denoting that the arranger must be a governmental body. The service arranger could be a municipality, a special district or county, or the service recipient himself in the case where a household or commercial establishment decides to hire a private firm to collect its refuse. The last descriptor is *service type.* With regard to refuse collection, service type refers to classes of refuse, i.e., bulk items, leaves, litter baskets, mixed household refuse. A particular city may and often does have different service providers for different types of refuse.

For each class of recipient and type of waste, one can develop a matrix of service arranged by service provider. The resulting cells are the arrangements possible for refuse collection. Figure 1 shows such a matrix. As can be seen, several entries are either not applicable or no examples could be found. Of the possible arrangements, five were found to dominate on the local level. These are the municipal, contract, franchise, private and self-service arrangements. Table 1 gives the definition of each of the five major types. Under municipal collection, the municipality arranges for the pick up of refuse and actually picks up the refuse itself through a department of streets, sanitation, public works, etc. Other examples of public agencies that may engage in refuse collection are counties and special districts. (The public arrangement will be referred to as "municipal" for the body of the chapter.) Under contract collection, a public agency contracts with a private firm to provide refuse collection services to the town. Collection is mandatory and the public agency (city, town, or county) takes the full responsibility for financing the service either through the general fund or by billing service recipients directly. A franchise is similar to a contract. A firm is given the exclusive right to collect refuse in a given area of a town, county, etc.; however, the firm bills the residents directly. Collection may be mandatory or not. Furthermore, frequently there is a franchise (license) fee that must be paid to the franchising agent for the right of having the franchise. The private arrangement is the case where firms are permitted to compete without any assigned territories. There may or may not be various forms of licensing and rate regulation. Each firm negotiates directly with its customers and fees are paid directly to the firm without any direct governmental intervention. Self-service is where the individual

Figure 1. SERVICE ARRANGEMENTS FOR SOLID WASTE COLLECTION

Service Arranger	Service Provider → Local Municipality	County	Another Government	Special District	Private Firm	Service Recipient	Voluntary Association
Municipality	municipal (New York)	inter-governmental contract	inter-governmental contract	(Des Moines)	contract (Boston); franchise—mandatory (San Francisco)	NA	
County		County				NA	
Special District	NA	NA	NA	special district (Indianapolis)	special district contract (Jersey City)	NA	
Voluntary Association					association contract (Houston)	NA	voluntary association
Service Recipient					franchise—non-mandatory; private (St. Paul)	self-service (Eugene, Ore.)	voluntary service

Table 1. DEFINITIONS

MUNICIPAL:	Collection by city agency.
CONTRACT:	Collection by private firm, hired and paid for by city.
FRANCHISE:	Collection by private firm, in exclusive territory assigned by city; firm paid directly by its customers.
PRIVATE:	Firm without exclusive territory sells services to customers and is paid directly by them.
SELF-SERVICE:	Generator of waste hauls it away.

transports the waste to the disposal site without the assistance of a governmental agency or outside private hauling firm.

Two important points about these organizational forms must be kept in mind. (1) They are listed in the order of the degree of control a public agency has over the collection service. Thus, under public or municipal collection, the governmental agency can be said to have a monopoly over collection. Under contract collection, the public agency exercises considerable control over the private refuse collecting firm through the contract document, and mandatory collection laws, and there is a control over payment. With franchise collection, particularly nonmandatory franchise (where residents are not legally compelled to subscribe to an organized collection service), governmental oversight is reduced. A local government, through the franchise agreement, can specify level of service and rates to be charged. However, it has no direct control over the billing arrangements nor how many residents in an area receive service. Finally, under private arrangement, there is open competition among firms with little regulatory control save for licensing and the establishment of standards. Individuals make their own arrangements with the collection firm of their choice or they can choose to self-haul. (2) As has become obvious by the above discussion, there are three different arrangements by which the private sector can provide service: contract; franchise; and private, open competition.

WHO COLLECTS SOLID WASTE: NATIONWIDE PATTERNS

After conceptualizing a model of the possible organizational structures for refuse collection, the research team undertook to determine their frequency of use among localities throughout the United States.

DATA COLLECTION METHODOLOGY

To obtain necessary information, it was decided to undertake a telephone survey of municipalities. City managers, mayors, public works directors or sanitation superintendents were contacted by trained interviewers from Columbia, International City Management Association, and Public Technology, Inc. The survey was carried out by telephone instead of mail to ensure (1) a high response rate, and (2) accurate responses. The basic telephone sample was drawn from all local government jurisdictions with populations over 2,500 located within Standard Metropolitan Statistical Areas (SMSAs). To be eligible, a SMSA had to have a population of less than 1.5 million and be located entirely within one state. These restrictions were mandated by the National Science Foundation. Given these restrictions, 2,060 communities in 200 SMSAs were eligible. Of the 2,060 jurisdictions, 252 were central cities and 1,808 were satellite cities or townships.

The eligible central cities were divided into two parts, those which used a municipal agency to collect residential refuse and those which relied on the private sector. Of the central cities that used a municipal agency, 41 were chosen at random. In these 41 SMSAs, the central city and all eligible satellite cities were called. In the remaining 159 SMSAs, each central city and every other eligible satellite city was called. Responses from these satellite cities were then double counted to create the data base of 2,060 cities (minus eight cities which were eliminated due to invalid responses), upon which tabulations were based.[1] The total number of cities in the telephone sample was 1,377. This represents a response rate of 99.9%. (One community could not be reached despite repeated attempts.) It should be noted that the sample is biased, by design, toward central cities and suburbs, ignoring rural areas and communities below 2,500 population. It should also be noted that very large cities were excluded by the study. The largest city in the sample had a population of 717,000.

FINDINGS

This section will report the general findings regarding arrangement types and their distribution. (See Savas and Niemczewski, 1976; Savas, 1977: Chap. 4.) Table 2 shows the percentage of cities in which a given service deliverer is found by type of service. In examining residential refuse collection, it was found that of 2,060 municipalities reporting, 37.3% have mixed refuse collected by the municipality, 65.1% have it collected by a private firm, and 18.3% have self-service. (Numbers sum to greater than 100% because a city may have more than one arrangement, i.e., a city may license private firms but also allow self-hauling.) For institutional wastes, 34.4% of the cities in the sample used municipal agencies to collect, 64.9% used private firms and 6.4% permitted self-hauling. For commercial wastes, 31.4% of the cities used municipal agencies, 74.5% used private firms, and 16% allowed for self-hauling. Finally, for industrial wastes, 22.6% of the cities used municipal agencies, 74.5% had private firms, and 16.0% permitted self-hauling.

As is evident from the table, the dominance of the municipality as a service provider declines as one moves down the column. The vast majority of cities surveyed rely on municipal work forces to clean streets and remove litter from parks and other public spaces. However, only 37% of cities surveyed have

Table 2. NUMBER AND PERCENT OF CITIES, BY SERVICE PROVIDER, FOR EACH TYPE OF SERVICE RECIPIENT

Service Recipient	Total number of Cities*	Service Provider							
		Municipality		Private Firm		Service Recipient		Other	
		No.	Per-cent	No.	Per-cent	No.	Per-cent	No.	Per-cent
Streets	1,591**	1,467	92.2%	57	3.6%	NA***		72	4.5%
Parks and Public Spaces	1,644**	1,352	82.2	185	11.2	NA		126	7.7
Litter Baskets	1,383**	1,147	82.9	193	14.0	NA		55	4.0
Residential									
Bulk	1,814	920	50.7	734	40.5	439	24.2	16	0.9
Mixed Refuse	2,060	769	37.3≠	1,342	65.1	377	18.3	23	1.1
Multiple Dwellings	1,745	645	37.0	1,213	69.5	18	1.0	8	0.4
Institutional	1,798	618	34.4	1,167	64.9	115	6.4	46	2.6
Commercial	1,992	626	31.4	1,697	80.7	84	4.2	8	0.4
Industrial	1,453	328	22.6	1,083	74.5	233	16.0	6	0.4

*Excludes the cities that are surveyed but responded "don't know" for service provider.

**Excludes the cities that were surveyed but responded "no one" for service provider.

***NA = Not applicable.

≠ That is, 37.3% of 2,060 communities have government agencies which collect at least some of the residential mixed refuse.

municipal work forces which participate in residential refuse collection. The municipality's role diminishes even further regarding institutional, commercial, and industrial collection. The pattern nearly reverses itself when one examines the private sector. Collection by the private sector dominates among private sector recipients. In residential collection, private hauling firms provide service in 66.7% of the cities studied. The role of the private sector declines as one examines collection from public areas, e.g., streets, parks, and litter baskets.

Another way of presenting the roles of various service providers is to examine the percentage of population served by each major provider. Table 3 shows the percentage of population receiving solid waste collection by service provider and class of service recipient. The table indicates that 63.2% of the sample population lives in jurisdictions where at least some of the residential mixed refuse is collected by the municipality. This contrasts to the finding shown in Table 2 that 37% of cities surveyed had municipal collection systems. The variance in the two figures is accounted for by the fact that more people are served by public agencies because large cities are more likely to have municipal collection systems.

Table 3. PERCENT OF POPULATION LIVING IN CITIES THAT HAVE THE INDICATED SERVICE PROVIDER, BY TYPE OF SERVICE RECIPIENT

SERVICE RECIPIENT	SERVICE PROVIDER			
	Municipality	**Private Firm**	**Self-Service**	**Other**
Streets	89.9%	1.4%	NA**	3.1%
Parks	81.8	4.0	NA	8.7
Litter Baskets	80.6	5.2	NA	2.6
Residential				
Bulk	62.1	29.1	17.5	1.7
Mixed Refuse	63.2*	47.2	12.6	1.9
Multiple Dwellings	56.6	63.3	0.4	——
Institutional	48.3	58.6	7.2	2.0
Commercial	51.6	81.4	4.6	——
Industrial	24.0	69.9	14.5	0.3

*That is, 63.2% of the population in the sample live in a city where municipal workers collect at least some of the residential mixed refuse.

**NA = Not applicable

NOTE: Row totals exceed 100% in some cases because more than one service provider is to be found in some cities. Row totals are less than 100% for the first three rows because some cities have no regular street cleaning service, no litter basket service, etc., and because some cities responded "don't know" about these services.

Table 4. NUMBER AND PERCENT OF CITIES IN WHICH CLASS OF SERVICE RECIPIENT IS SERVED BY ONLY A SINGLE ARRANGEMENT

Service Recipient	Total		Municipal		Contract		Franchise		Private		Self-Service	
	No.	Per-cent	No.	Per-cent	No.	Per-cent	No.	Per-cent	No.	Per-cent	No.	Per-cent
Streets	1515	73.5	1462	71.0	53	2.6	NA	NA	NA	NA	NA	NA
Parks and Public Spaces	1506	73.1	1333	64.7	173	8.4	NA	NA	NA	NA	NA	NA
Litter Baskets	1316	63.9	1131	54.9	185	8.9	NA	NA	NA	NA	NA	NA
Residential												
Bulk	1489	72.3	766	37.2	150	7.3	52	2.5	291	14.1	230	11.2
Mixed Refuse	1637	79.5	666	32.3	394	19.1	99	4.8	435	21.1	10	.5
Multiple Dwellings	1569	76.2	511	24.8	241	11.7	130	6.3	777	32.9	10	.5
Institutional	1580	76.7	503	24.4	201	9.8	107	5.2	708	34.4	61	3.0
Commercial	1567	76.1	353	17.1	136	6.6	135	6.6	935	45.4	8	.4
Industrial	1235	60.0	224	10.9	78	3.9	84	4.1	742	36.0	107	5.2

154   THE POLICY CYCLE

Table 4 adds the dimension of service arranger. It includes only those municipalities reporting a single arrangement for a class of service recipient. Thus, looking at the mixed residential refuse entry, one observes that 32.3% had municipal collection and 45.0% of cities relied on the private sector. Of the private sector arrangements, the "private" arrangement was the most prevalent (21.1% of cities surveyed), the contract arrangement second most prevalent (19.1% of cities surveyed), and the franchise arrangement the least prevalent (4.8% of cities surveyed). The private arrangement is used most frequently for the collection of refuse from multiple dwellings, institutions, industries, and commercial establishments.

With respect to service level, it was found that 59.7% of all cities have once-per-week collection of residential refuse. With respect to cities with municipal collection, it was found that a minimum of twice-per-week collection is provided in slightly over half such cities as compared to 26.4% of cities relying on the private sector or self-service arrangements. Pickup occurs at curbside in 53.8% of cities and from the backyard in 10% of cities with the remaining cities using other sites such as front yard.

Finally, for residential refuse collection, cross tabulations were run to observe whether organizational arrangement was associated with region, population of city, and form of government. Table 5 shows the results. With respect to population size, as a city's population size increases, it is more likely to have municipal collection of its household refuse. With respect to region, the North Central and the Northeast have the highest perponderance of private (open competitive) and self-service arrangements. The South, strikingly, has predominantly municipal arrangements; 73% of all residential refuse collection arrangements are municipal. The Western region has the next highest percentage of municipal arrangements and the highest concentration of franchise arrangements in the entire country. If one groups municipal, contract, and franchise collection systems into a category entitled "government control" and categorizes private and self-service arrangements as "minimal government control," regional patterns become even more striking. In the Northeast and North Central regions, 42.9% and 37.5% of arrangements are under government control. In the South and West, these percentages rise to 86.2% and 70.4%, respectively. (See Table 6.) No immediate explanation is evident for the particular pattern. There is some reason to believe that southern cities in the late 19th century assumed responsibilities for refuse collection due to the constant threat of epidemics of yellow fever, typhoid, etc.[2] The presence of franchise arrangements in the West may be attributable to the newness of cities and thus, their desire to implement more "business-like" arrangement types.[3]

With respect to the association of form of government to service arrangement type, no particular pattern emerges. The relevant literature might lead one to believe council-manager cities would rely less on the municipal arrangement and more on the contract and franchise arrangement. (See Clark, 1975; see also Alford and Scoble, 1965; Kessel, 1962.) Except with the franchise arrangement, this hypothesis does not hold up.

Table 5. SERVICE ARRANGEMENTS FOR COLLECTION OF RESIDENTIAL MIXED REFUSE

	Total		Municipal		Contract		Franchise		Private		Self-Service		Other	
	No.	Per-cent	No.	Per-cent	No.	Per-cent	No.	Per-cent	No.	Per-cent	No.	Per-cent	No.	Per-cent
Total	2,540	99.9	769	30.3	437	17.2	151	5.9	786	30.9	377	14.8	20	.8
Population Group														
>500,000	15	100.0	8	53.3	1	6.7	1	6.7	2	13.3	1	6.7	2	13.3
250,000–499,999	25	100.0	18	72.0	1	4.0	1	4.0	3	12.0	1	4.0	1	4.0
100,000–249,999	97	100.0	63	64.9	8	8.2	2	2.1	15	15.5	7	7.2	2	2.1
50,000– 99,999	175	100.0	87	49.7	23	13.1	15	8.6	28	16.0	21	12.0	1	.6
25,000– 49,999	204	99.9	64	31.1	42	20.6	18	8.8	53	26.0	27	13.2	0	
10,000– 24,999	503	100.1	179	35.6	113	22.5	39	7.8	117	23.3	54	10.7	1	.2
5,000– 9,999	640	100.0	178	27.8	110	17.2	24	3.8	219	34.2	107	16.7	2	.3
2,500– 4,999	881	100.0	172	19.6	139	15.8	51	5.8	349	39.6	158	18.0	11	1.2
Geographic Region														
Northeast	983	100.0	186	18.9	218	22.2	18	1.8	383	39.0	176	17.9	2	.2
North Central	720	100.0	142	19.7	98	13.6	30	4.2	332	46.1	108	15.0	10	1.4
South	470	100.0	343	73.0	48	10.2	14	3.0	33	7.0	27	5.7	5	1.1
West	367	100.0	98	26.7	73	19.9	89	24.3	38	10.3	66	18.0	3	.8
Metro/City Type														
Central	313	99.9	192	61.3	28	8.9	17	5.4	46	14.7	24	7.7	6	1.9
Suburban	2227	99.9	577	25.9	409	18.4	134	6.0	740	33.2	353	15.8	14	.6
Form of Government														
Mayor-Council	882	100.0	373	42.3	212	24.0	45	5.1	181	20.5	65	7.4	6	.7
Council-Manager	726	100.0	321	44.2	124	17.1	88	12.1	101	13.9	87	12.0	5	.7
Commission	67	100.0	34	50.7	15	22.4	2	3.0	9	13.4	4	6.0	3	4.5
Town Meeting	112	100.0	16	14.3	16	14.3	2	1.8	43	38.4	35	31.2	0	
Rep. Town Meeting	20	100.0	4	20.0	2	10.0	0		8	40.0	6	30.0	0	
Don't Know	733	100.1	21	2.9	68	9.3	14	1.9	444	60.6	180	24.6	6	.8

NOTE: This table shows the distribution of *arrangements*, not the distribution of *cities*. The total number of arrangements is 2,540 in the 2,060 cities.

In summary, the following points can be made with respect to arrangement types, public and private:

1. More cities use a form of private collection for residential refuse collection than a municipal agency. The same is true for commercial and industrial collection, although not for collection of institutional wastes or wastes from municipal properties.

2. In terms of population served, more people are serviced by municipal agencies for residential collection due to the fact that larger cities tend to use municipal agencies.

3. The Northeast and North Central regions lean to private collection for residential collection. The South has the heaviest concentration of cities which rely on municipal refuse collection. The West has the highest concentration of franchise arrangements of any region.

Table 6. PERCENT OF ARRANGEMENTS WITH STRONG AND MINIMAL GOVERNMENT CONTROL BY REGION [1]

Geographic Region	Total Number of Arrangements Reported	Percent of Government Control	Percent of Private and Self-Service
Northeast	983	42.9	56.9 [2]
North Central	720	37.5	61.1
South	470	86.2	12.7
West	367	70.9	28.3

1. Table derived from numbers in Table 5.
2. Numbers do not sum to 100% because "other" arrangements were excluded.

THE RELATIVE EFFICIENCY OF ALTERNATIVE ORGANIZATIONAL ARRANGEMENTS FOR REFUSE COLLECTION

The above sections have delineated the basic components of the service delivery structure for refuse collection and described the pattern of use of these arrangement types across a nationwide sample of local jurisdictions. While it is interesting to understand the various types of organizational structures that exist, a more important question remains to be asked. Are there any relevant differences in the way in which these arrangements provide service? This section will address the issue of the evaluation of major organizational arrangements that were described above.

A local service delivery system can be evaluated on the basis of three criteria: (1) Is it efficient, i.e., does it carry out its objectives for the least cost; (2) Is it effective, e.g., is the service being delivered according to certain standards of quality; and (3) Is it equitable, e.g., is the same level of service being provided across income, racial, and age categories for an equal or proportional amount of financing effort per unit of service output.[4] To address these issues, it was decided to concentrate solely on residential refuse collection. The initial phase of the research focused on the first criteria, that of efficiency. The current research effort is examining the issues of effectiveness and equity.

Before reporting the findings on efficiency, the definition used should be made clear. Efficiency was defined in terms of cost per unit output of the service to the household. Cost of service to the household had to be further operationalized, given the mix of arrangements possible. For municipal collection, cost was defined as the actual cost of the service regardless of the means used to finance the service, taxes or user charges. For collection by private firms, cost was defined as the price charged to householders. In each case, disposal costs were excluded. Output was defined as number of tons collected, and number of households served.

DATA COLLECTION

To obtain and compare costs, a total of 315 cities were studied, including 102 municipal arrangements, 92 contract (and mandatory franchise) arrangements, and 121 private (and nonmandatory franchise) arrangements. The cities were randomly selected after stratifying by population, size, and region. The sample chosen had to be small enough to be feasible for on-site visits, but large enough to be satisfactory for statistical analysis. Both the contract and private sample were also drawn at random from cities having those arrangements stratified by region and population size.

The problems in collecting data were significant. Cities do not actually know their true costs of refuse collection. The number reported in the city budget frequently excludes fringe benefits, overhead, vehicle depreciation, rent on buildings, etc. Furthermore, no city uses an accounting system exactly like any other city. In fact when comparing budgeted costs, it was found that on average actual cost was 30% greater than the figure shown in the budget (Savas, 1977:200). For cities serviced by a private firm, the situation was somewhat simpler. One needed only to obtain the price charged to the householder, exclusive of disposal costs, or the amount paid by the city to a contractor, exclusive of disposal costs.

Trained interviewers conducted on-site audits of all municipal systems, using a specially designed detailed form to ensure the uniformity of costing methods. Two-person teams spent one to three days collecting necessary information. To obtain accurate information on prices charged to householders by private firms, the private firms, a group of householders served by the firm, and relevant city officials were contacted by telephone or mail. If a hauler served the city under contract or franchise, the city was contacted, a copy of the contract agreement was secured, and the firm was contacted by telephone to secure necessary information.

FINDINGS

Three basic questions presented themselves: (1) Did average cost vary by arrangement type; (2) Did economies of scale exist with regard to refuse collection systems; and (3) Did management practices vary by service delivery system?

Average Cost by Arrangement Type.

Focusing first on the average annual per household costs, it was found that the mean annual cost of municipally provided residential refuse collection was $32.08 per household. For each city in the sample having municipal collection, costs were calculated for wages, fringe benefits, operating expenses, overhead, and vehicle depreciation. On the average, it was found that 57% of cost was attributable to wages, 12% to fringe benefits, 16% to operating expenses, i.e., maintenance, insurance, etc., 9% to overhead costs, and 6% to depreciation of equipment (Stevens and Savas, 1977:200-205). Combining wages and fringe expenses, it becomes obvious that over two thirds of the cost of municipal refuse collection is associated with the cost of direct labor. The mean annual cost per household of contract collection was found to be $28.00 per year and of private collection, $45.00 per year.

Disaggregating the sample into three population categories and examining average cost of the household per ton, it can be seen that mean cost per ton varies from a low of $18.09 (for contract cities with populations in excess of 50,000) to a high of $30.81 (for private collection in excess of 50,000 population). For each population grouping, private collection has the highest mean cost per ton (see Table 7).

Table 7. COST/TON FOR COLLECTION (Number of cities in parentheses)

Arrangement	Population		
	Under 10,000	10,000 to 50,000	Over 50,000
Municipal	$22.48 (29)	$19.47 (18)	$25.87 (46)
Contract	18.86 (10)	21.77 (16)	18.09 (12)
Private	28.39 (19)	23.08 (33)	30.81 (10)
ALL	23.79 (58)	21.80 (67)	25.22 (68)

Although the evaluation of mean annual costs permits one to draw some tentative conclusions about the impact of size of city and arrangement type on cost, it is not very meaningful. Clearly service level, e.g., point of pick-up and number of times per week refuse is picked up, must be controlled for. Municipal collection systems tend to have higher service levels than do systems in which service is provided by the private sector. The comparison is also obscured by the fact that region has an effect on collection systems. Southern cities tend to have municipal collection systems and a higher than average collection frequency. However, the wage scale in southern cities is lower than that in other areas of the country. It was not possible to hold all relevant variables constant and still have cell entries of significant sizes to make statistical comparisons.

To take into account all relevant variables which could affect refuse collection costs, an econometric model was constructed.[5] A basic purpose of the model was to evaluate the association of organizational arrangements to total cost and management practices. The equation contained only those variables, hypothesized to have a strong impact on refuse collection costs, which were outside a manager's direct control. These were (1) the prevailing wage of the community, (2) quantity of refuse collected, (3) city population size, (4) density, and (5) weather conditions. A sixth variable, service level (frequency of collection and location of pick up point), was also included. Service level was not considered to be immutable;however, efficiency of a system should be evaluated within a given service level.[6]

It should be noted that there are clearly other factors reflecting managerial control which also affect cost. These include absentee rates, presence of labor incentive systems, crew sizes, and type of equipment (size and loading location). While it has been shown that these factors do influence cost, they were deliberately not held constant in the analysis so that one could compare high and low cost cities in terms of these indices, and observe whether differences in management factors were related to arrangement types.

A Cobb-Douglas production function was used to relate total cost to the independent variables. The model was estimated separately for those cities reporting quantity of refuse in cubic yards and those reporting in tons with similar results. (Stevens, 1976). Costs to the household for each arrangement type were then compared.

In terms of cost per household, it was found that private collection was significantly more costly than contract collection. Disaggregating the sample by population categories, additional findings emerged. No significant difference was found between the municipal and private collection arrangement in terms of cost for cities with less than 20,000 population or more than 50,000 population, nor between municipal and contract collection for cities less than 50,000 population. But for cities over 50,000 population, contract collection was significantly less expensive than municipal collection: the cost per household for municipal collection in such cities was found to be 29% (37%) greater than the corresponding cost of contract collection on the basis of refuse generation data in terms of tons (cubic yards). Table 8 shows the general findings concerning cost by arrangement type and city size. Table 9 shows predicted annual cost per household by arrangement calculated using the regression equation for cities of various population sizes, a given service level, and a reasonable set of values for factors which must be held constant.

Economies of Scale.

Before discussing the possible reasons behind the efficiency differences that were found, one should make explicit the findings on economies of scale implied in the above discussion. In general, cost to the household decreases for

Table 8. SIGNIFICANT DIFFERENCES IN PER HOUSEHOLD COSTS FOUND THROUGH REGRESSION ANALYSIS

Service Arrangement	Under 50,000 Population	Over 50,000 Population
Municipal	Significantly lower cost than private.* Not significantly different from contract.	Significantly higher cost than contract. Not significantly different from private.
Contract	Significantly lower cost than private. Not significantly different from municipal.	Significantly lower cost than municipal or private.
Private	Significantly higher cost than contract. Significantly higher cost than municipal.*	Significantly higher cost than contract. Not significantly different from municipal.

*There is additional evidence that for cities under 20,000 there is no significant difference in cost between municipal and private arrangements.

Table 9. PREDICTED[1] ANNUAL COST PER HOUSEHOLD FOR ONCE-A-WEEK CURBSIDE COLLECTION OF REFUSE

Arrangement	Population				
	3,000	15,000	30,000	60,000	90,000
Contract	$23.25	$17.77	$17.30	$18.40*	$18.26*
Municipal	25.51	19.51	19.55	23.77**	23.59**
Private	29.49**	22.55**	25.10**	24.10**	23.92**

1. Substituted values equal
    prevailing wage = $600/month
    density = 600 households per square mile
    amount of refuse collected = 1.5 tons per household per year
    temperature variation = 15°C
    total refuse generated = 0.5 tons per capita per year

 *Significantly different from the cost of municipal collection at the 99% level.

 **Significantly different from the cost of contract collection at the 99% level.

any service arrangement as the market served increases to 20,000 individuals. Small cost savings may be achieved for further increases in scale up to 50,000 individuals. There is no indication that diseconomies set in for markets larger than 50,000 population, although no city above 717,000 population was studied. Figure 2 shows the shape of the average cost function for the three arrangement types. Values used are from Table 9.

Factors Affecting Cost

The private arrangement had consistently higher costs, despite the fact that firms operated in an open, competitive environment. The cost can be attributed to

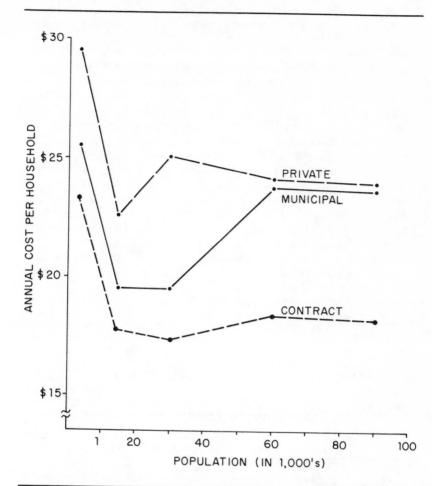

Figure 2: **ANNUAL COST PER HOUSEHOLD FOR ONCE-PER-WEEK CURBSIDE REFUSE COLLECTION ESTIMATED HOLDING WAGE RATE, REFUSE PER HOUSEHOLD, DENSITY, SERVICE LEVEL, AND TEMPERATURE VARIATION CONSTANT**

two factors: (1) billing expenses, and (2) nonexclusivity within a market area. Such firms usually are responsible for billing their customers. Firms under contract and municipal agencies usually do not incur this expense. If municipal agencies do bill, they can minimize the cost by billing simultaneously for other services. An informal canvassing of private firms indicated that up to 15% of total cost might be spent on billing and the collection of fees. In addition, firms under a private arrangement do not service an exclusive territory. Given that their customers may be scattered randomly throughout a city, such firms have higher costs in servicing them.

The difference between municipal and contract collection in larger cities was the most striking finding. One would expect municipal costs to be lower because municipalities neither pay taxes nor make profits. In addition, in both types of arrangement, the provider serves an exclusive area so neither has an advantage in that respect. To shed some light on the difference, management practices and production techniques were examined. As Table 10 shows, there are consistent differences in the indices of management between the contract and municipal arrangements. For cities of all sizes, the contractor uses a significantly smaller crew and a significantly larger collection vehicle than does the municipal collection agency. The absentee rate is significantly higher among public refuse collectors in cities sampled than in private firms. Moreover, these differences increase in magnitude with increases in city size. A further difference in production techniques occurs only in the sample of large cities. In cities with populations greater than 50,000, the private firm under contract with the city is significantly more likely than is the public collection agency to use vehicles which can be loaded conveniently by the driver of the crew, that is, front- or side-loading. These results hold even when cities providing only backyard collection are considered. Even in this case, the private firms use front- and side-loading vehicles almost twice as frequently as do public agencies. In short, whether because of political constraints, or whatever, labor productivity is lower in the municipal refuse-collection agencies that were sampled than in the private firms that were sampled, and this difference increases with city size.

Table 10. MANAGEMENT FACTORS IN REFUSE COLLECTION

Management Factor	Population of City < 50,000		Population of City > 50,000		Backyard Collection Location	
	Municipal	Contract	Municipal	Contract	Municipal	Contract
Crew size	3.08	2.15	3.26	2.15	3.04	1.98
Truck capacity (cubic yards)	19.04	22.21	20.63	27.14	19.90	23.5
Absentee rate	11%	7%	12%	6%	12%	4%
Percent of vehicles load—at front and side	26%*	23%*	13%	44%	16%	30%
Percent of cities with incentive system	57.1%	80.3%	80.4%*	85.7%*	72.7%*	86.7%*

*The difference between municipal and contract collection is not significant at the 95% confidence level. All other differences between municipal and contract collection are significant at the 95% confidence level.

SUMMARY AND CONCLUSIONS

In summary, the following points can be made about the cost and productivity of various residential refuse collection arrangements.

1. On average, it is more costly to the household if a private firm does not pick up refuse from every resident in a given area.

2. On average, cities of populations of 50,000 and above have significantly lower cost if they employ a contract arrangement for residential refuse collection than if they employ a municipal or private arrangement.

3. On average, firms under contract employ more efficient management practices than do municipal agencies, regardless of the size of the city.

4. Small adjacent cities might consider forming a single refuse collection market of 20,000 to 50,000 population in order to capture the available economies of scale.

Given the findings above, several courses of action are open to local officials desiring to reduce costs while maintaining a suitable level of service.

The first step for any city is an accurate determination of the cost of service for its residents. If it is a municipal service, it is crucial that all costs, not only those included in the budget, be taken into account. Specifically, a comprehensive cost analysis should include not only the more obvious costs of wages, fringe, operating expense, overhead, and vehicle depreciation, but also the costs of garage and office construction, land values of such properties and taxes forgone on them, underfunding of pension funds (i.e., the city putting less in the pension fund than it will eventually have to pay out), etc. Similarly, if the city has a contract, franchise or private arrangement, it must obtain the exact amount the contract is costing its citizens, including any costs of monitoring or regulating the private firms. The next step is to evaluate alternatives, comparing total costs of each system. Such alternatives may include the current system modified by changes in labor practices or production techniques, but different institutional arrangements should also be evaluated.

With respect to institutional arrangements, our findings indicate that larger cities above 50,000 in population can expect to achieve significant savings by changing to a contract arrangement, given the suitability of local conditions and contract letting procedures of at least average effectiveness. A large city of greater than 100,000 population might consider contracting out a few districts (each larger than 50,000) and retaining one or more districts under its own control. This can ensure a healthy competitive environment between the public and private sector while still capturing the advantages of economies of scale. Minneapolis is an example of such an arrangement. (Savas, 1976). Boston contracts out the service by district. Oklahoma City, as a result of the Columbia study, switched from a municipal system to one where it contracts out two districts out of the five into which the city is divided. (Solid Waste Management Journal, 1978:42-43, 86).

This chapter has reported on a major research undertaking which sought to identify and evaluate alternative organizational arrangements for an essential local service - - residential refuse collection. Additional research questions immediately suggest themselves: (1) Does effectiveness and equity vary by arrangement type; and (2) why do some cities adopt and implement innovative and cost effective refuse collection techniques and others do not? Subsequent research currently underway at the Center for Government Studies will address these issues.

NOTES

1. To further check weighting procedure, the results from calling every eligible satellite city in the 41 SMSAs were halved and added to the surveys in the 159 SMSAs where every other eligible satellite city was called. The results were almost identical to those obtained by doubling the results of the satellite cities in the 159 SMSAs.

2. From correspondence with Professor W. J. Wicker, Institute of Government, University of North Carolina at Chapel Hill, May 1976.

3. Terry Clark associates political systems in newer cities with a lesser reliance on patronage and a more business-like orientation than older Northeastern and Midwestern cities. See Clark, 1975:53-54. The public works department has traditionally been a source of patronage jobs. In franchising the refuse collection service, this source is removed. Thus, it could be said that cities that have contract or franchise arrangements have a more "business-like orientation" than those which use a municipal agency to collect refuse.

4. See Price (1974) for a detailed definition and discussion fo the equity in public works srvices.
services.

5. Details regarding the development and specification of the econometric model can be found in Stevens, 1976.

6. Frequency and point of pick-up have both been shown to affect cost. It would not be meaningful to permit these to fluctuate and then attempt to reach a conclusion as to the effect of arrangement type on cost. See Stevens, 1976 for a full discussion of this issue.

REFERENCES

ALFORD, R., and SCOBLE, H. M. (1965). "Political and socioeconomic characteristics of American cities." Pp. 82-97 in Municipal yearbook 1965. Chicago: International City Management Association.
CLARK, T. N. (1975). Cities differ—But how and why? Report submitted to Office of Policy Development and Research, U.S. Dept. of Housing and Urban Development, HUD/RES 1310, September.
Committee on Economic Development (1976). Improving productivity in state and local government. A state by the Research and Policy Committee. New York: author.
KESSEL, J. H. (1962). "Governmental structure and the political environment." American Political Science Review, 56(September):615-620.
OSTROM, E. (1975). "Interorganizational arrangements in urban police services. Paper prepared for the International Institute of Management Conference on Interorganizational Decision-Making and Public Policy, Berlin, June 17-21.
PRICE, W. (1974). "Social equity and the delivery of public works services." Paper

presented to the International Public Works Congress, Toronto, Canada, September.

SAVAS, E. S. (1976). "An empirical study of competition in municipal service delivery." Research paper no. 136, Columbia University Graduate School of Business, July.

———— (1977). The organization and efficiency of solid waste collection. Lexington, Mass.: D.C. Heath.

———— (1978). "The institutional structure of local government services: A conceptual model." Public Administration Review, 385 (October):412-419.

———— and NIEMCZEWSKI, C. (1976). "Who collects solid waste?" Pp. 167-172 in Municipal yearbook 1976. Washington, D.C.: International City Management Association.

Solid Waste Management Journal (1978). "Oklahoma City three-way split—Refuse burden shared by city and two private haulers." 21,3(March):42-86.

STEVENS, B. J. (1976). "Scale, market structure and the cost of refuse collection." Research paper no. 107, Columbia University Graduate School of Business, July.

———— and SAVAS, E. S. (1977). "The cost of residential refuse collection and the effect of service arrangement." Pp. 200-205 in Municipal yearbook 1977. Washington, D.C.: International City Management Association.

PART IV
IMPLEMENTATION

7

IMPLEMENTING PUBLIC SERVICE EMPLOYMENT

DONALD C. BAUMER

Smith College

INTRODUCTION

The public service employment (PSE) programs to be examined in this chapter are part of the Comprehensive Employment and Training Act of 1973 (CETA), and are best understood in the context of the long legislative history of CETA. CETA emerged from the Congress in late 1973 after many years of debate over manpower reform. It ushered in a new approach to the delivery of manpower services by eliminating the existing collection of categorical programs in favor of a system which distributed block grants determined on a formula basis to local governments called prime sponsorships. The chief elected officials of these governmental units (states, cities and counties) were designated as the prime

AUTHOR'S NOTE: *Support for the research reported in this chapter was provided by the Office of Research and Development of the Employment and Training Administration, U.S. Department of Labor (Grant No. 21-39-75-10), a grant from the State of Ohio, and by the Hershon Center of Ohio State University. I would like to acknowledge my associates on the CETA Implementation Study at Ohio State University: Randall Ripley, Director, Matthew Filipic, Grace Franklin, Janet Galchick, Mary Marvel, William Oiler, Carl Van Horn, Jack Wichita, and Richard Wright. Special thanks go to Grace Franklin who offered valuable editorial comments of both a technical and substantive nature, to Hallie Francis who typed an earlier version of this paper, and to Norma Lepine and Agnes Shannon who typed the final version. The opinions expressed here are, of course, those of the author alone.*

sponsors, and had the authority to design a mix of manpower programs that best suited local needs.

CETA was the first "special revenue sharing" program to be enacted, which marked it as part of the Nixon Administration's attempt to redesign intergovernmental relations through an approach called "New Federalism." One of the key assumptions underlying the "New Federalism" was the belief that the federal government was too large and complex to administer some types of domestic programs properly, and that local governments could do a better job of administering these programs.

Advocates of the "New Federalism" contended that local officials were "closer to the people" than bureaucrats in Washington, and this closeness would help to ensure that the programs established were in line with local needs. Architects of the "New Federalism" planned two major forms of programmatic innovation. First, they sought to establish a general revenue sharing program which would make federal funds available to local governments with very few regulations governing the specific purposes for which these funds could be used. (This program passed in 1972, see Nathan et al., 1975, for details.) In addition, a number of "special revenue sharing" programs were planned. In these programs the federal government would specify a general purpose for which funds would be spent (manpower, housing, education). Existing categorical programs in each of these areas would be combined under one funding package, and local officials would be responsible for choosing the specific types of programs to be operating in each locality (see Reagan, 1972:89-141 for a discussion of "New Federalism").

The executive-legislative maneuvering over manpower reform that eventually resulted in CETA began in 1969. The Administration favored a radical form of decentralization which would give almost total authority for the administration and design of manpower programs to local elected officials, preferably the state governors. This meant that ongoing categorical programs[1] would be consolidated under one umbrella, and block grants would be given to the states for the operation of the manpower programs judged to be most effective in meeting local need. Congressional Democrats seemed willing to give up most of the categorical programs (although many of their reform proposals, especially in the Senate, did include provisions protecting favorite categorical programs), but only under certain conditions. First, they favored a continued and significant federal role in overseeing the planning and operation of locally designed programs. Second, they wanted to decentralize authority below the states, to the city and county level. Finally, they sought to include a public service employment component in the reform package. (For an extended account of the history of manpower reform, see Davidson, 1972.)

PSE played a central role in the debate over manpower reform from the beginning. The Administration's first reform proposal, the Manpower Training Act (MTA), followed the lines just described. Administrative authority was to be decentralized to the state level with minimal federal oversight, and the categorical programs were to be eliminated (Davidson, 1972:18). The MTA was rejected by Congressional Democrats, who went to work on a counterproposal. What eventually emerged from a House-Senate conference was a slightly modified version of the Senate bill developed by Senator Gaylord Nelson (Chairman of the Senate Subcommittee on Employment, Manpower and Poverty) and his staff, which was called the Employment and Manpower Act (EMA). The EMA designated local governments as the principal administrative agents, guaranteed a role for Community Action Agencies, protected a few "successful" categorical programs, and included a multibillion dollar PSE program (Davidson, 1972:32). Republicans, especially in the House, strongly opposed the EMA. The bill passed easily in the Senate, and won narrowly in the House (177-159), only to be vetoed by the President. In explaining his veto, Nixon voiced strongest objections to the PSE component of EMA. He referred to PSE jobs as "WPA type jobs" and said that a large PSE program would mean "Dead-end jobs in the public sector" (Davidson, 1972:62-66).

Democrats in Congress were bitter about the EMA veto. They felt they had gone more than halfway in meeting the Administration's demands for decentralization and decategorization, and believed the criticisms of PSE to be unjustified. Unemployment rose steadily in 1970 and 1971, which put the Congress under increasing pressure to act. Nelson and his people went to work again, and came up with the Emergency Employment Act of 1971 (EEA). The possibility of a Presidential veto was uppermost in the minds of those who wrote the EAA, and it was worded in a way to make it minimally offensive to the Administration. The bill stressed the temporary nature of the jobs and the ultimate goal of placing those hired into unsubsidized employment, which was intended to assuage Nixon's concern over creating permanently subsidized makework jobs. Support for the EEA was very strong in Congress, and it easily passed both houses, despite some obstacles created by the Administration. Faced with high unemployment and a carefully worded piece of legislation, Nixon finally signed the bill into law.

The Public Employment Program (PEP) created by the EEA was authorized for two years and carried a budget of $2.25 billion (Levitan et al., 1972:259). The program was designed to serve three major purposes. The first was to provide counter cyclical relief during a period of high unemployment. This was to be coupled with an effort to supply needed public services to especially depressed areas. Finally, the program was supposed to help disadvantaged, chronically unemployed people by giving them a job.

EEA was generally perceived to be a success. Its new delivery system, which relied on city and county governments to implement the program, showed an impressive ability to act promptly. In the first six months after the initial appropriation was made, 127,000 people were hired (Levitan and Taggart, 1972:16). Furthermore, the jobs appeared to be worthwhile ones, and city/county department supervisors were generally happy with the quality of the work performed by those hired. There was no evidence to support the allegation that the jobs were "makework" (Levitan and Taggart, 1974:22).

Some aspects of the PEP program were not so positive. The actual counter cyclical impact of the program appeared to be quite limited. Peak enrollment in the program reached 185,000, which meant that if every enrollee had been part of the labor force before entering the program, the net reduction in aggregate unemployment would have been 0.2%[2] (Levitan and Taggart, 1974:12). Service to the disadvantaged was not terribly impressive either. Nationally, 40% of those hired were reported as economically disadvantaged,[3] but this figure seems to have been inflated. A more accurate estimate may have been about 17% (see Levitan and Taggart, 1974:26). EEA results were good enough, however, to increase Congressional support for PSE being a part of any comprehensive manpower legislation.

Efforts to achieve manpower reform continued between 1971 and 1973, but failed. In 1973 both sides began to employ pressure tactics to get what they wanted. The Administration announced that it would begin to implement reforms by administrative regulation. However, an extension of the Manpower Development and Training Act of 1962 (MDTA) was needed in order to do this. The Administration was also working to phase out EEA. The House reacted by extending MDTA, but with a provision explicitly prohibiting the Administrative reforms that had been proposed. Meanwhile, the Senate passed an EEA extension. Finally, representatives from both sides met to fashion a compromise. The eventual result of this compromise was the Comprehensive Employment and Training Act, signed by the President on December 28, 1973 (see National Journal Reports, 1973:299; Van Horn, 1976:18-19).

It is apparent that both sides involved in the compromise made concessions in arriving at CETA. The Administration realized its goal of manpower reform by dismantling most of the categorical programs and by giving primary control over the planning and operation of manpower programs to local elected officials. However, federal oversight in the form of reviews of local plans and the monitoring of local operations was maintained, which satisfied Congressioanl Democrats. The Administration also gave in and accepted public service employment as part of the CETA package.

CETA has been described as being organized around three major themes: decentralization, decategorization, and citizen participation (Van Horn, 1976: 24-28). Decentralization was achieved by giving formal administrative authority over local manpower programs to the chief elected officials of cities or counties with a population of 100,000 or more.[4] Decategorization basically took place under Title I, or the Comprehensive Services title, which was originally seen as the principal component of CETA. The former categorical manpower programs, most of which were authorized under MDTA or the Economic Opportunity Act of 1964 (EOA), were consolidated under Title I of CETA. Title I made it possible for prime sponsors to chose the types of programs and operators that would be funded in their locality.[5] Citizen participation was to be achieved by the establishment of citizen advisory councils in each prime sponsorship. These councils were supposed to be involved in planning and operational decisions in an *advisory* capacity, which the Democrats in Congress hoped would serve to check the discretion of local elected officials and help to ensure local accountability.

Title II of CETA called for the establishment of a public service employment program. The PSE program under Title II resembled categorical progams in some respects: it had its own source of funding (Title II allocations were separate from those for Title I), and federally established regulations governed many aspects of the program. However, Title II was clearly different from categorical programs in other respects. Local officials had a great deal of latitude in designing many aspects of the program, and could even decide to use Title II funds for non-PSE programs.

Full implementation of the CETA system began in July, 1974. The Title I allocation for that year was approximately $1.6 billion. Congress authorized two allocations for Title II which amounted to $600,000,000.

By December, 1974, the unemployment rate had increased substantially, reaching a 13 year high of 7.1%. Both Congress and the Ford Administration went to work on a new public employment program. The Administration favored a public works approach, which would be administered separately from CETA. Congress rejected this plan in favor of an expanded public service employment program under CETA (see National Journal Reports, 1975:53). On December 31, 1974, President Ford signed the Emergency Jobs and Unemployment Assistance Act, which became Title VI of CETA. The bill authorized $2.5 billion for public service jobs to be spent in the 18-month period from January, 1975 to June, 1976. Title VI also included provisions which greatly expanded federal unemployment insurance coverage (see Congressional Quarterly Weekly Reports, 1974:3367).

The additon of Title VI made PSE a much more prominent part of CETA. The combined Title II and VI allocations for FY 1975 totaled nearly $1.6 billion making the PSE component roughly equivalent to Title I. In FY 1976, PSE allocations were up to just over $2 billion, while the Title I allocations remained about the same.

The primary goals of the EEA PEP program continue to be pursued by CETA's PSE programs—providing counter cyclical relief, supplying needed public services, and employing disadvantaged, chronically unemployed people. One of the critial tasks of this study will be to assess the emphasis given to each of these goals during the implementation of CETA PSE programs. Specific attention will be focused on determining the extent to which disadvantaged persons were served in the programs, and to discussing some aspects of the counter cyclical impact of PSE programs. This chapter will also address the issue of decentralization by describing the role of the Department of Labor (DOL) in the implementation process, and by analyzing some of the critical program design decisions made by local implementors.

Because national and state data were not always available in the form that allows for intensive investigation of some of these important issues, five sites selected from the state of Ohio serve as the primary units of analysis in some sections. The five sites include three cities, Akron, Youngstown, and Canton, and two counties, Portage and Stark. The sites exhibit a number of similarities and differences in size, political, economic and social conditions. Some of the important characteristics of the sites are shown in Table 1.

A DESCRIPTION OF CETA PUBLIC SERVICE EMPLOYMENT

The delivery system established for Title II and VI programs differed from that described earlier for Title I where units of government with populations of

Table 1. CHARACTERISTICS OF THE RESEARCH SITES

	Type of Government	Party ID of Chief Elected Official(s)	Partisan Make-up of City Council		Population	% Black in Population	% Below Poverty Level	Unemployment Rate	
			# Dem	# Rep				Jan. '75	Jan. '76
Akron	Mayor-Council	Republican	12	1	275,420	18	8	9.3	10.7
Youngstown	Mayor-Council	Republican	7	0	139,702	25	10	13.1	12.6
Canton	Mayor-Council	Republican	10	5	109,939	13	8	8.4	11.3
Portage County	3 Member Commission	All Democrats	——	——	125,868	2	4	10.1	11.8
Stark County	3 Member Commission	2 Democrats 1 Republican	——	——	262,271	3	4	7.1	9.5

Sources: Secretary of State, Ohio, Official Roster of Federal State and County Officers, 1975-1976, and Official Roster of Municipal and Township Officers, 1974-1975; U.S. Census Reports, Commerce Department, 1970; Ohio Bureau of Employment Services, Monthly Unemployment Reports; Bureau of Labor Statistics, Employment and Earnings, Vol. 22, December, 1975, Vol. 23, December, 1976.

100,000 or more called prime sponsors were responsible for administering local programs. A "Program Agent" designation was created and applied to any city or county with a population of at least 50,000. The prime sponsors retained formal responsibility for PSE programs operating within the prime sponsorship, but the program agents were given the "administrative responsibility for developing, funding, overseeing and monitoring" local PSE programs (The Regulations: section 96.22). Thus, Title II and VI funds are earmarked for program agents and prime sponsors serve as little more than a pass-through for these funds. The relationship between prime sponsors and program agents varies, but in most cases the CETA Title I programs are operated through the prime sponsor administrative machinery and PSE funds are passed on to the eligible program agents, which operate the programs using their own city or county staffs.[6]

The purpose of Title II is summarized in the Act: "to provide unemployed and underemployed persons with transitional employment in jobs providing needed public services in areas qualifying for assistance and, wherever feasible, related training and manpower services to enable such persons to move into unsubsidized training not supported by this Title" (Section 201). Most early observers did not consider Title II to be primarily counter cyclical in intent, but rather aimed at disadvantaged and chronically unemployed people. Title VI, on the other hand, was always regarded as a counter cyclical program, In Title II emphasis was placed on serving "the most disadvantaged in terms of the length of time they have been unemployed and their prospects for finding employment" (The Regulations: section 96.30). For Title VI the emphasis changed to favor victims of the economic downturn in late 1974 and early 1975. Title VI states that "special attention" should be given "to serving those who have exhausted or are not eligible for unemployment benefits" (The Act: section 602d).

This apparent difference in intent, however, had little effect on most local implementors. Soon after the passage of Title VI both programs were viewed by most local implementors as being essentially the same, which meant that, for the most part,they were implemented as counter cyclical programs.

Originally, there were a number of other differences in the Title II and VI legislation and the regulations. Some of these differences remain;others were gradually eliminated during FY 1975 and 1976. One basic difference that remains is the way Title II and VI funds are allocated. Title II funds only go to areas experiencing a rate of unemployment of at least 6.5% for three consecutive months during the year in which the funds are allocated. Title VI funds are allocated through a complicated formula that rewards areas of high unemployment, but every area in the country receives some Title VI money.

Eligibility requirements for Title II and VI also differ. To be eligible to participate in a Title II program, a person must reside in an area with a rate of unemployment of 6.5%, and be unemployed for 30 days or underemployed. Anyone within the jurisdiction of a program agent was eligible to participate in the orginal Title VI program as long as they were unemployed for 30 days or underemployed. Title VI also included a provision that allowed program agents with rates of unemployment above 7% to reduce the length of unemployment necessary to qualify for the program to 15 days.

The first set of Title II regulations included a nonmandatory goal of placing 50% of the Title II participants served each year into unsubsidized employment. (This rate of placement was required under the Emergency Employment Act of 1971, the immediate predecessor to CETA PSE.) When Title VI was passed, the placement goal for both Title II and Title VI was modified with inclusion of new provisions emphasizing that the placement goal was not a requirement, and establishing a process by which prime sponsors could waive the goal altogether.

Some important features were common to both Titles II and VI as originally passed: public service jobs could be provided by either public or private nonprofit agencies; participants were to receive the same wages, fringe benefits, promotional opportunities, and working conditions as other persons employed in similar jobs by the same employer, as long as the wages did not exceed $10,000 annually; 90% of all PSE money spent at the local level had to be spent on participant wages or fringe benefits, thus setting a 10% ceiling on the amount that could be spent for program administration; and all PSE jobs were supposed to be net additions to those which would have otherwise been available, which meant that no existing worker could be displaced, nor could PSE jobs be substituted for existing jobs.

The last aspect of PSE policy mentioned above concerns what is called "maintenance of effort" (see The Regulations: section 96.24). As CETA was being implemented in FY 1975 and 1976 Congress and the DOL devoted a great deal of attention to clarifying what constituted a maintenance-of-effort violation because some program agents had used substantial portions of their PSE funds to rehire laid-off municipal employees. This practice was never prohibited, but a series of restrictions were placed on program agents who decided to spend their PSE money in this way.[7] However, efforts to reduce the number of rehires in some of the large cities in the East and Midwest which made visible and extensive use of PSE funds for rehires were not very successful through FY 1976.

ROLE OF THE DEPARTMENT OF LABOR IN CETA PSE[8]

Once Congress passed the CETA PSE legislation, the Department of Labor assumed a major role in making sure the programs were administered in a way that reflected Congressional intent. The national office of the DOL had primary responsibility for writing the regulations for PSE programs, allocating PSE resources (both those allocated by formula and discretionary funds), and communicating national policy to local implementors through the regional offices.

Table 2 shows the national, state, and local allocations for Titles II and VI for Fiscal Years 1974, 1975, and 1976, and the dates in which these allocations were announced. By linking the dates with the allocations much of the general history of the implementation of Titles II and VI can be told.

In the first and second quarter of FY 1975 only Title II was operative. Because of the late announcement of the FY 1974 allocation, both the FY 1974 and 1975 Title II funds were available to be spent in FY 1975. In addition, the DOL allocated $240,000,000 to phase out the old PEP program under EEA. Despite the availability of over $700,000,000, the implementation of Title II proceeded slowly in the first half of FY 1975. By December, 1974, only 55,950 Title II participants had been hired.

The pace of implementation stepped up dramatically in January, February, and March of 1975 after the announcement of the first Title VI allocation. The combination of the Title VI, Title II, and EEA allocations represented a PSE effort of just under $2 billion for FY 1975. By June, 1975, there were 247,572 participants in Title II and VI programs, which represented an increase of over 190,000 since December, 1974.

By June, 1975, the pace of hiring began to slacken. Congress had not appropriated any new Title VI money and prime sponsors were being cautioned to plan to carryover unspent PSE funds into the next year. Just before the beginning of the new fiscal year new allocations were announced. These allocations amounted to roughly $2 billion for FY 1976. Most program agents were able to make a number of new hires in their Title VI program after the FY 1976 allocations were announced, but in some areas the funds received only allowed for the maintenance of the existing level of enrollment. By September of 1975, Title II and VI enrollments were up to approximately 300,000 and remained at that level through FY 1976.

In late FY 1976 the uncertain future of PSE funding caused prime sponsors and program agents another period of anxiety, wondering whether more PSE money would be allocated before they were forced to begin laying off participants. The Title VI extension was stalled in Congress and more money was needed almost immediately. Finally, in April, the Congress passed an Emergency Supplemental Appropriation which added $1.2 billion to Title II for the purpose of keeping all CETA participants working through December, 1976.

The phases in national PSE funding just described are reflected in the local funding as shown in Table 2. Four of the five sites had Title II programs in FY 1975, but these programs were relatively small. The first Title VI appropriation significantly increased the size of the local programs, and the FY 1976 PSE allocations further increased the level of PSE funding in all five sites. The Title II supplemental appropriation announced in late FY 1976 constituted between 40 and 60% of the FY 1976 PSE funding levels in the five sites.

The regional offices of the Department of Labor were given primary responsibility for communicating national policy to the prime sponsors, monitoring local operations, providing technical assistance, reviewing prime sponsor plans, receiving reports, and advising prime sponsors on programmatic decisions. Much of this burden rested on the shoulders of the federal representative assigned to each prime sponsorship.

Most regional offices and federal representatives adopted a policy of not interfering with programmatic decisions of CETA prime sponsors unless clear violations of federal regulations are involved. Therefore, federal representatives did not offer prime sponsors and program agents a great deal of guidance in developing the design of local PSE programs, unless an alternative being considered constituted a violation of the regulations. They occasionally responded to national priorities by taking on a more active role in influencing local decisions on certain matters (the most notable was their vigorous encouragement of prime

Table 2: CETA ALLOCATIONS FOR TITLE II AND VI FOR FISCAL YEARS 1974, 1975, AND 1976

| | Title II | | | | Title VI | |
	FY 1974	FY 1975	FY 1976	FY 1976 (Supplemental)	FY 1975	FY 1976
Date Announced	(June 1974)[a]	(Sept. 1974)	(June 1975)	(April 1976)	(Jan. 1975)	(June 1975)
Akron	$ 168,500	$ 235,059	$ 537,878	$ 1,536,508	$ 745,818	$ 2,070,143
Youngstown	206,000	267,552	357,813	1,005,423	627,201	1,993,030
Canton	76,300	76,829	175,810	599,560[b]	338,435	990,787
Portage County	176,753	168,202	297,715	850,457	487,255	1,186,880
Stark County	—	—	21,176	873,904[b]	342,789	1,571,763
State Total	$ 11,824,022	$ 11,370,978	$ 18,714,609	$ 52,736,006	$ 34,646,131	$ 72,817,983
National Total	$365,000,000	$350,000,000	$400,000,000	$1,200,000,000	$875,000,000	$1,625,000,000

a The Title II allocation announced in June of 1974 was $300,000,000. In September when the FY 1975 Title II allocation was announced, $65,000,000 was added to the FY 1974 allocation as a discretionary fund, which brought the Total FY 1974 Title II allocation up to $365,000,000.

b These FY 1976 Title II supplemental allocations had to be estimated. One prime sponsor staff could not reproduce exact amounts because they lumped the Title II supplemental funds with other unspent PSE funds after they submitted their plan. The figures shown in the plan did not total to the right amount.

Sources: The national and state figures come from the MIS Reference File (1976: 71:1035-1080). The program agent totals ar taken from the prime sponsor plans.

a   The Title II allocation announced in June of 1974 was $300,000,000. In September when the FY 1975 Title II allocation was announced, $65,000,000 was added to the FY 1974 allocation as a discretionary fund, which brought the Total FY 1974 Title II allocation up to $365,000,000.

b   These FY 1976 Title II supplemental allocations had to be estimated. One prime sponsor staff could not reproduce exact amounts because they lumped the Title II supplemental funds with other unspent PSE funds after they submitted their plan. The figures shown in the plan did not total to the right amount.

Sources: The national and state figures come from the MSI Reference File (1976: 71:1035-1080). The program agent totals are taken from the prime sponsor plans.

sponsors to increase PSE enrollment levels in the winter of 1975), but in general, they left most programmatic decisions to the discretion of local implementors. Consequently, federal representatives were perceived to have had little impact on the shape of most PSE programs (see Ripley et al., 1977).

National policy and resource allocation as communicated by the regional offices did have a major impact on local implementation activities. The early period (June to December of 1974) of slow PSE implementation was due, in large part, to the fact that most federal representatives were portraying Title II to the prime sponsors as a very restrictive program. They were insisting that PSE hiring be carefully monitored to ensure that only people from eligible census tracts were hired. They were also communicating the 50% transition goal as a requirement and asking prime sponsors to include the means by which this goal would be met in their Title II plans.

In January of 1975 the character of regional office communication changed noticeably. The regional offices began a new campaign of encouraging prime sponsors to hire people and spend PSE money quickly. DOL communications even contained the threat that Title II money not spent by the end of the fiscal year would be reallocated. The dramatic rise in PSE enrollments between December of 1974 and June of 1975 was a reflection of the impact that this new RDOL posture had on the pace of local implementation.

By May of 1975 the messages coming from DOL offices changed again. Prime sponsors were told to plan to carry over unspent Title II funds into FY 1976. The emphasis on spending and hiring had changed to one of maintaining existing levels of enrollment. This same emphasis continued throughout FY 1976.

The inconsistent nature of DOL communication was a source of constant complaints among the prime sponsors and program agents during FY 1975 and 1976. Even though many of the inconsistencies were due to changes taking place in Congress or the national DOL office, the local implementors usually blamed the regional offices. They also objected to other regional office policies. Staff people at the local level frequently complained about the limited amount of time they were given to plan PSE programs. Final plans were usually due at the regional offices less than a month after each new PSE allocation was announced. Local staff members also claimed that they received little or no useful technical assistance from regional office officials in designing their local programs. Many staff people insisted that the regional office could not legitimately complain about the poor design of PSE programs unless they were willing to offer prime sponsors more useful expertise and give them more time to plan the programs.

LOCAL IMPLEMENTATION[9]

The legislation and the regulations impose some restrictions on the options available to local implementors, but CETA prime sponsors and program agents will have a great deal of latitude in deciding how to spend Title II and VI funds. The existence of this local discretion has created a number of interesting implementation issues, which will be covered in this analysis of local implementation. In this presentation three different levels of data will be used: aggregate national figures, which include all prime sponsors in the country, aggregate figures for the state of Ohio, and data collected from the five sites described above.

WHAT ORGANIZATIONS GET PSE JOBS?

One decision that each program agent must make is how to distribute PSE jobs among the public and private nonprofit agencies in their jurisdiction that are requesting new positions. The potential employing agencies can be grouped into three categories. The first category includes city or county departments within the program agent's unit of government. The second covers all other public agencies (for example, Boards of Education, state agencies, and public housing authorities). The third category includes private nonprofit agencies (for example, community-based organizations and community action agencies).

The distribution of PSE positions among the three types of employing agencies for the state of Ohio and the five sites is shown in Table 3. The general pattern for both Title II and VI was for program agents to retain a high percentage of PSE jobs in city/county departments. This was particularly evident in Title II which was perceived as being the more permanent of the PSE programs. Other public agencies usually received a greater share of the PSE jobs not retained in city/county departments than the private nonprofit agencies. The percentage of funds going to these outside agencies increased slightly in FY 1976, when the total amount of PSE funding increased substantially.

There were exceptions to the dominant trend among the five sites. Canton and Portage County showed a more even pattern of distribution of avalable PSE jobs among the eligible employing agencies than the other sites and the state as a whole.

Decisions regarding the funding of employing agencies were determined by a number of factors. One important factor related to the specific actors involved in making PSE decisions. Where the elected officials personally participated in PSE decision making, city/county departments were usually favored. Elected officials acted in this manner because they recognized that PSE employees could be used to reduce the burden on regular employees, and/or to allow them to expand the services the city/county government could offer. In those cases where local elected officials did not participate directly in PSE decisions members of the program agent staff usually filled in. They were typically more interested in having a number of different types of agencies receive PSE jobs. However, it should be noted that even in these cases, PSE decision making was still confined within city or county government and could be influenced by the elected officials. The manpower advisory councils in the five sites did not participate, to any significant extent, in PSE decisions. Among the five sites, political official participation in decision making was greatest in Youngstown and Stark County. In the other sites staff members were responsible for most of the important decisions.

The fiscal condition of city or county government was another important factor which influenced the distribution of PSE job slots. Where local revenues were

Table 3. THE DISTRIBUTION OF PSE JOBS AMONG EMPLOYING AGENCIES

	FY 1975						FY 1976					
	Title II			Title VI			Title II			Title VI		
	%1	%2	%3	%1	%2	%3	%1	%2	%3	%1	%2	%3
Akron	86	14	0	59	29	12	100	0	0	60	23	11
Youngstown	100	0	0	92	8	0	100	0	0	21	16	16
Canton	100	0	0	39	32	30	100	0	0	63	23	30
Portage County	46	41	14	48	27	25	35	57	8	40	39	21
Stark County	—	—	—	100	0	0	50	22	28	62	16	21
Site Averages	78	18	4	62	25	13	81	15	5	52	29	19
State Averages	82	15	2	71	19	10	67	24	9	67	23	11

Key: 1 = City or county departments
2 = Other public agencies
3 = Private nonprofit agencies

Sources: Prime sponsor plans and program agent reports.

short, there was usually a high concentration of PSE jobs within the program
agent's unit of government. Both Akron and Youngstown had imposed a freeze on
creating new positions in city government due to the scarcity of local revenue.

Taken together these two factors account for much of the variation shown in
Table 3. High concentrations of PSE jobs in city/county departments are evident
where political official participation in PSE decisions was high (Youngstown and
Stark County) or where fiscal problems were apparent (Akron and Youngstown).
In the other two sites the jobs were spread out more evenly among the different
types of employing agencies.

WHAT KINDS OF JOBS ARE CREATED?

A second type of PSE program design decision that all local implementors must
face concerns the kinds of jobs that will be created. A number of considerations
came into play for those making this decision. Most local implementors
recognized the desirability of creating jobs that allowed participants to develop
good working habits and learn skills that would help them in finding future
employment, rather than simply creating a lot of labor and clerical positions. The
problem was that the disadvantaged were perceived as lacking the education or
the skill to perform these more demanding jobs adequately. Most staff members
said that basic, low skill positions were the only jobs in which the disadvantaged
could be hired and continue working. Furthermore, many political officials
expressed a preference for these jobs because they were expendable if PSE
funding was cut off.

In order to examine the patterns of PSE job creation in greater detail, the jobs
created in the five sites have been classified into six categories as shown in Table
4.[10] There was a general tendency for the cities to fund a high percentage of
laboring and service worker jobs, while the counties specialized in clerical jobs.
The percentage of professional and skilled labor positions was small in all cases,
but there was a slight tendency for the counties to provide more professional jobs,
and for the cities to have more skilled laborers.

Table 4. DISTRIBUTION OF PSE JOB TYPES (in percents)

	Type of Job					
	1	2	3	4	5	6
Akron	4	10	27	6	20	33
Youngstown	6	24	22	3	13	32
Canton	4	21	29	8	17	22
Portage County	12	19	20	1	29	19
Stark County	8	22	11	5	44	9
Average	7	18	23	5	23	26

Key: 1 = Professional
       2 = Paraprofessional
       3 = Service worker
       4 = Skilled laborer
       5 = Clerical worker
       6 = Laborer

Sources: Program agent reports

In order to probe more deeply into the question of how PSE jobs were distributed, the relationship between job type and employing agency was also investigated. Private nonprofit agencies were typically associated with high percentages of professional and paraprofessional jobs. City agencies employed high percentages of unskilled laborers, while county and other public agencies tended to favor the creation of a large number of clerical positions.

Another aspect of job creation is the wage rates established for PSE positions. Table 5 shows the wage distribution in the five sites. Not unexpectedly, wages were generally higher in the city sites than in the counties reflecting the impact of the increased presence of civil service job classifications and employee unions in the cities. Wage distributions were also related to the different types of employing agencies. Few jobs in city departments were found to fall in the lowest category. The other public agencies and the private nonprofit agencies in the city sites typically funded a large percentage of jobs falling into the highest and lowest wage categories. The county agencies of all types showed relatively high concentrations of jobs in the lower wage categories.

Table 5: DISTRIBUTION OF PSE WAGE RATES (in percents)

	1	2	3	4	5
Akron	22	13	26	21	17
Youngstown	6	22	35	20	18
Canton	21	12	27	24	16
Portage County	26	30	19	12	12
Stark County	26	21	17	11	8
Average	20	21	25	18	15

Key: 1 = Earning an hourly wage of between $2.01 and $3.00
2 = Earning an hourly wage of between $3.01 and $3.50
3 = Earning an hourly wage of between $3.51 and $4.00
4 = Earning an hourly wage of between $4.01 and $4.50
5 = Earning an hourly wage of $4.51 and above

Sources: Program agent reports.

In all five sites agency funding decisions and job creation decisions were made simultaneously. Thus, the patterns of job creation were the result of agency funding decisions because the employing agencies specified the types of jobs and wage rates that would be provided in their funding proposals. However, in most cases, the overall mix of jobs that would result was an important consideration for those reviewing agency funding proposals (this was particularly true in Portage County). Because of the close relationship between these two types of decisions, many of the same factors are important in explaining both. High political official participation in PSE decisions and/or fiscal problems were associated with high concentrations of PSE jobs in city or county departments. In the case of the cities (Akron and Youngstown), this meant that a great many of the PSE positions would be in the labor and service worker categories because a relatively high percentage of the regular city jobs were of this type, and because these kinds of jobs were most severely affected by the hiring freezes. In Stark County political official involvement meant that a premium was placed on creating expendable PSE positions within county government, which led to a high percentage of clerical and laboring jobs. Where neither of these two factors were present (Canton and Portage County), PSE jobs were more evenly distributed among the types of employing agencies, and a more balanced pattern of job creation resulted.

PSE wages were determined primarily by the types of jobs created and the wage structure of the employing agency. Some employing agencies did develop means of avoiding the provision in the regulations stating that PSE participants were to receive "the prevailing rate of pay for persons employed in similar occupations by the same employer" (Section 96.34), but in most cases the wages were determined in the manner specified in the regulations. Deviation from the prescribed method of establishing PSE wages was most common in the private nonprofit agencies. The city and county departments and the other public agencies usually had standardized job titles and wage schedules which meant that failure to comply with the regulations could often be detected. Many of the private nonprofit agencies were free to establish their own wage schedules for PSE employees (subject, of course, to the $10,000 ceiling), particularly when there were no comparable positions within the agency.

WHAT PEOPLE GET THE JOBS?

The data shown in Table 6 demonstrate that nationwide, the typical PSE client is a white male between the ages of 22 and 44 with at least a high school degree.[11] This closely parallels Levitan and Taggart's (1974:18) findings for the PEP program under EEA. Ohio totals resemble those for the nation, but the state tends to serve more blacks, fewer women, and fewer economically disadvantaged participants.

National client service patterns have not changed a great deal over time. Since December, 1974, aggregate client characteristics for Title II show small increases in service to people between the ages of 22 and 44, and those with at least a high school degree. Service rates for women have also increased slightly, while service to the economically disadvantaged has declined. For Title VI there was a substantial increase in service to women between June, 1975 and March, 1976, and small increases in service to blacks and those with a high school education or more (for details, see Ripley et al., 1977).

The data for the five sites illustrate how client service patterns can vary. They also suggest that local implementors have a great deal of discretion in determining the types of clients that will be served in their programs. Service rates to women in Title II programs were generally low in the five sites, but they were much higher in the county sites in Title VI programs. Service to blacks was higher in the cities than in the counties and in Title II than in Title VI. All of the sites except Akron tended to serve those between 22 and 44 at a rate that equaled or exceeded the state and national averages on both titles. This same pattern held with regard to service to those with at least a high school degree with Akron now conforming to the trend in the other sites. Service to the economically disadvantaged varied

Table 6: AGGREGATE CHANGE IN TITLE II AND VI CLIENT CHARACTERISTICS FROM DEC., 1974 TO JUNE, 1975 TO MARCH, 1976

Site	Title	Sex % Female			Race % Black			Age % Between the Ages of 22 & 44			Education % with H.S. Degree or More			Income Status % Economically Disadvantaged		
		12/74	6/75	3/76	12/74	6/75	3/76	12/74	6/75	3/76	12/74	6/75	3/76	12/74	6/75	3/76
Akron	II	34	43	24	78	67	51	73	67	58	84	88	85	85	79	74
	VI	NA	56	34	NA	47	43	NA	60	62	NA	94	83	NA	77	53
Youngs-town	II	NA	28	40	NA	48	47	NA	72	67	NA	88	89	NA	9	12
	VI	NA	28	25	NA	32	39	NA	78	73	NA	91	87	NA	9	14
Canton	II	20	25	21	68	71	67	52	58	64	64	75	74	12	8	36
	VI	NA	41	31	NA	30	39	NA	72	71	NA	53	88	NA	27	32
Portage County	II	57	33	24	16	10	9	57	75	68	78	78	88	56	47	35
	VI	NA	44	45	NA	9	9	NA	63	70	NA	83	87	NA	34	53
Stark County	II	NA	NA	17	NA	NA	0	NA	NA	66	NA	NA	83	NA	NA	50
	VI	NA	46	50	NA	9	13	NA	54	65	NA	95	87	NA	5	17
State Average	II	27	33	31	47	40	35	64	62	66	67	72	74	36	43	40
	VI	NA	35	34	NA	27	25	NA	62	64	NA	77	77	NA	37	39
National Average	II	35	35	37	24	23	25	62	63	64	71	75	75	48	45	45
	VI	NA	29	35	NA	21	23	NA	65	65	NA	74	77	NA	44	44

NA = Not Applicable. Title VI was not enacted until December, 1974, so there was no activity in this program in any site in December, 1974. Youngstown did not get its Title II program going until after December, 1974, and Stark County was not eligible for Title II funds in FY 1975.

Sources: Program agent reports and state and national aggregates of prime sponsor quarterly reports.

significantly. Service rates to this group exceeded the state and national averages in Akron, Portage County, and in the Stark County Title II program (which was very small), were slightly below these averages in Canton, and were well below state and national averages in Youngstown, and in Stark County's Title VI program.

The client service data presented in Table 6 suggest that many of the CETA PSE clients would not appear to fit the description of "the most severely disadvantaged." A number of factors help to explain why this was the case. The most often cited factor is a practice known as "creaming." Most employing agencies are given a choice from a number of referrrals in selecting a person to fill a PSE opening. What usually occurs is that the agency officials choose the most experienced and highly qualified candidate referred to them. The incentives to do this are obvious, and the net result is that prime aged, experienced, well educated applicants are systematically selected.

Local PSE administrators can counteract agency creaming if they establish a tightly controlled participant selection process. In Akron, for example, all applicants referred to PSE opening in city departments had to go through the city civil service system. A special scoring system was developed for PSE applicants whereby they were rewarded for being poor, members of minority groups, and having special needs. The PSE staff was then able to use this system to contol referrals to the employing agencies, and better ensure that some needy people were served. The Portage County staff developed similar controls over the selection process, and used this control to pursue the same type of client service goals. In Canton the local staff voiced a commitment to serving the disadvantaged, but the selection process was very loosely organized, and the staff was never quite able to control the types of people entering the program. As a result, service rates to the economically disadvantaged were significantly lower in Canton than in Akron and Portage County.

It was not only the degree of control over the selection process that was important, but also the ends for which the control was used. In Youngstown the Mayor was very much in control of the selection process, but service to the economically disadvantaged was very low. This same pattern of high political official involvement in participant selection being associated with low rates of service to the economically disadvantaged was repeated in Stark County.

Another factor typically cited to explain variation in local client service patterns is the demographic make-up of the CETA eligible population in the different localities. To test the hypothesis that local demography determines PSE client service patterns, estimates of the characteristics of the local pools of CETA eligibles[12] were compared to those of people serviced in PSE programs in each site. There was a reasonable fit between eligible populations and those served with regard to race, and within some age categories. But there was a very clear pattern of underservice to those with less than a high school education and to people over 45.[13] Women were underserved in all the city sites. There was also an obvious pattern of overservice to those with more than a high school education. Overall, the data did not lend a great deal of support to the argument that client service in PSE programs is determined by local demography.

A final set of factors that many staff people contend have a profound impact on client service patterns are the program design decisions just described. Thus, agency funding decisions and patterns of job creation are said to be closely related to client service patterns. In order to test this perception, the relationship between the sex, race, and income status of PSE participants in the five sites, the kinds of jobs and wages they received, and the type of employing agency in which they worked was examined.

The clearest pattern that emerged from this analysis involved service to women. Most female PSE participants were employed in clerical positions, and service to women was very low in skilled and unskilled laboring jobs. This pattern held across the different categories of employing agencies. Some women were employed in professional and paraprofessional jobs, but the percentage of women in these jobs was much higher in the other public and private nonprofit agencies than in the city/county departments. Women were also concentrated in the lowest wage categories, and very few women were in the highest paying jobs. Portage County was the only site that deviated from this pattern, which suggests that employing agencies followed traditional hiring practices unless specific steps were taken to overcome these practices. (Portage County made such an effort).

There was also a less apparent, but generally observable tendency for black and economically disadvantaged participants to be disproportionately represented in the lower skill jobs (labor, clerical, and service work), while being under-represented in the professional and paraprofessional jobs. This job pattern meant that service rates for these groups decreased in the higher wage categories. This relationship was more visible for blacks than the economically disadvantaged, and held principally for jobs sponsored by city/county departments, while being absent or even reversed among private nonprofit and other public agencies.

This discussion of PSE client service supports a number of conclusions. In general, the most severely disadvantaged are not being served in PSE programs. There is, however, a great deal of variation among local program agents on this score, and some enroll many more needy applicants than others. Service to the economically disadvantaged seems to be based primarily on the type of participant selection process that is established locally. Variations in service to other categories of participants appear to be due primarily to to other factors. Employing agency creaming appears to have its greatest effect in determining the educational background of PSE participants, and, to some extent, their age. Local demographic conditions are most influential in controlling the racial composition and some aspects of the age distribution of PSE participants. Program design decisions have their greatest impact in limiting service to women, but they were also related to service to blacks and the economically disadvantaged. This last set of relationships led to the identification of at least one clear client service problem in PSE programs. Women are not only relegated to certain types of jobs, but also receive consistently lower wages than male enrollees. Blacks also appear to be victims of this same pattern of service, but the differences between black and white service are less sharply defined than in the case of males and females.

EMPLOYMENT EFFECTS OF PSE PROGRAMS

Given the strong counter cyclical emphasis attached to CETA PSE programs during FY 1975 and 1976, it is important to explore the potential and actual effects of programs of this type on unemployment. In Table 7 the number of PSE jobs is related to the number of unemployed persons for the nation and in the five sites in order to examine the potential for direct unemployment reduction associated with PSE programs.[14] As the figures show, the highest national enrollment level of just over 340,000 represented approximately 4.7% of the unemployed population in January, 1976. This meant that CETA PSE had the potential for reducing the national unemployment rate by 0.3%. The number of jobs created in the five sites ranged from 2.85% to 3.65% of the unemployed population in each jurisdiction, while the unemployment reducing potential ranged from 0.26% in Stark County to 0.45% in Canton. These figures demonstrate that like the PEP program under EEA, the direct unemployment reducing impact of CETA PSE programs was not great.

The actual unemployment reducing impact of PSE programs is determined by a number of other factors besides the relationships shown in Table 7. The unemployment reducing impact of these programs declines in proportion to the number of people who are hired who were not previously part of the labor force, if the Bureau of Labor Statistics' method for determining the rate of unemployment is taken as the standard. Nationally, for Titles II and VI combined, 14% of the participants were reported as being outside the labor force at the time they were hired in FY 1976.

The unemployment reducing potential described in Table 7 does not take into account the increased impact that results from PSE participants being placed into an unsubsidized job. Participants moving from CETA jobs into unsubsidized jobs increase the unemployment reducing impact of the programs because the position vacated can be filled by another unemployed person.

The percentage of PSE participants (combining Titles II and VI) placed into unsubsidized jobs after being enrolled in PSE programs was 7% in FY 1975 and 14% in FY 1976. (Interestingly enough the 14% national placement figure for FY 1976 matches the percentage of participants who were outside the work force before receiving their PSE job which suggests that the effects of these two factors may simply have cancelled each other out.) Placement rates in the five sites were generally close to the national average, but, of course, significant variation was present. Placement rates varied from a low of zero to a high of 20% in FY 1975, and from a low of 8% to a high of 23% in FY 1976.

These data point to the conclusion that program agents in the five sites and throughout the country achieved only marginal success in placing PSE participants. There were a number of obvious incentives for employing agencies to pay little attention to placement. Like any other employer, officials in these agencies preferred to have a stable work force of experienced employees. Many employing agency officials indicated in interviews that they planned to absorb many of the PSE employees in their agency, but that they would not do so as long as CETA funds continued to be available. After January of 1975 pressure by federal officials to achieve placement results was virtually nonexistent. Agency officials and local staff members also cited high rates of unemployment and various agency hiring procedures and requirements as contributing to the low placement rates. What all this seemed to add up to was, that in the absence of federal pressure to move prople out of PSE jobs, most program agents were apt to follow the line of least resistance and operate their PSE programs with little emphasis on placement.

The experiences in the five sites do point out a number of means by which some placement activity could be achieved. One method was to secure pledges from employing agency officials that a certain number of people assigned to them would be placed, and then make follow up efforts to ensure that placement results were obtained. Another method was to threaten to cut off, or actually defund some employing agencies, which then forced the agencies to absorb the people they wanted. A final method was to hire experienced workers and rely on them to find their own unsubsidized jobs.

A final factor which has a great effect on the actual unemployment reducing impact of PSE programs is maintenance of effort or "substitution." The real unemployment reducing impact of these programs depends on the extent to which the jobs created constitute increases in the employment opportunities that would have been available if no PSE funds had been received. If local governments are using PSE funds to provide jobs they would have funded through local revenue had there been no PSE, then the unemployment reducing impact of these programs is greatly reduced. If, on the other hand, PSE money is used to provide jobs which represent net additions over what would have otherwise been available, the estimates of the unemployement reducing impact of PSE programs shown in Table 7 would be very close to the actual impact.

Undertaking the kind of analysis that would be necessary to arrive at an exact figure to describe the extent of substitution was beyond the scope of this research effort.[15] However, some impressionistic judgments on this subject, based on interviews with local staff members and employing agency officials, can be offered. When most of the PSE positions were originally created, there was an effort made to see that the jobs involved duties that were not part of the previous operations of the employing agency. Over time there was a strong tendency for PSE people to move into the regular routine of the employing agency, and become indistinguishable from the regular employees. In many cases this represented a subtle form of substitution in that employees that might have otherwise been hired using local revenue were being displaced by PSE employees. This type of substitution seemed to be more prevalent in city and county departments than in the outside employing agencies, especially in those municipalities suffering from fiscal shortages. Another common form of substitution took place in employing agencies which normally hired seasonal employees (park and recreation departments). These agencies often employed full time CETA people to perform the tasks formerly assigned to seasonal workers, which allowed them to divert that part of their budget normally spent on summer help into other areas. The attention of regional office officials was focused on the issue of rehires, and these less obvious maintenance-of-effort questions received very little federal attention.

Table 7. THE POTENTIAL DIRECT UNEMPLOYMENT REDUCING IMPACT OF PSE PROGRAMS

	# of PSE Jobs March, 1976	# of Unemployed in Jan. 1976	% of Unemployed That PSE Jobs Represent	Potential % Reduction in Un-employment Rate
Akron	411	12,560	3.27	0.30
Youngstown	234	7,516	3.11	0.35
Canton	205	5,623	3.65	0.45
Portage County	223	6,546	3.41	0.41
Stark County[a]	317	11,116	2.85	0.36
Nation	344,461	7,316,000	4.71	0.37

a The Stark County total includes the PSE jobs provided by two cities in the county, which were program agents. These cities accounted for 83 of the 317 jobs attributed to Stark County. These cities were included in the county total for this table because unemployment data for the county with these cities excluded was not available.

Sources: Ohio Bureau of Employment Services, Monthly Unemployment Reports. Program agent reports, and national aggregates of prime sponsor reports; Bureau of Labor Statistics, Employment and Earnings, Vol. 22, December, 1975, Vol. 23, December, 1976.

CONCLUSIONS AND RECOMMENDATIONS

The PSE experience in FY 1975 and FY 1976 indicates that local elected officials and their PSE staffs generally operated the programs with very little interference from outside groups. The federal presence in local decision making was found to be minimal. (See Ripley et al., 1977; Van Horn, 1976, for a similar conclusion.) Many federal officials expressed negative views regarding the direction being taken in local programs, but considered most questions of program design to be something for local decision makers to decide. Even though many federal officials stated a preference for greater emphasis on serving the disadvantaged in PSE programs, they did not often attempt to enforce their point of view. Their attitude, like that of most local actors, was that PSE was something for the elected officials and city/county governments to handle on their own. There was also very little evidence that the manpower advisory councils or the public at large contributed any significant input into PSE decisions.

In two of the five sites examined closely in this study, the local elected officials were personally involved making most of the important PSE decisions. Such involvement was associated with high concentrations of PSE jobs in city/county departments and low rates of service to the economically disadvantaged. Although some of the elected officials interviewed expressed some negative opinions about PSE, the program was quite popular among most city and county officials. (This observation is supported by another PSE study, see Manpower Development Corp., 1976:1.)

The domination of local elected officials and city/county governments over PSE decisions did not produce totally negative results. Both the EEA and CETA experience indicated that local governments can move quickly and respond to a sense of urgency (see Levitan and Taggart, 1974:14). As described earlier, over 190,000 people were hired in the last six months of FY 1975 in response to DOL emphasis on rapid hiring. Local governments do appear to be ideally suited to the task of sponsoring the rapid creation of a large number of public service jobs. However, the limited participation of outside groups in PSE decision making raises serious doubts about the extent of local accountability in PSE programs, which was frequently cited by proponents of revenue sharing as an important justification for decentralization.

In terms of the types of people employed, CETA PSE is not being used to serve the most severely disadvantaged.[16] PSE was often implemented more as a distributive rather than a redistributive program.[17] This finding contributes more support to a developing pattern in which programs that give local officials the discretion to determine the types of people who will be served have been consistently directed away from serving the disadvantaged segment of society (see Nathan et al., 1975: Nathan et al., 1977; Berke and Kirst, 1972; Van Horn, 1977).

National DOL attention was focused primarily on the counter cyclical side of the program, especially after the passage of Title VI. This emphasis was reflected in the regional office activities, and filtered down to many program agents as well, but this attention proved to be incompatible with some of the other PSE goals. The counter cyclical aspect of the program prompted the DOL to loosen some of the early restrictions attached to Title II, and was used as a justification for the limited time given to program agents to develop PSE plans. The result was, in many cases, poorly designed PSE programs and low rates of service to the economically disadvantaged. These outcomes raise doubts about the wisdom of attaching so much importance to the counter cyclical aspect of PSE, given the modest unemployment reducing potential of the programs.

The stress on quick hiring also had a detrimental effect on placement in the program. Under the urgency of speedy hiring, the placement goal was abandoned. This led many programs agents to ignore the possibilities for future placement in deciding where to locate PSE positions. The counter cyclical push also meant that very little PSE money was spent on job development activities for PSE enrollees. This was defended in FY 1975 by the existence of high rates of unemployment, which, it was claimed, made placement virtually impossible. When economic conditions improved in FY 1976, the number of placements also increased, but not as much as might have been expected. By that time many employing agencies had become dependent on their PSE employees, and did not want to give them up. With the continued availability of funding and no restrictions on the length of time a person could hold a PSE job, there was little incentive to move people out of the program.

Maintenance of effort or substitution is a serious problem in PSE programs. The practice of rehiring laid off employees was the focus of most national attention, but is probably not as serious as the less obvious forms of substitution which take place over time. Those who have studied this problem agree that, if local governments are relatively assured of continued PSE funding, widespread substitution is the inevitable result (see Fechter, 1975: Levitan and Taggart, 1974:17). The observations offered in this study suggest that by the end of FY 1976 the gradual process of substitution was well underway in many municipalities.

What many of these concluding observations point to is a pattern that has become very familiar to those studing the policy process in the United States. Congress, in an attempt to respond to the demands of various groups, and working within a context of limited resources, formulates a bill that seeks to kill two, three, or more birds with one stone by packing a number of goals or objectives into the same program. Limited attention can be given to the question of whether the goals are compatible during the legislative stage of the program's development because the major hurdle to be faced at this point is securing passage of a bill that addresses as many of the demands as possible. It then becomes the unenviable task of federal officials in the department responsible for implementing the program to devise regulations and strategies that will ensure that the program is implemented in a way that satisfies congressional objectives. It is almost inevitable that at this point one or more of the principal goals of the program will be emphasized at the expense of others. Therefore, it is not difficult for policy analysts and other interested parties to identify features of the implementation process which fail to live up to the standards set forth in the legislation.

The implementation process for CETA PSE followed this pattern. Federal officials at the national and regional levels seemed primarily interested in promoting rapid hiring in late FY 1975, shifting their emphasis to one of encouraging local program agents to maintain peak enrollments through most of FY 1976. This meant that very little was done to ensure that those most in need were served, to promote placement, or to prevent substitution. The discretion given to local implementors in a special revenue sharing program such as CETA added further opportunities for selective emphasis to be given to programmatic goals. The five sites included in this study included cases where local implementors had been fairly successful in responding to most of the principal goals of the program, and others where very little attention was paid to the major congressional objectives. This suggests that more effective federal enforcement of national objectives is needed in some areas, but not in others.

There are a number of concrete steps that federal officials could take to improve various aspects of the implementation of PSE programs. First, federal officials should become more directly involved in advising local implementors on matters of program design. This advice would not need to be binding, but would at least ensure that the federal position was known to those at the local level. There were many local officials observed in this study who were not consciously seeking to undermine national objectives, but simply did not know how to set up a PSE program so that national local goals would be fulfilled. Second, federal officials should aggressively monitor local client service records and insist on certain minimum service levels for groups identified as having disproportionately high rates of unemployment. Program agents failing to meet these minimum service levels should be given a reasonable period of time to correct the service gaps, after which funding would be withheld. Third, a new placement requirement should be imposed (50% may be too high, but at least 25% should be attainable). Placement might be further encouraged by establishing a special incentive fund to reward program agents achieving high placement rates.

To conclude, it seems that the unresolved conflicts which were built into the legislation itself made it certain that the implementation of CETA PSE would be, at best, partially successful. However, it also seems that more could have been done to fulfill national programmatic goals if federal officials had pursued a policy of vigorous, but selective enforcement. This analysis of local implementation indicates that decentralized delivery systems have been used successfully in some localitites, but decentralization is by no means a panacea for the problems that have plagued the implementation of federal programs.

NOTES

1. Categorical programs are programs having a specific funding authorization, with federally established guidelines governing most aspects of program operation, and in most cases, a delivery system established for the program, and a specific intended clientele. Most of the categorical manpower programs were authorized under the Manpower Development and Training Act of 1962 (MDTA) and the Economic Opportunity Act of 1964 (EOA). Some of the specific programs that were operating prior to the passage of CETA included: MDTA institutional training, Neighborhood Youth Corps (NYC), Operation Mainstream, New Careers, Jobs Optional Program (JOP), and the Job Corps.

2. This calculation is based on the assumption that all the jobs created represented net increases in the supply of jobs that would have been available, if there had been no PSE program. A number of economists have suggested, however, that many of the jobs would not be net increases, but cases where federal funds had been substituted for local funds. Estimates on the extend of substitution in PSE programs range from 40% to 90% of the jobs created. See Fechter (1975).

3. The term "economically disadvantaged" refers to a person who is a member of a family which receives welfare payments, or whose annual income does not exceed the poverty level (The Regulations: Section 94.4r). The poverty level in July, 1975 was an annual income of $5,050 for a nonfarm family of four.

4. Uncer CETA three distinct types of prime sponsorships can be formed. The first is a single jurisdiction with a population over 100,000. The second is a combination fo jurisdictions called consortia, in which at least one of the jurisdictions involved has a population over 100,000. Finally, there are balance of state prime sponsorships, which include all the cities and counties in a state with populations below 100,000 which are not part of another prime sponsorship.

.5 Prime Sponsors could choose to fund programs falling into four broad categories: Classroom Training, On-the-Job Training, Work Experience, or PSE. Also the prime sponsors could choose to use agencies that had formerly been categorical operators, run the programs themselves, or find new operators. Some of the common categorical operators included Boards of Education, Employment Security (ES) offices, Community Action Agencies, and various community-based organizations such as local Urban League organizations or branches of the Opportunities Industrialization Center (OIC).

.6 The five sites included in this study were all program agents. The sites were contained in three prime sponsorships. Akron and Portage County were part of the Akron Tri County Manpower Consortium. Canton and Stark County were part of the Canton-Stark-Wayne Manpower Consortium. Youngstown was included in the Northeastern Ohio Manpower Consortium. Stark County includes the city of Canton and two other cities that qualified as program agents (Massillon and Alliance). Therefore, the Stark County program agent described in this chapter was actually a balance of county operation, which did not include these three cities.

7. Some of the important restrictions placed on the practice of using PSE funds to rehire laid-off municipal employees were the following: First, program agents had to show that the lay-offs were "bona fide," which menat that they were based on a legitimate shortage of local revenue. Second, no PSE participant could be hired in the "same or substantially equivalent job" in a department where regular employees had been laid-off unless all the regular employees were rehired first (The Regulations: Section 96.24d). In April of 1976 a new provision was added stating that the number of rehires should be consistent with the percentage of the total unemployed population in the locality that such laid-off employees constituted. If this percentage was less than 10%, then a maximum of 10% of the PSE participants could be rehires (Section 96.24e, paragraph 1). The June regulation qualified the 10% restriction by stipulating that prime sponsors who planned to allot more than 10% of their PSE positions for rehires had to submit a request to the Regional Administrator documenting the reasons for this plan, and obtaining his permission before they could go ahead (Section 96.24f, paragraph 2).

8. This section is based on interviews with regional office officials in all 10 regions in the country. The presentation describes the general pattern of regional office activity that was observed, but there were certainly exceptions to the patterns described.

9. The obsrvations offered in this section are based on interviews with local implementors in all 17 prime sponsorships in the state of Ohio, and in 15 additional prime sponsorships spanning all 10 regions in the country. The special focus will be on the five

sites introduced earlier. Interviews were conducted with staff at both the prime sponsor and program agents level, with local elected officials, members of the manpower planning councils, and employing agency officials.

10. These categories are loosely based on U.S. Department of Commerce Bureau of the Census Occupational classifications. The professional category followed the guidelines of the Bureau of the Census classifications for professional occupations. The paraprofessional category was basically used for all nonprofessional, nonmanual labor and nonclerical positions. The category of service again followed the Bureau of Census guidelines, and includes mostly janitors and maintenance workers, protective service workers, and health and recreational aides. The skilled labor category was slightly more broadly defined than the Bureau of Census listing of craft occupations. It includes all the crafts, and some noncraft occupations requiring formal skills. The clerical category includes secretaries, clerks, typists, etc., and follows the Bureau of Census guidelines. The laborer category was used only for jobs with titles that were specifically "laborers" or "semi-skilled laborers."

11. The March, 1976 figures are reported in Table 6 rather than the June, 1976 figures because the March reports were the last in which Title II and VI enrollees were clearly separated. When the Emergency Supplemental Appropriation was passed in April, 1976, it allowed for the free transfer of Title VI participants into Title II. Thus, by June a number of former Title VI participants were counted as part of Title II. Also total enrollments for the two-year period of FY 1975 and 1976 reached a peak in March, 1976.

12. The estimates of the demographic composition of the CETA eligible populations in the five sites were derived from the Ohio Bureau of Employment Services (OBES) Employment Service Automated Reporting System (ESARS). The figures are based on the composition of the "active file" kept by OBES offices serving the populations included in the five sites. These active files contain all persons who have sought job placement assistance from OBES, and have not been removed from their list of people still seeking employment. The figures reported should not be considered exact descriptions of the composition of the CETA eligible population in each site for a number of reasons. First, the active file includes some people who are not unemployed, but simply seeking new employment. OBES officials estimate that this group represents about 10% of the active file. The active file also excludes an important group of CETA eligibles—those who have given up active job search. Thus, the figures probably underestimate the real incidence of need in the five sites. Finally, the figures are reported by area office, and there is no guarantee that a person registering at a particular office actually resides in the jurisdiction where the office is located. Despite all of these problems the ESARS data is still the best available estimate of local need because it is much more current than the alternative: the 1970 Census.

13. The terms "overserve" and "underserve" do not necessarily carry any normative implication as used here. These are simply summary terms which refer to the fit between the characteristics of those served in the program and the characteristics of the estimated eligible populations. Thus, a group is overserved if a higher percentage of that group is included among those served in CETA programs than is present in the estimated eligible population. Underservice describes the opposite situation.

14. I have used the terminology "direct unemployment reduction" to distinguish between the short-term and long-term effects of the program. The direct unemployment reducing potential refers to the unemployment reduction that results immediately, and as a direct result of a PSE program. There are also multiplier effects from a program such as this which further increase the overall unemployment reducing impact of the program. These multiplier effects are not considered in this analysis.

15. Arriving at a precise figure to describe the extent of substitution in a PSE program is very difficult. One reason the maintenance of effort question is so difficult to study is that one must make an assessment of an imaginary state of affairs (that is, what conditions would have been like if no PSE program had been instituted). Alan Fechter (1975) has analyzed the findings of previous studies of substitution (see Gramlich [1969], National Planning Association [1974], and the National Science Foundation [1976]), and applied them to PSE programs that are structured in a manner similar to CETA PSE. He estimates that, in the short run, 50% of the jobs created in these programs represent substitutions, and that this percentage increases the longer such programs continue in the same form. If these estimates are correct, the real unemployment reducing impact of PSE programs would be less than one half of the estimates shown in Table 7. (Johnson and Tomola [1977], analyzing CETA PSE, arrive at substitution estimates similar to those offered by Fechter. For a critique of their model, see Wiseman [1976].)

16. Other studies of PSE have arrived at this same conclusion. See Ripley et al. (1977), Levitan and Taggart (1974), and the Manpower Development Corp. (1976).

17. Lowi (1964:690-691) describes three broad types of governmental policy: distributive, redistributive, and regulatory. Redistributive policies address divisions in social classes. There are "have" versus "have not" questions. Ripley and Franklin (1976:18) define redistributive policy as involving "a conscious attempt by the government to manipulate the allocation of wealth, property, rights, or some other value among broad classes or groups in society."

Distributive policy, according to Lowi (1964:690), is synonymous with patronage "in the fullest sense of the word." Ripley and Franklin equate it with "governmental subsidy." Such policies "are made individually without consideration for their interrelation or overall impact; there is no sense of competing for limited resources" among those seeking redistributive subsidies (1976:18).

Regulatory policies are "governmental actions that extend government control over particular behavior of private individuals or businesses" (Ripley and Franklin, 1976:18). Such policies "are distinguishable from distributive in that in the short run the regulatory decision involves a direct choice as to who will be indulged and who deprived" (Lowi, 1964:690-691).

REFERENCES

BERKE, S. J., and M. W. KIRST (1972). Federal aid to education: Who benefits? Who governs? Lexington, Mass.: Lexington.

Congressional Quarterly Weekly Reports (1974). Volume 32, No. 51.

DAVIDSON, R. (1972). The politics of comprehensive manpower legislation. Baltimore: Johns Hopkins Press.

FECHTER, A. (1975). Public employment programs. Washington, D.C.: American Enterprise Institute for Public Policy Research.

GRAMLICH, E. M. (1969). "The effect of federal grants on state-local expenditures: A review of the econometric literature." In National Tax Association, Proceedings of the Sixty-second Annual Conference on Taxation.

JOHNSON, G. E., and TOMOLA, J. D. (1977). "The fiscal substitution effect of alternatives approaches to public service employment." Journal of Human Resources, XII (Winter):3-26.

LEVITAN, S., MANGUM, G., and MARSHALL, R. (1972). Human resources and labor markets. New York: Harper and Row.

LEVITAN S., and TAGGART, R. (1972). The EEA, an interim assessment. Washington, D.C.: American Enterprise Institute for Public Policy Research.

_____ (1974). The emergency employment act. Salk Lake City, Utah: Olympus.

LOWI, T. J. (1964). "American business, public policy, case studies, and political theory." World Politics, 16 (July):677-715.

Manpower Development Corp., Inc. (1976). "Public service employment in the Carolinas: Current utilization and the potential for expansion in selected communities." Report submitted to the Office of Research and Development, United States Department of Labor.

NATHAN, R. P., DOMMEL, P., LIEBSCHUTZ, S., MORRIS, M., and associates (1977). Block grants for community development, first report. Washington, D.C.: U.S. Department of Housing and Urban Development.

NATHAN, R. P., MANUAL, A. D., and CALKINS, S. E., (1975). Monitoring revenue sharing. Washington, D.C.: Brookings.

National Journal Reports (1973). Volume 5, No. 9.

_____ (1975). Volume 7, No. 2.

National Planning Association (1974). An evaluation of the economic impact project of the public employment program. Washington, D.C.: National Planning Association.

National Science Foundation (1976). The economic and political impact of general revenue sharing. Washington, D.C.: U.S. Government Printing Office.

REAGAN, M. D. (1972). The new federalism. New York: Oxford University Press.

RIPLEY, R. B., and FRANKLIN, G. A. (1976). Congress, the bureaucracy, and public policy. Homewood, Ill.: Dorsey.

RIPLEY, R. B., and others (1977). The implementation of CETA in Ohio. Washington, D.C.: U.S. Government Printing Office.

U.S. Congress (1973). Public Law 93-203. The Comprehensive Employment and Training Act. 93rd Congress, 1st Session. Washington, D.C.

U.S. Department of Commerce (1972). Public use samples of basic records from 1970 census. Washington, D.C.: U.S. Department of Commerce.

VAN HORN, C. E. (1976). Intergovernmental policy implementation: The comprehensive employment and training act. Unpublished Ph.D. dissertation, Ohio State University.

_____ (1977). "Decentralized policy delivery: National objectives and local implementors." Paper delivered at the Workshop for Policy Analysis in State and Local Government, State University of New York at Stony Brook, May 22-24.

WISEMAN, M. (1976). "Public employment as fiscal policy." Brookings Papers on Economic Activity, I:67-104.

8

FEDERAL AUDITORS AS REGULATORS:
The Case of Title I of ESEA

F L O Y D E. S T O N E R

Marquette University

INTRODUCTION

In the years since Title I of the Elementary and Secondary Education Act was passed in 1965, federal audits of the program have constituted an unwelcome intrusion into a political system based on unwritten goals and unpublicized alliances. The impact of the audits on state and local administrators raises questions concerning accountability in the federal system. This chapter represents an initial exploration of these issues in the context of a single domestic policy.

Theodore Lowi (1969) describes and Murray Edelman (1964) explains a phenomenon of increasing frequency in the United States: ambiguous and symbolic legislation resulting in varied and idiosyncratic administration of public policies that greatly benefit established interest groups. For Lowi, this system of "interest-group liberalism" is unfortunate because it means that elected representatives do not make decisions. For Edelman, the situation is understandable because it enables these politicians to provide benefits to important political supporters while reassuring the mass public that their interests are protected and "good" is being done. Neither writer expects much change.

AUTHOR'S NOTE: *An earlier version of this chapter was presented at the 1977 Annual Meeting of the American Political Science Association, Washington, D.C., September 1-4, 1977.*

Title I has many of the characteristics cited above: ambiguous statutory language and much administrative discretion. However, some of the administrators are not performing in the manner expected. Rather than simply carrying out the desires of congressmen and interest group representatives for a low profile distribution of funds to the existing educational system, these administrators have attempted to establish a national program with specific goals designed to reform that system. The attempt probably would have been inconsequential were it not for the auditors. Federal auditors in both the General Accounting Office and Executive Branch agencies constitute an obstruction to the smooth functioning of the system of "interest-group liberalism."

For Title I to conform to the model described by Lowi, there should be few clear standards formulated by administrators, and those that are established should benefit organized groups. However, some Office of Education administrators developed program requirements designed to redistribute both resources and political influence in local school districts. Once established, the Health, Education and Welfare Audit Agency (HEWAA) auditors utilized these requirements in their audits of states' administration of the funds. Their audits were broader in scope than the fiscal audits performed in the Department of Health, Education, and Welfare before 1965. They performed compliance audits to determine whether states and localities had spent the federal funds on programs designed to achieve the goal established by Congress. Their primary sources for the operationalization of the congressional goal were the Title I program requirements with which a number of influential congressmen disagreed. This type of input was new to the system of interest-group liberalism; it had a major impact.

This chapter had its origin in a study of the political history and implementation of ESEA Title I (Stoner, 1976). The information presented and the questions developed are based on that research, during the course of which the importance of the auditors became apparent. The data utilized was of two types: (1) public documents and published research, and (2) 89 open-ended interviews conducted with persons connected with Title I at the federal, state, and local levels.

TITLE I OF THE ELEMENTARY AND SECONDARY EDUCATION ACT OF 1965

Title I of the Elementary and Secondary Education Act of 1965 authorized the most direct federal involvement in local public education in United States' history. It is also the most heavily funded title of the act, which provides funds to school districts in 95% of all counties in the country. The organizational hierarchy designated to administer this program parallels the federal structure with distinct national, state, and local administrative agencies. The language of the title emphasizes aid to educationally deprived children by funding programs formulated by Local Education Agencies (LEA) to overcome the particular handicaps of deprived children in individual localities. These programs must be approved by State Education Agencies (SEA). The Office of Education (USOE) has general responsibility for implementing and administering this venture into educational federalism.

Although categorical aid for educationally deprived children in areas of concentrations of poverty is the purpose stated in ESEA Title I and reemphasized in the 1973 report by the National Advisory Council on Education of Disadvantaged Children, the legislative situation in which it passed was complex and the statutory language unclear. One congressional staff person who was intimately involved with the bill in 1965 asserts that Title I was carefully designed to approximate general aid to education in the distribution of funds, while emphasizing the language of compensatory education to save congressmen from charges of "federal meddling in local education." This language was viewed by most congressional proponents of the bill as the means of passing a federal aid to education bill after 100 years of failure (Eidenberg and Morey, 1969:77-80; Munger and Fenno, 1961: Thomas, 1975:38). The other titles were also important, but Title I was the largest and the most important title (Murphy, 1973:162-163). The fundamental issue in 1965 and still today is the dichotomy between categorical and general aid (Thomas, 1975:38). The principle of federal aid to education has been established, but the form that it should take has been hotly debated (Thomas, 1975:76;Congressional Record, March 12, 1974:H1673).

The general aid/categorical aid conflict was not readily apparent during the drafting and passage of the Elementary and Secondary Education Act. President Lyndon Johnson established only one major requirement for the education bill that he wanted to sponsor. He asked Douglas Cater, Lawrence O'Brien, and Commissioner of Education Francis Keppel to devise "legislation that Congress would pass' (Murphy, 1973:164). The Democratic majority of the House Education and Labor Committee, the committee in which many previous pieces of legislation designed to provide general aid had died, expressed similar sentiments. Two individuals who were working in the House at the time later wrote that "the Democratic membership of the education committee in the House (where the key battle was to be fought) by and large took the position that they would be able to support any legislation that carried the endorsement of the Administration and the principal interest groups" (Eidenberg and Morey, 1969:76). The bill's drafters had a relatively free hand, provided they could gain the support of the two primary interest groups, the National Education Association, and the National Catholic Welfare Conference (later called the United States Catholic Conference).

The NEA and NCWC were important because they represented the primary stumbling blocks to the achievement of this long sought goal: general aid to education. The National Education Association had previously opposed any proposals that included funds for parochial schools; the National Catholic Welfare Council just as strenuously had opposed bills that would fund only public schools (Price, 1961).

There was one other problem area faced by the drafters of ESEA: the issue of federal control. Support for local control of education had bedeviled general aid proposals since 1870 (Lee, 1949:165). However, if the two primary interest groups could be placated, the persons charged with devising legislation that would pass believed that they could succeed in passing it (Eidenberg and Morey, 1969:79-80). It was an important issue, however, and it would have great relevance for the role of the auditors in the years that followed passage.

ESEA Title I was passed, and President Johnson signed it into law on April 11, 1965. However, the means whereby this drive for federal aid to education was brought to fruition set the stage for years of conflict during implementation that were not expected by most of the congressmen influential in the passage of the bill.

The device utilized to gain the support of the NEA and the NCWC was the concept of "child benefit." While the Title I funds would obviously be spent in school systems, the policy statement emphasized the needs of "educationally deprived" children in "local educational agencies serving areas with concentrations of children from low-income families"(Public Law 89-10, Title I, Sec. 201).[1] The formula for the computation of local school district funding levels used the number of children from poor families and those receiving Aid to Families with Dependent Children. The emphasis on poor children was politically potent, both because of the publicized concern about poverty in 1965 and because the concept sidestepped the issue of parochial aid. Title I funds aided the child, wherever he attended school. In that sense it was categorical aid.

However, the hearings on ESEA held by both the House General Education Subcommittee and the Senate Education Subcommittee provided convincing evidence that the congressmen influential in the area of education policy believed that Title I was general aid under another name.[2] The hearings also contain evidence of the compromise between the two interest groups that resulted in their support for the bill, but which would have interesting ramifications later. One key point in the bill was the provision that "special educational services and arrangements" would be provided by the LEA for educationally deprived children in private schools (Public Law 89-10, Title I, Sec. 205(a)(2)). This provision was what guaranteed the support of the NCWC. However, Carl Perkins, Chairman of the General Education Subcommittee made it quite clear that he believed that the money provided to the public schools under Title I would not be restricted to certain uses, and Secretary of HEW Celebreeze agreed:

> Chairman Perkins: Now, could this legislation, particularly under Title I, actually increase the range of choices open to the local autonomy enjoyed under this proposal and actually create more freedom on the part of the local school administration?
>
> Secretary Celebreeze: That is absolutely right and that is one of the purposes of the act: to strengthen the local school system. [House Hearings, 1965:14.]

The Administration's testimony supported the belief of many congressmen that Title I would fund clearly defined special programs for the educationally disadvantaged in parochial schools, and that it would fund whatever the local educational decision makers wanted in public schools (House Hearings, 1965: 980-981).

The situation was the same in the Senate, though stated even more clearly. Senator Dominick elicited from Secretary Celebreeze agreement that Title I funds could be used for anything in public schools, including construction of gymnasiums and cafeterias, and then:

> Going back to this private-public school question my understanding from your presentation and from a brief summary of the bill is that the general grants under Title I apply only to the public schools.

> Secretary Celebreeze: That is right.

> Senator Dominick: That the monies which are to be made available to the private schools come in the form of special assistance or special programs or library services or things like that?

> Secretary Celebreeze: To the pupils rather than to the schools, Senator. [Senate Hearings, 1965:499.]

For the congressional proponents of Title I, the problem that the policy addressed was the "fiscal crisis" faced by public schools, particularly those with low property tax bases. Chairman Perkins clearly stated this position during the hearings:

> The whole impact here is the concentration of low-income families in the school districts that cannot provide adequate service for these youngsters. So, we follow the same guidelines that we set up in the [aid to school districts "impacted" by Federal installations] legislation all the way through. There is no Federal control. We just make sure that the funds get into the school districts where the impact actually exists. [House Hearings, 1965:1962-1963.]

The representatives of the two primary interest groups involved in the drafting process agreed. The goal of almost all concerned was legislation that would deliver dollars to financially strapped school systems. The symbol of the educationally deprived impoverished child was the means to pass the bill. As Chairman Wayne Morse of the Senate Education Subcommittee said: "Let us face it. We are going into federal aid for elementary and secondary schools . . . through the back door" (Congressional Record, April 7, 1965:S7313).

TITLE I, INTEREST-GROUP LIBERALISM, AND THE WAR ON POVERTY

At the time of its passage, ESEA Title I was a clear example of a policy produced by a system based on interest-group liberalism. Organized private groups were the primary influences on the drafting of the bill. The statutory language was extremely ambiguous (with the significant exception of the formula by which the funds were to be distributed at the local level). Discretion was granted to educational administrators at the federal, state, and local levels (House Hearing, 1965:146). This administrative structure was an example of the "creative federalism" disparaged by Lowi because definitive national goals could not be sought and federal decisions would not be made by Congress.

Because all the attributes of interest-group liberalism appeared to mesh in a single policy, one would expect that administrators would simply take the Title I funds and distribute them to the states for redistribution to those school systems that qualified under the formula. One would expect few requirements to be attached to the use of the money at the local level. One would certainly not expect to find large sums of money spent by Local Educational Agencies to be disallowed by federal auditors on the ground that they had not been spent in accord with the "intent of Congress." The hearings and committee reports of 1965 indicate that the congressmen influential in education policy wanted the money spent as the state or local administrators desired. However, something happened to the congressmen's desire for general aid in the process of implementation.

A most fascinating account of the first four years of Title I was written by its first division program director. John Hughes, in collaboration with his wife Anne, carefully delineated the means whereby a small group of administrators sought to develop the program in a direction that was not desired by congressional proponents, the interest group representatives, or most of the influential administrators in the Office of Education. The Hugheses detail an extended struggle between general aid supporters (whom they term "traditionalists") and advocates of Title I as the means "to modify the system to serve the special needs of the poor as a target population" (1972:33). These "reformers" faced an uncongenial group of top-level administrators (1972:38):

> Title I's program mission was already generally assumed by the traditionalists who were advising Keppel on policies to be followed in implementing ESEA. In their opinion, Title I's mission was to assure that the funds flowed as freely and smoothly as possible into the coffers of the nation's school systems with the minimum number of strings attached. In short, Title I—if not quite yet general aid—was to become so in due course. If the "child benefit" theory had been used to sell Title I to the Congress, the idea of specifically serving the target population, as defined in the allocation formula, with special programs to meet special needs was not a major consideration.

However, the means to challenge the general aid supporters did exist in the ambiguous legislative language. Further, a rationale was developed to justify the challenge. In the spring of 1965, one reform-oriented member of the Division of Program Operations (the division administering Title I) met with two other OE administrators and presented the argument upon which the reformers built their case. First, he argued, the Title I legislation and hearings clearly demonstrated Congress' intention to fund special programs for children in parochial schools under Title I. Second, it was obvious that OE should treat all children equally. Therefore, OE should require special programs for educationally deprived children in public schools (personal interviews, May and July 1976). With this rationale as a base, the reformers set about developing formal requirements for implementation.

A crucial decision regarding implementation was made by someone in OE based on the line of reasoning just presented. The determination of grant entitlements was separated from the development of basic criteria for state approval of LEA applications: "grants were to be made to school districts in accordance with measures of economic need, children were to participate in the program's benefits solely on the basis of relative 'educational disadvantage' " (Bailey and Mosher, 1968:103). Hughes and Hughes (1972:38-39) report that OE reformers hoped that "through the development of judicious policies and requirements, the Title I funds could serve not only the specific needs of poor children but as a change agent as well."

Had the desires of the congressional supporters of Title I been followed by the administrative unit charged with its implementation, control of the funds would have been held legally by the states and actually by the local districts. While the funds are granted to the states, state administrators are required to distribute them to local districts according to a specific formula. In order to receive the money, state administrators must sign assurances that they will administer the program in conformance with the intent of the law. To receive the funds to which they are entitled under the formula, local districts must submit an application to the state administrators (Title I is, after all, a categorical grant program). Where was the source of leverage for the reform-oriented administrators in Washington?

Title I contained one primary provision that complicated its implementation: Section 205(a) included a parenthetical phrase that reserved to the Commissioner of Education the power to establish "basic criteria" to be followed by state administrators when approving the applications from LEAs. President Johnson had been told that the provision was an assurance demanded by the NCWC as a guarantee that promises made at the federal level could not be abrogated at the state or local levels. The NCWC wanted to be certain that federal sanctions could be applied if they did not receive Title I funds (personal interview, July 1976). During debate on the bill, this provision was the focus of much concern by those who feared "federal control" of local public education (for example, House Hearings, 1965:146-147). During implementation the fears of those who opposed the provision were realized. Without the provision, OE could only have written checks. With it, administrators in OE had an instrument with which to attempt reform of the "education establishment."

FEDERAL IMPLEMENTATION OF TITLE I

The conflict between the general aid and the categorical aid proponents was based on two differing conceptions of the "poverty problem" facing public education. If one believed that the problem of local schools was insufficient funding for school districts, then federal funds without strings attached was a reasonable answer. If, on the other hand, one believed that the "poverty problem" was both an unwillingness and an inability to deal with poor children in local schools, then a tightly controlled categorical grant program provided the only hope for change. Simply to give callous and incompetent administrators more money would only result in their failing to reach poor children at a higher level of expenditure.

The reformers in OE did not share the faith in state and local administrators that had been evidenced by the congressmen. Therefore, the first five years of implementation of Title I encompassed a series of attempts by these individuals to tighten the "basic criteria" pertaining to state approval of LEA applications. If defeated by congressional and interest group pressure, they would try again later. They frequently succeeded. Over time, more and tighter requirements for LEA participation in Title I were included in the regulations, guidelines, and program memoranda that states were expected to monitor.

At the heart of the reformers' program was the desire to concentrate the Title I funds on a relatively small number of children in such a manner that these funds would supplement the state and local expenditures on the same children (Murphy, 1973:177-178). In other words, local public school districts were required to submit applications for their Title I funds to the states in which they outlined the special programs that had been designed for the carefully identified educationally deprived children. These children were chosen from particular schools that were "targeted" because the number of children from low income families was higher than the district average. By 1970, after much conflict both in OE and between OE and Congress, these requirements had been firmly established.

Establishing the requirements was not an easy task for the reform-oriented administrators. However, achieving compliance by local administrators would prove to be even more difficult. In fact, the difficulties faced by a poorly staffed division of program administrators in their attempts to enforce unwelcome requirements on state and local administrators may be one reason for the fact that the reformers were able to establish the requirements. It was undoubtedly assumed by many that the states and localities that so desired would simply fill out the required forms and then ignore the program requirements during implementation. Indeed, this practice was most common in the early years of Title I (Hughes and Hughes, 1972:77-80).

Had the administrative system of internal auditing in OE not been changed in 1965, it appears unlikely that Title I would have ever become tightly controlled categorical aid in the reform model except on paper in the formal requirements. It is not totally clear whether the process of tightening up will continue. However, in the case of Title I at least, the role of the auditors has been central.

PUBLIC AUDITING AND ESPECIALLY HEWAA

The field of public auditing has changed dramatically since World War II. Prior to that time, the "proper" function of the government's auditors was the performance of fiscal audits to investigate the regularity of public expenditures (Pois, 1975:245). Since 1945 this conception of the role of public auditors has changed, with the General Accounting Office both exemplifying the change and causing it to a certain extent. According to Pois, certified public accountants were hired in increasing numbers to staff the GAO after 1945. At the same time (and perhaps led by the CPAs, though Pois is not clear on this point) some members of the GAO sought to develop a greater role for it. In order to do so, GAO members had to expand upon statutory language that "reflected a perspective that was entirely financial in nature" (Pois, 1975:248). They did expand upon that language, and the results were first evidenced in the Comprehensive Audit Manual (Pois, 1975:248):

> Our audits are not restricted to accounting matters or to books, records, and documents. The scope of these audits is much broader and may extend into all significant aspects of an agency's operations.

The thrust for an expanded role came from the GAO, not from Congress.

This expanded role of the GAO was formally expressed recently in the "Standards for Audit of Governmental Organizations, Programs, Activities & Functions," issued in 1972. In the "Foreword" to that document it is noted that (U.S. Comptroller General, 1972:i):

> Auditing is no longer a function concerned primarily with financial operations. Instead, governmental auditing now is also concerned with whether governmental organizations are achieving the purposes for which programs are authorized and funds made available, are doing so economically and efficiently, and are complying with applicable laws and regulations.

Further, this statement of an expanded scope for audits was not intended to apply only to GAO; it was intended to apply to all audits of "all government organizations, programs, activities, and functions," no matter who performed them (U.S. Comptroller General, 1972:1). These standards apply to HEWAA in their audits of HEW programs, including Title I.

The HEWAA was formed in 1965, the same year that Title I was passed by Congress. It was formed by consolidating 15 separate audit organizations that had previously been located in various program offices within HEW. However, the consolidation did not merely move the auditors in Washington into new offices, it also resulted in an expansion of the audit staffs at the 10 HEW regional offices. New auditors were hired in what was essentially a new agency in 1965. In Washington the Audit Agency was organized into five operating divisions headed by assistant directors: State and Local Audits, University and Nonprofit Audits, Social Security Audits, Installation and Management Audits, and Audit Coordination (McMickle and Elrod, 1974:111).[3] These auditors are responsible for auditing all HEW programs.

Of particular interest for this chapter is the Division of State and Local Audits, because ESEA Title I is included in this category. While HEWAA is HEW's *internal* auditor at the federal level, it functions as an *external* auditor for state and local grantees of Title I funds. The distinction is important. Internal audits are performed primarily to improve management control by providing independent and objective information concerning programs to management. External audits stress accountability (McMickle and Elrod, 1974:61-65). Therefore, the role of the HEW auditor, at least in the case of the state and local program such as Title I, can be most ambiguous. If the federal program managers (the Office of Education in this case) do not disseminate clear requirements to the state and local grantees of federal funds, or if there are different interpretations of the law between Congress and OE, one would expect significant variations in the uses to which the funds would be put at the state and local level. The auditors who then audit these states and localities must identify some standards to use in an external audit of the states and localities. If deviations from these standards are identified and are tied to expenditures that are questioned by the auditors, these "audit exceptions" are referred to the Office of Education by the HEWAA for resolution.

AUDITS OF TITLE I

In the first years of Title I there was little audit activity, with three state audits in 1967 and 11 in 1968 (Pollen, 1975:4). No specific action was taken by OE officials on the basis of these audit reports. However, the reports were used by a group of civil rights activists who had pooled their resources to support an investigation of Title I. With the HEW audits as the data base, Martin and McClure's study had a major impact on the general aid/categorical aid conflict being waged over the implementation of Title I. It did so by focusing attention upon violations of the regulations and guidelines upon which the audits were based. The Martin-McClure study (frequently known as the Washington Research Project) was based squarely on the reform interpretation of Title I as change agent that had been written into the regulations and guidelines (1969:29):

> The Title I *Regulations* are very clear about the purpose of the legislation. It is to provide educational assistance to educationally disadvantaged children in order to raise their educational attainment to levels normal for their age. Title I *programs* must be directed to the "special educational needs" of disadvantaged children. [Emphasis added.]

Here is a prime example of the way in which the language used to skirt the church-state issue in 1965 has affected implementation. The 1965 legislative record included discussion of programs in connection with schools though the legislative language was ambiguous on this point; this 1969 expose emphasized the failure of many administrators to develop specific programs for the disadvantaged in the public schools.

The researchers documented numerous examples of general aid which fell into four basic categories (Martin and McClure, 1969:5):

> 1. Title funds purchase services, equipment, and supplies that are made available to all schools in a district or all children in a school even though many children reached are ineligible for assistance.

> 2. Title I funds are spread around throughout all poverty-area schools instead of focusing on those target areas with high concentrations of low-income families.

3. Title I funds are not going to eligible children at all.

4. Title I State administration funds support non-Title I operations of State departments of education.

Such expenditures, while congruent with the desires of many congressmen, were not permissible even under the rather ambiguous regulations formulated by USOE.

Technically, the area desk officers in OE were responsible for the violations documented by HEW's auditors. It was (and is) the responsibility of these desk officers officially to accept the written assurances of state Title I coordinators that the programs funded by Title I in their states were in compliance with the regulations. However, three to five desk officers for more than a billion dollars distributed throughout the United States were just not equal to the task of ascertaining definitely what was done with the money. Additionally, most of their superiors were not interested in enforcing compliance to a categorical aid interpretation. Finally, at least some states deliberately overlooked the violations perpetrated by local districts and "covered up" general aid expenditures. One lawyer who was preparing a lawsuit against some Mississippi Title I officials testified before the Senate Education Subcommittee in 1969. He emphasized the importance of the orientation of the state administrators (Senate Hearings, 1969:357):

> What we found is that the State office is nothing more than a mail drop. The State coordinator has testified that he makes no inquiry to determine . . . whether projects that are paid for out of Title I funds in black or disadvantaged schools are the same sort of things that are paid out of State and local money. He never looks at audits of the school districts to determine where the State and local money is going in other districts.

In this case and in others the auditors found serious violations of the regulations. The area desk officers had merely accepted the state assurances of compliance.

The issue upon which the attention generated by the audit revelations became centered was known as "comparability." Comparability refers to the principle developed in OE that districts should expend state and local funds equally among all schools within a district before adding the Title I funds in "target" schools for specific children. In other words, Title I money was to supplement, not supplant, state and local expenditures on eligible children. This specific issue had not been addressed in the 1965 law. Rather, the law prohibited the reduction of state aid to the districts:

> Sec. 207(c)(1): No payments shall be made under this title in determining the eligibility of any local educational agency in that State for State aid, or the amount of that aid, with respect to the free public education of children during that year or the preceeding fiscal year.

(2) No payments shall be made under this title to any local educational agency for any fiscal year unless the State educational agency finds that the combined fiscal effort (as determined in accordance with regulations of the Commissioner) of that agency and the State with respect to the provision of free public education by that agency for the preceding fiscal year was not less than such combined fiscal effort for that purpose for the fiscal year ending June 30, 1964.

These provisions of the law only concerned maintenance of the state and local fiscal effort evidenced prior to the first year's funding, and continued state expenditures in all districts. Criterion 7.1 of Progam Guide #44, on the other hand, stated that for any given year the state and local expenditures should be generally equal among all schools *within* a district. This requirement was ignored by almost everyone until the Martin-McClure investigation focused public attention on the violations of it. Congress had not originally mandated comparability; OE had formulated the provision requiring that state and local expenditures be generally comparable among all schools. (One person who had been very active on the House side asserted that no one in Congress had been concerned with strict comparability in 1965 (personal interview, March 1976).)

School districts would not have had a problem with the "supplement, not supplant" requirement if it had not been for the "targeting" requirements, and vice versa. If school districts had been permitted to simply add federal funds on top of state and local funds (as most congressmen intended), they would have no difficulty. Alternatively, if they had been permitted to "target" funds to particular schools as they had been doing, they would have had no compliance problems. However, the combination of comparability and targeting requirements was designed to increase the concentration of funds, and this tightly structured categorical aid produced the audit exceptions.

The point here is that the auditors provided the means to an end desired by some persons, and their influence could not have been predicted in 1965. Under the system of internal audits in OE before 1965, the auditors had been located in the program offices and had performed fiscal audits. This type of system was obviously what Chairman Perkins had in mind when he said (House Hearings, 1965:195):

I read the language in the bill just like the witness reads the language. The Department provides certain criteria to see that the money reaches the school districts we are seeking to reach, the impoverished *districts* ,and at the same time, to maintain fiscal accounting of the funds. [Emphasis added.]

Had the orientation of the HEWAA not been changing from fiscal to compliance and performance auditing, it is reasonable to assume that Perkins would have had what he sought. However, the audits performed by the Audit Agency were expanding in scope at the same time that the reformers were establishing their interpretation of Title I in the Regulations, Guidelines, and program materials. The early audit reports were embarrassing to the congressmen and the members of OE who shared their general aid orientation. There was little that anyone could do, however, but seek to minimize the impact of the auditors. An OE report released in 1975 indicates that that is exactly what was done.

The "Study of the Audit Resolution Process in the U.S. Office of Education" was written by Dr. David S. Pollen, Chairman of the Title I Audit Hearing Board. The Audit Hearing Board was established in 1972 as financial audit exceptions reported by HEWAA began piling up in OE for resolution. (One person closely involved stated that the Hearing Board's purpose was simply to prevent the audits from becoming issues in court cases (personal interview, June 1974).) Pollen's study provides some interesting insight into the role of the auditors in this program.

There are several primary points to be made about the audits and the impact of the reports in OE. First, the audit exceptions are primarily based on the reform-oriented requirements that target funds within school districts, thus forcing changes at the local level if the school districts comply (Pollen, 1975:51):

> Review of numbers of audit reports makes it evident that there are several major, recurring, issues which generate a very large percentage of the Title I fiscal exceptions taken by HEWAA auditors.
>   These issues are five in number, including
> supplanting
> comparability
> general aid
> ineligible children
> target areas

Second, assuming that some reformers still remain in OE (many left during the Nixon Administration), Pollen's findings concerning support for the validity of the audit exceptions are instructive. He found that the Title I staff were much more likely to support the HEWAA's findings on noncompliance with the program requiremnts than were the bureau-level administrators. Pollen further noted that knowledge of the political consequences of pressing the states for repayment of disallowed funds was a major reason for high-level OE administrators' avoidance of actually requiring the funds to be repaid (1975:68).

Finally, Pollen's study documents a fragmented and uncoordinated "system" for audit resolution in the Office of Education (1975:29-37). Given the political history of Title I, it seems reasonable to conclude that such a nonsystem is the only way for OE "traditionalists" to deal with the politically sensitive audit exceptions that are based on an interpretation of Title I that both they and a number of influential congressmen find objectionable. No one can stop the auditors from auditing Title I, and it seems likely that major audit exceptions will continue to be reported. Therefore, an attempt to defuse the situation is to be expected.

CONCLUSIONS

Federal auditors operating under the standards formulated by the GAO constitute a disturbing element in the established relationships evident in various policy areas in the United States. The emphases on "compliance," "economy," "efficiency," and "effectiveness" necessarily involve the auditors in interpretations of congressional intent and evaluations of performance (U.S. Comptroller General, 1972:2). If the auditors continue to expand their role in the compliance/ performance direction, programs of the type authorized by the legislation described in this chapter will be constantly subjected to searching investigation by auditors who seek clear standards for the performance of their function.

The audiors do want to expand their role. The heading to one of the sections of Dr. Pollen's report (1975:52) is illustrative:

HEWAA, Like GAO, Understands Its Official Mission To Go Significantly Beyond the Limits of Assuring Narrow Fiscal Accountability for the Expenditure of Federal Funds

Such an expansion will lead to the establishment of clear federal goals through the audit process unless authorizing legislation is made more explicit in its grants of power to state and local entities. This outcome will result because, by auditing to certain criteria, the auditors will hold state and local officials accountable to those criteria. Even if the fiscal exceptions are rarely upheld, it seems probable that the anxiety and adverse publicity faced by a noncompliant grant recipient will tend, over time, to result in program modifications designed to satisfy the auditors. If such a situation develops since the auditors do not have time to audit all aspects of all programs, their choice of audit criteria and operationalization of those criteria will effectively define the program for grant recipients. Effective accountability will be defined by the auditors.

At the same time that the auditors are defining the program for grant recipients, they are also providing unwanted information to congressmen. Audit exceptions faced by constituents are always unpleasant, and audit exceptions based upon an interpretation of a public policy with which one does not agree are even more irritating. Attacking the auditors (proponents of accountability) directly would be difficult; seeking to influence their auditing practices indirectly would open congressmen to charges of attempting to politicize the independent position of the goverment's auditors. The only solution may be for less ambiguous (and symbolic) legislative language.

Auditors are not only important, but their importance is increasing. The implications of their expanded role are difficult to discern. If Title I is not a totally deviant case, and the recent focus on Medicare and Medicaid audits indicates that it is not, then the influence of the auditors in HEW certainly deserves more analysis. Given the importance of GAO in the development of public auditing in general, the functioning of GAO itself and its influence on other departmental audit agencies should be investigated.

Finally, the potential for differential audit impacts should be explored. It may be that as states tighten up their program requirements in the directions desired by the auditors, only some local administrators may actually comply. It would be particularly interesting if the deviations were systematic with urban areas remaining noncompliant while the rest of a state complies. Such a situation seems most probable. If true, categorical grants to states are always block grants to cities.

NOTES

1. This approach was justified by many on the basis of Everson v. Board of Education. In a 5-4 vote the Supreme Court upheld the constitutionality of a New Jersey state law that subsidized the costs of transportation of children to nonpublic schools. The Court ruled that the primary object of the law was public safety, not aid to private education, and therefore it did not violate the First Amendment.

2. Senator Robert Kennedy was not an enthusiastic supporter of Title I because he did not share the faith of his colleagues that more money for education would have much impact on students from poor homes. However, most of his influence was exerted before the bill reached Congress (McLaughlin, 1973:3-7).

3. The Health, Education, and Welfare Audit Agency was placed under the direction of an Inspector General in 1977. It is not clear yet what impact this change in organizational structure in Washington will have on the performance of audits in the regions or the resolution of audits in Washington.

REFERENCES

BAILEY, S. K., and MOSHER, E. K. (1968). ESEA: The Office of Education administers a law. Syracuse: Syracuse University Press.

EDELMAN, M. (1964). The symbolic uses of politics. Urbana: University of Illinois Press.

EIDENBERG, E., and MOREY, R. (1969). An act of Congress. New York: W. W. Norton.

HUGHES, J. F., and HUGHES, A. O. (1972). Equal education. Bloomington: Indiana University Press.

LEE, G. C. (1949). The struggle for federal aid. New York: Teachers College, Columbia University.

LOWI, T. J. (1969). The end of liberalism. New York: W. W. Norton.

MARTIN, R., and McCLURE, P. (1969). Title I of ESEA: Is it helping poor children? Southern Center for Studies in Public Policy and the NAACP Legal Defense and Education Fund, Inc., December.

McLAUGHLIN, M. W. (1973). "Evaluation and reform: The case of ESEA Title I." Ed. D. dissertation, Harvard University.

McMICKLE, P. L., and ELROD, G. (1974). Auditing public education. Montgomery, Ala.: Alabama Department of Education.

MUNGER, F. J., and FENNO, R. F. (1961). National politics and federal aid to education. Syracuse: Syracuse University Press.

MURPHY, J. T. (1973). "The education bureaucracies implement novel policy: The politics of Title I of ESEA, 1965-72." Pp. 160-198 in A. P. Sindler (ed.), Policy and politics in America. Boston: Little, Brown.

POIS, J. (1975). "Trends in General Accounting Office audits." Pp. 245-277 in B. L. R. Smith (ed.), The new political economy. New York: John Wiley.

POLLEN, H. D. (1975). "Study of the audit resolution process in the U.S. Office of Education." Unpublished internal USOE document, August.

PRICE, H. D. (1961). "Race, religion and the Rules Committee." In A. F. Westin (ed.), The uses of power. New York: Harcourt, Brace and World.

STONER, F. E. (1976). "The implementation of ambiguous legislative language: Title I of the Elementary and Secondary Education Act." Ph.D. dissertation, University of Wisconsin-Madison.

THOMAS, N. C. (1975). Education in national politics. New York: David McKay.

U.S. Comptroller General (1972). "Standards for audit of governmental organizations, programs, activities and functions."

U.S. Congress, House (1965). Aid to elementary and secondary education, Hearings before General Subcommittee on Education on H. R. 2361 and H. R. 2362. 89th Congress, 1st session.

U.S. Congress, Senate (1965). Elementary and Secondary Education Act of 1965, Hearings before Subcommittee on Education on S370. 89th Congress, 1st Session.

9

CAPTURE AND RIGIDITY IN REGULATORY
ADMINISTRATION: An Empirical Assessment

JOHN P. PLUMLEE

Southern Methodist University

KENNETH J. MEIER

University of Oklahoma

Concern with economic regulation in the United States has a nature somewhat akin to Carroll's Cheshire cat, that is, it fades in and out at unpredictable intervals. Currently regulation is "in" and has become highly visible. Both the Ford and Carter Administrations have grappled with regulatory issues, and the clear implication is that regulatory reform is an idea whose time has come— maybe (Herman, 1976; Wellborn, 1977). No one believes that major changes in the regulatory arena will come easily, but the problems engendered by economic regulation and suggestions for their solutions have been vigorously discussed from a variety of perspectives.[1] Scholarly approaches to the regulatory dilemma have focused on such pertinent issues as the role of regulation in the social control of business (Holton, 1969; Harber, 1969; Gruchy, 1974; Nadel, 1975) and in the creation of economic inefficiencies and distortions (Noll, 1971; Weidenbaum,

AUTHOR'S NOTE: *This is a revised version of a paper presented at the Annual Meeting of the American Political Science Association, Washington, D.C., September 1-4, 1977. The authors are grateful to Paul Sabatier, Walter Roettger, and Roger Noll for their helpful comments and suggestions.*

215

1975). Related to these concerns is still another issue, one that has important administrative as well as political and economic implications. This is the issue of institutional responsiveness in regulation (Cary, 1967; Hall, 1961; Leone, 1972): where does the "public interest" lie in regulation and how can it be achieved in the regulatory process?

An important analytic thread that appears in discussions of institutional responsiveness is the frequently stated assumption that regulatory agencies must inevitably become the "captives" of the interests they were established to regulate (Salamon and Wamsley, 1976; Zeigler and Peak, 1972). The further assumption is that the loss of agency independence through such capture has important consequences for public policy. As the U.S. Comptroller General (1977:43-44) expressed this concern in a report to Congress:

> The question of independence involves the ability of the regulatory decisionmakers to operate an environment free from outside pressures. The aim is to achieve regulation that is in the interest of the Nation and not a particular industry, firm, region, or partisan group. Of paticular concern is undue influence from outside parties who are in no way accountable to the electorate.

Although the term "capture" is imprecise, generally it implies that a regulatory body has undergone a serious goal distortion wherein demand for active regulation in the public interest has been superseded within the regulatory organization by regulation in the interest of the regulated. Since the publication of Bernstein's (1955) *Regulating Business by Independent Commission,* the idea of agency capture has also been linked with the concept of an organizational life cycle intrinsic to all regulatory agencies. This perspective asserts that agency capture and organizational rigidity—an internal "slowing down" of the agency— are functions of the age of the regulatory agency (Moore, 1972; Simmons and Dvorin, 1977).

In spite of the widespread acceptance of this idea, the concept of agency capture as the end result of an inherent organizational life cycle has only recently been subjected to limited empirical testing.[2] This chapter is a further empirical examination of the concept of agency capture and the associated phenomenon of organizational rigidity. In this chapter, a synthetic model of the regulatory agency life cycle is derived from the theoretical models of Bernstein (1955) and Downs (1967). This synthetic model posits recursive relationships between the age of the agency, the nature of an agency's political support, the degree of "captivity" of an agency, and the organizational rigidity of the agency. Since political support can come from the regulated (specific support) or broader interests (diffuse support), the model contains five variables. Each of these variables corresponds to the elements of agency capture and rigidification as they are specified in the conceptual schemas of Bernstein and Downs. Following a more complete discussion of the development of the ideas of Bernstein and Downs, we evaluate the synthetic model derived from their works through the use of path analysis.

BERNSTEIN AND DOWNS:
TWO MODELS OF ORGANIZATIONAL LIFE CYCLES

In his influential and seminal work, Bernstein argued that all independent regulatory commissions follow the same historical pattern of development. In his view, this pattern resembles the human life cycle with four phases: gestation, youth, maturity, and old age (1955:74). Regulatory agencies are created among strong political forces that both support and oppose regulation. During the agency's youth the conditions which nurtured the origin of the agency fade in importance, and public support for regulation, including the immediate support of the President and Congress, begins to lag. This decline in diffuse public support is not matched by the decline in specific opposition by the regulated interests so that pressures counter to vigorous regulation are felt within the agency.

The environmental changes that occur in an agency's youth lead to the third stage in the life cycle, maturity. The agency must try to survive in a hostile environment where Congress, the President, and the public do not particularly care, or are not aware of, what the agency does or does not do. At the same time the organized interests, those being regulated, would like to eliminate the agency or subvert its influence. Since an agency without political support has little chance of survival, the agency must seek support from its environment. The most obvious source of such support is the regulated industry, since the agency's actions are unimportant to most other people. The agency and the regulated interest gradually arrive at a rapproachement wherein the agency lessens its regulatory vigor and protects the industry from the rigors of competition while the industry supports the agency in its political struggles (Bernstein, 1955:76-78). During this phase regulatory failure appears and is characterized by the following phenomena (1955:87-94):

> (a) Lawyers, economists, and other technical specialists dominate the agency. Many groups of specialists are able to veto or at least stifle the other's policy proposals, thus requiring a precedent for any action.
> (b) Reliance on precedent and judicialized procedures slow the regulatory process and create backlogs. Backlogs tend to prevent the agency from looking forward and planning its regulatory policies.
> (c) Increased backlogs and close relationships with the regulated motivate Congress and the President to deny the agency resources it needs to solve its workload problems. Budgets decline either absolutely or relatively as inflation reduces the agency's resources.
> (d) The above factors reinforce the agency-industry relationship creating an interdependence that includes the recruitment of agency personnel from the regulated industry. The industry, in turn, becomes a retirement haven for those executives who have left the federal service.

These phenomena culminate in a condition which can be termed organizational rigidity (1955:90):[3]

> The close of the period of maturity is marked by the commission's surrender to the regulated. Politically isolated, lacking a firm basis of public support, lethargic in

attitude and approach, bowed down by precedence and backlogs, unsupported in its demands for more staff and money, the commission finally becomes a captive of the regulated groups.

Finally, in old age, the situation gradually worsens. As the agency ages, so do its personnel who become less aggressive and opt for a conservative approach to policy decisions. The interest relationships become cemented in, and the regulated industry and the agency cooperate in a symbiotic relationship where both can survive though not necessarily prosper.

Many of the attributes of Bernstein's conceptualization of the regulatory commission life cycle were subsumed in a broader theory of bureaucracy developed by Downs (1967) in his now-classic book, *Inside Bureaucracy*. The major causal underpinning, according to Downs, of the growth and decline of public agencies (called "bureaus" by Downs) is the presence of exogenous factors in the bureau's environment. These exogenous factors include the bureau's need for political support and the results of the bureau's quest for such support. The youth of an agency is spent in developing automatic generators of support because survival is dependent upon such support. Officials in new bureaus place a high priority on creating the conditions most conducive to bureau survival, even if this means some sacrifice in performance of the agency's social function (Downs, 1967:7-10).

The early life of a bureau is critical for its survival. It must reach the minimal size and age levels which allow it to be large enough to render useful services and old enough to have established routinized relationships with its major clients. A bureau is vulnerable between the time of its origin and immediately before it attains its survival threshold. The critical variable is what Downs calls the power setting of the bureau: "If its suppliers or beneficiaries are strong and well-organized in comparison with its rivals and sufferers, then it will probably quickly gain a clearly autonomous position" (1967:10). Downs describes a dynamics of growth for bureaus. Growth is accelerated when the social functions of the bureau become important. This growth will bring those officials that Downs describes as "climbers" into the organization. The innovativeness and aggressiveness of these officials will cause the organization to grow still further. This type of growth is rapid for a while, but is soon inhibited by other factors coming into play. These factors include internal and external conflicts with other bureaus and with rival officials. Additionally, achieving impressive results becomes difficult as the agency increases in size and unwieldiness. As growth is slowed, another effect, the process of deceleration, appears which involves a change in the composition of bureau personnel from predominantly "climbers" to predominantly "conservers." Such a change reduces the ability of the bureau to innovate and its desire to expand functions (1967:10-14). All of these effects cause agencies to become more conservative as they age, meaning that the organization has a lessened will to take risks or engage in new patterns of behavior. The result is organizational rigidity.

While the phases of the life cycle described by Downs are not as clear-cut as those developed by Bernstein, the general trend from youthful vigor to entrenched old age and rigidity is evident in both models. Downs does not deal specifically with the notion of agency capture, but both Downs and Bernstein agree that the power setting of an agency plays a crucial role in determining whether agencies remain fairly flexible and able to meet new challenges or become increasingly bureaucratized and dependent on precedent as a guide for action. Thus Bernstein and Downs are in agreement on a number of fundamental points with regard to the cyclic nature of organizational existence. Table 1 displays the major characteristics of organizational life cycles as they are posited by Bernstein and Downs.

The conceptualization of Bernstein and Downs find additional support in the literature of bureaucracy and policy-making. The interaction of organization and environment has been the focus of extensive scholarship with emphasis placed on the efforts of public organizations to generate political support from their external environments (Ripley, 1975; Katz and Kahn, 1970; Long, 1962; Niskanen, 1971; Rourke, 1969; Warwick, 1975). The need to attract political support is seen by Bernstein and Downs as the ultimate source of the forces impelling agencies through the organizational life cycle. The argument advanced is that regulatory agencies are forced to accommodate private interests because they cannot gain sufficient support from the public, the President, or the Congress once the symbolic demand for regulation is satisfied and the agency becomes embroiled in obscure and routine tasks. The regulatory agencies must then seek to maintain organizational integrity by cultivating political support from the regulated interests. The "aging" process, then, can be thought of as the successive abandonment or closure of other lines of environmental support to the agency and the almost total dependence on one source of support. This closure can never be complete, but it can become so predominant that it shapes the main patterns of agency behavior.

In essence, then, this is the life cycle theory of regulatory organizations. The inability of an agency to gain political support from the more "public-regarding" sectors of its external environment (i.e., the President and Congress) cause it to turn to more "private-regarding" interests which are directly affected by the agency's function. The organization and the clientele interpenetrate one another to the extent that they have goals which are virtually indistinguishable. The agency loses the will and incentive to act in a fashion which would be inimical to the narrow interests of its clientele. The agency becomes passive, conservative, and demonstrates a "benign neglect" of larger public values.

A SYNTHETIC MODEL OF THE RIGIDITY CYCLE

In line with the considerations discussed above, we have extracted the important variables involved in regulatory agency life cycles and constructed a synthetic model which incorporates these variables. The first variable in the model is the chronological age of the agency. The second variable is the degree of diffuse political support for the agency, that is, the support given the agency by the President and Congress. The third variable is the specific political support the

Table 1. SUMMARY OF LIFE CYCLE MODELS

	Gestation	Youth	Maturity	Old Age
BERNSTEIN Theory of Life Cycle of Regulatory Commissions	1. Reform groups agitate for regulation 2. Emphasis on legislation	1. Animosities of period of origin do not immediately disappear 2. Agency begins with crusading spirit 3. Loss of support begins through inattention 4. Private interests find ways of checking agency activity	1. Spirit of controversy fades 2. Reliance on procedure 3. "Police" attitude replaced by "business management" attitude in agency 4. Marked passivity 5. Developments concerning staff, work load, appropriations 6. Commission surrenders to regulated interest	1. Passivity continues 2. Commission becomes protector of industry 3. Budgetary decline 4. Poor management, doubt about regulatory objectives 5. Failure to keep pace with change 6. Phase continues until emergency calls attention to failure ot the commission
DOWNS Theory of Life Cycle of All Public Organizations	1. Bureaus created in one of four different ways: a. Routinization of charisma b. Out of nothing by certain social groups c. By splitting off from an existing bureau d. Zealot entrepreneurship	1. Youth, maturity, and old age not clearly distinguished 2. Every bureau initially dominated by advocates or zealots 3. Bureau must attain initial survival threshold. It will be opposed by functional rivals or by powerful social agents if it tries to regulate or inhibit their activities 4. Character of power setting determines agency autonomy 5. Accelerator-decelerator effect causes "ratchet movement" in bureau growth rather than smooth curve 6. Growth indicated by climber/conserver ratio 7. Specific effects of age 8. Law of Increasing Conservatism 9. Age lump phenomenon 10. Bureaus unlikely to die once they have attained survival threshold 11. Bureaus threatened with shrinkage or extinction will seek to develop new functions to prevent such eventualities.		

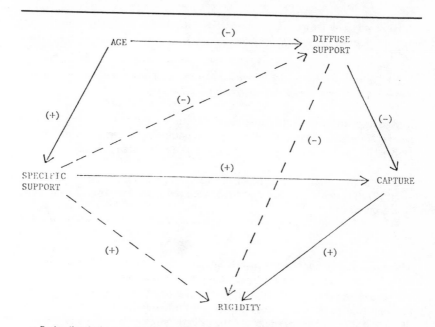

a. Broken lines indicate relationship implied but not specifically in the life cycle theory. The positive or negative sign in parentheses indicates predicted direction of relationships.

Figure 1: A SYNTHETIC MODEL OF THE REGULATORY AGENCY LIFE CYCLE

agency receives from the regulated interest. The fourth variable is the degree of agency capture, which may vary from nearly total dependence to nearly total independence. The fifth and final variable is the degree of organizational rigidity experienced by the agency—a slowing down of agency internal processes which presumably leads to a diminished ability of the agency to respond to new challenges or demands.

These five variables are combined to create the model shown in Figure 1. Age is the key variable in this model, because age affects the degree of diffuse and specific support and through change in political support has an impact on the degree of agency capture. Age also affects organizational rigidity, although this relationship is mediated by political support and agency capture. The impact of age on the degree of captivity and rigidity is indirect. The model assumes that the intervening variable of political support is what actually causes growth or diminishment of agency captivity and/or rigidity. This relationship is obscurely stated in Bernstein, but we believe he clearly implies the formulation discussed here. Several other relationships not specifically addressed by Bernstein or Downs are also possible within the boundaries of the model developed here. These possible relationships are denoted by the broken lines in Figure 1.

From inspection of the model and from our prior knowledge, several hypotheses related to the organizational life cycle of regulatory agencies can be generated. We are most directly concerned with four of these.

H1. *The greater the age of the agency, the lower the diffuse support for the agency.*
H2. *The greater the age of the agency, the greater the specific support for the agency.*
H3. *The less the diffuse support of the agency, the greater the degree of clientele capture.*
H4. *The stronger the interdependent relationship (capture) between the agency and the regulated interest, the greater the rigidity of the agency.*

In addition to the major hypotheses above, other relationships within the model can be treated as plausible alternative hypotheses. These relationships are denoted by the broken lines in the figure and can be stated verbally as follows:

H5. *The greater the specific support for the agency, the less the diffuse support.*[4]
H6. *The greater the specific support for the agency, the greater the rigidity of the agency.*
H7. *The lower the diffuse support for the agency, the greater the degree of agency rigidity.*

These alternative hypotheses merely specify some of the possible linkages not directly included in the model. Specifically, they link diffuse and specific support with agency rigidity of both types of political support irrespective of any impact that is mediated through agency capture. If these relationships are strong, then one could surmise that agencies can be directly affected by a rigidity syndrome without having to pass through an intervening stage of capture.

The relationships displayed in the synthetic model we have developed are recursive. While strong arguments could be made that some of these relationships are nonrecursive, we have chosen to maintain the recursivity of the model in order to conform as closely as possible to the theory from which the model was derived. Bernstein and Downs are fairly specific about the nature and direction of the relationships they posit, and we remain close to these sources.

SELECTION OF THE AGENCIES

We have selected seven regulatory agencies of the federal government to test our hypotheses. Although resource limitations prevented collecting data for the universe of federal regulatory agencies, we did try to select agencies that were representative of this universe in several important respects. Not only were regulatory commissions selected, but departmental agencies involved in regulation are included in the sample. The sample includes both old and new agencies. We chose some agencies which have been established fairly recently, such as OSHA, as well as some which have been in existence long enough to have reached "maturity" or old age, such as the FCC. Agencies whose origins were so far in the past as to preclude any opportunity for collecting data were excluded from our sample.[5] Finally, we chose agencies headed both by multi-member commissions and individual agency chiefs to control for the effects of differing structures and styles of agency leadership. Overall, we feel that the agencies selected as a data base are fairly representative of the various characteristics that are postulated to affect the rate of agency decline. The agencies selected and the year they were established[6] are the Civil Aeronautics Board (CAB), 1938; the Federal Communications Commission (FCC), 1934; the Federal Trade Commission (FTC), 1914; the National Labor Relations Board (NLRB), 1935; the Federal Aviation Administration (FAA), 1958; the Occupational Safety and Health Administration (OSHA), 1970; and the Packers and Stockyards Administration (PSA), 1967.

MEASURES OF THE VARIABLE

Two strategies of measurement are feasible for a longitudinal analysis of the type undertaken here. Given the need to develop several indicators of each variable (age, diffuse support, specific support, capture, and rigidity), either factor analysis or additive index construction can be used to combine the indicators into the variables needed for analysis. Factor analysis has the advantage of reflecting multidimensional concepts as multidimensional variables, but this procedure also weights the indicators by the altheoretical concept of variance maximization. Additive index construction permits the analysis to be sensitive to theory in weighting the factors, but forces the variables into a unidimensional form. At the relatively crude level of theory testing that the data in this chapter permit, we believe the flexibility offered by factor analysis must yield to the advantages of additive index construction. Consequently, each variable, with the exception of age, is constructed from an additive series of indicators each "weighted" according to the specifications of the theory. The construction of each of the variables of the model is discussed briefly below.

Age

Bernstein states explicitly that age is equivalent to chronological age rather than to some multidimensional concept such as maturity.[7] Age is the number of years since the creation of the agency.[8]

Diffuse Political Support

Diffuse support is the encouragement, particularly in terms of resources, that a regulatory agency receives from political actors other than the regulated industry. Since the general public is mainly unconcerned with or unaware of the impact of most regulatory agencies, the major sources of diffuse support are the President and Congress. Since a major resource these institutions have is the power of the purse, we have focused on the allocation of budgetary resources as our indicators of support. The indicators are (a) the growth rate in Congressional appropriations, (b) the success rate in Congressional appropriations (i.e., percentage of budgetary requests that is granted), (c) the growth rate in Presidential budget requests for the agency, (d) the rate of personnel growth in the agency, and (e) the rate of growth in higher civil service and executive positions (GS-14 and above) in the agency. These indicators were standardized and summed to create the measure of diffuse support.

Specific Political Support

Specific support is the political support given to regulatory organizations by the regulated interests. One arena in which specific support for regulatory agencies is visible on an annual basis is in testimony before Congressional appropriations subcommittees.[9] Thus, the two indicators of specific support used are the number of interest groups testifying with respect to the regulatory agency and the ratio of supportive to negative testimony based on a content analysis of subcommittee prints. These indicators were standardized and summed to form the measure of specific support.

Capture

Capture is the displacement of the agency's public interest goals by those of private interests. The most desirable measure of capture would be a content analysis of agency decisions to determine the impact of these decisions on the public and the regulated. Sabatier (1975) takes essentially this approach in his admirable analysis of the concept, "agency capture." His study, however, dealt empirically with only one agency over a relatively brief period of time. For our multiagency study we have selected another approach to the problem of measuring agency capture. We have examined the crossover of personnel between the regulated interest and the regulatory agencies, and approach which has substantial grounding in previous literature (see Graham and Kramer, 1976; Hadwiger, 1976; Herring, 1936; Stigler, 1975). The two specific indicators of capture used in this study are the percentage of agency executives recruited from the regulated industry and the percentage of agency executives who are employed in the regulated sector after their term of public service. Again, our procedure was to standardize and sum these indicators to create the measure.

Rigidity

The concept of rigidity concerns the policy-making performance of the agency. Rigidity implies that the agency becomes slow, is unresponsive to external demands, and has a lowered quantity and quality of policy outputs. Our indicators attempt to tap the inability of an agency to respond to new environmental demands. However, some suggestive output measures are also included. Our measures for this variable include the percentage of backlogged cases, a ratio of agency efficiency (the ratio of cases disposed per year to total manpower in the agency), the rate of turnover among agency executives,[10] the average age of agency executives,[11] the percentage of agency executives with legal training,[12] and the percentage of agency executives with prior expertise in the regulatory field. Rigidity is assumed to be associated with the growth of backlogs, executive turnover, increasing age of executives, legal training, and prior regulatory experience. Efficiency was given a negative weighting and together these indicators formed our standardized measure of agency rigidity.

THE NATURE OF THE DATA

The data used in this chapter are derived from four main sources: the annual reports of the respective agencies, the *Budget of the United States Government* for the years concerned, annual issues of the *Government Organization Manual,* and prints of the annual budgetary hearings before the relevant subcommittees of the House Appropriations Committee. Standard biographical sources such as *Who's Who in America* were also consulted. One data point was collected for each year of each agency. In some cases, complete data for all the years of an agency's existence could not be obtained, either because the documents were not issued or were not available. A major problem arising in the use of workload data was a tendency for agencies to change the format and frequently the contents of their annual reports, our primary source.[13] To a lesser extent, a similar problem existed in the use of budget data. An attempt was made for all agencies to find indicators for a long enough period to establish some pattern. In attempting to conform to this criterion, some available data had to be excluded from our analysis. Enough data was obtained, however, to produce indicators for almost all of the variables for all the agencies surveyed.[14]

DATA ANALYSIS AND INTERPRETATION

After developing the five composite variables to be used in the synthetic model, a multiple regression analysis was run to assess quantitatively the impact of the variables upon one another with respect to theoretical predictions. At this stage of building the model our chief concern was to determine whether the predicted positive or negative direction of the relationships between each set of variables held empirically. We were, of course, also concerned with the strength of the association between the sets of variables as indicated by the size of the path coefficients derived from the regression equations. The predicted relationships are indicated in Figure 1 by plus and minus signs along the causal pathways. For example, the predicted relationship between agency age and diffuse support is negative, implying, according to the life cycle theory, that diffuse support should decline as the agency gets older.

The path coefficients of the model for all seven agencies aggregated together are presented in Figure 2. The most arresting feature of this model is that only one of the relationships shown, the positive relationship between age and specific support, $p=.21$, is in the direction predicted by the theoretical model. All the other predicted relationships are reversed. However, the associations between age and diffuse support, $p=.07$, and between specific support and capture, $p=.05$, are so weak that one can argue that these variables are unrelated. The absence of any strong relationship between specific support and capture is revealing given Bernstein's strong emphasis on this association. Specific support is apparently not so closely related to the phenomenon of agency capture as would be expected on the basis of the model. The path coefficients connecting diffuse support with capture, $p=.34$, and capture with rigidity, $p=.28$, are fairly high, casting even greater doubt on the predictions of the theory. Indeed, based on the empirical

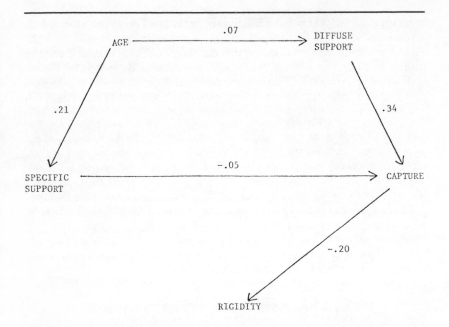

Figure 2: PATH COEFFICIENTS DERIVED FROM DATA FOR ALL AGENCIES

values of the path coefficients, one could easily conclude that increasing diffuse support is associated with agency capture. Although this relationship is counter to theoretical expectations, it makes some substantive sense if we consider the trend toward across-the-board increases in all agency appropriations. Almost all these agencies have received budgetary increases every year without much consideration of their actual performance. This budgetary largesse permits the agencies to grow, and in growing to increase their hiring from the regulated industries as well as to provide a larger pool of ex-officials to move into the regulated industry at the end of their public service careers. This pattern would be reflected as a positive relationship between diffuse support and capture.

The negative rather than the expected positive relationship between capture and rigidity may be an indicator of the increased knowledge of the industry and of high management skills that experienced "industry men" bring to their regulatory service. Thus, agencies, even though they may be undergoing a process of capture, may also remain fairly efficient, especially if they are dealing with highly routinized work patterns suitable for the promulgation of long-term standard operating procedures. In short, contrary to Bernstein's position, captured agencies may not necessarily be rigid ones given an environment that does not demand excessive change.

These findings provide some justification for rethinking some of the relationships extracted from Bernstein and Downs. Before drawing final conclusions, however, the empirical relationships for each individual agency must be examined for two reasons. First, the aggregation of individual agency data into a summary model has the effect of diluting the variation in the variables and, thus, obscuring what might be strong relationships within individual agencies. The second, more substantive, reason is that our theory does not assume a uniform process of aging across the separate agencies. Neither Bernstein nor Downs asserts that agencies proceed through the life cycle at a uniform pace. If individual agencies age at different rates, then combining all agencies into a single model will not provide accurate estimates of the impact of aging.

Table 2 depicts in tabular form the path coefficients for each of the individual agencies for which enough data was available to calculate the regression equations. Examining this table reveals that only in the relationship between age and specific support does the predicted direction hold true for all of the agencies. Specific support does increase with age in each of the four cases, although we note that the strength of that positive relationship varies rather widely, from $p=.02$ to $p=.32$. This finding supports the theory's prediction that agencies seek to increase specific group support. Contrary to theoretical expectations, however, is the finding that agency capture is not an inevitable consequence of the increase in specific support for an agency. Only in the data from the FTC does the predicted relationship hold with any degree of strength. Even this must be regarded as an anomalous finding, since the FTC has a more widely dispersed and varied clientele than any other of the agencies represented here.

Table 2. PATH COEFFICIENTS OF INDIVIDUAL AGENCY MODELS

Predictor Variables		Agency			Dependent Variables
	CAB	FCC	FTC	NLRB	
Age	.15	−.24	.44	−.31	Diffuse Support
Age	.10	.02	.21	.32	Specific Support
Diffuse Support	−.31	−.22	.24	.30	Capture
Specific Support	−.24	−.06	.25	.01	Capture
Capture	−.23	.33	.03	−.40	Rigidity

The relationship between diffuse support and capture for the individual agencies is consistently stronger than the relationship between specific support and capture. Since specific support and diffuse support are essentially independent (see Table 3), the phenomenon of agency capture as we have conceptualized it appears to depend more on an agency's status with the President and Congress than it does on its association with the regulated interest. Rourke (1969) contends that bureaucratic power stems from such sources as agency leadership, agency expertise, and agency vitality, in addition to clientele support. The effect of these

Table 3. PATH COEFFICIENTS FOR IMPLIED RELATIONSHIPS[a]

Predictor Variables			Agency			Dependent Variables
	All Agencies	CAB	FCC	FTC	NLRB	
Specific Support	−.04	−.03	.05	−.02	.05	Diffuse Support
Diffuse Support	−.15	−.13	−.17	−.02	.03	Rigidity
Specific Support	−.04	.08	−.17	−.18	.05	Rigidity

[a]Implied relationships are those represented by the broken lines in Figure 1.

additional variables, not clearly expressed in the Bernstein and Downs model, might account for the less-than-expected impact of specific political support on agency capture. Diffuse support might arise from the effects of leadership, expertise, and vitality as they are perceived by the President and Congress over and above the impact of specific clientele support. If this is the case, clearly a more elaborate model is in order to capture the effects of these elements. Such a model would deemphasize the role of specific support except as it is mediated through its impact on the President and Congress.

Table 2 also indicates that in the individual agencies age has somewhat more of an impact on both specific and diffuse support than it does in the aggregated model. The largest coefficient among the agencies with respect to these variables is p=.44 between age and diffuse support in the FTC. This relationship may spring from the broadening of functions on the part of the FTC over the years since its establishment, as well as from the more aggressive stance taken by the agency in the late 1960s and early 1970s. The diverse involvements of the FTC and its recent image as a protector of the consumer may have led to a higher visibility and regard for the agency with both the President and Congress. In this sense, these figures seem to support Bernstein to some extent, who argues that the routinization of function which comes with age will reduce the interest and support the agency receives from all but a narrow clientele. This syndrome can be avoided, as Downs argues, if the agency can periodically revitalize itself and find new functions, which seems historically to have been the case with the FTC much more so that with either the NLRB or the FCC, although recent changes within the FCC may point to a revitalization in the latter agency.[15]

We observe a similar ambivalence with regard to the relationship between capture and rigidity in the individual agencies. No clear-cut pattern seems to emerge here, but the relatively strong negative path coefficients in the CAB and in the NLRB as well as the very weak positive coefficient in the FTC makes us unwilling to accept completely the equation of capture and rigidity which is implicit in Bernstein. In the two agencies where the capture-rigidity relationship is reversed, particular circumstances offer some explanation. The NLRB was placed in an environment with built-in competition between management and labor to prevent the agency from becoming a handmaiden to either of these interests. The CAB was developed to serve a managerial function for the airline industries and, to that extent, was "born captured," a nuance not reflected in the non-output-oriented data employed in this chapter. The FCC, with a strong relationship in the expected direction, is probably closer to the situation Bernstein had in mind when developing his life cycle model, an agency that has beocme increasingly attentive to and dominated by the regulated industry over a long period of time.

The variation in the relationships among these variables across the several agencies emphasizes the importance of the unique developmental history and environmental circumstances associated with each regulatory agency. Differences in such factors as, for example, clientele structure and the task environment of the agencies undoubtedly influence the complex chain of causation which connects aging to agency capture and rigidity. Airline route and fare regulation by the CAB, for example, is a different kind of activity, involving a variety of different skills and perspectives, than is the management of union elections by the NLRB. Aggregate analysis has obvious limits when dealing with the complexities of economic regulation. A revised version of the life cycle model, therefore, must be able to distinguish the different circumstances of regulatory agency creation. Some agencies such as the CAB, for instance, are created to serve expressly as industry "managers," consequently, they will not necessarily face initial industry hostility and opposition. The industry may even request such regulation. Such a regulated industry may ultimately develop s. If resource provision does not keep pace with an expanding agindustry has experienced a period of regulation. The implication is clear: the life cycle model should not be construed as a predictor for the behavior of all regulatory agencies as they grapple with the complexities of their tasks.

We stated earlier that some implicit relationships that are not discussed by Bernstein and Downs can be derived from our model. Our examination of these relationshps is shown in Table 3. Overall, the "strongest" relationships in the predicted direction are those reflecting the impact of diffuse support on rigidity. In general, as diffuse support declines, agency rigidity raises, a process occurring independently of agency capture. This relationship is logical given the role of the President and Congress in providing agency resources. If resource provision does not keep pace with an expanding agency workload, then at some point, barring dramatic increases in efficiency, the agency will fall behind in processing its workload. This process is probably related more directly to trends in the expansion of the economy and a consequently greater workload imposed on the agency than to whether or not the agency is captured.

Table 3 also shows that the relationship between specific support and rigidity is very weak ($p = -.04$ for the aggregated agency model), indicating again that the impact of specific support on rigidity comes through the resource allocation process rather than in any direct fashion. Our examination of Table 3 shows that the relationships directly enumerated by Bernstein and Downs in their models are relatively more important than the relationships they omitted. Some marginal relationships exist that bear on the theory, but none are strong enough to provide a drastically different interpretation from that given to the major linkages enumerated in Figure 1.

SUMMARY AND CONCLUSIONS

This study has focused on four major hypotheses. The hypotheses and the findings relevant to each one merit recapitulation.

H1. The Greater The Age Of The Agency, The Lower The Diffuse Support For The Agency

This relationship holds in only two cases and strongly only in one, therefore, we conclude that diffuse support is more likely to increase for an agency over time than to decline. Our data do not let us completely separate substantive support in Congress from the overall secular growth of the governmental budget with respect to the regulatory agencies, but our feeling is that specific clientele support (see below) by the regulated industry is translated into more diffuse Congressional and Presidential support through the characteristic pluralism of the policy process.

H2. The Greater The Age Of The Agency, The Greater The Specific Support For The Agency.

This is the only finding that unequivocally supports the original theory. It is also in some senses the least surprising. The generation of political support by public organizations is a basic activity that virtually all agencies must undertake in order to survive in a political climate ideologically hostile to government bureaucracy.[16] Of course, for a public organization such specific support is valuable only if it is translatable into diffuse support (i.e., maintenance and growth of funding levels).

H3. The Less The Diffuse Support For The Agency, The Greater The Degree Of Clientele Capture.

The evidence for this proposition is somewhat conflicting, indicating a rather wide variation among agencies with respect to the expected pattern. Agencies, as we have seen, are sometimes captured even when diffuse support does not decline. This finding may again be an artifact of the overall governmental trend toward increased budgets, but it may also reflect an attempt by policy makers to placate cohesive and active clientele groups by supporting the agency that provides regulatory benefits to the clientele. Finally, we should note that Congressional decision makers may in fact be concerned that the potential for agency capture exists in the regulatory arena, but they may be unsure of the appropriate methods for dealing with this problem. Without knowing what the effects of "de-capturing" the agencies might be, maintaining the status quo becomes the safer policy.

H4. The Stronger The Interdependent Relationship (Capture) Between The Agency And The Regulated Interest, The Greater The Rigidity Of The Agency.

Rigidity does not seem to follow necessarily from captivity, and, indeed, captivity may have some effects in lessening rigidity. Rigidity as we have employed it refers to work and personnel movement within an agency. Had we measured rigidity more in the direction of the effects of the policy outputs of the agency, this relationship might have been somewhat different. In any event, we do not necessarily expect rigidity to follow from agency captivity. Rigidity, it appears, may grow within an agency regardless of the status of its relationship with its clientele.

We have not exhausted all possible empirical tests of the synthetic model developed here. Clearly, the indicators need to be refined. One major shortcoming is the absence of good indicators of the policy impacts of an agency's decisions over time. Such indicators would permit more refined measures of both capture and rigidity. Within the limitations imposed by our data, however, our analysis demonstrated the need to reconsider our usually unqualified acceptance of the life cycle model of regulatory agency behavior. Regulatory agency patterns of behavior are more flexible, varied, and complex than Bernstein suggested. As a metaphor, the life cycle model remains a useful conceptual and pedagogical device. As a predictor of actual historical agency behavior, however, it falls somewhat short. The public policy debate over institutional responsiveness in the regulatory arena should be sensitive to the nuances of the varying contexts of regulation lest the "obvious" solution of "deregulation" turn out to create more problems than it solves.

NOTES

1. In his review of the status of contemporary attempts at regulatory reform, Wellborn (1977) identifies three general orientations toward regulatory questions. He designates these as the traditionalist, the restrictivist, and the populist. Our catalog of orientations toward regulation is stated somewhat differently, but covers essentially the same concerns.

2. But see McGraw (1975) for an extensive discussion of the concept of regulatory capture. Sabatier (1975) also discusses this concept and develops an empirical test for it. His approach is different from our approach here and in our earlier paper (Meier and Plumlee, 1978) on this same subject. Sabatier pursues an in-depth case study of one agency while we use aggregate analysis of data derived from the lifespan of several agencies.

3. Bernstein does not specifically use the term "rigidity." We have taken this term from Downs and applied it to the similar organizational phenomena described by Bernstein as being part of the overall syndrome of "capture."

4. This hypothesis has evoked some controversy. A fairly strong argument can be made that the relationship between these two sets of variables should be positive. "It's

entirely reasonable to expect an agency with strong support from regulated groups to have increasing appropriations over time—particularly if it is a managerial agency in an increasingly complicated field" (Sabatier, private communication, 1977). Rourke (1969) points out that seeking support from the public at large and from other attentive publics is not mutually exclusive. However, our argument in this chapter is that the predicted effects we identify follow the stated or implied relationships in the theories we are examining. Bernstein particularly implies that a decline in diffuse support sets in for an agency about the time that specific (interest group) support for the agency begins to increase. In that case, the relationship would be negative, as we have shown. In any event, the empirical results based on the indicators used in this chapter show that these variables are essentially independent (see Table 3).

5. The Interstate Commerce Commission and the Food and Drug Administration were two agencies which fell into this category.

6. The date of founding an agency is not always easy to ascertain. Many regulatory agencies, such as the FCC and the FAA, had predecessor agencies and staffed themselves from these previously existing organizations. For simplicity, we collected our data from the year the agency as it is presently designated was created. For an opposite approach (for a somewhat different purpose), see Kaufman's (1976) study of an organizational mortality.

7. Ripley and Franklin (1975) have developed a much more cmplex concept, which they call agency maturity, involving four dimensions: age, size, complexity, and experience. Future research into organizational life cycles would benefit from the use of this or a similar complex notion of agency age.

8. See note 6 above.

9. The data actually used was derived from a content analysis of testimony before the House Appropiations subcommittees. A more complete exploration of specific support than we have undertaken here would include analysis of testimony before the Senate Appropriations subcommittees and the relevant policy committees in both houses.

10. Downs argues that one manifestation of rigidity is the increase in the rate of departure of agency executive personnel (especially those ambitious types he calls "climbers") as the agency runs into constraints on its initial growth. Those that remain tend to be more conservative in orientation (see note 11 below).

11. As the agency gets older, the average age of its employees should increase. "This tends to increase the influence of conservers in the bureau, for many officials . . . are likely to become conservers as they grow older" (Downs, 1967:20).

12. We included this indicator on the assumption, derived from Mosher (1968), that agency rigidity might be encouraged by the predominance of professional legal norms and an "overjudicialized" approach to regulatory problems, an approach institutionalized within the agencies by a dominant career system excluding entry by any but those having professional legal training and/or backgrounds.

13. The tendency for agencies to change the manner in which they reported their activities, as well as occasional changes in the nature of agency activities, led to another problem. This was the problem of data comparability. Data comparability is especially acute with respect to agency workload data, in that activities cannot always be simply and directly compared across agencies. For instance, the issuance of a cease and desist order by the FTC cannot be meaningfully compared to the processing of a broadcasting application in the FCC in terms of the content of these activities. Some kinds of activity are routine while others are nonroutine, which is not always clear to the outsider. Cross-agency comparisons of workload data must therefore be considered with some skepticism. Other indicators, such as those dealing with agency elites, agency budgets, and perhaps agency political support do seem to be more comparable and can be treated accordingly.

14. Data on all indicators was obtained for all agencies with the exception of backlog data for the FAA and OSHA and of backlog and efficiency data for the PSA.

15. See Wellborn (1977) for this and some other examples of recent changes in the regulatory atmosphere among federal agencies.

16. An interesting theoretical development of this point can be found in Salamon and Wamsley (1976).

REFERENCES

BERNSTEIN, M. H. (1955). Regulating business by independent commission. Princeton: Princeton University Press.

CARY, W.L. (1967). Politics and regulatory agencies. New York: McGraw-Hill.

DOWNS, A. (1967). Inside bureaucracy. Boston: Little, Brown.

GRAHAM, J. M., and KRAMER, V. H. (1976). U.S. Congress. Senate. Committee on Commerce. Appointments to the regulatory agencies: The Federal Communications Commission and the Federal Trade Commission (1949-1974). Committee Print. Washington, D.C.: U.S. Government Printing Office.

GRUCHY, A. G. (1974). "Government intervention and the social control of business: The neoinstitutionalist position." Journal of Economic Issues, 8 (June):235-249.

HADWIGER, D. F. (1976). "The old, the new, and the emerging United States Department of Agriculture." Public Administration Review, 36 (March/April):155-165.

HALL, H.M., Jr. (1971). "Responsibility of President and Congress for regulatory policy development." Law and Contemporary Problems, 26 (Spring):261-282.

HARBER, J. W. (1969). "Competition and the regulatory process." Quarterly Review of Economics and Business, 9 (Autumn):57-64.

HERMAN, W. R. (1976). "Deregulation: Now or never! (or maybe someday?)." Public Administration Review, 36 (March/April):223-228.

HERRING, E. P. (1936). Federal commissioners. Cambridge: Harvard University Press.

HOLTON, R. H. (1969). "Business and government." Daedalus, 98 (Winter):41-59.

KATZ, D., and KAHN, R. S. (1970). "Open systems theory." Pp. 127-146 in O. Grusky and G. A. Miller (eds.), The sociology of organizations. New York: Free Press.

KAUFMAN, H. (1976). Are government organizations immortal? Washington, D.C.: Brookings Institution.

LEONE, R. C. (1972). "Public interest advocacy and the regulatory process." Annals of the American Academy, 400 (March):46-58.

LONG, N. E. (1962). The polity. Chicago: Rand McNally.

McGRAW, T. K. (1975). "Regulation in America: A review article." Business History Review, 49 (Summer): 159-183.

MEIER, K.J., and PLUMLEE, J.P. (1978). "Regulatory administration and organizational rigidity." Western Political Quarterly, 31 (March): 80-95.

MOORE, J. E. (1972). "Recycling the regulatory agencies." Public Administration Review, 32 (July/August):291-297.

MOSHER, F. C. (1968). Democracy and the public service. New York and London: Oxford University Press.

NADEL, M. V. (1975). "The hidden dimensions of public policy: Private governments and the public-making process." Journal of Politics, 38 (February): 2-34.

NISKANEN, W. A., Jr. (1971). Bureaucracy and representative government. Chicago and New York: Aldine-Atherton.

NOLL, R. G. (1971). Reforming regulation: An evaluation of the Ash Council proposals. Washington, D.C.: Brookings Institution.
RIPLEY, R. B. (1975). "Policy-making: A conceptual scheme." Pp. 1-20 in R. B. Ripley and G. A. Franklin (eds.), Policy-making in the federal executive branch. New York: Free Press.
_____ and FRANKLIN, G. A. (1975). Policy-making in the federal executive branch. New York: Free Press.
ROURKE, F. E. (1969). Bureaucracy, politics, and public policy. Boston: Little, Brown.
SABATIER, P. (1975). "Social movements and regulatory agencies. Toward a more adequate—and less pessimistic—theory of 'clientele capture.'" Policy Sciences, 6:301-342.
SALAMON, L. B., and WAMSLEY, G. L. (1976). "The federal bureaucracy: Responsive to Whom?" Pp. 151-188 in L. N. Rieselbach (ed.), The responsiveness of American institutions. Bloomington, Ind.: Indiana University Press.
SIMMONS, R. H., and DVORIN, E. P. (1977). Public administration: Values, policy, and change. Port Washington, N.Y.: Alfred.
STIGLER, G. J. (1975). The citizen and the state: Essays on regulation. Chicago and London: University of Chicago Press.
U.S. Comptroller General (1977). Government regulatory activity: Justifications, processes, impacts, and alternatives. Washington, D.C.: General Accounting Office, June.
WARWICK, D. P. (1975). A theory of public bureaucracy: Policits, personality, and organization in the State Department. Cambridge: Harvard University Press.
WEIDENBAUM, M. L. (1975). "The case for economizing on government control." Journal of Economic Issues, 9 (June):205-281.
WELLBORN, D. M. (1977). "Taking stock of regulatory reform." Paper presented at the 1977 annual meeting of the American Political Science Association, Washington, D.C., September.
ZEIGLER, L. H., and PEAK, G. W. (1972). Interest groups in American society. 2d ed. Englewood Cliffs, N.J.: Prentice-Hall.

PART V
UTILIZATION OF
POLICY EVALUATION

10

THE FEDERAL DECISION
TO FUND LOCAL PROGRAMS:
Utilizing Evaluation Research

RITA MAE KELLY

Rutgers, The State University of New Jersey

BRUCE FRANKEL

Rutgers, The State University of New Jersey

UTILIZING EVALUATION RESEARCH IN FEDERAL FUNDING DECISIONS

In the 1960s the stress upon the use of independent, "hard-nosed" evaluation of public programs led to the hope that economic rationality and planning, programming, and budgetary systems would gain parity with "politics" in federal program decision-making. By 1970 this optimism declined; many observers concluded that the gap between evaluation data, economic rationality, and the decisions of federal bureaucrats was unbridgeable (Weiss, 1972; Weiss and Rein, 1970; Williams and Evans, 1969). The purpose of this chapter is to use path analysis techniques to assess the direct and indirect effects that evaluation research data produced by a third-party independent evaluator (ABT Associates,

AUTHOR'S NOTE: *This is a revised version of a paper presented to the American Political Science Association at its annual meeting in Washington, D.C., September 4, 1977.*

Inc.) had on the funding decisions made by federal policy makers in the OEO (now CSA) Office of Economic Development about Community Development Corporations—the specific programs used to attain the OEO program objectives. Our basic thesis is that evaluation research data on past performance does have an impact on funding decisions, but that the impact is indirect and of lesser importance than the local programs' organizational and ideological readiness to achieve the desired federal objectives in the future.

THE NORMATIVE VIEW OF THE APPROPRIATE ROLE OF PROGRAM EVALUATION IN AGENCY DECISION-MAKING

A literature has evolved on the appropriate role of quantitive evaluation in a decision-making process. The normative theory holds that evaluation of policy alternatives and of implemented programs serves to make decisions more rational. Planner Britton Harris (1965), economists Nathaniel Lichfield and Julius Margolis (1963), and systems analyst Russel Ackoff (1963) agree that evaluation can demonstrate the best policy alternative given prescribed policy goals. This knowledge is indispensable to the discovery of the logical relationship between means and ends, and is essential to the claim that the choice over means has led to a rational decision.

Harris asserts that the evaluation of programs serves to rejuvenate the planning process. The knowledge of program failure suggests to the policy analyst that the problem and its alternative policy solutions ought to be reformulated. Facts are to confront the decision maker with his/her mistakes and result in budgetary reallocations and program re-design; accordingly, successful programs are rewarded with increased budgets and partial program failures are rehabilitated through a rearrangement of program operations and personnel.

Yet the literature leaves unresolved a normative dilemma. Should funding decisions be based on an assessment of where they are needed or, rather, where they will yield the greatest expected results? Clearly, these are conflicting criteria, because highly successful programs diminish the need for future funds; alternatively, programs which have proven to be unproductive place substantial demands on public funds based on the extent of an unremedied problem. We attempt no resolution of this normative issue, only to test the extent to which evaluation research has been utilized in decision-making. The subject of our chapter is empirical not normative.

ACTUAL USE OF EVALUATION RESEARCH IN DECISION-MAKING

As already indicated, one of the chief goals of evaluation research is "to supply information that allows policy-makers, planners, and professionals to make rational decisions about social-development and human-resource programs and thus to maximize the expenditure of economic and human resources" (Bernstein and Freeman, 1975:1). From this perspective evaluation research is essentially a management tool, "an input into making decisions about support of competing programs" (1975:4), rather than primarily a means of assessing the broader societal value of the program. The value of evaluation research thus becomes viewed primarily in connection with the extent to which its results are utilized in decision-making. (As is pointed out elsewhere this need not be the only use of evaluation research, however. See Kelly, 1977.)

What does the record reveal about the use of evaluation research in decision-making? Below are quotations from some recent students of this question.

UNDERUTILIZATION

Much of our discussion has assumed that there are two stock characters (with a few supporting players) in our cast—an evaluator who produces research results of some degree of cogency and an agency policy maker who proceeds to ignore them. [Weiss, 1972:121.]

Currently the lack of utilization, particularly the failure of evaluation to significantly effect public policy, is causing the greatest concern. [Sullivan, 1976:27.]

Despite the potential use of evaluation, the actual impact remains meager at best. The possibilities of evaluation research are appreciated. But, as already noted, there have been few cases of actual effective utilization of evaluation research for expected purposes. [Bernstein and Freeman, 1975:5.]

Since 1968, interest has grown in the development of methods to determine the effectiveness of crime control programs. . . . The tool of evaluation has yet, however, to play a major role in the management of criminal justice programs. [Gardiner, 1975:177.]

The evaluation of services integration projects, not surprisingly, has proved to be exceedingly difficult. . . . Because of this, and despite the attention paid to the evaluation of services initiatives, we do not yet have the persuasive data and analyses to fully support administrators at the state and local level in their services integration efforts. Nonetheless, there are a number of important evaluations that, while not definitive, have yielded useful information about the nature and difficulties of services integration. [Morrill, 1976:53.]

APPROPRIATE LEVEL OF UTILIZATION

Evaluation results do achieve appropriate utilization. Richardson (1972) offers one example. Evaluation of the National Defense Education Act loans to students who undertake a career in teaching suggested that this had not been a significant incentive. It was possible to conclude, with the concurrence of the Congress, that the feature should be eliminated, and it was. Lynn (1972) gives further illustrations of HEW utilization of health care services to an array of educational assistance programs. Effective utilization of evaluation among federal agencies was reported by Riecker (1974) when those agencies participated in the evaluation. Beigel (1974) illustrates how local program self-evaluations can have meaningful impact on policies and practices. Both Weiss (1972) and Ciarlo (1974) stress that the evidence of effective utilization of evaluation becomes much clearer if one maintains observation over a sufficiently extended period. [Davis and Salasin, 1975:72.]

OVERUTILIZATION

Mushkin (1973) has called attention to numerous instances of well-known evaluations of major programs which were methodologically or conceptually unsound. In
some instances decisions to terminate or reduce programs have been justified on the
basis of those evaluations. It is a clear lesson rather than just greater use. [Davis and
Salasin, 1975:622.]

LEVEL OF KNOWLEDGE

As the quoted studies indicate there is no universal agreement that evaluation
research has become widely or wisely used in decision-making. In this regard
evaluation research seems to fare similarly to social science research in general.
As Caplan, Program Director, Center for Research on Utilization of Scientific
Knowledge, University of Michigan, has noted (1976:187): "Furthermore,
social science utilization in policy-making is complex and not a subject on which *a
priori* assumptions can be expected to shed much light. In consequence, we know
very little about what information gets used, by whom, for what purposes and with
what, if any, impact."

In his own study of 204 policy makers (either political appointees immediately
below the cabinet rank or high-level civil servants during October 1973 to March
1974), Caplan found that in 20% of those instances where social science
knowledge was used it came from program evaluation research. Only general
social statistics from surveys, censuses, and so on ranked higher—32% (1976:
188). Yet again there is no clear indication from Caplan of the precise use made of
the social science data. Elsewhere Caplan and Barton (1976) report that some
social science data having ostensibly high probability of use by policy makers,
such as *Social Indicators 1973,* were used more for speech-writing purposes than
for policy-making.

USE IN FUNDING DECISIONS

In searching the literature for how evaluation research has been or is being used
by decision makers as a guide to funding decisions—the focus of our study—we
find both less research and less information. Lehne and Fisk concluded that
(1974:133) "proposed changes in funding appear to be unrelated to the impact of
policy analysis." They suggest that funding decisions by nature require a political
strategy that accommodates diverse interests, groups, and bureaus, not an
analytical strategy based on long-range planning and sophisticated evaluation of
the impact of each option.

Winnie (1972), in the findings of a study conducted in the fall of 1971 under the
auspices of the International City Management Association and the Urban
Institute, reported, however, that of the slightly more than 350 cities greater than
50,000 and counties of more than 100,000 in population that responded about
55% reported using some type of effectiveness measurements in the preparation
of their local government budget. Obviously, such effectiveness measures need

not have been derived from evaluation research per se nor does use in budget preparation necessarily indicate that the effectiveness data were used as a guide during specific funding decisions.

The Comprehensive Employment Training Act (CETA) program provides us with at least one concrete example of structural limitations to using evaluation research performance data in formulating specific funding decisions. After demonstrating the operational criteria of a performance rating system for federal job training programs, Menzi (1975) concluded that its utility in funding decisions was severely limited by the formula nature of CETA block grants. At best evaluation research could be employed to re-design training programs. Need, as clearly reflected in the block grant formula, was the paramount funding criterion, not past program performance.

AN ANALYTICAL MODEL FOR ASSESSING UTILIZATION OF EVALUATION RESEARCH

To investigate possible direct and indirect effects of evaluation research data on funding decisions, it is necessary to have a clear conceptual picture first, of the administrative arrangements within which the evaluation research effort and results develop and flow, and, second, of the probable relationship of various variables likely to influence decision-making. A map of the administrative arrangement is depicted in Figure 1. As can be seen, the Director of the Office of Economic Development, the person having the most individual influence on funding decisions, is the most removed from the evaluation research effort in the Office. The figure suggests that the likelihood of evaluation data having a strong direct effect on funding decisions is small. The evaluation research data on the effectiveness of the CDCs is not the only input into the management decision-making process. Political pressures, funding considerations based upon employment and regional needs, staff capability and morale, and other influences compete with such information. Moreover, the path of influence of the evaluation data results goes to the director of the OED very indirectly. The evaluation reports go first to the monitors in the Planning, Development, and Evaluation Division of the OED. Once approved by these monitors, the evaluation reports are given to the OED operation analysts, who are officially the organizational equals of the monitors in the PDE Division.

The operation analysts reach conclusions about each CDC's success not only on the basis of the evaluation data, but also via similar types of external and internal information, pressures and considerations affecting the Director's final funding decisions. Once the monitors' own general conclusion of each CDC's success to date and likelihood of successful future performance is made, the Director is informed; thus, he receives a more comprehensive view of each CDC than the evaluation reports alone could provide. The Director also, of course, has access to the evaluation reports and can be directly and independently influenced by them.

The administrative structure relating evaluation results and funding decision makers, and considerations of the inherent difference between past performance

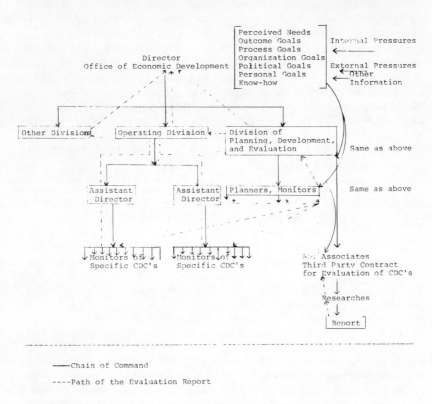

SOURCE: Portions of this figure are adapted from a comparable figure in Bigelow and Ciarlo, 1976: 374.

Figure 1: MANAGEMENT STRUCTURE AND THE EVALUATION FEEDBACK PROCESS.

and estimates about future performance lead to the development of the causal model depicted in Figure 2. It posits that evaluation research data have an independent impact upon decision-making and that they may also have an indirect effect mediated by three intervening variables: (X_5) OEO Monitor's General Perceptions of Each CDC's Past Impact on the Target Area; (X_4) OEO Monitors' Perception of Each CDC's Goal Orientation; and (X_2) OEO Monitors' Perception of Each CDC's Overall Success. It also depicts the option that considerations of organizational and ideological readiness to perform in the future will have an equal or greater direct and/or indirect impact upon the funding decision. Consideration of organizational and ideological readiness for future performance is treated as being independent and uninfluenced by evaluation findings on past performance.

In addition to attempting to discern the indirect ways in which evaluation data affect funding decisions, the research reported here examined the following

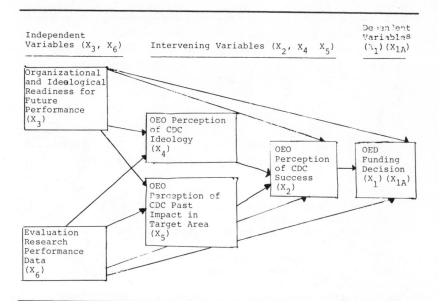

Figure 2: MODEL OF HOW EVALUATION DATA INFLUENCES FUNDING DE-
CISIONS

hypotheses about the funding decisions for the local community development
programs we reviewed:

Hypothesis 1. The OEO perception of the local program's overall success is the best
individual predictor of funding decisions made on CDCs.

Hypothesis 2. The organizational and ideological readiness of the CDC for future
performance is the next most important determinant of the funding decision.

Hypothesis 3. CDCs with a strong community development orientation will have a
higher funding level than those with a capitalist or more narrow economic
orientation.

Hypothesis 4. The OEO perception of both the CDC ideological orientation and its
past performance is more important to the funding decision than direct empirical
measures of ideology and success.

Hypothesis 5. The indirect impact of evaluation research on the decision to fund each
CDC is not as great as the path commencing with a measure of the organizational
and ideological readiness of the CDC to act.

RESEARCH DESIGN AND METHODS

We approach the problem of assessing the effect of evaluation research data on
funding decisions by developing a path network of direct and indirect causal
relationships between the funding decision (our dependent variable) and the
selected independent and intervening variables depicted in Figure 2. The

principles of path analysis are applicable to such a complex causal structure. A multistage, multivariate path model will allow us to explicate indirect as well as direct pathways through which evaluation research data can influence funding decisions. The multiple regression technique upon which path analysis is based will allow us to test specific hypotheses about the relative explanatory importance of the various variables in our causal model.

ASSUMPTIONS UNDERLYING THE ANALYSES

In using path analysis and restricting ourselves to the use of one indicator for each of our variables, we necessarily make the following assumptions:

(a) The impact of evaluation research on funding decisions is isomorphic with evaluation data scaling the success of each project on the key indicator (see below for its delineation). Specifically, we assumed that the indicator of each individual project's success developed by the evaluators is linearly related to the funding the project received.

(b) Funding decisions are assumed to be the dependent variable and evaluation results are assumed to be not dependent on any other decision variables represented in the system.

(c) Relationships between the variables in the system are assumed to be additive as well as linear.

(d) Other causes of each variable in the system are assumed to be uncorrelated with the other variables in the system.

(e) Uni-directional causation is assumed for all variables depicted.

PROGRAMS STUDIED

The programs selected for study are 19 Community Development Corporations (CDCs) funded initially under the Office of Economic Opportunity (OEO) and since 1974 under the Community Services Administration. The federally funded CDCs are particularly useful for analyzing the questions posed in this study because the ideological commitment to community economic development posited by the federal monitors within OEO and CSA clearly differs from the ideological stress of the Office of Minority Business Enterprise program of the Department of Commerce (see Kelly, 1977:chap. 2) and the ideology of many local businessmen.

The possibility for ideological variation among local programs is great. As Garn (1975:565) has noted, there are at least three ideological stances a CDC can take: (1) it can be an economic and social institution designed to pursue essentially political objectives in neighborhoods; (2) it can be a rather traditional type of economic institution that pursues primarily economic objectives; or (3) it can be an institution which makes trade-offs between economic gains, attaining political clout, and community development. The relative sharpness of these options means that ideological differences between federal and local program decision makers can be more easily operationalized than would be the case for many other federal-local programs. In addition, data on past performance exist (Abt, 1972, 1973), as does data on the federal monitors' perceptions of local

CDC's objectives, general success, past impact in the target area, and oranizational readiness (Kelly, 1977), producing a unique data base for assessing the main features of our model.

To complete the desired analyses for this study on use of evaluation research data in funding decisions, information from the following three different data sources was needed: (1) the data from Abt, third party evaluation of past CDC performance (for details, see Abt, 1972, 1973); (2) data on surveys completed by the senior author for studies of the official leadership of CDCs for the Center for Community Economic Development, a research support firm of the CDCs, which included data on OEO/CSA monitors' perceptions and independent measures of organizational and ideological readiness for future performance (for details, see Kelly, 1977); and (3) the OEO/CSA data on actual level of funding (see CED Newsletter, 1976). While the data source on funding decisions included all CDCs funded between 1971 and 1975 by OEO/CSA, the Abt and Kelly data bases were selective, overlapping only for 19 CDCs.

Abt, concentrating on the earliest funded CDCs, included 30 CDCs in their 1971-1972 data collection effort. Kelly, seeking to include all 35 CDCs still being funded in 1973, gathered data on 26 CDCs in 1973. Thus, the sample frames for selecting CDCs to be studied were different. The extent to which the sample of 19 CDCs used here is representative of all CDCs is not known. It seems to be representative of the modal CDC funded from 1968-1969 to 1976, however, The CDCs lost by using only the CDCs studied by both Abt and Kelly, as our conceptual model requires, are the CDCs most recently funded, many of them serving Spanish-speaking target areas in medium size cities and some of the oldest and most highly funded CDCs, such as the Bedford-Stuyvesant Restoration Corporation in Brooklyn, New York, and the Harlem Commonwealth Council in Manhattan, New York. Hence, the CDCs not included tend to represent those on the extreme in terms of age and size of total funding received from OEO/CSA to date.

The Abt evaluation of CDC performance concerned data up to about mid-1972. These Abt results were made available to OEO officials in late 1972 and early 1973. The Kelly survey of OEO officials recording their perceptions of individual CDCs took place in late summer of 1973. Hence, the OEO officials had available to them the evaluator's assessment of past performance as well as their own unique data frames of reference. All monitors were expected to review the evaluation reports. The decisions regarding the amount to fund a CDC were made at various time points in 1973 and 1974.

The specific CDCs, including the total funds (in thousands of dollars) each had received in biannual Fiscal Year 1974-1975 and the percentage increase in funding between biannual FY 1974-1975 and biannual FY 1972-1973, are as follows:

Table 1. CDC FUNDING

Urban (N=10)	Absolute Funding Received Fy 74-75	% Increase in Funding FY 74-75 FY 72-73
Hough Area Development Corp., Cleveland, Ohio	1500	5.6
United Durham, Inc., N.C.	1300	14.4
North Lawndale EDC, Chicago, Ill.	3000	4.8
People's Involvement Corp./People's Development Corp., Washington, D.C.	0	0.0
Denver CDC, Denver, Colo.	1187	9.5
East Boston CDC, Boston, Mass.	1500	15.0
Circle Venture Capital Fund, Boston, Mass.	160	2.3
East Central Citizens Organization (ECCO), Columbus, Ohio	0	0.0
Greater Memphis Urban Development Corp., Memphis, Tenn.	0	0.0
Mexican-American Unity Council, San Antonio, Tex.	3000	13.6
Rural (N=9)		
Home Education Livelihood Program (HELP), N.M.	1500	14.7
Community Investment and Development, Inc., Ark.	400	3.3
Southeast Alabama CDC	200	40.0
Northeast Oklahoma CDC	0	0.0
Adela DC, Utah	1500	15.1
Seminole Employment and Economic Development, Inc., Fla.	1358	13.6
Impact Seven, Inc., Wisc.	1200	12.0
Midwest Minnesota CDC	2050	23.6
Lummi Indian Tribal Enterprises, Wash.	5873	25.4

DESCRIPTION OF PATH MODEL BY VARIABLES SELECTED

Table 2 identifies the variables selected for analysis.

DEPENDENT VARIABLE: FUNDING DECISION

Two measures of funding were used. The first employed in the path model was the measure of absolute funding received for each CDC in FY 1974-1975 (X_1), the last year for which data was available on the 19 corporations. The second measure (X_{1A}) was the ratio of the dollar amount of the FY 1974-1975/FY 1972-1973 biannual funding multiplied by 100. The reason for averaging biannually is that the CDCs usually were funded on that basis. The range of X_{1A} was from 0, as four CDCs were terminated, to 40%; the average was a 12% increase. The range for actual dollars received in FY 1974-1975 (X_1) was from $0 to $5,873,000 as received by Lummi Indian Tribal Enterprises in Washington State; the average absolute funding received was $1,354,105 with a considerable standard deviation of $1,442,701. The funding data was taken from the March 1976 *Center for Community Economic Development Newsletter* (pp. 10-11).

Rita Mae Kelly and Bruce Frankel

Table 2. LEGEND OF VARIABLES IN PATH MODEL

X_1 = T score: Absolute Level of CDC Funding FY 74-75

X_{1A} = T score: Present Increase in CDC Funding Level between FY 74-75 and FY 72-73

X_2 = T score: OEO perception of CDC success

X_3 = T score: Index of Organizational Readiness

X_4 = T score: OEO perception of CDC ideology

$\{$/T score: (1/Turnover rate of CDC Board of Directors) $]$
$+$/T score: (CDC Board Ideology/STD. Deviation of the Ideology Votes)$]$ ÷ 2

$$\left\{ \begin{array}{l} (PR_{X1} + PR_{X6} + PR_{X7} + PR_{X10} + PR_{X11}) - \\ (PR_{X2} + PR_{X3} + PR_{X4} + PR_{X5} + PR_{X9}) \end{array} \right]$$

	(1st parentheses)	(2nd parentheses)
weighted so that priority rating	1=3	−3
	2=2	−2
	3=1	−1

X_5 = T score: OEO perception of CDC impact on community economic development

X_6 = T score: Evaluation by Abt—2 Factor Judgment

$\{$(T score: dollar value of property acquired by CDC ÷ total amount of funds for the CDC) +
(T score: private sector funds leveraged ÷ SIP dollars) ÷ 2

Because the 19 CDCs came into existence at different times, both X_1 and X_{1A} are useful measures. Both measure a decision to fund subsequent to the submission of Abt's evaluation to OEO. Each adds information revealing a different dimension of the funding decision.

The decision as an absolute level of funding reveals, fundamentally, OEO's budgetary commitment to invest in each CDC; this measure addresses how resources were allocated. Alternatively, the decision as a relative change in funding over a policy-relevant time directly measures the impact on funding of the explanatory variables; it discounts for the phenomenon that CDCs in existence for a longer period of time or serving impact areas of greater need tend to have the most absolute funds.

Shown in the "Results" is a consistent path using either dependent variable. X_1, as a measure of absolute funding, demonstrated the path of greatest explanatory power statistically, but X_{1A} has theoretical utility also.

INDEPENDENT VARIABLES

To explain this funding decision, two principal paths were constructed. One originated with the Abt evaluation (X_6) and was filtered through OEO's perception of two phenomena: the CDC's past impact in the target area (X_5) and the CDC's overall success (X_2). Alternatively, the other path began with a measure of probable future success which did *not* consider Abt's performance data. Here, the independent variable of the actual organizational and ideological readiness of each CDC to operate (X_3) was filtered through two intervening variables: OEO's perception that the CDC would operate consistent with OEO program goals (X_4) and OEO's perception of CDC success (X_2).

As variants of these initially recognized paths are paths leading from the two independent variables to alternate intervening variables. That is, evaluation research (X_6) impacts OEO perception of the CDC ideology (X_4); and, the readiness of the CDC to perform has a bearing on OEO's perception of the CDC's past impact (X_5).

For all paths the logic of the model holds that CDC success should be rewarded; the distribution in the paths holds that the perception of success may be based on different types of information.

EVALUATION RESEARCH PERFORMANCE DATA: ABT EVALUATION OF PAST PERFORMANCE

Although, as Lehne and Fisk suggest, the basic difficulty of finding a link between evaluation research and specific funding decisions might be that funding decisions require a stress on balancing political interest and need rather than a stress on performance optimization, the nature of the research produced is also an important factor (Weiss, 1972:110-128; Davis and Salasin, 1975:623). Rationality in decision-making is related to the use of specific information. Some types of evaluation research, such as what Suchman (1967) calls summative research, usually provide an either-or-choice for high level policy makers. Should or should not a program be funded? If the summative evaluation concludes the program is effective in achieving the stated policy goals, then it seems "rational" to fund, continue, or expand such a program. If the conclusion about impact is negative, then it would be "irrational" to adopt positive funding policies.

When the evaluation research is not summative, but rather formative (that is, when it examines success and impact of a variety of techniques, options, and processes of projects within a larger program to provide feedback on operating and developmental questions), then the likelihood of impact upon specific funding decisions would seem to rise. However, because the recommendations are not of an either-or nature and are not as obvious to outside observers, such impacts of evaluation research are harder to identify.

For evaluation data to be used for funding decisions concerning which of the existing CDCs ought to be continued, stressed, or phased down, the data have to be a relative comparison of the extent of successful goal attainment; that is, to say that CDC A did meet some actual standard which CDC B did not is by itself not too helpful. The OED simply is not going to eliminate a significant minority of its CDCs because the CDCs had not met an absolute standard set by an evaluator or the Planning, Development, and Evaluation Division of the Office. Hence, to be useful the data must enable at least an ordinal ranking of the CDCs on the relative attainment of given goals. In our judgment, the Abt evaluation produced such data only on the relative success of each CDC to stimulate the flow of capital in the target area.

As already stated, this chapter investigates the effect of a $2 million evaluation of CDCs by Abt on funding decisions for these CDCs made by the Office of

Economic Development of the Office of Economic Opportunity (now of the Community Services Administration). As Yin and Yates have noted (1975:246), the Abt evaluation "stands as an acceptable piece of work," but is weak in both design and methodology. The evaluation is useful for our purposes primarily because it did systematically address the three major goals outlined for the CDCs in the authorizing legislation: (1) establishing community control over the CDC, (2) launching an operating demonstration program, and (3) stimulating the flow of capital to the target area. In our assessment of the impact of the Abt evaluation on the OED funding decisions, we will use only the Abt data related to the stimulation and flow of capital. The reasons for this limitation are several. First, such data represent "hard," economic findings producing a comparable measure of the effectiveness of each CDC on one of the most important objectives of the enabling legislation. Second, these data represent the type of relative success measure needed, while the more general discussions on community control and so on do not. This decision to focus on only one of the chief goals logically requires us to admit that whatever conclusions we reach about the impact of the Abt evaluation research on the OED funding decision understate the probable actual impact. In other words, whatever impact we find, direct and indirect, ought to be multiplied by some unknown quantity. We should also stress that the primary objective of the evaluation was not to produce data for OED budgetary allocations. It was more for the purposes of obtaining baseline data for future evaluations, assessing program progress to the date of the evaluation, and to pinpoint program areas needing improvement.

THE EVALUATION VARIABLE, X_6

As Table 2 describes, this independent variable was composed of two performance indicators. One was the proportion of dollar value of property acquired and developed by the CDCs relative to the total amount of funds the CDCs has received through FY 1973. Another was the proportion of private sector funds leveraged in relation to the total SIP (Special Impact Program) dollars in FY 1973. Both are the best quantitative representations of performance in achieving community economic development in the ghettos, particularly for the urban CDCs (see Faux, 1971:32-47).

INDEX OF ORGANIZATIONAL READINESS, X_3

The other independent and alternative origin in our path model was the readiness of the CDCs to operate (X_3). Its inclusion is fundamentally based on our own assessment of its importance in addition to its reference in an established literature. Stein (1973, 1974) contends that the changing of directors was usually traumatic for CDCs and often involved extreme disruption for them. The index of organizational readiness was composed of two factors: (1) the stability of the director, or the reciprocal of the average annual turnover rate for directors, and (2) the consensus among members of the CDC board to set goals congruent with the OEO ideology of community development. This ideology is explained in

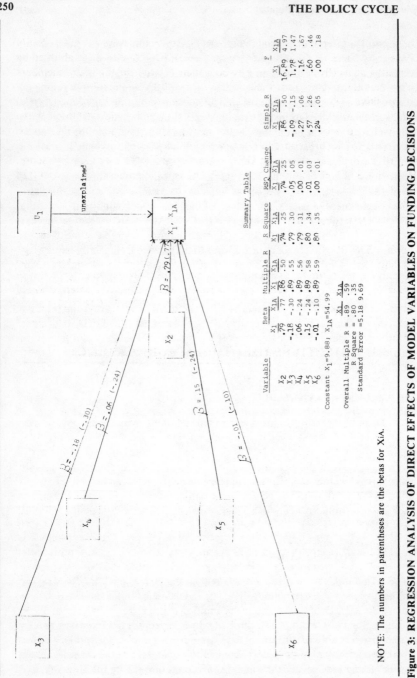

NOTE: The numbers in parentheses are the betas for X₁ₐ.

Figure 3: REGRESSION ANALYSIS OF DIRECT EFFECTS OF MODEL VARIABLES ON FUNDING DECISIONS

describing the intervening variable X_4 below. Both factors were weighted equally in the index. The ideological orientation of each CDC board was established by weighting goals (from $+3$ to -3) by both their priority among board members (absolute value of 1 to 3) and their contributions toward community development (the positive versus negative scores). The consensus among board members in setting goals was measured by the reciprocal of the standard deviation among the 546 weighted scores given by board members in prioritizing CDC goals. According to this procedure, a board with a high level of agreement to act but toward goals inconsistent with OEO's orientation would receive a low score. High scores reflect a consensus among CDC board members to carry out that community development ideology established by OEO, the funding agency.

INTERVENING VARIABLE: OEO PERCEPTION OF CDC IDEOLOGY, X_4

The Kelly fall 1973 survey requested the rankings for the top three priority objectves from both OEO monitors in their perception of each CDC goal orientation, and from the board members themselves. Table 3 presents the eleven objectives presented to both groups. Our path model considered the perception of OEO monitors regarding the ideological orientation of each CDC (X_4) as an intervening variable, and the actual goal orientation of board members is presented as part of independent variable X_3.

Table 3. OBJECTIVES IDENTIFIED FOR THE CDCs

1. Creating jobs;
2. Developing profitable businesses;
3. Reducing unemployment;
4. Providing manpower training and development;
5. Providing opportunities for local individual ownership of businesses and property.
7. Reducing community deterioration (developing land, resources, and property);
8. Reducing community dependance on outsiders;
9. Increasing incomes of those already employed;
10. Reducing number of people leaving the area; and
11. Getting outside institutions to aid in community development.

Of these 11 objectives the following were identified as indicating a community development preference: 1, 6, 7, 8, 10, 11. Votes of the OEO monitors were weighted so that a top priority for a community development goal represented a value of 3 and the top priority for a noncommunity development goal represented a value of -3. Given this scale, the mean was $+.158$ with a standard deviation of 1.463. This suggests a slight orientation of the average CDC, from OEO's perspective, toward community development and highly dissimilar ideologies among the 19 CDCs.

The reason for selecting CDC ideology as perceived by OEO monitors as a key intervening variable in explaining funding decisions is evident from the history and legislative intent of the federal community economic development program. In 1968 Congress rejected the manpower focus developed by the Department of Labor in administering Title I of the Economic Opportunity Act as amended in December 1966. In doing so, Congress transferred authority for a new focus in the enactment of Title VII, enunciating the goals and eligible activities under the Special Impact Program.

In July 1972, Title I-D was superceded by Title VII of the Economic Opportunity Act, which enunciates the goals of the Special Impact Program. Section 711 states that the purpose of the program is to provide assistance to community corporations and other organizations which (1) "are directed to the solution of the critical problems existing in particular communities or neighborhoods"; (2) "are of sufficient size, scope and duration to have an appreciable impact . . . in arresting tendencies toward dependency, chronic unemployment, and community deterioriation"; and (3) "hold forth the prospect of continuing to have such impact after the termination of financial assistance under this title."

The activities which may be funded, according to Title VII, are: (1) "economic and business development programs . . . to start, expand, or locate businesses in or near the areas served so as to provide employment and ownership opportunities for residents"; (2) "community development and housing activities which create new training, employment, and ownership opportunities and which contribute to an improved living environment"; and (3) "manpower training programs for unemployed or low-income persons which support and complement economic, business housing, and community development programs."

Not only does Faux, in his 1971 study of the emerging hope presented by the CDC program, indicate the preference of OEO for community development, but Abt in their 1973 report documents and summarizes the importance of this ideology:

> The aims of the original enabling legislation, however, very clearly recognized that a *specific* focus on unemployment was not appropriate to the task. The Senate Committee on Labor and Public Welfare, in hearings of September 29, 1966 concerning the Economic Opportunity Act Amendments of 1966, (in report #1666 of the 89th Congress, 2nd Session) clearly specified a comprehensive attack in four "areas of unique problems." These were a) unemployment; b) dependency and welfare; c) breakdown of social services; and d) physical deterioration. Four desired benefits were spelled out: 1) improvement in social development; 2) creation of economic, social, and physical community improvement; 3) training and employment of residents; and 4) emphasizing participation of private enterprise.

INTERVENING VARIABLES: OEO PERCEPTION OF CDC OVERALL SUCCESS (X_2) AND IMPACT IN TARGET AREA (X_5)

As part of the 1973 national study of the role of CDC board members in producing CDC organizational success, OEO monitors of each CDC were asked, among other things, to rate on a 20-point scale their assessment of (1) how successful the CDC had been in achieving its goal (X_2), and (2) how great an impact the CDC had had to 1973 on community economic development in its target area (X_5). These assessments were used as indicators of the federal perception of overall local program performance. The OEO perceptions of the success of the CDCs ranged from 03 to 19; the mean was 10. The OEO judgments of the impact of the CDCs on community economic development up to 1973 ranged from 00 to 20; the mean was 8. These two indicators were kept separate in the analyses under the assumption that perception of past performance was only one component of probable future success. The OEO perception of overall success is considered the best indicator of OEO's assessment that the particular CDC is likely to be successful ultimately.

RESULTS

The effect of evaluation research (X_6) and organizational and ideological readiness (X_3) on the decisions to fund each CDC (X_1) is demonstrated through both the direct impact and the indirect impact through path analysis.

DIRECT IMPACTS

To examine the direct effects of each variable in our model on the OED funding decision, a simple multiple regression was performed. In our final path model (see Figure 4), the resulting betas are the path coefficients for the direct paths of each individual variable. To simplify our presentation and to make the path model in Figure 4 easier to understand, the results of our regression analysis of relative direct effects are presented first in Figure 3 with the standard information about regression results presented at the bottom of the figure. The findings indicate that our model was able to explain 80% of the variance in absolute funding and 35% in the change in the funding level between FY 1974-1975 and FY 1972-1973.

The multiple regression assessing the direct effects of each variable while controlling for the others in the model produced support for the hypotheses examined.

The analysis completed on all 19 CDCs revealed that evaluation research data had a negligible direct effect on the OED specific funding decisions for these CDCs. When the impact of the other variables in our model are controlled for, the direct relationship of evaluation research data on the funding decision is the smallest of all paths leading directly to the funding decision (the Pearson r was .24; $p = 0.16$ for absolute funding; $r = .05$ for the change in funding). Factors other than the third party evaluation had significantly greater influence over OEO's funding decision.

Hypothesis 1 was clearly confirmed as the OEO monitors' perception of the local program's overall success was found to be the best individual predictor of the funding decision made on CDCs (beta = .79 for absolute funding and .77 for the change since FY 1972-1973). The CDC's organizational and ideological readiness to perform as desired in the future was also found to be the next most important variable reflecting the funding decision; this confirms our second hypothesis. In contrast to our expectations, however, the impact was negative (beta = − .18 for absolute funding and − .30 for the change in funding).

As this same beta of −.18 indicates, the third hypothesis that the CDCs with a strong community development orientation will have a higher funding level than those with a capitalist or more narrow economic orientation was not supported.

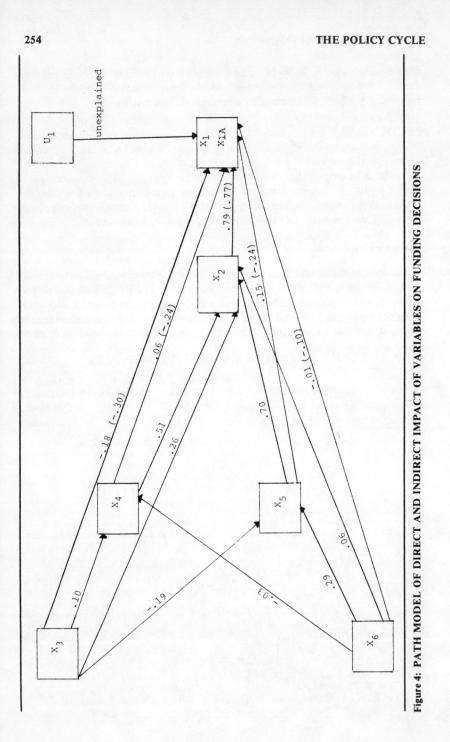

Figure 4: PATH MODEL OF DIRECT AND INDIRECT IMPACT OF VARIABLES ON FUNDING DECISIONS

The negative value of this beta, in fact, suggests the opposite. It appears that a readiness for economic development was more important for funding than an overall comprehensive community development orientation.

Additionally, betas from this same regression show that the OEO perception of the CDC's ideological orientation (X_4) is of considerably less importance to the funding decision than the empirical reality of that ideology (X_3); OEO's general perception of the CDC's past impact on the target area (X_5) is relatively more important than empirical evaluation research data on specific past performance (X_6). This last finding confirms our fourth hypothesis that federal decisions to fund are more firmly grounded on the funding agency's *perception* of expected success of each project than less subjective evidence of the same.

INDIRECT IMPACTS

One of the main objectives of our study was to ascertain the nature, extent, and paths of the indirect effects of evaluation research data on funding decisions. To do this the causal path model in Figure 4 was developed and calculations of the impact of each path upon the funding decision were made. The paths and their respective relative impacts are as follows:

Table 4. PATHS AND THEIR RELATIVE IMPACTS

Path	Absolute Funding	Path Coefficients	Relative Increase in Funding
X_6 — — — → X_1 =	−.01	$X_{1A}=$	−.10
$X_6 \, X_2$ — — — → X_1 =	.05	$X_{1A}=$	.05
$X_6 \, X_5 \, X_2$ — — — → X_1 =	.16	$X_{1A}=$	.16
$X_6 \, X_4 \, X_2$ — — — → X_1 =	−.0	$X_{1A}=$	.01
$X_6 \, X_4$ — — — → X_1 =	.00	$X_{1A}=$	.07
$X_6 \, X_5$ — — — → X_1 =	.04	$X_{1A}=$	−.07
Total Effect =	.23	$X_{1A}=$	.10

The path analysis revealed the indirect impact on OEO funding decisions of the quantitative evaluation of the CDCs performed by Abt (X_6). The best path was $X_6 \, X_5 \, X_2 \rightarrow X_1$ with the evaluation performance data affecting the funding decision most being the means of first influencing the OEO monitors' perception of the CDC's past impact and, secondly, the OEO monitors' overall perception of the CDC's success.

The indirect impact on the OEO funding decision was greater from a path originating with the alternate independent variable of organizational and ideological readiness. The path $X_3 \, X_2 \rightarrow X_1$ produced an impact on funding 31% larger than the best path from X^6 (coefficient =.21; cf. .16). This suggests that the factors of the ideology and the organizational readiness of the CDC may have had a larger impact on OEO's funding decisions than those including hard-nosed evaluation performance data.

IMPACT OF RURAL/URBAN LOCATION ON FINDINGS

Economic development problems and their solutions can vary dramatically from rural to urban areas. For this reason alone it would be wise to consider if the Abt index of past performance was more relevant to one area than the other. However, the number of cases is too small to do this empirically. We should note, nonetheless, that the evaluation data undoubtedly had a greater impact upon the funding of urban than rural CDCs. One explanation of why is the history of the OED CDC program. Initially the Special Impact Program was designed for urban riot-torn areas. Rural areas were included on a substantial scale largely to obtain political support from key congressional leaders with rural constituencies (Kelly, 1977). The stated goals, however, were not altered substantially because of this political compromise. The criteria that Abt used in its evaluation were more appropriate for urban than rural areas. Hence, it ought not be surprising that evaluation data on performance would be used more for urban funding decisions.

CONCLUSIONS

Although the literature and professional knowledge present clearly how useful evaluation research can be in decision-making, they leave largely unresolved how, and even if, it has been used. When this empirical issue has been addressed, present knowledge has provided us with examples in which evaluation studies have been underutilized, overutilized, and utilized at the "appropriate level."

The gap in knowledge we have attempted to close does not involve *how much* program evaluation research has been used in reaching decisions, but in *how* it has been used. A path analysis was used to estimate the direct and indirect ways in which evaluation data influenced OEO funding decisions for CDCs.

The model constructed statistically explained 80% of the variation of OEO's absolute funding decisions and 35% of the relative increase in funding. The variable accounting for most of this explanation was the OEO monitors' overall perception of CDC success. Evaluation data on performance by itself accounted for relatively little of the explanation. Nonetheless, the findings show that performance data did affect this success perception as well as other intervening variables in the model. Thus, it was utilized in the funding decision, but in an indirect rather than a direct way.

In more theoretical terms, our model of how evaluation performance data is related to funding decisions raises a basic issue yet to be resolved. In the past an implicit assumption seems to have been made that future success is directly related to past performance and that ability to perform in the future is directly related, perhaps on a one-to-one basis, with past performance. Our model does not make this assumption. Our findings have not supported this assumption. The model and findings suggest that it might be just as rational to make separate judgments about ability to perform in the future and past performance. In several instances judgments about these two variables might well contradict each other. If such contradictions exist, it would seem more rational to base funding decisions upon ability for future performance. The issue is: Do we need to reconsider past definitions about rational uses of evaluation research? It might be that its use in funding decisions has been greater than thought, but in ways different from that described in existing decision models.

REFERENCES

Abt Associates, Inc. (1972-1973). An evaluation of the special impact program. Phase I Report, 4 vols., Phase II Report, 4 vols.; and Final Report, 4 vols. Cambridge, Mass.: Author.

ACKOFF, R. (1963). "Toward quantitative evaluation of urban services." Pp. 91-117 in H. Schaller (ed.), Public expenditure decisions in the urban community. Baltimore: Johns Hopkins Press.

BERNSTEIN, I. N. and FREEMAN, H. E. (1975). Academic and entrepreneurial research: The consequences of diversity in federal evaluation studies. New York: Russell Sage.

BIGELOW, D. A. and CIARLO, J. A. (1976). "The impact of therapeutic effectiveness data on community mental health center management." Pp. 371-382 in G. V. Glass (ed.), Evaluation studies review annual, Vol. 1. Beverly Hills, Cal.: Sage.

CAPLAN, N. (1976). "Social research and national policy: What gets used, by whom, for what purposes, and with what effects?" International Social Science Journal, 28:187-194.

_____ and BARTON, E. (1976). Social indicators 1973: A study of the relationship between the power of information and utilization by federal executives. Ann Arbor, Mich.: CRUSK-ISR.

DAVIS, H. R., and SALASIN, S. E. (1975). "The utilization of evaluation." Pp. 621-666 in E. L. Streuning and M. Guttentag (eds.), The handbook of evaluation research, Vol. 1. Beverly Hills, Cal.: Sage.

EDWARDS, W., GUTTENTAG, M., and SNAPPER, K. (1975). "A decision-theoretic approach to evaluation research." Pp. 139-182 in E. L. Streuning and M. Guttentag (eds.), The handbook of evaluation research, Vol. 1. Beverly hills, Cal.: Sage.

FAUX, G. (1971). CDC's: Hope for the future. New York: Twentieth Century Funds.

GARDINER, J. A. (1975). "Problems in the use of evaluation in law enforcement and criminal justice." Pp. 177-184 in K. M. Dolbeare (ed.), Public policy evaluation. Beverly Hills, Cal.: Sage.

GARN, H. A. (1975). "Program evaluation and policy analysis of community development corporations." In G. Gappert and H. M. Rose (eds.), The social economy of cities. Beverly Hills, Cal.: Sage.

HARRIS, B. (1965). "New tools for planning." JAIP, XXXI, No. 2 (May):90-95.

KELLY, R. M. (1977). Community control of economic development: A study of the boards of directors of community development corporations. New York: Praeger.

_____ (1977). "Evaluation research, public policy, and theory: Interfaces to be developed." Paper presented at 1977 Annual Meeting of the American Political Science Association, Washington, D.C., September.

LEHNE, R. and FISK, D. M. (1974). "The impact of urban policy analysis." Urban Affairs Quarterly, 10 (Dec.):115-138.

LICHFIELD, N. and MARGOLIS, J. (1963). "Benefit-cost analysis as a tool in urban government decision making." Pp. 118-146 in H. Schaller (ed.), Public expenditure decisions in the urban community. Baltimore: Johns Hopkins Press.

MENZI, D. (1975). "Developing a performance rating system for manpower training programs." Evaluation, 2(2).

MORRILL, W. A. (1976). "Services integration and the department of Health, Education, and Welfare." *Evaluation* 3:1-2.

SCHALLER, H. (ed.) (1963). Public expenditure decisions in the urban community. Baltimore: Johns Hopkins Press.

STEIN, B. (1973). Throw the rascals out. Cambridge, Mass.: Center for Community Economic Development.

_____ (1974). The people's development corporation. Cambridge, Mass.: Center for Economic Development.

SUCHMAN, E. (1967). Evaluative research. New York: Russell Sage.

SULLIVAN, E. A. (1976). "Evaluation: What is the current status." Paper presented at the 1976 Annual Meeting of the Southern Political Science Association, Atlanta, Georgia, November.

WEISS, C. H. (1972). Evaluation research. Englewood Cliffs, N.J.: Prentice-Hall.

WEISS, R. S., and REIN, M. (1970). "The evaluation of broad-aim programs: Experimental design, its difficulties, and an alternative." Administrative Science Quarterly, 15:97-190.

WILLIAMS, W., and EVANS, J. W. (1969). "The politics of evaluation: The case of Head Start." Annals, 385:118-132.

WINNIE, R. E. (1972). "Local government budgeting, program planning, and evaluation." Urban data service. Washington, D.C.: International City Management Assoc., May.

YIN, R. and YATES, D. (1975). Street-level bureaucracy. Lexington, Mass.: Lexington.

11

USE OF EVALUATIONS IN AID: The Influence of Roles and Perceptions

DOUGLAS H. SHUMAVON

Oklahoma State University

INTRODUCTION

Throughout the past 10 to 15 years departments and agencies of the United States government have attempted to develop and use more systematic methods to understand how well they are operating their programs, to analyze the effectiveness of their efforts, and to gather information for planning future activities. Reports on the related evaluative research of these governmental entities are numerous and informative; but most end with a pessimistic appraisal of what has been accomplished to date (Rivlin, 1970). During this past decade and a half, the national government has attempted to expand its capability to understand how well it has been carrying out its activities and responsibilities through evaluations. The objectives of this chapter are to study the evaluation efforts within the Agency for International Development in order to identify the various kinds of evaluations conducted within the agency, to examine the use of those evaluations in project design and approval processes, and to analyze the influence of actors' perceptions of evaluations on the utilization of evaluative data and analysis.

Evaluation research is characterized by the application of social science research for the purposes of analyzing the effects of governmental intervention in complex societal situations. Evaluations are distinguished from monitoring

AUTHOR'S NOTE: *This chapter was prepared for delivery at the 1977 Annual Meeting of the American Political Science Association, Washington, D.C., September 1-4.*

systems. The latter are administrative devices used to assess compliance with management controls and regulations, and as such are focused on the nexus of inputs with the outputs of an agency. Evaluations, on the other hand, focus on the outcomes that result from agency activity and the impact of those outcomes on the environment within which the project functions.[1]

The Great Society Programs of the mid-1960's and the resultant proliferation of social legislation sparked a new interest in evaluation research. Those involved in the early anti-poverty programs recommended that such programs should be treated as experiments with an emphasis on evaluative research accompanying those experiments (Wholey, 1970: 15-16). Since the late 1960s, legislation from Congress has increasingly included mandatory evaluations for many different programs and projects (Public Affairs Center, 1975).

What has this increased interest and growth in evaluations brought us? Do we understand more now than we did 10 years ago? Is the information being used to improve governmental projects and programs? Some of the questions raised about governmental intervention have not been significantly answered even with systematic evaluations. According to Alice Rivlin, we know more today about the nature and prevalence of social problems in our society. We also know more about the initial distribution of costs and benefits of social action programs. But we know little about the impacts of different programs, and we do not have a great deal of knowledge on how to improve the effectiveness of the programs already in action (Rivlin, 1970:7). If we are to better understand what difference evaluations have made in governmental activity and the potential for using that information in decisions, a fundamental series of questions must be addressed. How are evaluations used? What makes evaluations useful instruments in decision-making? What influence do evaluations have in the design and implementation of projects? What are the limitations of evaluations? How could evaluations be better incorporated into governmental activity to improve project design?

To work, evaluations must convey messages about the project or program such that action can be taken. While that action may be positive (changes in program direction, continued funding) or negative (termination of the project or major cutbacks in funding), the key to successful evaluation is the utilization of the research findings. Research on the topic of evaluations has not always addressed the question of utilization, but several basic themes on the study of evaluations seem to be recurrent. The literature tends to accentuate the negative, i.e., most identify obstacles to utilization. For the sake of clarity I have identified three categories of concern which are frequently addressed: the design of evaluations, the internal dynamics of the organization, and political considerations—the environment within which the organization functions. The first of these, the design of evaluations, draws attention to the choice of methodology and the topic of organization goals (Coleman, 1972; Weiss and Kein, 1970; Scriven, 1972; Moursund, 1973). The internal dynamics refer to the interpersonal aspects of conducting evaluations and the element of timing so that evaluations can be use in making decisions about the future (Caro, 1971; Rodman and Kolodny, 1971; Freeman and Sherwood, 1965). The final category refers to the political and public environment within which the organization carries out its responsibilities (Davis and Salasin, 1975).

A fourth concern, not frequently mentioned in the literature, but nonetheless important, involves the role of evaluations. The utilization of evaluations can be significantly influenced by how the organization's members' perceptions vary in what evaluations should do and how the information should be used. Different members of an organization receive copies of the evaluations and the analyses or recommendations from those evaluations. That information may be stated from a certain perspective. For example, the function implied or expressly stated in the design of the evaluation may be to gather information for project redesign. Yet a potential user of the evaluation may perceive the role of the evaluation to be gathering information on the contribution the project under study has made to social improvement or economic development. If this is the case, the potential user of the evaluation may consider the information collected unimportant and useless. Conversely, if the perceptions of the role of the evaluation are the same for both the conduct of the evaluation and the potential user of the evaluation, it is more likely that the information provided through the evaluation will be utilized.

Several questions must be addressed to determine the importance of the role of evaluations. How can different role perceptions be identified? What are the factors that determine the role perceptions of evaluations? What are the specific consequences in the utilization of evaluations if there are different perceptions of the role of evaluations within a single organization? While some studies have suggested the existence of different perceptions of the role of evaluations by different sectors (e.g., Congress versus the agency, or the agency versus the public at large), there has been little public information about the different role perceptions existing within a single agency. In this study the various perceptions of the role evaluations by actors working at different levels within the Agency for International Development are identified, and through the study of the design and approval of an AID loan to the National Community Development Service of Bolivia, the influence of the perceptions of actors on the actual use of information for evaluations are assessed.

EVALUATIONS IN AID

Beside the previously noted distinction between monitoring and evaluations, AID further distinguishes between regular and special evaluations. Regular evaluations, the major concern of this study, are systematic evaluations, usually but not exclusively conducted at the project level, and are based on the design of a specific project. The responsibility for conducting these evaluations may be at the project, mission or AID/Washington level, but generally it is within the purview of the project manager. Special evaluations also are generally project oriented, but they are less formally structured, more ad hoc, and trouble shooting in nature. Special evaluations may be called for when specific problems are feared or identified in order to isolate areas where changes can be made to alleviate problems.

The AID *Evaluation Handbook* (1974:3) suggests three criteria for project evaluations: effectiveness, significance, and efficiency. These criteria serve as the basis for addressing the following questions about AID-funded projects:

EFFECTIVENESS Are the targets for outputs and purposes being achieved? What are the reasons for success or failure?

SIGNIFICANCE Will the achievement of the targets contribute to economic development or other high goals beyond the project purpose? To what extent? What are the activity's advantages over possible alternatives? What about side effects?

EFFICIENCY Do the benefits justify the cost? Are there more efficient means of achieving the same targets?

The effectiveness criterion concerns itself with the success of a project. By implication it also encompasses the notion of project design, particularly from the perspective of how project objectives are identified and the ability to design a project capable of reaching those objectives. The significance criterion deals with project impact. It also deals with the larger question of models of intervention, which are applied in various nations where AID funds projects. The efficiency criterion implies the use of economic standards in assessing a project's design and implementation.

There are several functions which may be performed by evaluations in AID. These functions provide the link between the role and the use of evaluations. AID has identified three functions for evaluations: project redesign, project replicability, and project economic feasibility. Each function is a potential use of evaluations. The project redesign function is an attempt to clarify the direction of a project during implementation, such that, if it becomes apparent there are difficulties in executing the project according to the original design, the evaluation can provide information and guidance for restructuring the project prior to its completion. Project replicability emphasizes the collection of information about the impact of the project on the target population. If a proper mix of inputs capable of achieving the level of social and economic development sought through foreign assistance programs can be identified in a given project, then there exists the possibility of transferring that mix to other similar situations. Project economic feasibility emphasizes the provision of information which can show the relative cost effectiveness of various alternative project designs, thus attempting to identify the most economical means for achieving the project goals.

AID, BOLIVIA, AND
THE NATIONAL COMMUNITY DEVELOPMENT SERVICE

The relationship between the United States government and Bolivia in the area of foreign assistance began with technical assistance as early as 1942. The first major expansion of the relations between these two countries followed the Bolivian revolution of 1952. In 1954 a financial capital assistance program was initiated and the Food for Peace Program was started in 1961. In the late 1960s a financial assistance program was started which included direct support of the central government's budget. Since 1962 the U.S. government has provided $410 million in loans, grants and consessional sales of agricultural commodities (November 1973 data). More than $160 million in loans were authorized during the Alliance for Progress Program and since the new funding categories established with the 1973 Amendments to the Foreign Assistance Act, $64 million have been authorized under the Education and Human Resources Development category (June 1976 data). U.S. government assistance was interrupted during the leftist Torres regime between 1969 and 1971 when relations between the United States and Bolivia deteriorated drastically, but it has increased substantially since the current regime of Col. Hugo Banzer Suarez came to power in a bloody coup in 1971.

The National Community Development Service (NCDS) is a rural development, self-help oriented agency within the Ministry of Peasant Affairs and Agriculture of the government of Bolivia. Started in 1964, NCDS experienced a large growth in the early 1970s primarily due to technical and financial support through AID grants and loans. AID's involvement began in 1966 with technical assistance. Disbursement of a project loan to NCDS of $915,000 began in July 1972 and overlapped with the initiation of a second project and an additional $3 million loan in September 1972. With the initiation of the first and second AID loans, used in large part to fund sub-projects (individual community-level projects selected in cooperation between the community members and NCDS personnel), the NCDS placed its primary emphasis on the construction of a social infrastructure.

During the early 1970s NCDS began to place an emphasis on the development of economic, rather than social infrastructure projects. These projects included small irrigation systems, roads, and bridges and a variety of agricultural projects. NCDS realized that although social infrastructure was still needed and was relatively easy to promote, the construction of such projects did not materially increase the economic well being of peasantry still largely surviving on a subsistance-based form of agricultural production. NCDS leadership, at the urging of AID, began to espouse a preferred emphasis on economic infrastructure that would more directly and immediately increase the economic well being of the peasantry.

Coinciding with the change in focus from social to economic infrastructure, the AID mission in Bolivia had identified, as an area for future AID activities, assistance to small farmers and the development of cooperatives.[2] The AID project manager of the community development project began the initial steps of the design for a new project with the NCDS in the area of cooperative development in late 1973. By mid-1974 the mission had submitted a project proposal, which after three reviews in Washington was approved in December 1975. The final project proposal included a $7.5 million loan and an accompanying $2.29 million grant.

This study uses the design and approval of the cooperative development project with the NCDS of Bolivia to analyze the role of evaluations and determine how that influences utilization. To determine the preferences for evaluative information and the influence of those preferences on the utilization of evaluations in the design and approval processes, interviews were held with the major actors involved. Three levels of analysis are used. The first is with the project manager who was responsible for the implementation of the community development project and the design of the cooperative development project both implemented by the NCDS. The second level is that of the employees in the AID mission in Bolivia, the field office responsible for the operations of all AID projects in Bolivia. The third level is AID/Washington, particularly those in the Latin American Bureau—the level at which the major funding decisions regarding the approval of all projects in Latin America take place. In addition to the interviews, questionnaires were mailed to overseas personnel. Various AID and NCDS documents were also used.

EVALUATION AVAILABLE TO DECISION MAKERS

During the design and approval processes of the cooperative development loan, agency decision makers had access to both systematic and ad hoc evaluations. The data and analyses from the NCDS evaluation system were the only information available from systematic evaluations.

As a condition to the second loan, AID/Washington required the NCDS to set aside a specific amount of funds in the area of technical assistance for the design and implementation of an evaluation system. The NCDS contracted with a private firm for the assistance in July 1973, and the design was completed in mid-1974. A year later data were collected and analyzed by NCDS personnel on projects constructed in 1972.

The evaluation system was designed to collect information on various projects constructed by the communities with the NCDS's technical and financial assistance. The thrust of the evaluation was to collect information relating to the effectiveness criterion. Each project type had a separate, extensive series of questions relating to two major success indicators: (1) user rates—with measures of the various uses of each project, and (2) maintenance and upkeep indicators with information about the community contributions to ensure the continuation of the project after construction. All projects also had data collected about the contribution of both the community and NCDS in project preparation and construction. The analysis involved the comparison of like projects and identified the factors influencing the outcome which were controllable by NCDS, and the extent to which those factors were influential in determining the success of the project. Additional data were also collected on each project which provided new and useful information for NCDS about the extent of their operations.

Several ad hoc studies were also available during the new project's design and approval. First, two special evaluations looked in detail at the institutional capacity of the NCDS and made assessments about the potential for implementing the new loan. Furthermore, in compliance with the requirements for project documentation several additional studies were completed which assessed the socio-economic setting of the proposed project. Beyond these more formal, but not systematic studies, regular reporting and monitoring devices, including audits, were available to decision makers.

THE PROJECT LEVEL

The first chore is to identify the preference for the role of evaluations by the project manager. A manager's major responsibility during tenure at a particular post is to implement a single project. The manager may also assume the responsibilities of project design. In the case of the NCDS project manager, most of his time was spent managing the community development project's implementation. During the latter part of his tenure in Bolivia, he also assumed the major responsibility for the design and approval of the cooperative development loan. These two responsibilities prompted different responses about evaluations and their usefulness and resulted in different uses in practice.

The AID *Evaluation Handbook* suggests that information generated through project evaluations addressing questions related to the effectiveness criterion can be used to redesign projects during their implementation. Such evaluations can assess the achievement of targets for outputs or purposes and the analysis can point to the factors influencing success or failure. This analysis can point to the factors influencing success or failure. This analysis might suggest necessary changes in the input mix. When asked to identify the most useful information for evaluating a project, the manager indicated "money movements," "types of projects," and information from host country staff—information generated through monitoring rather than evaluation devices. When asked to identify three criteria he would use to evaluate a project, the first criterion he identified was the achievement of agreed upon objectives, which corresponds to the effectiveness criterion suggested by the agency. In practice, the project manager relied on monthly reports he prepared, monthly sector meetings within the mission, and to a lesser extent, Project Appraisal Reports, a static assessment of progress on implementation. He did not use the information from the NCDS evaluation system that was available to him.

The apparent discrepancy between the agency's expectations, the project manager's perception of useful information, and his actual use of evaluations in meeting his implementation responsibilities deserves futher examination. The manager's implementation necessitate the demonstration of his ability to manage the project. Given the project design, the manager must show his superiors how he has managed those aspects of the input mix under his control in order to achieve the projected output targets. In AID it is assumed that the good manager correctly manipulates those variables to achieve the stated goals. The design hypothesizes that achievement of these targets will achieve the project purpose, which will contribute to the project goals, but variables other than those controlled by the manager are assumed to be responsible in explaining the linkage. In demonstrating his capabilities to manage the inputs, the project manager turned to the most readily available information—that generated from the regular reporting documents—which demonstrated progress in implementation of the project. To succeed in his capacity within the mission, the project manager must provide information which he perceives will reflect favorably upon the work he has done.

The project manager did not use the information generated through the employment of the effectiveness criteria in the NCDS evaluation system. When asked about this, he said that the information became available far too late in the funding life of the project to be of any practical use. At first glance, it would appear that the Wholey et al; (1970) emphasis on poor timing as an explanation for the non use of evaluation data holds true in this specific example. However, this does not fully explain the apparent discrepancy between the project manager's perceptions of useful information and the agency's expectations of evaluations. The project manager might still have utilized the information after it became available, and when interviewed he indicated that information provided through evaluations could be helpful. But when he was asked to select the most useful information in evaluating a project, he chose the kind of information most readily available through monitoring devices rather than evaluations.

Several additional factors reflect upon this discrepancy between the agency's intended use of project evaluations seeking to provide information related to the effectiveness criterion and the project manager's reliance on information generated through monitoring devices for evaluating a project.

First, because of the pressure on the project manager to demonstrate his managerial capabilities, there is incentive for him to concentrate on the kind of information which reflects on his abilities. If he can manage the inputs to produce the expected outputs, he has done a good job. This is done by gathering information which is easily accessible—information generated through regular reporting or monitoring devices. There is no incentive for him to utilize evaluations which reflect upon variables outside his control—even though there is an expressed agency preference for managers to seek and use such information.

Second, because of the timing of the analysis by the NCDS evaluation system, we have insufficient experience upon which to judge the design of the community development loan in its projection to achieve certain levels of social and economic development. In other words, because the information was generated so late in the life of the project, and because the project manager opted not to use the information for project redesign purposes at that time, we cannot test the linkages between outputs and purposes and purposes and goals. For such an analysis to be useful, information would have to be available shortly after the start of implementation. In a four-year project, as was the case with the community development loan, information would be needed (at the very latest) after the completion of the second year of the project's execution. This would allow at least two years for the changes to be manifested in project outputs. However, there still remains the question of how much change might occur as a result of project execution during the first two years. To determine if the targets for outcomes have been achieved, some time must lapse between completion of the project and the manifestation of the results. In the case of the NCDS evaluation system, for example, three years had lapsed between project execution and the evaluation of the project (1972 to 1975). Even this is a short period. In addition, often a project takes up to a year or two to reach its peak implementation schedule. Because of this, AID often withholds funds, which results in light disbursement at the beginning of a project and heavier disbursement near the end.

This represents an interesting paradox relating to evaluations and their usefulness. If evaluations are completed in time to be useful for project redesign purposes, they may be based upon insufficient experience—there might not have been enough time elapsed to permit the manifestation of the project's impact on its intended beneficiaries. Stated another way, the information included in evaluations that are appropriately timed for project redesign may not accurately reflect the true impact of the project. Whether project redesign is undertaken or not, the time necessary for the impact of a project to manifest itself in a community may necessitate evaluations which take place sometime after the completion of the project. Certainly, information generated after the completion of the project is inapplicable for redesign purposes; but such information is supremely important in determining the relevance of the project's design as a catalyst for social and economic development.

This further permits one to question the link between the short range objectives of the project manager and the longer range objectives of AID. The project manager attempts to demonstrate his capabilities as a manager of inputs to produce outputs. The incentive is to gather information he feels will provide his superiors with this knowledge. Yet, to measure the achievement of the agency's long range goals, it may be necessary to evaluate the impact of the project long after the project manager has left—and possibly even after AID has terminated the funding.

Third, the project redesign (from social to economic infrastructure) took place without the assistance of input from either the regular or special evaluations in the decision-making process. The decision to redirect the project from an emphasis in social infrastructure to economic infrastructure was based upon intuitive assessment and the anticipation of a possible future loan in the cooperative development area. While the project manager had strong intuitive feelings about expanding the role of the NCDS, the possibilities of a follow-on loan in the area of cooperative development generated enthusiasm for expanding the activities of NCDS in areas which would prepare them for this possible future work. But this change in direction even further complicates evaluations. If the evaluation system is designed to measure a set of goals and the goals change during implementation, the usefulness of analyses directed at the original goals would be correspondingly limited.

With respect to the significance criterion, the *Handbook* suggests that information generated from evaluations related to the significance criterion can be utilized for project replicability. The significance criterion is intended to generate information confirming or rejecting the hypotheses of the design employed in the project in terms of its contribution to social and economic change. If a project achieves the economic and social development anticipated, similar projects could be designed with greater confidence of achieving development goals. As was mentioned above, the project manager listed the most useful information in evaluating a project as that generated from monitoring and reporting devices. But he also identified one criterion he would employ in evaluations which corresponded to the significance criterion, the ability of the recipient agency to continue its activities at a similar level after AID funding terminated.

As in the case with implementation responsibilities, discrepancies appear between the agency-suggested uses of evaluations related to the significance criterion, the perceptions of useful information by the project manager, and the actual use of evaluations by the manager in meeting design responsibilities. In meeting those responsibilities, the project manager assumed a role of advocate

and defender of the proposed project. He had to demonstrate to others the strength
of the proposed project in the most appropriate fashion. In gathering support for
his position, the project manager extracted material from the special studies,
analyses, and special evaluations conducted during the design phases, as well as
from the NCDS evaluation system. He needed to respond to specific AID/
Washington inquiries during the review and approval process and he needed
general information that supported the design's logic and demonstrated the
potential for project success.

The NCDS evaluation system generated information about the relative success
of various sub-projects constructed by the NCDS. By identifying user rates and
calculating the quantity of contributions by communities, the NCDS evaluation
system established a list of sub-projects considered to be more successful than
others. It also identified some of the factors controlled by the NCDS which might
have contributed to that success. The project manager used this information to
support the logic of the new project's design and to justify the institutional
capacity of the NCDS in meeting the new requirements of the proposal. Even
though the NCDS evaluation system did not attempt to assess the project's
impact, which corresponds to the significance criterion, the project manager cited
several instances in which information generated through the system was actually
used in the new project design. These uses were primarily indirect. For example,
the popularity of the NCDS was the most appropriate agency to implement the
new loan. Similarly the NCDS capacity to evaluate was cited as an example of the
institutional capacity to assume responsibly the obligations of the proposed
project. Thus, while the data in the evaluation system was designed to measure
effectiveness, the project manager was motivated to utilize the information to
support the new project's design. This he did even though evaluations guided by
the *significance* criterion was suggested by AID/Washington as the most
appropriate means of generating information about project replicability.

In this case, the incentive worked in the opposite direction from the preceding
example of project implementation responsibilities. In meeting his project design
responsibilities, the project manager had incentive to use any and all information
that supported his proposal. Demands are placed on the manager to demonstrate
proof of the design in order to have it approved. These demands provide an
incentive to utilize information which supports the position established by the
mission. Thus the manager utilized information directed toward the effectiveness
criterion in justifying the new project.

In the preceding two examples, one can see that in meeting his project
implementation responsibilities, the project manager is imbued with the notion
that the manager must draw upon the types of information that will demonstrate
his ability to manage the inputs of a project and produce the anticipated outputs.
There is no incentive to seek information which reflects upon the longer range
considerations of an evaluation system because the manager may gather all the
information he needs through monitoring devices. The incentive is to produce the
anticipated results that are under the control of the manager. In identifying criteria
he would employ in evaluations designed to appraise project effectiveness, the
project manager made it clear that the most useful information came from
monitoring devices, not from systematic evaluations.

In meeting his design responsibilities, the project manager turned to any and all information he could generate to support the position that the proposed project's design was strong and should be funded. In this case, the incentive was to use all information—that generated from monitoring devices, special evaluations, special studies, and the NCDS evaluation system. While the design of the evaluation system did not include the significance criterion and was not intended for project replicability, there was incentive for him to use the information for that purpose anyway.

In the most common and generally the most time consuming responsibilities of the project manager, the incentives provided by the agency are greater for utilizing information demonstrating the application of his managerial skills. Conversely, the incentive in the design of new projects is to demonstrate the potential strengths of the proposals. In reviewing the proposal AID officials look to whatever evidence the manager may provide in support of his proposed project. But in following the agency's guidelines, they would presumably be most concerned with information systematically oriented toward the significance criterion.

THE MISSION LEVEL

Mission-level employees must concern themselves with the total picture of mission operations. They want information which will assist them in assessing the contribution of various projects to the general development of the host country. The incentive at the mission level is to provide AID/Washington with information reflecting first, the development within the principal sector (e.g., agriculture, health, education) identified in the mission's Development Assistance Program, and second, the collective results of their efforts in that sector to the social and economic development in the host country. This perspective, for example, explains the preference for information from evaluations that relates to the significance criterion. Such information would provide information about the relative benefits attributable to each project within the mission's operations. Whether or not designed with such intent, this information could provide the mission personnel with knowledge about the relative contribution of each project funded by AID.

Even in the area of financial considerations, the mission personnel reflect this broader perspective in their responses. The second most frequently identified criterion for evaluation suggested by mission-level employees was efficiency. But, as in the case of the "impact" criterion, they all stressed longer-term results. With respect to the disbursement of funds, the project manager emphasized information assessing the fact that funds were disbursed, and accordingly utilized information generated through monitoring devices. The mission personnel emphasized information assessing *how* those funds were disbursed. They utilized AID audits, also classified as monitoring devices, identifying to whom and for what purposes funds were expended. As to the results of fund disbursement, the project manager utilized information identifying immediate project results, e.g., the number of sub-projects constructed. Again, he utilized information generated from monitoring devices. In contrast, mission-level personnel stressed the utilization of information which assessed farther reaching results: project impact and cost-benefit analyses.

In both cases, the preference of mission-level employees which reflect this broader perspective present special problems for evaluations. First, for project impact to manifest itself, it may take several years beyond project completion to demonstrate the project's actual contribution to social and economic development. In the case of sub-projects which are "economically" oriented, e.g., sheep dips which enable local farmers to bathe their animals periodically to prevent disease, it may be possible to measure the number of animals bathed each year and the costs to each farmer per animal and tabulate the number of animal deaths per hundred and compare that to pre-sheep dip conditions. But even this would fall short of the economic contribution to the small farmer. It might be that more animals will increase the economic well being of the transporters from farm to market, rather than the farmer. When one contemplates the possible range of benefits which might be attributable to the education of youth, made possible by the construction of a school house, the amount of time necessary for these contributions to manifest themselves may indeed by longer than AID has been in existence. In short, the time for projects to make their impact and properly assess their contribution to social and economic development may take several years after the completed funding of projects.

The second problem which presents itself is the difficulty in assessing the relative contribution of various projects within the mission's purview. Suppose the mission, as in the case in Bolivia, has several projects within the agricultural sector which are all contributing to the development of the agricultural sector which, theoretically, will assist the country in economically developing itself. With project evaluations being designed for each project, there remains as many different measurement devices for the impact of the several projects as there are projects themselves. Stated another way, the problem of coordinating several impact assessments, each designed for a separate project, would be enormous, not to mention methodologically unsound.

A second conclusion discerned from the interviews and observations is the selective use by mission personnel of information and analyses provided through evaluations. In several cases mission-level employees selectively excerpted from studies and analyses either to include in the mission's submissions for the small farmer organization proposal or to attempt to discredit the information when it contained evidence contrary to the mission's position.

As the proposed project changed the direction and focus of the NCDS from community development to cooperative development, the mission was lacking information within Bolivia on a similar type of project. As a result, the mission personnel turned to an evaluation of the cooperative development activities of AID in Guatemala completed by the Latin American Bureau's Sector Analysis Division. The mission claimed that the Guatemalan study "helped to provide a data base for policy and project decisions relating to small farmer development programs with objectives of, *inter alia* increasing net incomes, production of farm commodities, and increasing employment opportunities for rural dwellers."[3] In attempting to demonstrate the validity of the Bolivian project's approach, parallels between both projects were drawn of both similar goals and a similar design.

However, when AID/Washington employees reviewed the project paper, several officials took note of the excerpted material. They doubted that the Bolivian project could achieve its anticipated results in such a short period of time—noting that the experience in Guatemala indicated that far more than the four years planned for the Bolivian project was necessary to establish a successful cooperative movement in a country.

Several of the special evaluations identified weak spots in the proposed project through deficiencies in the implementing agency. When those weaknesses were independently acknowledged by the mission they were addressed through corrective devices in the Project Paper; for example, the inclusion of "conditions precedent" to ensure higher salaries and thus increase the competence of employees. When mission personnel perceive criticisms in some of the special evaluations to be unjustly harsh or inconvenient, they were discounted. The mission would first attempt to show contrary evidence to the unpopular conclusions. If the conclusions could not be disproven, the mission would criticize the study—either the methodology was weak or the evaluator had "another axe to grind." Thus, whenever critical reports were prepared placing the mission in a defensive posture, the reports were undermined by one of two means: either discrediting the study by providing contrary evidence or discrediting the methodology, weakening the substance of the criticism.

The third example of the selective use of information, more spontaneous than either of the above, was the assessment made by a mission official of the data from the NCDS evaluation system and the costs associated with the benefits of social infrastructure sub-projects. While no attempt was made in the analysis to relate the benefits to the costs, an assessment of this nature was made by one of the mission officials. During the final stages of the approval process when the mission was requested to relinquish its position for the inclusion of funds for social infrastructure projects in the loan, little objection was made by mission personnel. As in the preceding cases, the information provided through the evaluation system was interpreted by the official according to the perspective through which he assessed projects (in this case relating benefits to costs). The assessment at the time of the presentation of the analysis was not enough to exclude from the proposal a request for the social infrastructure funds. But when challenged in the final stages, resistance to the exclusions was not great.

Mission-level employees indicated a preference for evaluative information relating to the significance and efficiency criteria. In meeting their project oversight responsibilities, mission personnel concern themselves with several projects and the collective contribution of those projects in achieving social and economic development within the host country. The selection of evaluative information relating to the significance criterion reflects this broad concern with development. Even in financial considerations the mission-level employees reflect this breadth. While the project manager's perspective is one of "money movement"—that funds were disbursed—the mission's perspective is *how* those funds were disbursed.

These three examples demonstrate the selective use of information by mission-level employees, all relating to the new project's design. Again, the question is one of incentive. In the case of the Guatemalan project, mission-level employees used a portion of the findings which justified their positon—they must convince AID/Washington officials of the logic of their proposal to get it funded. Therefore, they provide information which demonstrates replicability. The choice of the Guatemalan project is not surprising as the proposed project was similar in many ways. On the other hand, inclusion of data from the NCDS evaluation system is reflective of their need to provide whatever information they can muster to support their position. While the information from the Guatemalan evaluation was from a replicable project, mission-level employees included data and analysis from the NCDS evaluation system in the proposed project's documentation. This they did inspite of the fact that the two project's documentation. This they did inspite of the fact that the two projects were not replicable and the data collected from the NCDS evaluation system were related more to the effectiveness than the significance criterion.

THE WASHINGTON LEVEL

AID/Washington-level employees indicated the most useful information in evaluating project proposals related to the capabilities of the proposed implementing agency. Two other kinds of useful information included that relating to the logic of the design of the project and that relating to the socio-economic setting of the project. When asked to identify the criteria they would employ in evaluating a project, the two most frequent responses were the effectiveness and the significance criteria.

The information actually utilized by AID/Washington employees in formulating opinions favoring or disfavoring the loan was largely generated by the mission and made available through the project paper, the final document submitted by the mission for review by Washington. The second most frequently identified source of information was that generated by the first-hand observation of some Washington-based officials who visited Bolivia during the design and preparation of the project's documentation. While some Washington-based officials were aware of the evaluation component of the NCDS, none had seen or used the data and analysis from the NCDS evaluation system. Almost all Washington-based employees had reviewed the project documentation, although in varying degrees, and most aware of the special evaluations included therein.

There appeared to be a general skepticism about project evaluations by most of the Washington-based employees who were interviewed. The most common response was that such evaluations were limited in their scope and not capable of providing information about the most substantive questions involving the model of intervention employed in a project. Project evaluations were thought to be management devices for the project manager and were limited to providing information capable of permitting some fine-tuning of the project, or for redesign purposes.

It was generally felt that there was a need for information from evaluations which could assist in determining the agency's general strategy on intervention and in new project design. But those interviewed felt that there was little of this kind of information one could anticipate from project evaluations. Sector assessments, on the other hand, were perceived to be capable of providing this kind of information. But the Sector Analysis Division pointed out some dilemmas in generating such information. In their work, whenever their analysis challenged the status quo or the conventional folk-wisdom of the agency, the Sector Analysis Division was considered to be too threatening and it generally took someone with a particularly receptive ear to consider altering projects based on these results. Conversely, many wondered what the division was actually doing when the results produced through their systematic research merely confirmed the conventional folk-wisdoms of the agency which already governed agency activities.

Again, as in the case with the preceding levels of analysis, confusion abounds in the perceptions and usefulness of evaluations. AID/Washington employees felt that the most important criteria were effectiveness and significance. In actual use, however, the only sources of information were those provided in the project paper and first-hand observation, which did not include details of the NCDS evaluation system. Nonsystematic evaluations were included, but none had seen or used the NCDS evaluation system data and analysis. The most useful information in evaluating a project in the review process was related to either the institutional capacity of the proposed implementing agency, the actual design of the project, or the socio-economic setting of the project. This hardly seems surprising because the information included in the project paper contained the kind of information indicated to be useful.

One of the more interesting patterns of these interviews was the skepticism about project evaluations. Most of the Washington-based officials felt that project evaluations were suited as management tools for project redesign and fine-tuning during a project's implementation. A criticism about project evaluations was that they were unable to provide information that could assist in project design or in general intervention strategy. Yet collecting information related to the significance criterion would provide data permitting assessment of the impact a project had in contributing to social and economic development, and would also provide information relevant to the intervention efforts of the mission.

CONCLUSIONS

In summary, at each level of the organization a preference for information relating to different criteria has been identified. The project manager indicated that his preference for criteria in evaluating projects was meeting project objectives; but in actual use the project manager referred to regular reporting documents or monitoring devices. This is not surprising because there is incentive for him to produce information which reflects upon his ability to manage the inputs to produce the outputs. In meeting his design responsibilities, however, the manager utilized information from whatever sources he could to demonstrate the logic of the proposed project's design. The incentive for the project manager is to demonstrate the potential for success of the proposed project from whatever sources possible. In this case he used information from the NCDS evaluation system which generated information applicable to the effectiveness criterion, even though the agency suggests the most applicable information would most likely be generated from the application of the significance criterion.

At the mission level, mission personnel expressed a preference for information reflecting a broader perspective than that of the project manager. The preference for criteria suggested by the mission personnel is that reflecting project impact and that reflecting some cost-benefit analysis. However, mission-level employees demonstrated the selective use of information from available evaluations. In support of the proposed project's design, mission personnel selectively included portions of comparable studies to support the mission's perspective. When presented the information from the NCDS evaluation system, one mission employee suggested the applicability of cost-benefit analysis. The incentive at the mission level is to demonstrate that the mission's selection of projects is appropriately directed at resolving the mission's identified host country development problems. This was evident in the mission's preference for information which reflected the larger perspective. In the mission's project design contributions, the employees were also advocates and thus turned to evaluation information which best supported the mission's proposal, even if it involved selectively utilizing data and analysis from evaluations.

The interviews with AID/Washington personnel involved with the design and approval of the proposed loan suggested that the most frequently relied upon information was that generated by the mission and submitted in the documentation or that first-hand observation gathered by those who visited Bolivia. The preference for evaluative information from those employees suggests, however, that information reflecting on the significance criterion would be the most useful. Most felt that project evaluations were not capable of providing this broader perspective, and many expressed a general skepticism for either special or regular evaluations generated from the mission. While there was a preference for information allowing for better project design of assisting in the development of strategies of intervention, AID/Washington employees who produced such information considered themselves caught in an awkward situation. The work they produced that confirmed conventional folk-wisdom among their colleagues was not considered to be productive (we knew that already), whereas when their conclusions challenged conventional folk-wisdom, they were considered to be too threatening.

There are two basic findings from this study which lead to the following recommendations. First, different preferences for evaluations reflecting information relevant to different criteria were found at each of the three levels of the organization. Second, feelings about the most useful information for evaluating a project influenced the use of evaluations *and* other sources of information.

To provide evaluations with the potential for more utilization, careful consideration must be made of the preferences for evaluative information at various levels of the organization. If evaluations are to be used for project redesign and fine-tuning, the evaluation should reflect the weighting of questions toward the effectiveness criterion. If, on the other hand, evaluations are to be used for project replicability, the evaluation should reflect the weighting of questions toward the significance criterion. Finally, if evaluations are to be used to determine project economic viability, then the evaluation should reflect the weighting of questions toward the efficiency criterion. If project evaluations are expected to have relevance and use at each level of the organization, they must take into account the preferences for evaluative information at each of those levels.

There also appears to be a need for incentive to use evaluations. At each level of the organization, available information from evaluations was used when an appropriate incentive existed. Conversely, when evaluations were available but not used, the incentive provided by the organization was not necessarily conducive to the use of evaluations; rather, incentive was more conducive to the use of information provided through monitoring or regular reporting devices.

While this study was limited to a single experience—the design and approval of the small farmer organization loan for the NCDS—it has provided an opportunity to look at the importance of the perceptions of actors in the organization on the role of evaluations. It has also demonstrated the importance of incentives as another factor influencing the utilization of evaluative data and analysis. An expanded study to include more than one case is needed to provide more information regarding the generalizability of this research.

NOTES

1. Levy et al. (1974) provide this useful distinction between inputs on the one hand, and outputs, outcomes, and impact on the other. AID uses a similar distinction, although with different wording: inputs, outputs, purposes, and goals. The agency classifies project inputs into three groups: cash, manpower, and materiale.

2. The title of the loan was Small Farmer Organizations. The thrust of the loan was rural cooperative development. The terms are used interchangeable throughout the chapter.

3. AID. Project Paper of the Small Farmer Organization Loan.

REFERENCES

Agency for International Development (1974). Evaluation handbook—second edition. Washington, D.C.: U.S. Government Printing Office.

CARO, F. G. (ed.) (1971). readings in evaluation research. New York: Russell Sage.

COLEMAN, J. S. (1972). "Reply to Cain and Watts." In P. H. Rossi and W. Williams (eds.), Evaluating social programs: Theory, practice and politics. New York: Seminar.

DAVIS, H. R., and SALASIN, S. E. (1975). "The utilization of evaluation results." Pp. 13-26 in E. Streuning and M. Guttentag (eds.), Handbook of evaluation research. Beverly Hills, Cal.: Sage.

FREEMAN, H. E., and SHERWOOD, C. C. (1965). "Research in large-scale intervention programs." Journal of Social Issues, 21:11-28.

LEVY, F. S., METSNER, A. J., and WILDAVSKY, A. (1974). Urban outcomes. Berkeley: University of California Press.

MOURSUND, J. P. (1973). Evaluation: An introduction to research design. Monterey, Cal.: Brooks/Cole.

Public Affairs Center (1975). Social research and public policies, the Dartmouth/OECD conference. Hanover, N.H.: Dartmouth.

RIVLIN, A. (1970). Systematic thinking for social action. Washington, D.C.: Brookings Institution.

RODMAN, R., and KOLODNY, R. (1971). "Reorganizational strains in the researcher-practitioner relationship." In F. G. Caro (ed.), Readings in evaluation research. New York: Russell Sage.

SCRIVEN, M. (1972). "The methodology of evaluation." Pp. 123-126 in C. H. Weiss (ed.), Evaluating action programs: Reading in social action and education. Boston: Allyn and Bacon.

WEISS, R. S., and REIN, M. (1970). "The evaluation of broad-aim programs: Experimental design, its difficulties and an alternative." Administrative Sciences Quarterly, 15:97-109.

WHOLEY, J., et al. (1970). Federal evaluation. Washington, D.C.: Urban Institute.

PART VI

TERMINATION

12

A THEORY OF POLICY TERMINATION

PETER deLEON

The Rand Corporation

I can think of no one objective that will possibly be raised against this proposal, unless it should be urged that the number of people will be thereby much lessened in the kingdom. This I freely own, and was indeed one principal design in offering it to the world.

> "A Modest Proposal"
> Jonathan Swift (1729)

WHAT IS POLICY TERMINATION?

With due respect to those who have described implementation as "the missing link" in policy analysis,[1] it is clear that public policy termination has been much less attended, much less linked to policy analysis. The recent outpouring of literature on implementation has greatly increased this disparity.[2] This chapter addresses this imbalance by asking a series of policy-related questions about termination, such as: What is meant by policy termination? Where and how does it fit into a general model of the policy process? Is termination important, and, if so, why? And, finally, how might one devise incentives to encourage the process and politics of termination, thus making option more accessible the policy makers?

AUTHOR'S NOTE: *This article was prepared for delivery at the 1977 Annual Meeting of the American Political Science Association, Washington, D.C., September 1-4. The views expressed here are the author's own, and are not necessarily shared by Rand or its research sponsors.*

Before considering the policy implications of termination and how termination might affect and be affected by policy planning, execution, and evaluation, we must arrive at some agreement on what is meant when we talk about termination, both in the general sense and in the more specific policy sense.

The American Heritage Dictionary definition of termination is quite explicit and unexceptional: "The spatial or temporal end of something; . . . conclusion or cessation. A result or outcome of something." Within the bounds of this definition, we can observe numerous personal and organizational examples of the termination act that have received a great deal of study. Divorce, death, retirement, coup d'etat, bankruptcy, revolution, and surrender can all be viewed as termination for particular programs or policies. Public policy termination is more complex than the personal types and much less studied. It can be initially defined as "the deliberate conclusion or cessation of specific government functions, programs, policies, or organizations."[3] The definition is at once too restrictive, for it excludes changes in policy emphasis or jurisdiction. The March of Dimes did not conclude its operations with the discovery of the Salk polio vaccine, nor did the U.S. Army Horse Cavalry canter off into the sunset with the advent of the mechanized army.[4] To include these sorts of phenomena, we need to appreciate the concept of "partial termination," in which specific government functions, programs, policies, or organizations significantly redirect their activities so as to remain operant, that is, to justify their continued existence. The termination/partial termination distinction will be examined later in the chapter.

A second fundamental question regarding policy termination is where it fits in the policy process, which implies a formulation of a model of the policy process. The absence of such a model or one that does not acknowledge the importance of termination would naturally result in the neglect of the termination process. Drawing largely upon the earlier theoretical framework of Harold D. Lasswell,[5] Brewer has offered a six-step, highly interactive, model of the policy process that allows us to observe the role and contribution of policy termination:[6]

— Initiation/Invention
— Estimation
— Selection
— Implementation
— Evaluation
— Termination

Very briefly, the first step includes the individual and organizational recognition of a societal problem, the definition of the policy objectives, and the generation of possible policy options. The estimation stage weighs each alternative's costs and benefits against the general policy objectives prior to the selection stage, in which the decision maker chooses among the policy options. The policy is translated into specific programs and carried out during the implementation stage. In the evaluation stage, the effects of the program relative to the policy objectives are assessed as well as any unanticipated consequences the policy may have produced. Finally, the termination stage is a recognition that a specific policy need (or should) not live forever; when a policy's objectives are reached and maintained, its relevance and applicability should be reconsidered and, if found redundant, outmoded, or dysfunctional, terminated.

Although termination represent the final step in the policy process, conceptually it should not be (although it too often is) something to be considered last. The initial recognition of the problem in the initiation/invention stage is directly analogous to a set of intellectual tasks that partially characterize termination. Both stages are predicated on the recognition of an imbalance between the political system and its relative domain or the demands upon the system and its capacity to respond adequately.[7] If a problem is seen to exist, then the policy process is initiated; if a given policy is evaluated as exacerbating the problem it was designed to correct, then the termination process is begun. Of course, the other reason for exercising the termination option is when the policy has been successful and the problem no longer exists. Between these two poles are a multitude of "fine tunings" or partial terminations, in which the policy is adjusted and refined to make it more responsive to the problem or to change the policy as the problem or the context itself is altered. In short, then, the termination stage can be treated as both an end and a beginning—an end to a program that has served its purpose, and a beginning to correct an errant policy or set of programs (deLeon, 1978).

THE STUDY OF POLICY TERMINATION

As just described, policy termination seems a rather benign, perhaps necessary, and certainly important stage in public policy planning. Yet this recognition has not been forthcoming, as demonstrated by the almost complete lack of literature specifically examining this topic. What might explain this peculiar oversight? Certainly a great deal has been written about certain types of termination activities. Every war fought has been ended somehow but there has been little attempt to treat the cessation of hostilities as a problem in policy termination.[8] Major government research programs have been abruptly stopped—such as the B-1 bomber, the supersonic transport, and the nuclear airplane[9]—but these have been treated as isolated case studies with little thought given to understanding the general problems and politics of termination.[10] The closing of mental health institutions has received a great deal of attention and is beginning to be treated as an examination of policy termination strategies, but one must be cautious about over-extending the lessons gleaned from a single issue area.[11] Again, what explanations might be offered to explain why this seemingly important aspect of policy has received so litte systematic, focused consideration?

Three principal reasons come to mind. First, strong negative connotations are generally ascribed to most acts of termination. For example, Westerners are almost pathologically unable to examine death with any great degree of analytic detachment.[12] Bankruptcy, coups, and surrender have pejorative overtones. For whatever explanations of cognitive dissonance one might wish to cite, it is clear that people do not like to think about the unpleasant. However plausible this reason might be, it must be viewed from a policy perspective as unacceptably myopic. In primitive cultures, death has been structured into one's set of life expectations; life is not static or immutable, a reality often lost on more modern cultures. As Herman Kahn (1960) has skillfully demonstrated, thinking about the unthinkable is not tantamount to inviting or even condoning it. To appreciate fully the policy process, the analyst needs to provide the appropriate mechanisms to accommodate the contextual facts of life—which perforce include termination— rather than continuing to be made insecure by them. Divorce, bankruptcy, and retirement were once tacit admissions of failure or an anachronism but, more recently, they are being viewed as opportunities for new and creative beginnings. Similar logic can be promoted regarding the termination of programs, policies, and organizations. As Biller (1976:137) states: "Ones's ability to take advantage of discovery is directly proportional to one's ability to terminate prior policy and organizational commitments."

A second possible reason why termination has received such sparse critical attention is that there simply are not enough cases upon which one can begin to generalize.[13] This empirical dearth would explain the existence of only a limited number of case studies and the lack of generalizations regarding termination. Kaufman (1976:77) writes that one of the reasons for publishing his study of termination "is to call attention to this gap." There is, of course, a great deal of validity behind this explanation. Kaufman (1976:35) was only able to identify 27 agencies out of his sample of 421 federal government agencies that have gone out of existence since 1923. Further, "one always suspects that each instance of the phenomenon is bound to be so idiosyncratic that no interesting generalizations will be possible" (Bardach, 1976:123). But if the previous explanation could be attributed to psychological reluctance, this excuse is comparable to analytic indulgence. As noted on virtually every page of this essay, there is already a sizable number of case histories of policy terminations, although they are not couched in those precise words. Policies fundamental to the nation;s political culture have been terminated[14] as well as major government institutions and their programs,[15] actions which have received extensive documentation. Kaufman (1976:65) notes that the number of terminated agencies he identified "though small, was not trivial. And if someday more frequent readings on the organizational population of the government are taken, there is reason to believe the death rate will turn out to be even higher." There appears, then, to be ample evidence to begin to describe termination conditions and strategies. Even more pressing, however, is the need. As Foster and Brewer (1976) caution, the exigencies of nuclear war do not permit the luxury of previous war termination strategies. Furthermore, governments' resources are increasingly restricted, which implies a cutback in their services. Funds are simply no longer available for organizations and policies that do not appear to be returning full value for their expenditure.[16] Therefore, the intellectual and political acts of termination must be confronted.

A third reason is that the intellectual problems presented by termination are very difficult, especially if one permits the incremental notions of policy adjustment and partial termination to enter into the picture. At what point does the "fine tuning" of policy implementation become partial termination? When does reorganization become termination? There is little question that the study of termination is difficult, not only because of the limited number of examples, as we have noted above, but—even more important— the political act of termination itself is very difficult. Policy researchers have been reluctant to approach an area in which findings are likely to lie fallow. Until we can appreciate what makes termination appear—and usually be—so intractable, we can hardly expect to find creative work on the topic. Therefore, let us examine what it is about the act of termination that has rendered it so immune from the usual list of policy options and, as a result, scholarly dissection. Before examining the obstacles to policy termination, it is important to pause momentarily and discard the semantic convenience "policy termination," disaggregating it into function, organization, policy, and program termination. At the same time, we will examine the effect of time upon policy termination.

TYPES OF "POLICY" TERMINATION

Earlier, the generic "policy termination was adopted as a shorthand device. Under this rubric, "policy" was meant to include governmental functions, organization, and programs as well as policies themselves.[17] We will now treat each of these individually because they represent different facets of the policy termination process and present different requirements. Admittedly, in practice it may be difficult to differentiate among them: the Veteran's Administration cannot be clearly distinguished from various veteran'sbenefit programs. Still, in many instances, the distinctions are entirely appropriate and important to recognize. It is useful, if only for the sake of the expositon, to view each of these separately so that the different methods of improving termination discussed in the final section can be appropriately matched with the different types of "policy" termination.

FUNCTIONS

A "function" is defined as a service provided by the government for its citizens. It transcends organization and policies; a number of agencies and their respective policies can all serve the same function. For instance, one function of the federal government according to the Constitution is the regulation of interstate commerce. There are many federal agencies and an even greater number of policies designed to regulate interstate trade. Still, the regulation of interstate commerce may be viewed as a singular government function.[18] It is important to distinguish functions from organizations, policies, and programs because functions appear to be the most resistant to termination attempts. One of Kaufman's findings (1976:64) was that "the functions performed by the agencies were even more enduring than the organizations themselves. In most of the twenty-seven [agency] deaths, the activities were not terminated; they were reassigned or taken up by other units, for the most part."

This relative permanence of functions is not difficult to understand. Generally speaking, the government will only dispense with services or functions if the society lacks either the assets or judgment to provide itself with the necessary services. Economists have identified a category of "public goods" that can be considered governmental functions; national defense is a function that has outlived any number of reorganizations of the national defense establishment (Ries, 1964). Jurisdiction over interstate regulatory matters and the redistribution of wealth and income are other instances of government functions. Additional examples from the state and local levels of government are easily identified, e.g., the regulation of public utilities and the provision of sanitation services and housing codes.

These functions or obligations are assumed by the government as a result of the demands of its citizens, and are "instituted because they fill a need not otherwise met, . . . Terminating them would therefore cause hardship and even suffering, the effects of which radiate outward through the society" (Kaufman, 1976:64). It is, therefore, not surprising that governmental functions would have the hardiest aptitude for survival, the greatest tendency toward posterity.

The implications for the policy analyst are clear. If he is to unsheath the termination sword, the function dragon is the most difficult to slay. More concretely, functions, almost by definition, serve a public purpose or fulfill a pressing need more directly and visibly than an organization and its various policies. To act against a governmental function is the hardest of the "policy" termination acts. As such, the analyst should recognize that he will have to present an exemplary effort (i.e., evaluate the policy termination and offer a comprehensive policy analysis for his proposed replacement) if he is to succeed.

ORGANIZATIONS

Organizations are groups of individuals that constitute what we call institutions. Organizations are created to respond to a specific need although they may—and probably will—expand their domain over time. They are designed to last and, as we shall see, they do precisely that. We need not anticipate the arguments presented in the following section that explain this longevity. Although organizations are rarely subjected to complete termination, it should be clear that they are more susceptible than governmental functions.

POLICIES

Organizations select and implement policies, which are generalized approaches or strategies toward solving a particular problem. Although an organization can expend significant amounts of its resources devising and executing appropriate policies, it should be stressed that policies are easier to terminate than the sponsoring organization itself for four reasons. First, unless the policy and the institution are exactly coincident or inextricably interwoven, the organization will act to preserve the whole—i.e., itself—before saving its component parts. The organization would prefer to forsake some of its policies rather than have the organization itself terminated. Second, in all likelihood, the policy cannot avail itself of as many allies as can the larger parent organization. In the simple calculus of power politics, policies have fewer chips to expend on their survival. Third, policies are easier to evaluate relative to a given objective than an organization, which could have multiple policy objectives. Criteria are more available for the analyst to measure the policy's relative ineffectiveness and to support his termination case. In this sense, it becomes much more vulnerable than the parent organization. And, fourth, most policies will have already generated their own congeries of critics that can be expected to coalesce behind the termination proposal. Organizations, of course, also have a group of natural enemies. However, they are usually disposed against particular policies and therefore less likely to join a termination coalition against the organization.

The policy may be the optimal level for the analyst to concentrate on for his termination activities. As was just suggested, policies are more vulnerable to being ended than governmental functions or the institutions which are their sponsors. At the same time, they are sufficiently general and important that they represent worthwhile targets.

PROGRAMS

Of the four targets or levels of termination, programs are the easiest to end. Although they occupy the lowest stratum of the analyst's attention, individual programs have the fewest political resources to protect them and represent the smallest investment on the part of the organization. They are closest to the problem and therefore their impact can be most directly measured and, if found lacking, blame most easily affixed. On the other hand, the day-to-day minutia of program implementation might serve to shield from them the critical view of the analyst who may assume that the policy level is his appropriate level of attention.

This latter phenomenon is often the case, which is unfortunate for three reasons. First, programs often define the policy, a point implied by the incrementalist school of decision-making (Meltsner, 1976). Second, the ability to terminate programs can be seen as a means of partial termination, or adjusting a policy that may have only a few identifiable components that are deficient. To overlook a poor program and attempt to terminate the entire policy might perpetuate the program if the overall policy proves resistant to efforts to curtail it. Third, programs affect the clients more immediately than the policies. A poorly planned or executed program can literally hurt people. For these reasons, the analyst should not be hesitant to examine and terminate individual programs.

A MATTER OF TIME

A final diversion before addressing the issues of termination obstacles and corrective strategies concerns the question of time. Specifically, how does the tenure of an institution or policy affect termination? Although other variables can intervene, in general one can assume that the longer a policy or institution has been in existence, the more difficult it will be to terminate, ceteris paribus. This condition is largely because of the allies it will have been able to accumulate. Although a fledgling organization has some sponsors or assets (otherwise it would not have been created), older organizations almost certainly are better fortified to resist reform movements.

The major exception to this assertion would be the policy or bureaucracy that has seemingly been made obsolete by an altered political environment or technology. Federal agents from the U.S. Treasury are no longer necessary to enforce Prohibition legislation. However, if only one point is to be gained from this essay, it is the remarkable adaptability of organizations whose raison d'être has been apparently outmoded. Treasury agents now enforce firearm, drug, and tobacco laws. Again, Katzenbach's treatise (1958:121) on the U.S. Cavalry is to the point:

> The Horse Cavalry . . . maintained a capacity of survival that borders on the miraculous. The war horse survived a series of challenges each of which was quite as great as those which today's weapons systems present to today's traditional concepts. Like the mollusk, the Horse Cavalry made those minor adjustments that time dictated absolutely. Then it continued to live out an expensive and decorous existence with splendor and some spirit straight into an age which thought it a memory. Indeed, it is difficult to conceive of an institution that underlines so sharply the relativity of the concept of obsolescence.[19]

In short, to equate organizational age with biological age and assume, in turn, that an organization *automatically* grows more vulnerable as it grows older is an hypothesis not supported by the evidence.

The policy implication regarding termination and the age of an organization is that the analyst would probably have greater success in terminating a newer (rather than an older) policy. One important caveat is necessary. The very new policy or program is obviously the most vulnerable; it has not had time to generate any support beyond its orginal sponsors. However, its very newness should provide some measure of protection because it has not had the opportunity to be evaluated. The evaluation plans might not have been designed, no data collected, and there would have been little opportunity to judge how the policy has affected the problem in terms of the defined policy objectives. The analyst has a professional obligation to avoid the temptation to terminate programs just because they are vulnerable or because he "doesn't like them." At the very least, a policy should be given a chance to fail (which implies a chance to succeed) before it is a candidate for policy termination.

OBSTACLES TO POLICY TERMINATION

We can identify six reasons why policy termination has been particularly difficult to plan and execute in the policy arena:

(1) Intellectual reluctance;
(2) Institutional permanence;
(3) Dynamic conservatism
(4) Antitermination coalitions;
(5) Legal obstacles; and
(6) High start-up costs.

These obstacles inhibit—if not virtually prohibit—the political act of policy termination. Although they usually occur in combination, we will discuss them, somewhat arbitrarily, one at a time.

INTELLECTUAL RELUCTANCE

The first obstacle, already alluded to above, is that people do not readily confront issues pertaining to death. This reluctance is also applicable when dealing with organization termination, particularly if the observer has a vested interest (professional, emotional, intellectual, collegial and so forth) that makes his exercise particularly unpalatable or even painful. This inhibition often results in a complete failure to link the institutions's purposes and objectives to a changing contextual reality. Perhaps the most vivid example was the refusal of the world's armies to recognize that, prior to World War I, new technology—especially the machine gun and rapid fire artillery—had rendered the horse cavalry obsolete. Katzenbach (1958:122) comments:

> For the elite of the armies of the world, the cavalry, . . . these developments would seem to have been nothing short of disaster. For that proud and beautiful animal, the horse, has a thin skin and a high silhouette, and its maximum rate of speed on the attack is only 30 m.p.h. Especially in conjunction with barbed wire, automatically manufactured since 1874 and in military use at the end of the century, it is difficult to imagine a target more susceptible to rapid fire.[20]

Evidence of the reduced effectiveness and increased vulnerability of the cavalry garnered from the Crimean War with its infamous charge and slaughter of the light brigade, the American Civil War, the Boer War, and the Russo-Japanese War was discounted and the elan of the cavalry charge was retained as part of the arsenal of the Great War combatants.[21] Remarkably enough, the U.S. Army Horse Cavalry existed as an entity through the Second World War as well!

This explanation has important implications for the policy analyst. Cognitive reluctance to realize policy shortcomings is reinforced for the analyst because policies are typically designed to solve or at least reduce a specified problem; the options proposed and programs chosen are not selected with the thought that they will prove deficient. For this reason, little serious attention is paid to the question of failure or the later need for policy termination. The French never considered that the Maginot Line defenses would not defeat the German wartime offensive so there was no reason to countenance an alternative or fall back position should the Maginot Line fail. In sum, not only do people in general not like to consider termination options, but the professional egos of analysts increase the psychological obstacles necessary to deal with ending projects with which they have been associated.[22] Biller (1976:137) speaks for analysts everywhere:

> Having invested substantially in persuading ourselves and others of the efficacy of what was then proposed, and having secured the necessary "reform" resources to bring it into existence, it is little wonder that we defer recognition as long as possible if it does not work as anticipated; or that we prefer to note the surprisingly inconstant

nature of the world as an explanation of the troubles we then experience rather than looking to our own skill in the strategies we had earlier employed.

INSTITUTIONAL PERMANENCE

Policies and especially organizations are deliberately designed to endure. Organizations are created to perpetuate a service or relationship. This is even more the case regarding government or public organizations because they are created to institutionalize services deemed necessary, services whose demands are considered to outlast a single sponsor or bureaucrat. Indeed, such "organizations have as one of their principal *strengths* the ability to resist change and termination—that is, persist in the face of information that may warrant discontinuity" (Biller, 1976:137). The problem-solving, adaptive nature of the organization further immunizes it from easy termination. Should discrepancies arise between the organization's objective and its environment, the organization is designed to recognize, act upon, and reduce the problem before the threat can attain a magnitude that would endanger the institution's very existence, or at least its nominal jurisdiction in dealing with such problems.[23]

These tendencies are, to a large degree, proper and justifiable institutional objectives; major policies and institutions should not be transitory or ephemeral, nor should they meekly collapse under the threat of a new problem or altered conditions. The Tennessee Valley Authority clearly outgrew its original charter of a utility industry yardstick as it perceived new requirements resulting from the dams it was constructing (Selznick, 1949). This is not the time or place to debate the issues and values of organizational growth, adaptation, or permanence. The crucial point is not whether planned institutional longevity is good or bad, but simply that it is a fact of political, bureaucratic life. Organizations, their policies, and many of their programs are consciously designed for long life, possibly permanence (though few analysts pretend to such an extended time horizon)[24] and this renders the termination option extremely difficult to exercise. Indeed, if longevity were an institutional and policy goal, then one might view the study of termination as little more than an academic exercise (in the negative sense of the term). Simply stated, policy termination is not in the usual self-interest of the bureaucracy. Biller (1976:136) provides an overview to the issue of organizational permanence and its influence on our conception of termination.

[I]t is not surprising to find system designers choosing, in the name of making operation "easy," to focus on amortizing a long operational run by setting up standard procedures and templates that are as difficult as possible to change. . . . Coupled with our primary dependence in the public sector on administered bureaucratic organizations (that is, organizations designed to transcend the attributes of particular persons through modes of recruitment, socialization, succession and incentives, designed, given continued support, to run forever) it really is unremarkable that we have come to assume basic persistence and perpetuity rather than termination to be the appropriate assumption to be used in dealing with most public policies and organizations.

DYNAMIC CONSERVATISM

A third reason why organizations and policies are so resistant to termination is that they are dynamic entities. An organization has both the means and motivations to recognize when its objectives are accomplished or when there is a great disparity between the institution's policies and the directed policy goals. In either case, the organization can move to alter its objectives or possibly its effective domain.[25]

The successful completion of a policy objective is scarcely sufficient grounds for disbanding the organization. New objectives can be defined within the organization that require its continued existence. However, these new objectives may be beyond the organization's ability to attain. The United Nations police action in Korea had the specific mandate of driving the invading North Korean forces out of South Korea, but the achievement of that goal did not result in the termination of police action. Rather, the successful attainment of that objective encouraged the commander of the U.N. forces, General Douglas MacArthur, to define a new set of objectives, which included at least driving the Communist forces off the Korean peninsula. This expanded set of objectives led to the U.N. invasion of North Korea, the entry of Communist China into the war, and a longer, more costly American involvement than had been initially anticipated or would have been necessary had the achievement of the originally stated objectives been sufficient to terminate the hostilities (Rees, 1964). A more benevolent example of success not resulting in termination is the March of Dimes organization. After the discovery of the Salk vaccine, the March of Dimes charter—the cure or prevention of polio—was essentially fulfilled. However, rather than disband, the charity chose to redirect its attention to other, yet unconquered diseases. Nor did the WCTU disband after the passage of the Prohibition Amendment. Thus, there is little reason to suggest that the successful completion of an organization's original goals is sufficient, or even cause, to bring about its termination.

The contrary case—the inability of an organization to resolve a problem in its domain—is similarly unlikely to result in its termination. As noted above, organizations are generally resourceful enough to realize such deficiency exists and move to correct or ameliorate it. If proponents of a policy find themselves lacking allies in one organization, they may move to another, more hospitable agency. For example, advocates of performance contracting in education were unable to convince the Department of Health, Education, and Welfare of the efficacy of their programs so they took their case to the Office of Economic Opportunity (OEO), which was much more receptive. Thus, a policy which might have been terminated in one agency was able to relocate and prosper. If conditions change and social support wanes, an organization can easily change its original objectives and move to meet new demands; the YMCA is today more concerned with recreation facilities and less with Christian souls than its earlier manifestations.

Obviously, if an organization or policy is not performing to expectations, it is a more likely candidate for termination than if it were achieving some worthwhile measure of its defined objectives. The point here is not to deny that ineffective performance will not lead to termination; surely, it increases the probability for termination, although the increase may not be significant. The main point is that organizations, policies, and their contexts are dynamic, not static. Organizations can and will alter their sponsors, clientele, policies, and objectives if need be, thereby making it much more difficult to terminate them for failure to achieve an initially defined set of objectives (Hirschman, 1970).

ANTI-TERMINATION COALITIONS

A fourth obstacle to policy termination is that there are significant political groups that will be opposed to termination from both within and without the threatened agency. Each has its own assets and tactics, but they are particularly successful when they form coalitions to block threatened termination acts.

Internally, the members of the organization will work assiduously to develop new rationale why it should continue. They will procrastinate and compromise in hopes of temporarily placating and then outlasting the reform or termination initiative. At times, an organization might simply refuse to discontinue its programs. In the first instance, one can appreciate the efforts of American cavalry officers who argued that their horses were superior to tanks because horses did not need spare parts; they contended that God assured the Army that there would always be plenty of mounts, i.e., you could destroy a tank factory but not the procreation process (Katzenbach, 1958). In the second instance, one can cite the resiliency of the American SST proponents. Although the final tactic—refusal—is the least employed, it is clearly not beyond the bureaucratic ken. In November 1969, President Nixon "announced that the United States had decided to renounce the use of biological weapons" and ordered all stocks of such weapons destroyed. Dr. Nathan Gordon, the director of CIA's biological branch, ignored the order because of his department's interest in shellfish toxin, which, as he explained to a Senate committee, was excluded from the Presidential order because it was a chemical, not biological, toxin. The following February, a Presidential clarification ordered that all chemical and biological toxins were to be destroyed. Again the order was ignored because, in Gordon's words (Washington Monthly, 1975:39), "the second order was directed to the Defense Department and the CIA is not part of the Defense Department."

A fourth and relatively common strategy for a threatened agency or program is to recruit its external allies to apply whatever pressures they can to protect the organization or a specific program. Instances of these tactics are numerous; for example, the U.S. Navy has had little compunction when threatened with the closure of a navy yard against enlisting local support (i.e., the local labor unions and suppliers), industrial concerns, and the appropriate members of Congress. Whatever economic and operational efficiency arguments underlie the suggested closing of a base, they can rarely withstand the internal and external opposition that a large organization like the Navy can muster.

Similar arguments and pressures are often cited during the formative days of a policy as creating and defining the initial demand. This is the essence of group theory (Truman, 1951) and is reflected in "bureaucratic politics" (Allison,

1971). However, the arguments are much more forceful to the politics of termination than initiation for two reasons. First, the internal bureaucracy that would be opposed to termination actions is well entrenched (which Bardach (1977:128) defines to mean "having easy and regular access to powerful governmental allies"). The organization has had the opportunity to cultivate a number of clients or interest groups, all of which can be mobilized against whatever termination threats might appear. Second, these external allies can be particularly purposeful because they will have already benefited from the threatened agency's services. In the case of groups politicking for the initiation of a program, the external allies can only lobby on the basis of expectations. The former condition is clearly more conducive to strong advocacy. Often these outside interests are well organized (e.g., the automobile industry, the oil industry, labor unions) and have their own political credits which they can call due. These allies can include other government agencies, Congressional committees, and even other national governments. The British Government and U.S. State Department both lobbied strenuously against the Secretary of Defense's decision to terminate the Skybolt missile development program. (Neustadt, 1970).

LEGAL OBSTACLES

If these conditions and coalitions were not sufficient to inhibit any termination activity unless it possesses the most implacable credentials and allies, the fact that the federal government operates under the constraints of "due process" is a fifth factor that makes termination an even more difficult task. As Bardach (1977:129) points out, "the Administrative Procedures Act forbids the government to be 'arbitrary and capricious.' " Washington, D.C. Chief of Police Jerry Wilson's decision to abolish his department's motorcycle police squad was contested in the courts on the issue of whether Wilson could reclassify his employees' position (Shulsky, 1967). The embattled OEO employees won a federal court restraining order cancelling President Nixon's executive order that the OEO be disbanded and forbidding him to impound the agency's funding, and there is a current debate whether President Carter has the legal right to cancel all further development of the breeder reactor given that contracts have been signed.

HIGH START UP COSTS

The coalition of the internal and external elements that can be marshalled against an organization's or a policy's termination are formidable. They result in the sixth obstacle to policy termination, which can be called extremely expensive "start up cost" for anybody who wished to argue in favor of termination. These start up costs can be characterized as the political resources necessary to counter the coalitions enumerated above that shield organizations and progams from the termination axe. Start up costs must overcome the following four obstacles within the termination coalition. First, few agency heads or politicians want to admit that they were mistaken and the termination of a program is a tacit admission of such a failure. Second, many critics would only move to terminate a program if they could offer alternative programs to rectify the problem; the inherent complexity of some policy issues might well insulate organizations and programs from termination actions because attractive alternatives are not available. The lack of alternative energy resources that did not pollute the environment silenced many critics of nuclear power reactors until recently (Bethe, 1976). Third, as just suggested, to propose even the possibility of termination could provoke powerful protest. Only the most naive, arrogant, or confident analyst would consciously initiate a termination action knowing the maelstrom that must always assuredly follow. His potential allies would have similar reservations in joining him. Finally, the analyst recognizes that if he is successful, serious externalities could occur; for instance, the organization's morale may be crucially undermined and the government itself may suffer in its citizen's eyes.[26]

The combination of these four factors affecting start up costs means that the analyst who recommends termination must be quite certain of his evaluation measures and the efficacy of his proposed alternatives. Just as important, he must be sure that his appreciation of the general policy objectives is true, a situation often complicated by the reticence of decision makers to make their objectives operational or even well enunciated (Ikle, 1971). Furthermore, he must not only be able to demonstrate persuasively the existing program's deficiencies and why his proposed policy is more congruent with the policy objectives and more likely to be effective in terms of the problem and objectives; he should also have devised twin plans—a termination plan for the ineffective policy and an implementation plan for the new one. Barring these confidences, the high costs and political liabilites incurred by proposing policy termination make the recommendation of policy termination extremely difficult and unlikely.

SUMMARY

It is clear that policy termination is a rare political activity. The intellectual and political forces arrayed against termination are formidable. Unless the offending policy or organization is generally recognized as pernicious or dysfunctional, the analyst will have little initial support to justify his analysis and proposed courses of action.[27] For these reasons, the termination processes have seldom been exercised unless the target was extremely weak and isolated without powerful allies (the Washington motorcycle patrol is one example) or the consequences of permitting a policy to continue were consensually seen to run diametrically counter to the society's preference (as was the case during the late 1960s regarding the Vietnam war).

These difficulties would explain the earlier noted lack of termination case histories and even rarer attempts at generalization. Still, as argued earlier, many cases are already in hand, more are coming, and there is an increasing recognition of the necessity to understand the conditions, processes, and problems of policy termination. For example, as nuclear power reactors begin to approach the end of their designed life expectancy, they will have to be closed down and the radioactive parts of the reactor neutralized or safely disposed. Two reactors in the United States—one in Hallam, Nebraska, and the other in Detroit—have been shut down, but there is little documentation on the procedures that were followed, the criteria that were used to determine if the areas were safe, and the problems that arose. Welfare and education programs are similarly in need of termination guidelines.

Certainly the need for research on termination is clear and demanding. Just as certainly, the obstacles are imposing. The response from the policy analysis community should be two-fold: first, researchers should begin to collect appropriate studies and then to generalize about the termination process. This need for a theory is meant to structure both the intellectual tasks and the political actions that are required. Second, analysts must begin to include termination considerations and options in their policy planning processes, so that termination will no longer be a neglected policy consideration. The primary purpose of the chapter to this point has been to address the first response. Let us now turn to the second.

STRATEGIES FOR POLICY TERMINATION

This essay has discussed a number of issues related to policy termination, such as: What is it? How and where does it fit into the policy process? And why is it so difficult to perform? There is little to be gained, however, by the mere recognition of termination. The imperative for creative policy termination policies is apparent; the United States cannot afford all the weapons systems the Department of Defense wants nor all the social welfare programs proposed by interest groups and still maintain a viable economy. The inclusion of termination options into legislation is certainly useful but not sufficient. An example of this type of termination strategy is the current consideration of "sunset legislation" by many legislatures (see Simison, 1976; Cohen, 1977). The Federal Energy Agency (FEA) was mandated with a five-year lifespan, but at the end of its proscribed existence, Congress renewed the FEA charter; even after reviewing its extraordinary growth, the FEA's "sunset" clause was not exercised (see House, 1976). A similar amendment has been written into the legislation mandating the newly formed Department of Energy.

If termination strategies are not carefully formulated and implemented, they can undermine their purpose. Again, sunset legislation is a good example of termination tactics that could be counterproductive if they do not meet these tests. For instance, an agency that has to defend its existence could devote a sizable amount of its resources to that task. This reallocation is almost sure to decrease the resources being expended to address the problem areas under that agency's jurisdiction. Alternatively, it could obscure its activities in such a way that effective evaluation would be impossible. In both ways, sunset legislation could detract from the organization's capability to carry out its policy mandate.[28] Others suggest that sunset requirements are fundamentally biased against social legislation (Randall, 1977), or that they could create more problems than they solve (see Brewer, 1978, for an extremely critical evaluation of the Program Evaluation Act of 1977).

What then might be an appropriate set of termination strategies that serve the dual function of not interfering with the organization's or policy's ability to treat problem areas while making the evaluation and termination options more available?[29]

The most important step in improving termination opportunities is the recognition that termination is not the end of the world, either for concerned persons or vested organizations. Rather, termination should be viewed as an opportunity for improving a deficient condition or as representing a successful venture. This constructive approach is less alien to U.S. business firms than political bureaucracies. Even after a tremendous emotional and financial commitment, the Ford Motor Company did not permit the failure of the Edsel to drag out; it was cancelled less than two years after its initial introduction (Brooks, 1959). Not only should the analyst work to overcome his psychic inhibitions regarding termination, but the pejorative attitude toward those whose jobs require them to close down projects should be disavowed. Termination will continue to be an onerous and neglected process until the connotations of "hatchetman," "hired gun," and "program assassin" are abandoned. Although his advice is not guaranteed to be sanguine, the marriage counselor or management consultant is no longer considered persona non grata. A similar acceptance of public policy termination, the creative opportunities it offers, and those who implement it is clearly in order.

Before specific termination strategies (or at least their possibility) can be devised, termination must be recognized as an integral and beneficial part of the policy process.[30] This implies a great deal more than the understanding that programs can fail. It suggests that the possibility of failure should be realized from the very start of the policy process when the original policy alternatives are generated. Even though it might run counter to an analyst's professional ego, a well-designed policy analysis might include the presentation of the policy problem and options, an implemenation plan, the evaluation metric and methodology, and a termination option should the evaluation of the policy prove to be negative. The estimation process can weigh the termination option (i.e., is it a feasable alternative?) and the decision maker can base his selection partially on the ease with which the option can be invoked should the cause arise.

The analyst who proposes and develops termination contingencies must pay special attention to the evaluation stage because it provides him with the measures relative to the policy objectives that determine if the termination option need be exercised, or if partial termination can provide the necessary adjustments. In the public sector, the evaluation criteria are often difficult to define and hard to use. The insertion of political values makes firm evaluation criteria ever harder to utilize.[31] In private industry, the nominal objective—profits—and evaluation measures—dollars—are much more apparent. Ford's loss of over a third of a billion dollars within two years was a totally unambiguous indication that the Edsel was losing money and should be cancelled without delay. However, this ready metric rarely exists for most large government programs.[32] Thus, to call for better public policy termination strategies is, in effect, to call for better evaluation strategies, for, without the latter, the former would be based on little more than visceral impressions. Simply put, good termination strategies demand good evaluation strategies.

A third consideration before designing specific strategies to end an organization or a policy is what we might call the "political context" and "natural points" for termination.[33] The first suggests that the analyst should understand what groups oppose or favor a specific policy termination and why. This information would be pivotal in determining the termination strategy. "Natural points" suggest that there are times and places during a policy's lifespan that are more conducive to termination than others. The most obvious example of a natural time for ending a policy would be the change in a political administration when the new occupants have a public mandate to change or conclude the incumbents' policies.[34] Thus, President Carter, free of the political baggage of the preceding Republican administrations, terminated the production of the B-1. Similarly, a large turnover or reorganization in committee assignments in Congress might weaken an agency's legislative allies, thus rendering it more susceptible to terminations. Another point would be after a major personnel change in an agency; the Chief of Naval Operations made a concentrated (and successful) effort to terminate the Navy's sponsorship of the F-111 aircraft following the resignation of Secretary of Defense Robert McNamara (Coulam, 1977: Chap 5), and the FBI's questionable activites were revealed and curtailed after the death of its long-time director, J. Edgar Hoover. An example of a convenient place for terminating a policy might be within an executive agency, such as OMB, where the vested interests that would be present in the agency whose program is being terminated are precluded. The lesson here is quite straightforward: there are enough inherent obstacles to policy termination, so the analyst should avail himself of all the advantages he can muster.

With these considerations in mind, what are some stategies that would improve the chances for policy termination? One decision might concern the time horizon and whether the termination will be a gradual, decremental process or an immediate and total action. Brewer (1974) argues that this choice is usually forced by circumstances beyond the analyst's control; furthermore, the chosen time frame will call for significantly different tactics. The first is likely to be more successful because the programs's clients will have gradually transferred their requirements elsewhere and the sponsoring constituency's interest will have waned as the inevitable slowly becomes acceptable. More humanely, this decremental strategy allows those affected (both the staff in charge of the policy and those benefiting from it) to acquire alternative positions and resources. The second time frame is more abrupt, liable to meet with greater resistance, and require greater preparation should it be selected (Lambright and Sapolsky, 1976:202-204). For example, if the latter time horizon is chosen, the termination plan might prepare positions for the agency's staff prior to the termination announcement so that they do not view the end of their agency as tantamount to their being out of work. The affected organizations can be persuaded of the action's efficacy if they can be shown that there are sufficient alternative sources of supply; the military services did not object to the end of the universal military conscription because they were convinced they could recruit enough men in the all-volunteer service environment to meet their manpower requirements.

Biller suggests a number of particular strategies that provide positive incentives for policy termination and might prove appropriate for specific contingencies.[35] For example, he notes that organizations currently have little incentive to curtail their programs because any funds saved in this manner revert to the treasury at the end of the fiscal year. If agencies were allowed to retain the money saved from terminating a policy or program and reallocate it according to their internal priorities or even carry it over to the following fiscal year, they would have a greater incentive to cancel questionable programs. This would also permit an organization to maintain its bureaucratic presitge among its peers, which is usually adjudged by the size of its domain and budget (Downs, 1967).

Other suggestions include close analogies to private industry. For example, "as in bankruptcy experienced by private sector firms, there is a need for the appointment of referees able to protect legally the rights of multiple claimants (both funding sources and clients) when a public agency flounders" (Biller, 1976:146). Such an agency would make certain that a program's assets (money and personnel) could be equitably redistributed. It also would provide an incentive for the operating agency to terminate its own programs as soon as they proved deficient rather than waiting until it loses control of its assets. Thus, this approach would provide tangible incentives encouraging the sponsoring agency to engage in policy readjustment or even partial termination on its own initiative rather than postponing termination until the last possible moment and permitting a third party to reallocate its resources.

A third alternative would be to have a staff of "salvage specialists" who are trained in reallocating resources freed by policy terminations to other positions where they can do the most good. This would alleviate staff reluctance and uncertainties engendered by termination action and thereby help overcome internal resistance.

These strategies are not meant to provide a how-to-do manual with chapter and verse for every partial and complete termination scenario ("lock all doors," "turn out lights,"etc.).[36] They are rather meant to offer organizations internal incentive to correct—or if need be, end—their policies as they are evaluated to be dysfunctional. At present, virtually all institutional incentives are biased toward perpetuating an organization or its policies. If these alternative internal incentives can be operationalized, specific termination actions will be more readily forthcoming from both within and without the organization and with much less opposition(i.e., greater opportunity) than is currently the case.

CONCLUSION

This essay has attempted to demonstrate two ideas: first, policy termination is a grievously and "wrongly underattended" (Biller, 1976:133) issue in policy analysis; and, second, even though the obstacles that hinder or prevent policy termination are formidable, the potential payoffs are such that successful termination strategies can and should be devised to overcome these obstacles. There are three sequential tasks, then, that are required to make the transition from the implausible to the feasible. First, case histories of policy termination should be compiled. Second, based upon these, analysts can begin to acquire an understanding of the intellectual and political requirements for termination, which can serve as the foundation for a theory of policy termination. And third, based on the previous two, general incentive strategies and more specific tactics that promote termination can be set forth. This essay has offered a tentative first approximation on most of these points, but, clearly and urgently, much more need to be done.

NOTES

1. Hargrove (1975) is only one of many.
2. See, for example, Pressman and Wildavsky (1973); Bardach (1977) incisively surveys most of the implementation literature.
3. These can be treated as four distinct types of termination but, for our immediate purposes, they will all be grouped under the generic of policy termination. This grouping will be disaggregated later in the essay.
4. The latter episode, a classic study in termination, is described by Katzenbach (1958).
5. In Lasswell (1971), Chapter 2 is perhaps the most systematic statement of his policy process model.
6. Brewer (1974). A more thorough delineation of this model is found in Brewer and deLeon (forthcoming).
7. "Domain" in this case is similar to the usage in Thompson (1967), that is, the political area over which a political entity has recognized (although not necessarily undisputed) jurisdiction. Also see Easton (1965).
8. The major exception is Ikle (1971); a more recent and normative effort is Foster and Brewer (1976).
9. The Congressional decision to cancel the SST is described by Costello and Hughes (1976); and the atomic aircraft is treated by Lambright (1967). The cancellation of the B-1 is documented by Wade (1977).
10. A first attempt at this is provided by Lambright and Sapolsky (1976).
11. An optimistic straw in the wind is Bardach (1972). Also see Bradley (1976).
12. See Zilboorg (1943), and, from a cultural perspective, Choron (1963).
13. This is suggested by Bardach (1976) as guest editor of the special issue of *Policy Sciences* dedicated to the study of termination.
14. The Supreme Court's 1954 decision to ban school segregation by race is an example of a termination act that has had profound ramifications on virtually every segment of the society. Kluger (1975) documents the history of school segregation from *Plessy v. Ferguson* (1896) to *Brown*. Judicial rulings and later legislation on environmental issues have had a similar pervasive effect.
15. For example, the Office of Economic Opportunity, the lynchpin of President Johnson's War on Poverty, was abolished under President Nixon. See Levine (1970).
16. This is especially visible in the Department of Defense where new weapons systems are scrutinized for their cost-effectiveness. Organizations are also prone to a similar calculus; see Shulsky (1976).
17. Bardach (1977) distinguishes between policies, programs, and bureaucratic organizations.
18. Of course, these functions can be disaggregated until they are coincident with policies or programs, such as the confiscation of drugs at customs stations. Still, the identification of functions as a possible object of termination is valuable.

19. Katzenbach's thesis is supported by recent reports that the Rhodesian militia are using cavalry tactics to combat guerrilla incursions; the Rhodesian commander explained, "If you put a lot of modern technology on [the horse], it becomes a very effective weapon" (Burns, 1977:1).

20. The reluctance of European strategists to recognize the impact of rapid fire weaponry on warfare is described by Ellis (1975).

21. The demise of the horse cavalry as an offensive battlefield weapons systems was presaged even earlier; see the account of the Battle of Waterloo in Keegan (1976).

22. Barber (1961) adds religion and ideology to the list of psychological obstacles that can make alternative scenarios less available.

23. Organizational response to stress is the main concern of Cyert and March (1963), and Thompson (1967).

24. A possible exception: during the reign of Queen Victoria, an Englishman of sufficient means could purchase a 999 year lease on a box in Royal Albert concert hall.

25. Schon (1971) refers to this as "dynamic conservatism."

26. The feared loss of U.S. credibility was a key factor in Lyndon Johnson's decision to continue the American Vietnam commitment; see Halberstam, 1969.

27. Behn (1978) suggests that a possible termination strategy is to demonstrate a policy's harmful or malicious effects rather than its mere inefficiencies or ineffectiveness.

28. DeLeon (1977) examines some of the possible problems with the currently pending sunset legislation. This paper was presented as testimony supporting U.S. Senate Bill 2, the Program Evaluation Act of 1977.

29. Some government organizations are created with specified lifespans. Commissions to study particular problems (e.g., the Kerner and Murphy Commissions on race and U.S. foreign policy institutions, respectively) and disaster relief agencies fall into this category. Even here, term existence is occasionally problematic; see the *Sixteenth Annual Report of the Temporary Commission of the State of New York,* as noted in *The Washington Monthly,* Vol. 9, No. 4 (June 1977), p. 31. Still, in general, these organizations are so stipulative in their nature that they need not concern us here except to note that they do exist, even if only in rare circumstances for limited purposes.

30. To date, only the Lasswell and Brewer models accept this assertion. The otherwise excellent compilation of essays by Bauer and Gergen (1968) makes no reference to policy termination, an oversight rather typical of the policy process literature.

31. Titmuss (1971) skillfully weaves costs and ethics into his comparison of the U.S. and British systems for blood donations, thereby demonstrating the inherent difficulties.

32. Rivlin (1971) speaks eloquently to this problem. See her testimony on S.2 in U.S. Senate Subcommittee on Intergovernmental Relations of the Committee on Governmental Affairs (1977).

33. I am indebted to Robert K. Yin of The Rand Corporation for suggesting these concepts, albeit in a different context (see Yin, 1976).

34. Although, as Bardach (1977) notes, changes in administrations scarcely guarantee that new programs will replace outmoded ones.

35. This section is greatly indebted to Biller (1976:144-149).

36. Most organization development books deal at great length with reorganization or what we might call partial termination; to wit, Beckhard, 1969.

REFERENCES

ALLISON, G. T. (1971). Essence of decision: Explaining the Cuban missile crisis. Boston: Little, Brown.

American Heritage Dictionary of the English Language (1969). Boston: Houghton Mifflin.

BARBER, B. (1961). "Resistance by scientists to scientific discovery." Science, 184, 3479(September 1):596-602.

BARDACH, E. C. (1972). The skill factor in politics: Repealing the mental commitment laws in California. Berkeley: University of California Press.

_____ (1976). "Policy termination as a political process." Policy Sciences, 7, 2(June):123.

_____ (1977). the implementation game. Cambridge, Mass.: MIT Press.

BAUER, R. A., and GERGEN, K. J. (eds.) (1968). The study of policy formulation. New York: Free Press.

BECKHARD, R. (1969). Organization development: Strategies and models. Reading, Mass.: Addison-Wesley

BEHN, R.D. (1978). "Ten hints for the would-be policy termination." Policy Analysis, 4, 3(Summer):393-413.

BETHE, H. A. (1976). "The necessity of fission power." Scientific American, 234, 1(January):21-31.

BILLER, R. P. (1976). "On tolerating policy and organizational termination: Design considerations." Policy Sciences, 7, 2(June):137.

BRADLEY, V. J. (1976). "Policy termination in mental health: The hidden agenda." Policy Sciences, 7, 2(June):215-224.

BREWER, G. D. (1974). "The policy sciences emerge: To nurture and structure a discipline." Policy Sciences, 5, 3(September):239-244.

_____ (1978). "Termination: Hard choices—harder questions." Public Administration Review, 38, 3(May/June):338-344.

_____ and DeLEON, P. (forthcoming). The foundation of the policy sciences. Homewood, Ill.: Dorsey.

BROOKS, J. (1959). The fate of the Edsel and other business adventures. New York: Harper and Row.

BURNS, J. F. (1977). "Rhodesian cavalry in action again." New York Times, February 20, Section 1, p. 1.

CHORON, J. (1963). Death and western thought. New York: Collier.

COHEN, R. E. (1977). "Taking up the tools to tame the bureaucracy: Sunset legislation." National journal, 9, 14(April 2):514-520.

COSTELLO, J., and HUGHES, T. (1976). The Concorde conspiracy. New York: Charles Scribner's.

COULAM, R.F. (1977). Illusions of choice: The F-111 and the problem of weapons acquisitions reform. Princeton, N.J.: Princeton University Press.

CYERT, R. M., and MARCH, J. C. (1963). A behavioral theory of the firm. Englewood Cliffs, N.J.: Prentice-Hall.

DeLEON, P. (1977). The sun also sets: An evaluation of public policy. Santa Monica Cal.: Rand, P-5826, March.

_____ (1978). "Public policy termination: An end and a beginning." Policy Analysis, 4, 3(Summer):369-392.

DOWNS, A. (1967). Inside bureaucracy. Boston: Little, Brown.

EASTON, D. (1965). A systems analysis of political life. New York: John Wiley.

ELLIS, J. (1975). The social history of the machine gun. New York: Pantheon.

FOSTER, J. L., and BREWER, G. D. (1976). "And the clocks were striking thirteen: The termination of war." Policy Sciences, 7, 2(June):225-243.

HALBERSTAM, D. (1969). The best and the brightest. New York: Random House.

HARGROVE, E. C. (1975). The missing link: The study of the implementation of social policy. Washington, D.C.: Urban Institute.

HIRSCHMAN, A. O. (1970). Exit, voice, and loyalty: Responses to decline in firms, organizations, and states. Cambridge, Mass.: Harvard University Press.

HOUSE, K. E. (1976). "Getting entrenched: Energy agency spends much to insure a long life, foes say." Wall Street Journal, March 9, pp. 1, 19.

IKLE, F. C. (1971). Every war must end. New York: Columbia University Press.

KAHN, H. (1960). On thermonuclear war. Princeton, N.J.: Princeton University Press.

KATZENBACH, E. L. (1958). "The horse cavalry in the twentieth century. A study in policy response." Public Policy, 8:120-149.

KAUFMAN, H. (1976). Are government organizations immortal? Washington, D.C.: Brookings Institution.

KEEGAN, J. (1976). The face of battle. New York: Viking.

KLUGER, R. (1975). Simple justice: The history of Brown v. the Board of Education. New York: Alfred Knopf.

LAMBRIGHT, W. H. (1967). Shooting down the nuclear plane. Indianapolis: Inter-University Case Program, Bobbs-Merrill.

_____ and SAPOLSKY, H. M. (1976). "Terminating federal research and development programs." Policy Sciences, 7, 2(June):199-213.

LASSWELL, H. D. (1971). A pre-view of policy sciences. New York: American Elsevier.

LEVINE, R. A. (1970). The poor ye need not have: Lessons from the War on Poverty. Cambridge, Mass.: MIT Press.

MELTSNER, A. (1976). Policy analysts in the bureaucracy. Berkeley: University of California Press.

NEUSTADT, R. E. (1970). Alliance politics. New York: Columbia University Press.

PRESSMAN, J. L., and WILDAVSKY, A. B. (1973). Implementation. Berkeley: University of California Press.

RANDALL, R. (1977). "What's wrong with sunset laws?" Nation, March 19:331-334.

REES, D. (1964). The limited war. New York: St. Martins.

RIES, J. C. (1964). The management of defense. Baltimore: Johns Hopkins Press.

RIVLIN, A. M. (1971). Systematic thinking for social action. Washington, D.C.: Brookings Institution.

SCHON, D. (1971). Beyond the stable state. New York: Random House.

SELZNICK, P. (1949). TVA and the grass roots. Berkeley: University of California Press.

SHULSKY, A. N. (1967). "Abolishing the District of Columbia motorcycle squad." Policy Sciences, 7, 2(June):183-197.

SIMISON, R. L. (1976). "Cleaning house: New 'sunset laws' seek to curb growth of big government." Wall Street Journal, June 25, pp. 1, 25.

THOMPSON, J. T. (1967). Organizations in action. New York: McGraw-Hill.

TITMUSS, R. M. (1971). The gift relationship: From human blood to social policy. New York: Pantheon.

TRUMAN, D. B. (1951). The governmental process. New York: Alfred Knopf.

U.S. Senate Subcommittee on Intergovernmental Relations of the Committee on Government Affairs (1977). The Sunset Act of 1977. 95th Congress, 1st Session. Washington, D.C.: U.S. Government Printing Office.

WADE, N. (1977). "Death of the B-1: The events behind Carter's decision." Science 197, 4303(August 5):536-539.

Washington Monthly (1975). 7, 9(November):39.

YIN, R. K. (1976). R&D utilization for local services: Problems and prospects for further research. Washington, D.C.: Rand, R-2020-DOJ, December.

ZILBOORG, (1943). "Fear of death." Psychoanalytic Quarterly, 12:465-475.

13

IDEOLOGY AND POLICY TERMINATION:
Restructuring California's Mental Health System

JAMES M. CAMERON

University of California, Los Angeles

Most innovations in public policy are accomplished only with great effort. An innovation that entails a major redirection in policy generally means that part or all of the earlier policy is to be discontinued. The difficulties involved in policy innovation have been the object of much attention. But this interest has rarely extended to issues raised by the other side of the policy coin—what happens when a policy is discontinued? Termination refers to the cessation or redirection of policy. It may be the result of a deliberate effort to discontinue or phase out obsolete, unworkable, or unnecessary policy; or it may occur as an unanticipated consequence of policy innovation.

For the most part, termination has been ignored by those concerned with the analysis of public policy; the few studies that have focused on the cessation of policy have usually treated it as a unique event not subject to generalization or theoretical development. The neglect of policy termination is not particularly surprising since people are generally more interested in processes that *are* going to occur than those that are *not* (Biller, 1976). That is, termination is considered an act of history. What little attention has been accorded it has centered around political and organizational inertia factors that inhibit the process of termination. The intellectual focus of such inquiry has usually been concerned with the

AUTHOR'S NOTE: *This chapter also appears as an article in Public Policy (1978), Volume 26, No. 4, and is reprinted here by permission of John Wiley and Sons.*

development of strategies and tactics for terminating policies and programs.[1] These are important considerations but, to the extent that critical questions regarding the *outcomes* associated with the terminated policy are neglected, the analysis becomes very shortsighted.

The profound transformation of California's mental health system provides an excellent case study in policy termination. The state wants to get out of the mental health business. Other states, following California's lead, are also attempting to extricate themselves from the delivery of direct services to the mentally ill. Changes in California mental health policy have resulted in a rapid deinstitutionalization process, phasing out state hospitals and shifting the locus of responsibility to the local communities.

This chapter examines the processes of policy and organizational change that occurred with mental health reform and reveals a number of significant policy outcomes associated with that change. It attempts to show how the consequences associated with the redirection in policy are intimately related to the manner in which previous mental health policy was terminated. This chapter discusses how the numerous obstacles to the termination of policy diminish the prospect of policy innovation without the powerful force of ideological fervor. Ideology, it is argued, both reveals and obscures the underlying valuations within the social context. It is shaped by certain characteristics of the social structure, and its function in the mental health field is to augment and legitimize directions in public policy.

POLICY TERMINATION

The study of policy termination can be conducted most fruitfully by placing it within the context of the overall policy process. Brewer (1974), taking his cue from Lasswell's decision sequence, has identified six phases constituting the lifecycle of public policy: initiation, estimation, selection, implementation, evaluation, and termination. All of the steps are conceptually and operationally interrelated and overlapping with one another; aspects pertinent to one phase cannot be considered in isolation, independent of processes occurring in other phases. Accordingly, termination is conceived as systematically linked to the other phases in the policy sequence. In addition, Brewer's formulation provides a coherent framework for analyzing policy within the purview of the methodology of science. As such, it suggests that policy be viewed from an experimental perspective.

THE EXPERIMENTAL APPROACH

Public policy may be conceived as an experiment: a problem is identified or chosen; preferred outcomes are specified that provide criteria upon which to measure actual outcomes; alternative means of solving the problem are contemplated and calculated for their probable outcomes; a plan of action is selected as a working hypothesis; consequences of the implemented plan are observed and analyzed for their significance; the hypothesis is either partially or wholly confirmed or rejected on the basis of the evidence. It is clear, of course, that public policy, broadly conceived as a social experiment, differs substantially from a natural experiment. The subject matter and specific procedures of experimentation in the natural sciences are quite different from those embodied in social experimentation. But both entail the same logic of inquiry—the scientific method;[2] both consider the validity of an idea as dependent upon how it stands up to experience; both view the adopted intervention as a working or tentative hypothesis until the anticipated consequences which led to its adoption are squared with actual consequences. The relatively "clean" aspects of natural experiments cannot be duplicated for social experimentation. "Nevertheless," as Dewey (1938:508-509) explained, "every measure of policy put into operation is, *logically,* and *should* be actually of the nature of an experiment." Policy entails the selection of one idea among a number of possible alternatives, and its implementation is accompanied by observable consequences that may serve as indicators of the validity of the idea.

Several barriers to intelligent inquiry and careful appraisal of public policy combine to prevent policy from being viewed from the standpoint of an experiment. In addtion to the numerous procedural difficulties involved in social experimentation (e.g., problems of internal and external validity), policy makers are faced with often severe time constraints, and high levels of uncertainty with regard to outcome preferences and cause-effect relations. Further, an experimental approach is obviated by the nature of the policy-making and executing process which encourages policy makers to advocate a particular policy alternative as though success were certain (Campbell, 1971). Policy makers thus become inexorably committed to a particular alternative rather than to amelioration of the problem. Another inhibition to experimentation is the propensity of man to avoid the unsettling condition caused by doubt. According to Peirce (1966:99), "We cling tenaciously, not merely to believing, but to believing just what we do believe." Thus, although the experimental approach to policy is "self-corrective" in the sense that expected outcomes are always subject to revision by future evidence, it may also be viewed as potentially threatening to strongly held beliefs.

The most significant handicap that results from the failure to view policy from an experimental perspective is that policy is ultimately treated as a final solution. The image of policy as a solution rather than a working hypothesis usually reflects an implicit conception of the larger "theory" underpinning the policy as "true". That is, policy is regarded as the practical application of a holistic and universal theory. The theory may be internally consistent, but it is not context-specific, formulated in terms that connect it to a concrete spacio-temporal setting. Empty of empirical referents, the theory may be neither confirmed nor refuted; as such, it is nonscientific (Popper, 1966). The absence of an experimental approach is reflected by the absence of a critical examination of the belief system that gives policy its intellectual force.[3] To the extent that the system of beliefs upon which policy measures are based is not subject to continuous critical examination, it becomes a tenet of faith. Negative consequences of policy are rationalized or ignored. Like the system of beliefs from which it springs, policy becomes fixed and nonadaptive. The net effect of the policy-as-solution syndrome is the inhibition of innovation and change.

If policy is viewed as a working hypothesis, discriminative observations of the consequences that flow from policy serve to reduce uncertainty regarding outcomes. Hence, the risk to policy makers that generally attends significant policy innovation is similarly reduced. Moreover, a critical temper that accompanies an experimentalist attitude implies a movement away from what Peirce (1966) labeled "fixation of belief." The point is that an experimental approach not only facilitates innovation and change, it allows for these processes to be built on testable conceptual foundations. It encourages decision makers to redesign policy on the basis of (1) a careful analysis of the contextual significance of the consequences of earlier policy, and (2) a systematic assessment and comparison of a variety of policy alternatives in terms of their probable effects on individuals, organizations, and institutions. In the absence of an experimental approach, major redirections in policy occur not on the basis of sound judgment, but on the basis of other stimuli: a sudden crisis requiring an immediate policy response, or a popular belief system with a high degree of newly acquired ideological consensus.

RESISTANCE TO TERMINATION

Certain policy initiatives have a built-in transitory character in which the manner of their termination is institutionally prescribed. Such is the case when it is clear to relevant participants that the realization of specific outcomes will mean the ending of effort expended to achieve those outcomes. For example, the establishment of price controls during World War II, administered by the Office of Price Administration (OPA), was a temporary policy directed toward finite objectives with explicit provisions for termination; when prices stabilized after 1946, controls ceased and OPA was dismantled. Most policies, however, have neither finite objectives nor provisions for termination. Defense policy, of course, is a good contemporary example. Growing out of a specific, historical crisis, defense policy is accompanied by spending patterns that produce powerful vested interests dependent on their continuation and growth. As the entire economy becomes dependent on defense expenditures, cessation of policy becomes less and less feasible. By the time the conditions that led to the creation of defense policy have changed, the institutional mechanisms created to serve it have become part of the social structure and part of its ideological raison d'etre.

Many of the resistances to termination attending defense policy are paralleled, albeit on a lesser scale, by most other public policy. The implementation of policy entails a number of personal, organizational, and societal sunk costs that serve to ensure continuity. Biller (1976) has persuasively argued that resistance to termination is largely a product of organizational design that is explicitly engineered to be resistant to change. The filtering process of organizational information flows, organizational reward structures that serve to reduce risk-taking behavior, the elaboration of organizational routines, and patterns or resource allocation all derive from presumptions of persistence and perpetuity. In addition to organizational design factors, resistance may come from operators of existing policy who have a professional stake in continuity, and from clientele and other beneficiaries who may lose certain benefits if programs are discontinued. Termination presents a heavy threat to operators of existing policy. It reflects badly on those responsible for policy execution insofar as it implies inefficient allocation of resources or a lack of adaptive capability. Although existing policy may be clearly inappropriate, the multiple sources of resistance, coupled with the overarching threat of uncertainty that accompanies a major redirection in policy, produce a strong inhibition to termination.

Termination is rarely an explicit goal of policy innovation and change. Rather it is a political resultant, occurring as a neglected or ill-conceived after-effect of newly adopted policy measures. Even in the face of severe budget restraints, it is far easier, politically, to focus attention on what will be *created* than what will be *ended*. Hence, specific termination issues are generally ignored or left in an ambiguous haze during the selection phase of the policy process. Because the specific details of how a policy is to be actually carried out are left to the implementation phase, termination issues are not confronted until the newly adopted policy is irrevocably put into operation. The manner in which termination is to be accomplished has to be "invented" *after* the execution of the selected policy option has already begun. Not surprisingly, it often results in a patchwork, piecemeal process characterized by a vast array of unanticipated consequences. Thus, resistance to termination, as the counterpart of innovation, creates a policy scenario in which these two processes are often treated separately, when in fact logic dictates that they be considered as mutually interdependent.

TERMINATION AND IDEOLOGY

In the absence of an experimental approach to policy, an enormous amount of energy is required to move decision makers to adopt an innovative policy proposal. Faced by numerous resistances to change, not the least of which is a high degree of uncertainty, policy makers usually consider only those policy alternatives that approximate previous policies (Lindblom, 1968). How, then, does a new idea that significantly deviates from previous practices get adopted? In other words, lacking an experimental approach to policy, what other convincing forces are powerful enough to drive the political arena toward a radical redirection in policy?

Two basic forces may be identified: (1) a novel crisis requiring immediate action and (2) the force of ideology. By "crisis" is meant a sufficiently urgent emergency that captures the focus of attention and has the actual effect of an immediate policy response—an act of war, a natural catastrophic event, a major epidemic.[4] Such profound events are rare, however. More commonly, the necessary impetus for a significant redirection in policy is provided by ideology.

Policy change can frequently be traced to underlying changes in social structures. As the system evolves over time, certain characteristics of the changing social structure conflict with ongoing policy, which is in turn characterized by the absence of self-correcting mechanisms. A major shift in policy must be justified on the basis of a powerful system of beliefs that "matches" or has a close affinity with changing aspects of social structure. Ideology provides the intellectual and emotional pressure required to "convince" the system not merely to change itself, but to change itself in a particular way. Moreover, the system of beliefs, or ideology, must be sufficiently acceptable to relevant participants in the system to overcome the inertia of an earlier, competing ideology. Ideology therefore lends legitimacy to proposals for change. To the extent that it is characterized by a high degree of consensus, it may provide the policy arena with enough pressure for change—enough "energy"—to overcome the forces resisting change.

Thus, to overcome the barriers to terminating previous policy, and to gain authoritative approval for innovation, policy is formulated not on the basis of testable alternatives, but on the basis of a *particular* alternative. Legitimizing the proposal involves a systematic effort to delegitimize the policy it is designed to supplant. This frequently takes the simplistic form of "the right and the good" versus "the wrong and the immoral." It may have the positive effect of moving an otherwise intransigent policy-making arena, and it is a useful device for coalescing divergent economic and social interests into a concerted change-oriented action group. But the simplistic approach that gives ideology its coalescing force results in ill-considered policy choices: data that are inconsistent with the ideology are ignored or explained away; rigid adherence to credo becomes more important than inquiry into the potential effects of particular contingencies; overoptimism and the personal risks attending the prospect of failure lead to an implementation process characterized by disincentives for the recognition of failure. Ideas are slow to become accepted and, once accepted, exhibit a strong tenacity for survival. However, as Schon (1971:127) explained:

> Ideas in good currency emerge *in time*, and the situations to which they refer change underneath the very process of deliberation . . . By the time ideas have come into good currency, they no longer accurately reflect the state of affairs.

Ideology, upon which policy is justified, is generally formulated as fixed conceptual principles unrelated to specific, contextual variables. As a consequence, these underlying conceptions tend to be taken for granted once a policy alternative is selected. "Such conceptual generalizations," according to Dewey (1938:506), "*pre*judge the characteristic traits and the kinds of actual phenomena that the proposed plans of action are to deal with." This is extremely significant, because context-specific, problem-oriented inquiry is severely handicapped from the start. To the extent that the conceptual dimensions of policy are formulated on the basis of "sweeping universals," they are divorced from actual phenomena and therefore can be neither empirically verified nor refuted. Hence, negative consequences flowing from the actual operation of policy are not linked to the controlling ideas. The ideas may therefore retain their social validity long after the policy effects of those ideas are dysfunctional.

THE CHANGING IDEOLOGICAL CONTEXT IN MENTAL HEALTH

Mental health policy has always been formulated largely on the basis of prevailing ideological currents. Ideology refers to a shared system of beliefs and values that provides reasons for action with accompanying rules of logic. It emerges out of the social situation and provides a framework for viewing it. This holds for the generation of a scientific or professional belief system as well as a political doctrine. According to Vickers (1970:59), a professional orientation or ethic resides "in a set of readinesses to see and value and respond to its situation in particular ways." He calls this shared conceptual milieu an "appreciative system." As with other systems," it is resistant to change of a kind or at a rate which might endanger its own coherence." The change in California's mental health system resulted largely from the impetus provided by the ideology of community mental health. The only way to understand the nature and significance of the new mental health ideology, and its role in the policy process, is to trace the course of its development.

CONCEPTIONS OF MENTAL ILLNESS

The history of mental health policy reveals that changing ideological currents have reflected varying conceptions of the nature and causes of mental illness. Different conceptions lead to different implications for policy. What, for example, should be the scope of mental health programs? Should such programs be limited to persons who are clearly suffering psychiatric syndromes, or should they extend to persons with ordinary problems of living such as family stress, nervousness, job dissatisfaction, and so forth? Do social problems such as poverty and unemployment fall within the purview of mental health, or are they more significantly the province of other fields? How one views these policy issues is largely dependent on one's conception of mental illness. In spite of the wide array of viewpoints regarding the causes of mental illness, the appropriate criteria for establishing its occurrence and the means by which it can be ameliorated and controlled, it is possible to delineate four general conceptions of mental illness that constitute relatively distinct (if somewhat overlapping) perspectives—the disease perspective, the myth perspective, the psychoanalytic perspective, and the environmental perspective.

The disease perspective maintains that obvious disturbances in psychological functioning are pathological conditons. Although the process is far more judgmental than diagnosis in ordinary medical practice, and it is often difficult to justify mental illness objectively on a biological basis, psychiatric diagnosis and treatment are considered to be basically the same as other branches of medicine. The disease concept regards mental illness in a limited or specific way; it does not attempt to give a total explanation for the entire constellation of psychological difficulties. It insists that specific treatments be applied to particular disorders and encourages the search for correlations between behavior disorders and neurophysiological processes. Psychopathology is considered to be the result of the interaction between biogenetic and environmental influences. Insofar as mental illnesses are indeed considered illnesses in the medical sense of the term, the patient himself is considered the primary focus for treatment.

The myth perspective holds that what is generally designated as mental illness is actually deviations from conventional thinking and behavior. This perspective is represented by those who believe that those labeled "mentally ill" are as rational as everyone else, except that they view reality differently, and that the suffering in evidence is a result more of the label than of the underlying psychiatric condition. Although few mental health professionals subscribe to the myth perspective, this view has had considerable influence within the legal profession.

The psychoanalytic perspective is based on the belief that behavior is shaped by unconscious processes and that only by reconstructing the patient's personality development can one ascertain how the distrubed state of the patient developed. Inappropriate social functioning and psychological distress are seen as the responses of a distrubed personality in adapting to the environment. The psychoanalyst, through intensive and prolonged interaction with the patient, attempts to uncover those basic unconscious processes which have led to the personality disorder. Normal behavior and severely distorted behavior are analyzed from basically the same perspective—the development and adaption of the personality.

The environmental perspective views mental disorders as principally the result of environmental circumstances. The causes and the cure for mental disorders are conceived as related to the entire web of social relationships in which the individual is caught. Those who put forth an environmental perspective are likely to view the entire community as the locus of treatment, because they consider the incidence and prevalence of mental disorders to be the result of adverse environmental circumstances. A person's behavior is determined by the specific social environment within which he operates. Thus, any manifest problems in psychological functioning—whether mild neurosis or debilitating psychosis—are considered a function of the interaction of the individual with his environment. Treatment is oriented toward helping the individual adjust to his social environment or changing the environment that caused his problems.

The fundamental differences among the various conceptions of mental illness outlined above have significant implications for policy. If one accepts the myth argument that mental disorders are simply forms of social deviance and that the mental health system is basically a covert penal system designed to maintain order, then one may conclude that the mental health system should be dismantled altogether. On the other hand, if the genesis of mental illness is considered as rooted in early personality development, then the treatment of mental disorders would entail longterm intensive psychoanalytic therapy.

The disease conception, in defining mental illness from a comparatively narrow perspective, suggest orienting public policy toward retarding and ameliorating the disabilities of the mentally ill. If mental illness is defined on the basis of medical diagnosis of disease, and is considered fundamentally different from the ordinary problems arising out of the stresses and strains of modern society, then policy with respect to the seriously mentally ill would be based on different considerations from those given to general problems of living.

In contrast, the implications for mental health policy flowing from the environmental perspective suggest directing the focus of attention toward the general social environment that is considered the breeding ground for mental disorders. It is assumed that severe or chronic mental illness, as part of the same continuum as other psychological difficulties, is due largely to the absence of early intervention that might have prevented its development. Mental health policy should thus be oriented toward treatment of less severe psychological disorders and the modification of conditions that presumably lead to mental illness. This is precisely the orientation adopted by the community mental health movement.

HISTORICAL ANTECEDENTS

In tracing developments in the mental health field, one finds that conceptions of mental illness and treatment modalities have varied significantly over time. Indeed, historians have carefully documented how changing conceptions of mental illness have closely paralleled changes taking place in the sociopolitical context (Dain, 1964; Deutsch, 1937; Grob, 1966; Rothman, 1971). During the early 19th century the dominant social and political values were hard work, individualism, laissez faire, and Social Darwinism (Hofstadter, 1954). Social philanthropy and charity were in large part the social mechanisms for handling the problems of pauperism and insanity (Mohl, 1971). Public welfare policy was almost nonexistent, because the idea was contrary to the dominant social philosophy that prevailed at the time. As the concentration of the population in urban areas generated greater public awareness of bizarre behavior, the mentally ill were confined in poorhouses and jails where they suffered brutal cruelty and neglect. A reform movement, originating in Europe, was led by influential figures who urged policy makers to provide special facilities for these unfortunates. To convince the public that the welfare of the mentally ill was the proper domain of the public sector, the movement for reform had to be grounded on a sufficiently convincing theory; the vehicle was a change in people's perceptions of mental illness. Prior to this period it was widely believed that mental illness was incurable. During the early 19th century "the pendulum of opinion on this subject swung violently to the opposite extreme" (Deutsch, 1937:132). The view that mental illness could not be cured was supplanted by a "cult of curability."

The mental health reform movement proved to be a potent impetus toward redefining the role of state government with regard to the welfare of the mentally ill. The reform ideology embraced three interrelated themes, closely tied to the existing sentiments and values of the period, which gave it its social force: (1) scientific respectability, (2) religious righteousness, and (3) economy. Psychiatrists and other ideologues of the movement insisted that mental illness was curable in most or even all cases. This affirmation was coupled with a religious appeal to humanism. Because the insane can be cured of their suffering, the argument went, we cannot stand before God and allow them to be brutalized in poorhouses and prisons. But the kicker for policy makers was the appeal to economy. To continue placing the mentally ill in noncurative institutions where they would probably remain for life would mean increasingly heavy burdens on the public purse, whereas the construction of hospitals where the mentally ill could be easily and rapidly cured would result in great savings.

The new ideology, fueled by extravagant claims by professionals and justified on the basis of a social responsibility for the indigent mentally ill, resulted in a rapid proliferation of state mental hospitals. Between 1825 and 1865, the number of state mental hospitals grew from 2 to 62 (Dain, 1964). The early public mental hospitals, adhering to the concept of "moral treatment," experienced an initial period of success. Moral treatment was based on the assumption that kindness and humane treatment was the best way to alleviate mental disorder. During the initial "era of moral treatment," the medical model was employed. While accepting the idea that adverse environmental conditions played an important role, it was assumed that such factors led to some sort of brain dysfunction. Types of disorders were carefully differentiated, drugs and other forms of therapy were administered according to an individually tailored regimen, and a close doctor-patient relationship was provided. The optimism for recovery afforded by the medical approach to treatment engendered a positive climate for rehabilitation and probably accounts, to some degree, for the early hospital records of success.

But the period of moral treatment in public mental hospitals was short lived. Rapid industrialization and population growth contributed to a sharp increase in the number of hospitalized persons. To induce policy makers to provide more funds for expanding existing facilities and building new hospitals, reformers continued to hammer away at the curability theme by providing exaggerated and fabricated statistics showing remarkable recovery rates.[5] In spite of this effort, public mental hospitals soon degenerated into large custodial institutions without the resources or staff necessary to provide adequate treatment. Policy makers were willing to allocate a minimal amount of public funds for institutions for the mentally ill, but they were clearly opposed to making the kind of commitment that would have been necessary to maintain the high standards of care offered during the period of "moral treatment." Coupled with, and partly as a result of, the "custodialization" of the mentally ill, there was a gradual deflation of the "cult of curability." By 1850 "the pendulum began to swing back to the opposite extreme" (Deutsch. 1937:155). Declining confidence in the ability of mental hospitals to cure patients led to a protracted period of pessimism that lasted well into the 20th century. States continued to send their patients to mental hospitals, but the standards of success in these institutions were no longer related to treatment. "In effect their primary responsibility was not to their patients, but to society, which demanded some form of protection against the mentally ill" (Grob, 1966:356).

Why was mental health reform such a complete failure? Although policy makers were aware of the needs for making special provisions for the indigent insane during the early 19th century, the notion of public welfare conflicted with the prevailing social philosophy of the period. The reform ideology provided the necessary energy to resolve the philosophical conflict. The passionate appeal to humanistic principles of Christian righteousness legitimized the process. It provided the necessary *moral justification* for policy change, but it did not alter the basic underlying philosophy of the period—that the public welfare function of the state should be kept to the barest minimum. Nor did the ideology reflect a significant change in public morality. Ideologies need appropriate symbols, and these symbols evoke the emotions associated with the situation; but to mistake the symbol for the real thing is to fall prey to reification. The appeal to righteous indignation and Christian principles was consistent with the public's abstract sense of morality. But the abstract moral code to which the ideological symbols referred were divorced from and irrelevant to the actual operating values in the context.[6] Justifying policy on the foundation of religious abstraction gave the movement sufficient moral force, but it tended to obscure the real policy issues—protecting organized social life from the mentally ill at minimum cost.

In short, the significance of ideology for public policy can be discerned only by analyzing the function it serves. Mental illness as a social problem emerged with changes in certain characteristics of the social structure. Policy initiatives in the field not only required the force of ideology, but also required that it be composed of a particular belief system. Clothed in scientific respectability, and legitimized by an aura of moral responsibility, it offered the ideological energy necessary to initiate public policy. But the theory proved unrealistic, the moral imperative ephemeral, and the costs prohibitive. Overoptimism and oversimplification doomed the reform movement before it started. Nevertheless, it played a crucial role in society's effort to construct an acceptable mechanism for dealing with the problem of mental illness.

Conditions in state mental hospitals did not improve with the embracing of psychoanalytic theory by American psychiatrists beginning in the 1920s. Many superintendents of public mental institutions held "the conviction that many psychoses represented forms of adaptation to intolerable stresses of the personality, that mental symptoms were intimately related to the pre-psychotic personality of the individual, and that study of childhood development, especially family relationships, should be the basis for understanding the development of major personality problems" (Hendrick, 1958:260). But, as Freud had warned, psychoanalysis has little effect on, and is not meant for, the treatment of psychotics. The emphasis on psychoanalysis only tended to confirm the notion that the more serious forms of mental illness were inaccessible to treatment. Psychoanalytic theory was absorbed by and came to dominate medical psychiatry. The proliferation of the psychoanalytic approach, which was oriented to the neuroses and the milder forms of psychological disturbance, had the effect of moving the medical profession away from the kinds of disorders characteristic of patients in mental hospitals. The contradiction was one of the primary reasons for the development of the community mental health ideology. The psychoanalytic approach had the effect of moving the practice of psychiatry from the hospital to the community.

THE COMMUNITY MENTAL HEALTH MOVEMENT

Adoption of the psychoanalytic conception meant neglecting the state hospitals and focusing on the community, but it was poorly suited to providing *public* mental health care to persons in the community; that is, it was far too expensive and manpower was limited. In addition, the depression of the 1930s had a profound influence on the public's conception of the role of government in providing for public welfare. The new mental health ideology, therefore, has its roots in two historical developments: (1) the internal contradiction of the psychoanalytic approach, and (2) the birth of social welfarism.

In 1963 President Kennedy (1964:730) proposed a "wholly new emphasis and approach to care for the mentally ill." Congress subsequently passed the Community Mental Health Centers Act, which was to be a massive federal effort toward developing a community mental health system. Kennedy's proposal served as the catalyst for constructing a new ideological consensus with the force required to initiate a national policy innovation.

The community mental health movement must be viewed within the context of the larger effort of the federal government to deal with the growing disorder in the cities. The social reform legislation of the 1960s may be seen as directed at ameliorating the rapid growth of deviant behavior that emerged in the major cities. The social mechanisms for socialization and social order—the "pattern maintenance function" in Parson's (1951) terms—were ineffective in the large urban areas. The existing state and municipal government apparatus was unable to adjust sufficiently to the new and changing demands of the increasing lower status clientele. Inhibited by a variety of organizational and political constraints, municipal governments resisted expanding their social service domains to accommodate the changing urban reality (Piven and Cloward, 1972; Kirlin, 1973). Federal initiatives, therefore, circumvented the traditional municipal government apparatus and established a number of community-based programs directly. Community mental health programs played an integral part in the federal strategy. Like the other social welfare programs, community mental health was intended to be an important socialization mechanism. The community mental health movement can thus be seen as an instrument for social planning and social control, and the ideology as legitimizing this function.

Like earlier ideologies, the community mental health ideology is comprised of three interrelated themes: (1) scientific respectability, (2) moral righteousness, and (3) economy. The environmental conception provides the etiological basis; the notions of freedom from incarceration and the right of every citizen to treatment in his community provide the moral imperative; and the increasing cost of state hospital care supplies and economic rationale.

By conceiving all behavior as part of the same continuum, the focus is on early intervention and prevention (Caplan, 1961, 1964). A universal thread running through the prevention literature is the notion that community mental health is concerned with entire social systems. In their review of the literature, Kessler and Albee (1975:557) concluded that primary prevention has to do with "everything aimed at improving the human condition, at making life more fulfilling and meaningful." Prevention becomes synonymous with intervention aimed at redesigning the social structure of the community. The global nature of the new ideology is exemplified by the adoption of the "ecological" perspective as a primary conceptual foundation. Because behavior is determined by the specific social environment within which the individual operates, the job of creating a positive mental health environment entails influencing the structure and function of the social setting (Kelly, 1969). Accordingly, the mental health professional becomes a social change agent. Ideologues of the movement stress the importance of conceiving poverty programs and mental health programs as closely interrelated (Reiff, 1969). In addition, a large body of literature argues that influencing the political process is an appropriate task for community mental health professionals (Duhl and Leopold, 1968: MacDonald et al., 1974).

A direct implication of the community mental health movement has been a radical redefinition and expansion of the role of the mental health professional. Expansion of the domain of the mental health system to include the entire community spotlighted the inadequate supply of mental health professionals. The ideology provides the basic justification not only for expanding traditional mental health manpower (psychiatrists, psychologists, psychiatric social workers), but also for designing new professional roles to meet the greatly increased need for mental health services.

Set within the model of public health, the community mental health movement called for a shift in focus from treatment of the individual to intervention into community situations judged to be associated with mental disorder (e.g., poverty, racism, unemployment).[7] Moreover, the ideological thrust toward deinstitutionalization, which entailed moving patients out of hospitals and into the community, was coupled with a heavy emphasis on returning patients to their families. Stress on the primacy of the traditional family unit and the moral responsibility of the family to care for the patient provided both an ethical and economic justification for the movement. The system of beliefs and values that comprises the community mental health ideology was consanguine with certain characteristics of the emerging social structure of the 1960s. That is, out of a wide range of possible conceptions that society could have "chosen," the ideological components of the community mental health movement reflected significant changes taking place within the larger social context. As in the case of mental health reform during the early 19th century, the community mental health ideology served to legitimize a fundamental redirection in policy.

CONSEQUENCES OF IDEOLOGY-INDUCED TERMINATION

The ideology of community mental health proved to be a potent impetus for terminating mental health policy in California. By the mid-1960s, the state had already begun reducing its state hospital populations and was nurturing a fledgling community mental health system. The process of depopulating the state hospitals was augmented by the use of psychotropic drugs, which allowed many patients to function outside the hospital, and the availability of federal public assistance funds, which provided support for former patients (especially the aged) in the community. Pressure to redesign the system was stimulated by the State

Legislature and culminated in 1967 with the passage of the Lanterman-Petris-Short Act (L-P-S). The legislation, which did not take effect until 1969, imposed severe restrictions on the criteria for involuntary commitment of mental patients and transferred responsibility for all clients in the system to the local communities.

IDEOLOGY AND MENTAL HEALTH REFORM

Successful enactment of the reform legislation was largely dependent on a broad ideological base of support among relevant participants within the mental health context. A 1967 questionnaire survey of a representative sample of the "attentive public," reported by Bardach (1972), revealed a strong orientation toward the community mental health ideology. Although ideological conflicts existed, the new ideology clearly dominated the issue context. Despite the ideological shift that had occurred among the attentive public, the inertia of the existing system required a skillfully engineered legislative effort. The new law reflected the recommendations embodied in a study conducted by the Assembly Subcommittee on Mental Health Services (State of California, 1966) which initiated the reform effort. The widely disseminated report documented the abuses of involuntary commitments and linked the inadequacies of the state hospitals to the medical approach to treatment. Although it was clearly an ideological instrument carefully constructed to put forth a particular point of view, it formed the main body of analysis upon which legislation was formulated.[8] It served to define the problem, delineate those issues considered relevant, and set the parameters for discussion. The report successfully escalated the ideological debate between the traditional system (depicted as anachronistic and morally bankrupt) and the proposed alternative of a voluntary community-based system. Public debate tended to proselytize many of the uninitiated to the community mental health ideology and to augment pressures for reform. With considerable political acumen, the Subcommittee staff succeeded in minimizing political opposition and bolstering support for the proposal.

By focusing on the question of involuntary commitment and emphasizing that treatment should be a voluntary matter, the Subcommittee instigated a debate between civil libertarians arguing the legal rights of patients and those stressing a treatment perspective. As Arthur Bolton, senior consultant to the Assembly and principal architect of L-P-S, explained, "although *in practice* the commitment system was not too uncomfortable for most legal and mental health professionals, the latent *ideological* conflict was stimulated to create a climate for change" (ENKI, 1972:16). The issue for the civil libertarians was infused with an all-important moral imperative—individual liberty—the most sanctified of American traditions. If the Subcommittee had centered its attention on termination of the state hospitals, it would have faced considerable resistance. Abolition of involuntary commitment would, however, achieve essentially the same purpose since the hospital clientele was predominately this category of patient. By concentrating on the commitment issue, and capitalizing on the ideological thrust toward noninstitutional community-based care, the Subcommittee successfully generated enough moral indignation to alter the system radically. Thus a major policy innovation and the concomitant termination of previous policy occurred within a context in which traditional ideology was superseded by a new ideology that had gained a high degree of consensus.

The new law imposed very stringent conditions for involuntary commitment. A person could be detained involuntarily for as long as 17 days if certified by two mental health professionals that he was dangerous or gravely disabled (i.e., unable to provide for his basic survival needs.) Thereafter, he could be involuntarily detained for further treatment only after a thorough judicial review by the Superior Court. In addition, under the new system the counties were given ultimate responsibility for patient evaluation and treatment and for the planning of mental health services. To ensure the redirection of funds from state hospitals to local programs, the legislation provided for a single statewide funding arrangement in which the counties were to be responsible for 10% of the cost of their local programs and their residents in state hospitals. The remaining 90% of the cost for both state and local facilities was to be met by the state.

In spite of the clear intent of the new mental health law to redirect the flow of patients out of the state hospitals and into the communities, it was nowhere stated in the legislation that this was an intention. The question of the eventual termination of state hospitals was never addressed during the policy adoption phase, nor do the the the designers of the legislation acknowledge it as their intention. Assemblyman Lanterman, the main author of the new legislation, stressed the point (1976:6): "Never was it the concept to destroy the state hospitals, in any way." But a mental hospital with a drastically reduced patient population quickly becomes economically unfeasible to operate. Legislation designed to diminish the use of state hospitals would probably lead to their demise; yet the multiple problems associated with organizational termination escaped consideration by policy makers. Furthermore, the issue of alternatives to hospitalization for released state hospital patients was almost wholly neglected. Policy makers tacitly assumed that patients who were no longer receiving services in the state hospitals would receive more appropriate services on a voluntary basis in the community. Persons who are prone to be hospitalized (i.e., the more severely disabled) are, however, generally disinclined to seek outpatient services on their own. Because policy makers failed to address the termination aspects of the new mental health law, they were unable to project the consequences of putting the plan into operation.

PHASING OUT STATE HOSPITAL SERVICES

The new law was followed by a vigorous effort to deinstitutionalize. Within three years after L-P-S took effect the resident population of state hospitals had been sliced nearly in half. The multiple incentives designed to depopulate state hospitals and increase local mental health services led to a massive increase in expenditures for local mental health programs. Between fiscal years 1968 and 1973 local programs jumped from 21 to 64% of the state mental health budget. The closure of California's state hospitals began with the implementation of the new law. Between 1970 and 1973 five state hospitals closed their doors to the mentally ill. (One of them continued to admit penal code commitments only.)

Termination of hospital programs for the mentally ill proceeded with little planning and less coordination. Decisions by state officials were made without the participation of hospital administrators or local officials who had little advance notice of actual termination dates and received conflicting information regarding specific changes in programs. The protracted period of uncertainty experienced by hospital staff and the lack of consideration given to relocating hospital personnel in local programs had a devastating effect on the morale (State of California, 1974; Weiner, 1976).

The most serious effects were felt by the patients themselves. Many were indiscriminately transferred from one hospital to another—a procedure that can be particularly traumatic for patients (Marlowe, 1976). The succession of hospital closures resulted in the wholesale discharge of patients into communities that were ill-prepared to provide care for them. Very few intermediate care facilities were available and most patients were either placed in inadequate board and care homes or left to find their own living arrangements.

Patients were returned to communities that, for the most part, did not want them. Social and legal pressures were frequently brought to bear that served to exclude the mentally ill from the community. In many cases zoning laws and city ordinances were manipulated to restrict residential care facilities to certain neighborhoods. Studies of residential facilities for the mentally ill in California have suggested that many former mental patients were not really living in the community. Patients in boarding and family care homes were found to be isolated and excluded from their surrounding community, resulting in just another form of institutionalism at the community level (Aviram and Segal, 1973: Lamb and Goertzel, 1971, 1972). Segal and Aviram (1976) indicated in their study of the sheltered care service system in California that about 68% of the facilities serving the mentally ill also served the other groups, such as transients, the dependent aged, alcholics, and the mentally retarded. "As a general policy," they concluded (1976:123), "such care represents a return to the poorhouse approach, emphasizing aggregate care for all those unable to 'make it' in our society." Very few studies have investigated what happens to patients after they leave California state hospitals. One such study entailed a follow-up of chronic, long-term patients released from Metropolitan State Hospital in Los Angeles. It revealed that during the first few critical days after discharge these patients were extremely limited in their interaction with the environment. Nearly half spent less than 15 minutes per day in social interaction of any kind. Over half had a maximum territorial range of one block or less. Few individuals utilized existing community resources, and with rare exceptions, their daily activities consisted of little more than eating, sleeping, and watching television. The study concluded that the recently discharged, chronic patient lives a lonely, isolated, alienated existence (Strayer 1973).

In spite of the apparent lack of community alternatives to hospitalization for the mentally ill, the state continued to plunge ahead with its termination plans. An ad hoc committee of the State Senate, charged with investigating the proposed phaseout of state hospitals, uncovered problems with implementing the new law in nearly all its dimensions (State of California, 1974). In the face of severe legal restrictions on involuntary commitment, many severely disordered persons who were unable to adjust to community living were left to deteriorate in the community. Referring to the financial rewards to the counties for reducing use of state hospitals and the states's deliberately underestimated budget allotment of days of state hospital utilization, the Committee's report stated that "the present system of budgeting local programs appears to have resulted in denial of hospital care to patients whose condition warrants admission to state hospitals" (1974:14). It was found that money saved by closing hospitals was being diverted to programs designed for patients who were easier to treat and more professionally rewarding. Exposure to major problems involved in implementing the new law, however, did not lead to significant moves toward policy adjustment. With the new system firmly rooted in the ideology of community-based care, the focus continued to be on the development and expansion of autonomous local mental health programs and the concomitant reduction of state hospital services.

EXPANSION OF SERVICES

Although the restructured California mental health system was characterized by a paucity of community alternatives for the seriously disabled, the overall population receiving community mental health services was greatly expanded. County programs prior to L-P-S, funded on the basis of the 75% state and 25% county matching formula, were generally small programs serving an essentially middle class clientele. With the shift in emphasis to community-based care, outpatient services became available to much broader cross-section of the population. The implementation of L-P-S (which coincided with the introduction of the 90% state and 10% county funding arrangement) produced an explosive increase in the delivery of local mental health services. In Los Angeles County, for example, the caseload for outpatient services increased at a average annual rate of 60% between 1969 and 1975.

The changing complexion of the California mental health system reflected not only changes in the location and types of services, but in the type of patients receiving the bulk of those services. The tremendous expansion in outpatient services was largely directed toward a new population of mental health consumers for whom few services were available prior to L-P-S (ENKI, 1972): those who were less severely disorderd, and those who were amenable to service on a voluntary outpatient basis. Thus, the focus on community mental health resulted in the delivery of services to a previously underserved population—persons suffering some form of psychological distress for whom inpatient services were inappropriate. The benefits associated with the increase in community mental health services, however, do not appear to have been shared by those who were prone to be hospitalized—the more severely disabled.

AFTERCARE SERVICES IN LOS ANGELES COUNTY

A basic tenet of mental health reform was that the reduction in hospital services for the mentally disabled would lead to their receiving more appropriate services in the community. Yet by 1975 little or no systematic research had been conducted in California to determine the extent to which patients, who were no longer receiving services from state hospitals,were receiving them from the expanding network of outpatient services. Consequently, a study was conducted in Los Angeles County in an effort to bridge this critical research gap. With a population of nearly 8 million, Los Angeles County is by far the largest county in the state. It has over one third of California's population,commands over one third of its mental health budget, and has a well-established system of community-based care. Aftercare became subject to increased attention in Los Angeles County in 1974. The state legislature had enacted two bills designed to augment efforts by local programs to provide aftercare services: SB 2316 required that an individual aftercare plan be developed for each patient being released from an inpatient psychiatric facility, and AB 4513 increased the statewide mental health budget for 1974-1975 by $5.25 million for new and expanded aftercare programs. In order to capture a good portion of these additional funds, Los Angeles County developed, for the first time,a Continuing Care Plan (County of Los Angeles, 1974). The plan focused on the development of a comprehensive and integrated system of linkage between the many components of the mental health system. With increased formal attention accorded aftercare, it was expected that provisions for continuity of care for discharged state hospital patients would be well integrated by 1975, expecially since aftercare services were considered crucial for successful post-hospital adjustment.

The basic purpose of the study was to determine the extent to which released state hospital patients received mental health aftercare services in Los Angeles County within the first few months after discharge.[9] A 10% random sample was drawn from all Los Angeles patients discharged during a five-month period in 1975. Although the original sample consisted of 651 patients—373 diagnosed as psychotic, 73 as nonpsychotic, and 205 as drug dependent or alcoholic—the findings reported here include only the 446 patients diagnosed as psychotic or nonpsychotic.

In 1975 over half of California's state hospital admissions were from Los Angeles County. The study found that the typical patient is young and male, and is admitted involuntarily and remains in hospital only briefly (60% of the sample stayed in hospital 17 days or less). The "departure centers" at each of the two state hospitals serving Los Angeles County were the principal mechanisms for linking patients to appropriate community services. Only 35% of the patients, however, were referred by the departure centers to units in the community. In addition, only 30% of the patients had an Individual Continuing Care Plan written for them on discharge, although legislation in 1974 required that one be written for each patient discharged.

The county provides in its annual plan that discharged state hospital patients will receive aftercare services from both the Continuing Care Services Section (CCSS) of the State Department of Health and the county's own system of local mental health services. "Protective social services" offered by CCSS and a variety of treatment services offered by the county mental health program[10]are intended to be linked and interwoven so as to provide for an appropriate mix of continuing care services based on individual need. In practice, the county relies most heavily on CCSS for its aftercare services. Among those referred to community mental health units, the vast majority of referrals were to CCSS. The study found that, of the 446 patients discharged, 26% had one or more contacts with CCSS within one month of discharge, and 34% had one or more CCSS contacts within 4 months of discharge.[11]Only 12% had five or more CCSS contacts within four months of discharge. Utilization of services provided by the county's mental health system was much lower; only 11% utilized any of the non-inpatient services provided by the county within one month of discharge, and only 20% utilized these services within four months. Only 5% had five or more contacts within the county's system during the four-month period.[12]

Probably the most startling finding of the study was that almost none of the persons in the sample utilized county rehabilitation services, which include "day treatment" or "partial hospitalization." These are the set of services most readily identified as mental health aftercare services for former inpatients. Only 3% of the sample had one or more visits during the first four months after discharge. Consistent with the community mental health ideology, the county (and the state as a whole) has given this category of service a low priority.[13]

Less than half (46%) of the sample of 446 patients used any of the available non-inpatient services, either CCSS or county, within four months of discharge. Most of these had very few contacts with the system. Only 17% of the sample had five or more contacts of any kind within four months.

A large percentage of the sample—34%—was rehospitalized one or more times within six months after discharge. Patients who received a relatively large number of post-hospital contacts were significantly less likely to be rehospitalized than those receiving relatively few contacts. Among those receiving nine or more contacts within four months of discharge, 20% were rehospitalized, whereas among those who received between one and eight contacts, 41% were rehospitalized. This suggests that clients who receive relatively frequent community mental health services are a lower risk for rehospitalization.[14] Yet, as the study findings clearly indicated, little emphasis was really given to "continuity of care" for former hospital patients.

A primary goal of the county has been the reduction of inpatient services, "thus reducing the cost of chronic care to the County" (County of Los Angeles, 1972). Reducing the cost of care for the county's severely disabled would allow for the continued expansion of a variety of local programs. It does not appear, however, that concern for reducing the cost of care for these patients was accompanied by an equally compelling concern for providing them treatment at the local level. On the contrary, what little emphasis existed in providing aftercare for former hospital patients seems to have been not on treatment, but on traditional welfare services.

Because in practice CCSS (which is comprised almost wholly of psychiatric social workers) was expected to provide the bulk of aftercare services, its role would seem to be a critical one. In 1975, however, the client/staff ratio of CCSS in Los Angeles County was 56 to 1 (excluding supervisory and clerical personnel) (State of California, 1975b). This placed a heavy burden on CCSS staff, who were charged with providing continuing care services to those patients who were often the most difficult to reach. CCSS, whose budget is largely funded by the federal government, provides a host of important social welfare services to former hospital patients. Most mental health *treatment* services, on the other hand, are expected to be provided by the county's local mental health system. Patients who left California state hospitals in 1975, however, rarely *received* treatment in the community. The greatly expanded network of outpatient services was apparently oriented toward a type of patient different from those who were prone to be hospitalized. In principle, discharged state hospital patients and other indigent mentally ill persons for whom inpatient services were no longer an available alternative were to receive rehabilitation, psychotherapy, and other treatment services in the community. In practice, however, they were neglected by the mental health system under the presupposition that the primary responsibility for their care lay with the welfare system.

The primary mechanism for aftercare has been the existing stock of residential care facilities. These are mainly board and care homes that ordinarily operate on severely limited budgets. Relying on the patient's welfare check, they are able to offer very few services, usually no more than room and board. Patients who seek out counseling, therapy, or other services provided by community mental health facilities, are likely to receive them, especially if they are persistent and are not a nuisance.The severely disabled, however, are often not inclined to seek out services on their own. Consequently few former patients actually received these services.

FRAGMENTATION OF CONTROL

The lack of aftercare services for former hospital patients can be traced, in large part, to the pattern of radical decentralization that accompanied implementation of the new law. Although the legislature attempted to shore up certain provisions of L-P-S in order to induce the counties to increase their efforts in the provision of aftercare services, its efforts had little effect. Local programs, oriented toward the voluntary, easier to manage clients, had developed independently of the state hospitals whose programs were oriented toward the more seriously disordered. The counties' response to this new population was colored by a history of serving what was essentially another type of clientele. Organizational technologies had been constructed, roles elaborated, and routines established that were consistent with the new (and professionally exciting) approach of community mental health. Caring for the chronically mentally ill was not considered part of their professional domain.[15] In spite of the tremendous increase in state expenditures for local mental health programs—from $27.5 million in fiscal year 1969 to $185.5 million in fiscal year 1976—local programs were disinclined to target mental health dollars specifically to the types of patients who were prone to be hospitalized.

It is to be expected that when one level of government controls the purse strings for another, some degree of accountability will be exercised. In the California mental health system, however,the state relinquished control of programs in its effort to disengage itself from the delivery of direct services. The new mental health law was designed to provide for a single system of care in which the counties assumed responsibility for the provision of services. The manner in which the system was decentralized, however, precluded the state from exercising programmatic control. The county programs, which had traditionally functioned autonomously, were free to develop their patterns of service delivery unfettered by state intervention. The only significant pressure brought to bear on the counties was the statewide drive to reduce the use of state hospitals. As a result, local programs were not held accountable for the effectiveness of their programs or even the types of patients being served. The State Department of Health made little effort to determine how the system was actually functioning.[16] The absence of control over local programs was partly a reflection of a lack of interest. For example, the Department's Cost Reporting/Data Collection System was the principal source of hard information regarding the functioning of the system. Yet a study by the State Office of the Auditor General (State of California, 1975c:10) revealed that not only were the reports "not used at the local level for planning, control or any other aspect of management decision-making," they were rarely used by the Department itself.

State mental health administrators were consumed by a single purpose—reducing the use of state hospitals. Blinded by their procrustean determination to make the evidence fit the theory, they insisted that the phaseout in state hospitals was the natural result of the drop in hospital caseload. For example, in 1972 the state published a 190-page document detailing each county's service utilization trends and prefacing it with the proud claim that "outpatient and other services are precluding hospitalization" (State of California, 1972). No evidence was presented indicating the extent to which released patients were receiving post-hospital services. Yet the widely circulated report confidently asserted that the decline in hospitalization was evidence that local programs were removing the need for hospitalization. In reality, of course, the reduction in hospital caseload reflected changes in *policy*. It was self-delusion to pursue a policy of emptying state hospitals and then turn around and point to the reduced hospital caseload as a measure of successful local treatment.

PERSISTENCE OF IDEOLOGY

The manner in which termination of previous mental health policy was executed precluded an adequate assessment of the likely outcomes of the new legislation. The absence of an experimental approach to policy development and adaptation necessitated the force of ideology to drive the context toward change. Relying on ideology-induced change, however, tended to obscure the consequences of public policy. Wedded to a rigid conceptual framework whose validity was considered a foregone conclusion, policy makers assumed that unforeseen problems would work themselves out during the implementation phase. According to Lanterman (1976:6) the important thing was first to pass a law that would afford the mental patient all the rights of due process, "then provide the machinery of implementation later, which is the concept of let the dollar follow the patient." Lanterman's "concept of let the dollar follow the patient" was inappropriate, however; the concept did not match the realities. From one perspective the failure to consider the problems of implementation during the estimation and selection phases can be a useful strategy: If the termination effects of a policy innovation are systematically ignored, sources of resistance to the proposal may lie dormant during the crucial acceptance phase. On the other hand, termination is then likely to be a haphazard, poorly planned process in which potential consequences are not considered until they are experienced.

Policy makers designed a system that systematically obscured its own success or failure. For instance, insisting on the therapeutic value of the family and the community in general, policy makers in effect were able to diffuse the problem.[17] That is, by emptying the large and conspicuous state hospitals, upon which attention could easily be focused, patients disappeared into the community, thereby becoming "lost" to the system until they surfaced again in a state hospital. Not only were the consequences of policy difficult to determine, the influence of ideology served to isolate the conceptual foundation of policy from those consequences that did become apparent.

The newly acquired ideological consensus of the community mental health approach successfully replaced earlier ideologies and was sufficiently powerful to overcome existing resistances to termination. But the very strength of the new ideology produced a context that was, in turn, resistant to significant change. Considered immutable "truths," the conceptual underpinnings of policy remained insulated from critical appraisal. Recent events in California reveal that, in the face of severe problems associated with the phasing out of state hospital services, policy makers steadfastly clung to the precepts of community mental health. During the fall of 1976, after a spate of highly publicized deaths in the state hospitals, it was revealed that hospital conditions were far below minimum standards. After the enactment of L-P-S, the physical plants had been allowed to deteriorate, training programs were ended, and a general atmosphere of organizational strangulation enveloped the context. The relatively low salaries for hospital employees coupled with an organizational ambiance of slow degeneration produced a situation in which patient neglect was commonplace.[18] The controversy generated by patient deaths was interpreted as further evidence of the need to dismantle the hospitals completely. The state, which subsequently increased its efforts toward this end, was not prompted to examine the underlying conceptual basis of the reform legislation. Instead, it used the controversy as fuel in its continuing effort to move patients out of inpatient settings and into the community. By the end of 1977 the state, in cooperation with the counties, had developed plans to eliminate completely the use of state hospitals within four years.[19] Commensurate with this effort, the state also intends to terminate the role of CCSS and transfer its responsibilities to the local programs.

The state has maintained that treatment in the community is less expensive than treatment in state hospitals. Yet, all evidence points the other way. A single outpatient unit of service in Los Angeles County cost $41 in 1975,[20] nearly as much as an average per patient day in a state hospital (McAdams, 1976). County and private hospitals cost from two to four times as much as state hospitals per patient day (State of California, 1975a). To provide a full constellation of mental health and support services to the mentally ill in the community, it would apparently be far more expensive than the provision of state hospital services.[21] The focus of attention, however, has not been on how to *treat* former hospital patients in the community, but on where to *place* them. Completion of the process of hospital termination, therefore, has primarily involved attempts to increase the stock of residential facilities.

CONCLUSIONS

The change in California's mental health system resulted largely from the impetus provided by the ideology of community mental health. Control over mental health programs has been transferred from the state to the community; the emphasis has shifted from providing inpatient services to providing outpatient services; and the type of client for whom the system offers the bulk of its resources has changed from involuntary to voluntary. The phasing out of state hospital services has been heralded as a progressive leap forward. Considered as anachronistic vestiges of the past and subject to intense public scrutiny, they have been a favorite whipping boy of the system.

Deinstitutionalization, a concept increasingly in vogue not only in mental health but in other fields as well, such as criminal justice administration, has entailed the wholesale discharge of hospitalized mental patients. The policy is predicated on the belief that insofar as bad mental hospitals are harmful to patients, all hospitalization should be eschewed, and if unavoidable, then used for the shortest possible period. Public mental hospitals have indeed had deleterious effects on patients. Still, the fact that hospitalization of mental health patients has been abused does not make the public mental hospital an abuse. Community mental health ideologists, pointing to detrimental consequences that have accompanied hospitalization, frequently leap to the conclusion that the underlying problem is institutionalization per se. Thus the policy option of improving the quality of mental hospitals as a measure to improve the delivery of mental health services is not seriously considered. It has been delegitimized because of its incongruity with the basic assumption that institutionalization is, by definition, bad for patients. This position is buttressed by delegitimizing the conception of mental illness (the "medical model") that purportedly dominates the institutional environment.

The demise of the state hospital was expected to lead to the treatment of the mentally ill in the community. Unlike the hospital, it has been argued, the community is a natural setting, one that can facilitate the patient's return to reality. Expanding the field of "mental health" to include the entire community has meant a greatly increased role for the mental health professions. Professions, like organizations, seek to expand their domains. The focus of attention has shifted to a new and more professionally interesting clientele—voluntary patients, those who are more likely to be amenable to service. In one sense, what has occurred is an institutionally prescribed and ideologically sanctioned "creaming" effect, in which those who are the easiest to treat are the ones receiving service. The severely mentally ill, on the other hand, are more professionally frustrating; treating them has been largely eschewed with the reorganization of the mental health system.

The consequences associated with mental health reform in California can be traced to the manner in which previous policy was terminated. The political requirements of policy adoption, which inhibited an experimental approach to policy, necessitated that policy be justified on the basis of a powerful system of beliefs. Commensurate with changes taking place within the larger social context, community mental health emerged as the dominant ideology in the 1960s. To the extent that it attained a high degree of ideological consensus among relevant participants in the political arena, it provided the energy required to redirect the flow of public policy. In the face of multiple resistances to termination, policy makers focused attention on the adoption of new policy while systematically neglecting issues related to termination. Policy outcomes associated with termination, therefore, were largely unanticipated. Moreover, adherence to the precepts of ideology tended to insulate the conceptual underpinnings of policy from critical appraisal.

The outcomes associated with the termination of mental health policy in California should have implications not only for other states contemplating similar reforms, but for the termination of government programs generally. Recently, increased emphasis on "debureaucratization," "deinstitutionalization," and "decentralization" has contributed to an emerging interest in the termination of government programs. Although policy termination has received little systematic attention in the literature, it is quickly becoming an important issue for many government officials. On the face of continued public disenchantment with the performance of large bureaucracies and widespread support for efforts to reduce government expenditures, it seems likely that efforts to terminate outdated, unpopular, or inefficient programs will be increased. To the extent that the incipient interest in termination is not accompanied by careful appraisal of the likely outcomes attending terminated programs, the results could be less than positive, and even disasterous.

NOTES

1. See the collection of studies in the special issue devoted to termination in *Policy Sciences* (1976), 7 (June); see also Kaufman (1976).

2. The term "scientific method" is not meant to denote any particular set of techniques in the acquisition and interpretation of information on social phenomena. As Kaplan (1964) insists, the scientific method is not really a "method," rather it refers to a frame of mind and embraces all the techniques that scientists may find useful.

3. Policy failure can frequently be traced to inappropriate or inadequate theoretical underpinnings. In their devastating critique of the Economic Development Administration's effort in Oakland, Pressman and Wildavsky (1973) suggested that behind the failure to implement policy was a deficient economic theory.

4. The notion of crisis suggested here has to be distinguished from the conventional usage of the term. Most issues that draw public attention are referred to as "crisis" situations to dramatize their importance. In the field of health care, for example, periodic "crises" had led only to symbolic efforts at reform and have had little effect in changing the basic components of public policy (see Alford [1975]).

5. Two analyses of this process that derive somewhat different conclusions are provided by Deutsch (1937) and Bockoven (1963).

6. See Kaplan (1968) for an incisive discussion of a "dualistic code" and its significance for public policy.

7. This expanded view of mental health is reflected in the recently released final report of the President's Commission on Mental Health (1978:9), which emphasizes that public policy should be based on a "broad view" of mental health problems: "They must include the damage to mental health associated with unrelenting poverty and unemployment and the institutionalized discrimination that occurs on the basis of race, sex, class, age, and mental or physical handicaps. They must also include conditions that involve emotional and psychological distress which do not fit conventional categories of classification or service."

8. The principal documentation of the abuses associated with involuntary commitment was drawn from a statewide survey of commitment court hearings, which revealed that the average length of the commitment hearing was only 4.7 minutes (State of California, 1966:43). This figure was actually somewhat misleading because it did not take into account the consideration given the case before its appearance in open court, nor the fact that in many cases there was an extensive investigation by the county before the hearing (ENKI, 1972:14).

9. For a full report of the study, see Cameron (1977).

10. The county's mental health system is comprised of a vast network of county-administered and county-contract agencies that provide emergency, regular outpatient, and rehabilitation services.

11. A "contact" is defined as a day in which a social service contact occurred subsequent to discharge with either a client or significant other. For CCSS this also included telephone contacts.

12. Since the county screens patients before placing them in hospitals, hospitalization is generally preceded by an outpatient contact. Client contacts that led immediately to hospitalization were not recorded, as these were considered to be part of the overall process of hospitalization.

13. The county has consistently considered these types of services as its lowest priority, as implicitly revealed in its yearly plan. See County of Los Angeles, 1972:2.05; 1975:3.03; 1976:3.71.

14. For similar results of a study conducted in Kentucky, see Kirk (1976).

15. Other studies have indicated that severely disabled patients are generally given a low priority by community mental health professionals who would prefer to treat "good patients" and those who are more amenable to treatment (Hogarty, 1971; Taube, 1973; Lamb, 1976).

16. An extensive study of the Department of Health conducted by the Commission on California State Government Organization and Economy (State of California, 1976) was particularly critical of the perceived failure by the Department to administer mental health programs.

17. Many patients who previously would have been removed from the family situation now remain at home. One of the more tragic consequences of mental illness, however, is the disruption of the normal family unit. A growing body of evidence suggests that the presence of a psychotic person in the home is not only disruptive to the family as a whole, but is correlated with a high rate of mental illness among other family members (Arnhoff, 1975).

18. An investigation of state hospital conditions by the California Conference of Local Mental Health Directors (1977) uncovered gross inadequacies in nearly every

aspect of the state hospitals. The report concluded that conditions were intolerable and that state hospitals should be phased out.

19. Unlike the administration's announcement in 1973 of their intention to phase out all the state hospitals, the state in 1977 was, nominally at least, placing responsibility with the local programs to develop alternatives to hospitalization. Moreover, in contrast to the earlier effort, plans for elimination of state hospital services focused primarily on state hospitals for the mentally ill, thereby avoiding the political barriers to closure that might be imposed by groups representing the interests of the mentally retarded.

20. An outpatient "unit of service" is not the same as a "patient visit." A "unit of service" represents a face-to-face contact by a mental health professional with a patient or his "significant others." Frequently, a single visit to an outpatient clinic results in multiple units of service, especially in crisis situations. In some instances 15 or more units of service have been reported for a single outpatient visit (Fowler et al., 1976:13).

21. Studies in Los Angeles County have repeatedly suggested this to be the case (Haugen, 1973; Fowler, 1977; County of Los Angeles, 1977).

REFERENCES

ALFORD, R. (1975). Health care politics. Chicago: University of Chicago Press.

ARNHOFF, F. (1975). "Social consequences of policy toward mental illness." Science, 188(June):1277-1281.

AVIRAM, U., and SEGAL, S. (1973). "Exclusion of the mentally ill." Archives of General Psychiatry, 29(July):126-131.

BARDACH, E. (1972). The skill factor in politics: Repealing the mental health commitment laws in California. Berkeley: University of California Press.

BILLER, R. (1976). "On tolerating policy and organizational termination: Some design considerations." Policy Sciences, 7(June):133-149.

BOCKOVEN, J. S. (1963). Moral treatment in American psychiatry. New York: Springer.

BREWER, G. D. (1974). "The policy sciences emerge: To nurture and structure a discipline." Policy Sciences, 15(September):239-244.

California Conference of Local Mental Health Directors (1977). Report of the task force on state hospitals. Sacramento: Author, February 10.

CAMERON, J. M. (1977). Community mental health and the discharged state hospital patient. New Haven: Center for the Study of Health Services, Institution for Social and Policy Studies, Yale University, Working Paper No. 7-56, November.

CAMPBELL, D. (1971). "Reforms as experiments." In F. Caro (ed.). Readings in evaluation research. New York: Russell Sage.

CAPLAN, G. (1961). An approach to community mental health. New York: Grune & Straton.

_____ (1964) Principles of community psychiatry. New York: Basic Books.

County of Los Angeles (1972). Plan for mental health services, 1973-74, 1973-78. Los Angeles: Author, October.

_____ (1975). Plan for mental health services, 1975-76, 1975-80. Los Angeles: Author, June.

_____ (1976). Plan for mental health services, 1976-77, 1976-79. Los Angeles: Author, September.

_____, Department of Health Services, Mental Health Services (1974). "Continuing care plan for Los Angeles County." Los Angeles: Author, November 1 (mimeographed).

_____, Department of Health Services, Mental Health Services (1977). "Plan for reduction/elimination of state hospital utilization." Los Angeles: Author, August 16.

DAIN, N. (1964). Concepts of insanity in the United States. New Brunswick: Rutgers University Press.

DEUTSCH, A. (1937). The mentally ill in America: A history of their care and treatment from colonial times. Garden City, N.Y.: Doubleday.

DEWEY, J. (1938). Logic: The theory of inquiry. New York: Henry Holt.

DUHL, L. F., and LEOPOLD, R. L. (1968). Mental health and urban social policy. San Francisco: Jossey-Bass.

ENKI Research Institute (1972). A study of California's new mental health law, 1969-1971. Chatsworth, Cal.: Author.

FOWLER, G. (1977). A survey on needs for alternatives to hospitalization. Los Angeles: County of Los Angeles, Department of Health Services, Mental Health Services, Evaluation an Research Division, February.

_____, MOCHIZOKI, M., and ROSHAL, S. (1976). The crisis evaluation unit—an evaluation. Los Angeles: County of Los Angeles, Department of Health Services, Mental Health Services, Evaluation and Research Division, February.

GROB, G. N. (1966). The state and the mentally ill. Chapel Hill: University of North Carolina.

HAUGEN, R. (1973). A feasibility study of the closure of Metropolitan State Hospital. Los Angeles: County of Los Angeles, Department of Health Services, Mental Health Services, Evaluation and Research Division, April 16.

HENDRICK, I. (1958). Facts and theories of psychoanalysis. 3d ed. New York: Knopf.

HOFSTADTER, R. (1954). Social Darwinism in American thought. Rev. ed. New York: Braziller.

HOGARTY, G. E. (1971). "The plight of schizophrenics in modern treatment programs." Hospital and Community Psychiatry, 22:197-203.

KAPLAN, A. (1964). The conduct of inquiry. Scranton, Pa.: Chandler.

_____ (1968). American ethics and public policy. New York: Oxford University Press.

KAUFMAN, H. (1976). Are government organizations immortal? Washington, D.C.: Brookings Institution.

KELLY, J. (1969). "Ecological constraints on mental health services." In A. J. Bindman and A. D. Spiegel (eds.), Perspectives in community mental health. Chicago: Aldine.

KENNEDY, J. F. (1964). Message from the President of the United States relative to mental illness and mental retardation. 88th Cong., 1st sess., February 5, 1963, H.R. Document 58, reprinted in American Journal of Psychiatry, 120 (February):727-737.

KESSLER, M. and ALBEE, G. W. (1975). "Primary prevention." Pp. 557-591 in M. R. Rosenzweig and L. W. Porter (eds.), Annual review of psychology. Palo Alto, Cal.: Annual Reviews, 26.

KIRK, S. F. (1976). "Effectiveness of community services for discharged mental hospital patients." American Journal of Orthopsychiatry, 46(October):646-659.

KIRLIN, J. (1973). "The impact of increasing lower status clientele upon city government structures: A model from organization theory." Urban Affairs Quarterly, 8(March):317-343.

LAMB, H. R. (ed.) (1976). Community survival for long-term patients. San Francisco: Jossey-Bass.

_____, and GOERTZEL, V. (1971). "Discharged mental patients—Are they really in the community?" Archives of General Psychology, 24(January):29-43.

_____ (1972). "The demise of the state hospital—A premature obituary?" Archives of General Psychiatry, 26(June):489-495.

LANTERMAN, F. (1976). State Assemblyman. Sacramento: Interview Document, January 2.

LINDBLOM, C. (1968). The policy-making process. Englewood Cliffs, N.J.: Prentice-Hall.
MacDONALD, K. R., HEDBERG, A. G., and CAMPBELL, L. M., III (1974). "A behavioral revolution in community mental health." Community Mental Health Journal, 10(Summer):228-235.
MARLOWE, R. (1976). "When they closed the doors at Modesto." In P. Ahmed and S. Plog (eds.), State mental hospitals: What happens when they close. New York: Plenum.
McADAMS, L. A. (1976). "Cost per episode by modality of service for FY 1975." Los Angeles: County of Los Angeles, Department of Health Services, Mental Health Services, Evaluation and Research Division, E & R Notes, August 26.
MOHL, R. (1971). Poverty in New York. New York: Oxford University Press.
PARSONS, T. (1951). The social system. New York: Free Press.
PEIRCE, C. (1966). In P. Weiner (ed.), Selected writings: Values in a universe of chance. New York: Dover.
PIVEN, F. F. and CLOWARD, R. A. (1972). Regulating the poor: The functions of public welfare. New York: Random House.
POPPER, K. R. (1966). The open society and its enemies. Rev. ed. Princeton, N.J.: Princeton University Press.
President's Commission on Mental Health (1978). Report to the President, Volume 1. Washington, D.C.: U.S. Government Printing Office.
PRESSMAN, J., and WILDAVSKY, A. (1973). Implementation. Berkeley: University of California Press.
REIFF, R. (1969). Mental health manpower and institutional change." In A. J. Bindman and A. D. Spiegel (eds.), Perspectives in community mental health. Chicago: Aldine.
ROTHMAN, D. J. (1971). The discovery of the asylum. Boston: Little, Brown.
SCHON, D. A. (1971). Beyond the stable state. New York: W. W. Norton.
SEGAL, S., and AVIRAM, U. (1976). "Transition from mental hospital to community." Official Proceedings, 102d Annual Forum, National Conference on Social Welfare, San Francisco, May 11-15, 1975. New York: Columbia University Press.
State of California, Legislature, Assembly Interim Committee on Ways and Means, Subcommittee on Mental Health (1966). The dilemma of mental commitments in California. Sacramento: Author.
State of California, Legislature, Senate Select Committee on Proposed Phaseout of State Hospital Services (1974). Final report. Sacramento: Author, March 15.
State of California, Department of Health (1975a). "Schedule of patient care and treatment costs, effective July 1, 1975." Sacramento: Author, July 1 (mimeographed tables).
_____ , Community Services Section (1975b). "Services for the mentally disabled." Sacramento: Author (mimeographed).
State of California, Office of the Auditor General (1975c). A management review of the community mental health system. Sacramento: Author, February.
State of California, Commission on California State Government Organization and Economy (1976). A study of the administration of state health programs. Sacramento: Author, January.
STRAYER, R. (1973). "The first four days: A study of the recently discharged chronic, long-term psychiatric patient." Ph.D. dissertation, Claremont Graduate School.
TAUBE, C. (1973). Utilization of mental health facilities. DHEW Publication NIH-74-657. Rockville, Md.: National Institute of Mental Health.
VICKERS, G. (1970). Value systems and social process. Harmondsworth, England: Penguin.
WEINER, S. (1976). "The impact of closing DeWitt State Hospital." Pp. 65-82 in P. Ahmed and S. Plog (eds.), State mental hospitals: What happens when they close. New York: Plenum.

ABOUT THE CONTRIBUTORS

DONALD C. BAUMER is Assistant Professor of Government at Smith College. He has been involved with CETA research projects since the inception of the program, and has coauthored articles and monographs analyzing all facets of the implementation of CETA.

EILEEN B. BERENYI is Assistant Professor, Department of Public Administration, Maxwell School of Citizenship and Public Affairs, Syracuse University. Her areas of expertise include public budgeting and urban service delivery. She has been a Senior Research Associate at the Columbia University Graduate School of Business and served as a staff assistant in the office of the Mayor, City of New York and in the Office of the Health Commissioner of New York City.

JAMES M. CAMERON is Assistant Professor of Public Health at U.C.L.A. While a Research Associate at the Center for Health Studies at Yale University, he coordinated a project aimed at the development of a case-based prospective reimbursement system for health care. Dr. Cameron's current research interests include issues related to policy termination, health policy, and mental health policy.

PETER deLEON received his Ph.D. in policy analysis from The Rand Graduate Institute for Policy Studies. He is presently a member of the professional research staff at The Rand Corporation and an adjunct faculty member of the School of Public Administration, University of Southern California. Part of his research on policy termination was presented as invited testimony to the U.S. Committee on Intergovernmental Relations.

BRUCE FRANKEL is an assistant professor in the Department of Urban Studies and Community Development at Rutgers University. He has also served on the Rutgers faculties in urban planning and social work. As a public policy consultant, he reported on welfare reofrm to committees of primary jurisdiction in both Houses of the United States Congress. Further, he has counseled local, county and state governments in New Jersey on planning, housing, and social services. He authored reports for Rutgers University on both marketing and evaluating educational programs. The recipient of the Ph.D. degree in city planning from the University of Pennsylvania (1974), Dr. Frankel has published his research on a variety of topics including community development block grants and incidence analysis in various governmental and research institute reports and professional journals.

RITA MAE KELLY is an associate professor in the Department of Urban Studies and Community Development at Rutgers, The State University of New Jersey. From 1973 to 1975 she was director of a national survey of the leadership of community development corporations for the Center for Community Economic Development, Cambridge, Massachusetts. In 1967 she received a Ph.D. in political science from Indiana University. She has also been a lecturer in political science for the University of Maryland Overseas Division (1965-1967) and Seton Hall University (1974-1975), a Research Scientist at American University (1968-1969), a Senior Research Scientist for American Institutes for Research (1969-1972), a consultant to the Office of Economic Opportunity (1972-1973), and a consultant to various private and public research groups. Dr. Kelly has published a variety of books, articles, and monographs on several topics.

THOMAS LINDENFELD, formerly a research assistant of the Research Program in Criminal Justice, is now a student at the Woodrow Wilson School, Princeton University. His interests include prisoner release, half-way house programs, and campaign management.

JUDITH V. MAY is an urban policy specialist in the Department of Housing and Urban Development where she worked on the preparation of the Carter Administration's national urban policy and recently wrote a handbook for federal agencies on urban and community impact analysis. She received her Ph.D. in Political Science from the University of California at Berkeley and has written articles on citizen-participation, professional-client relations, and the classification of social service programs.

KENNETH J. MEIER is Assistant Director of the Bureau of Government Research and Assistant Professor of Political Science, University of Oklahoma. He has published articles in professional journals on representative bureaucracy, interest groups, budgeting, regulation and agricultural policy. He is the author of *Politics and the Bureaucracy.*

STEPHEN A. MERRILL received his B.A. from Columbia University and graduate degrees from Oxford and Yale University, where he also taught political science. He has been a Kellett Fellow, a Congressional Fellow of the American Political Science Association, and a Brookings Institution Research Fellow. He worked on the reorganization of the Senate committee system and subsequently joined the professional staff of the Committee on Commerce, Science and Transportation, where he specializes in science and technology policy.

ERIC S. MOSKOWITZ is on the political science faculty at the University of Illinois—Chicago Circle campus. The article included in this volume is part of a larger study of federal neighborhood preservation policy-making. His two primary areas of interest are urban politics and national policy-making in the United States.

STUART S. NAGEL is Professor of Political Science at the University of Illinois and a member of the Illinois bar. He is the coordinator of the *Policy Studies Journal* and the secretary-treasurer of the Policy Studies Organization and has been Series Editor of the Sage Yearbooks in Politics and Public Policy since its inception. He is the author or editor of *Policy Studies and the Social Sciences, Policy Studies in America and Elsewhere, Improving the Legal Process, Effects of Alternatives, Environmental Politics, The Rights of the Accused: In Law and Action,* and *The Legal Process from a Behavioral Perspective.* He has been an attorney to the Office of Economic Opportunity, Lawyers Constitutional Defense Committee in Mississippi, National Labor Relations Board, and the U.S. Senate Subcommittee on Administrative Practice and Procedure.

BARBARA J. NELSON is Assistant Professor of Public and International Affairs at Princeton University's Woodrow Wilson School. She is conducting a study, "Agenda Setting for Domestic Policy," which looks at how economic and political risk shifts back and forth from private to the public sector. Her American research on how child abuse went from being a private sector charity concern to a public sector social welfare issue is being extended to Great Britain and The Netherlands.

ELINOR OSTROM is Co-Director of the Workshop in Political Theory and Policy Analysis, and Professor of Political Science at Indiana University. She has written extensively in the area of criminal justice and has undertaken a number of research projects related to the effects of different ways of organizing police departments.

ROGER B. PARKS is Associate Director of the Workshop in Political Theory and Policy Analysis, and Co-Principal Investigator of the Police Services Study. He is the author of several articles dealing with police industry organization, police relations with crime victims, and police performance measurement. His current research is exploring the linkages between police organization and police performance in residential settings.

JOHN P. PLUMLEE is Assistant Professor of Political Science at Southern Methodist University. Dr. Plumlee has co-authored published papers dealing with the distribution of urban public services and with organizational models of regulatory administration. His current research interests include the assessment of the effects of productivity improvement in bureaucratic organizations and the role socialization of professionals (particularly lawyers) in administrative agencies.

NELSON ROSENBAUM is a political scientist who specializes in studies of environmental politics and policy. Educated at Princeton and Harvard, he currently serves as Senior Research Associate at the Urban Institute in Washington, D.C. He is the author of numerous prior works on land use and growth policy, including *Land Use and the Legislatures* and *Citizen Involvement in Land Use Governance.*

E. S. SAVAS is Professor of Public Systems Management and Director of the Center for Government Studies at the Graduate School of Business, Columbia University. He is also Associate Director of the Center for Policy Research, and was First Deputy City Administrator of New York under Mayor Lindsay.

DOUGLAS H. SHUMAVON received his B.A. in political science from California State University, Fresno, his M.A. in urban affairs and public administration from the American University, and his Ph.D. in political science is expected in 1978 from the University of California, Santa Barbara. He is currently an assistant professor in the Department of Political Science at Oklahoma State University and the Director of both the Master of Arts degree program in Public Administration and the Internship Program.

BARBARA J. STEVENS is president of Ecodata, Inc., an economic research firm specializing in analysis of urban service delivery. She has a Ph.D. in urban economics from MIT, has been on the faculty of Columbia University, and has published widely for both academics and practitioners in the area of solid waste, housing, and transportation.

FLOYD E. STONER is Assistant Professor of Political Science at Marquette University. He received his Ph.D. at the University of Wisconsin-Madison. His study of the passage and implementation of ESEA Title I was supported by a Post-Doctoral Fellowship at Michigan State University. Currently he is involved in research projects that deal with various aspects of public audits. He will be spending the 1978-1979 school year in Washington as an APSA Congressional Fellow.

GORDON P. WHITAKER is Assistant Professor of Political Science at the University of North Carolina at Chapel Hill. His research and teaching concern public service performance measurement the relationships between administrative structure and service quality and cost. He is currently completing a study of the activities of police officers on patrol. He has served as consultant to police and other public agencies and is coauthor (with Ostrom and Parks) of *Patterns of Metropolitan Policing* and *Policing Metropolitan America.*

AARON B. WILDAVSKY is a political economist currently on leave from the University of California, Berkeley. He is the author of numerous books and articles on politics and public policy.

Augsberg College
George Sverdrup Library
Minneapoli. .....sota 55454